Rhetoric and the Digital Humanities

Rhetoric and the Digital Humanities

Edited by

JIM RIDOLFO AND
WILLIAM HART-DAVIDSON

The University of Chicago Press Chicago and London

JIM RIDOLFO is assistant professor of writing, rhetoric, and digital studies in the Department of Writing, Rhetoric, and Digital Studies at the University of Kentucky and associate researcher at Matrix, the Center for Digital Humanities and Social Sciences at Michigan State University.

WILLIAM HART-DAVIDSON is associate professor in the Department of Writing, Rhetoric, and American Cultures and associate dean of graduate studies in the College of Arts and Letters at Michigan State University. He is also senior research associate for Writing in Digital Environments Research at Matrix.

The University of Chicago Press, Chicago 60637
The University of Chicago Press, Ltd., London
© 2015 by The University of Chicago
All rights reserved. Published 2015.
Printed in the United States of America

24 23 22 21 20 19 18 17 16 15   1 2 3 4 5

ISBN-13: 978-0-226-17655-0 (cloth)
ISBN-13: 978-0-226-17669-7 (paper)
ISBN-13: 978-0-226-17672-7 (e-book)
DOI: 10.7208/chicago/9780226176727.001.0001

Library of Congress Cataloging-in-Publication Data

Rhetoric and the digital humanities / [edited by] Jim Ridolfo and William Hart-Davidson.
   pages ; cm
   Includes bibliographical references and index.
   ISBN 978-0-226-17655-0 (hardcover : alk. paper) —
ISBN 978-0-226-17669-7 (pbk. : alk. paper) — ISBN 978-0-226-
17672-7 (e-book) 1. Humanities—Digital libraries. 2. Rhetoric—
Study and teaching—Electronic information resources. I. Ridolfo,
Jim, 1979– editor. II. Hart-Davidson, William, editor.
   AZ195.R47 2015
   025.06'0013—dc23

                         2014013080

♾ This paper meets the requirements of ANSI/NISO Z39.48-1992
(Permanence of Paper).

Contents

Introduction

JIM RIDOLFO

WILLIAM HART-DAVIDSON

The topic of the digital humanities (DH) has generated considerable research activity in rhetoric and writing studies in the last three years, as evidenced by the number of DH panels at major field conferences: the 2011 Conference on College Composition and Communication (CCCC) in Atlanta; the 2012 CCCC in Saint Louis; the 2011 Rhetoric Society of America Summer Institute in Boulder, which featured a DH workshop; and the Computers and Writing conference, which featured over a dozen sessions on DH at the 2012 meeting as well as town hall meetings on DH at the 2011 and 2012 meetings. Moreover, scholars working in either rhetoric studies or computers and writing (C&W) have received a number of National Endowment for the Humanities (NEH) Office of Digital Humanities (ODH) Digital Humanities Start-Up grants (e.g., Potts and Gossett 2012; Carter 2011; Ball, Eyman, and Gossett 2010; and Hart-Davidson and Ridolfo 2008) and a NEH Digging into Data grant (Rehberger 2010). Despite this burst in activity, to date there has been no book or collection examining the relation of rhetoric studies to the term *digital humanities*. In the collection *A Companion to the Digital Humanities*, Susan Hockey (2004) describes the origins of DH as evolving from a long tradition of humanities computing. Leading up to the recent history of the term *digital humanities*, since at least 1949 there has been a history of humanities computing that has focused on the use and development of "applications involving textual sources,"

1

and this research and development has "taken center stage within the development of humanities computing." As Hockey explains, in the 1990s interest in leveraging computational power to the coding and analysis of texts has expanded to include "the applications of computing to research and teaching within subjects that are loosely defined as 'the humanities'" (3). This general interest in the humanities and computation has produced what Susan Schreibman, Ray Siemens, and John Unsworth (2004), the editors of *A Companion to the Digital Humanities*, contend is a "discipline in its own right" (xxiii).

Despite the lengthy history of the term *digital humanities* outside rhetoric and writing studies, inside the field of rhetoric and writing studies there has been, up until recently, very limited mention of it. In a recent analysis of listservs such as TechRhet, Writing Program Administration (WPA-L), and H-Rhetor, we found that *digital humanities* is a recent term that emerged around 2008 in response to cross-posted messages such as job advertisements. For example, in a search of TechRhet, the premiere listserv in C&W, we found that in 2008 there were only six e-mails mentioning the exact phrase *digital humanities*, in 2009 there were only nine, in 2010 there were only seventeen, and in 2011 there were only sixty-four. Numbers on WPA-L and H-Rhetor were considerably lower than on TechRhet.[1]

For those in DH who are less familiar with rhetoric and writing studies, there are historical reasons why the term *digital humanities* is less prevalent in a field that has itself come to maturity and developed specializations with significant intellectual investments in digital technology over the last thirty years. One of these is the subfield of C&W, an area with an annual conference (Computers and Writing) that began in 1982, a peer-reviewed journal (*Computers and Composition*) in its thirtieth volume year, several book series, and numerous edited volumes to its credit. Over the last ten years, discussions related to writing in digital environments have become mainstream in composition and rhetoric, the area most closely associated with the teaching and learning of writing in postsecondary education and, in particular, the introductory writing curriculum in the United States. Another subarea of rhetoric and writing studies with long-running ties to digital technology as both object and medium of inquiry is technical and professional writing (TPW). TPW scholars are concerned with ways in which writing activity is practiced in workplace and community settings as well as with pedagogical and curricular issues related to preparing students for writing outside of school. As such, from the outset, TPW scholars have examined technology as part of writers' workplace contexts and looked to incorporate digital tools to extend the range of teaching and learning to include audiences and genres that students are likely to encounter in their working lives.

These rhetoric and writing communities share many of the intellectual values associated today with DH. The C&W community, in particular, embraces not only the analysis and critique of technology but also the making of digital tools—the "less yacking, more hacking" ethical imperative. The community's outstanding dissertation award is named for Hugh Burns, whose 1979 Ph.D. thesis is regarded as the first C&W dissertation. Burns's study evaluated students' use of heuristic software based on Aristotle's topoi and showed that well-constructed computer-assisted instruction could enhance the number and sophistication of ideas in students' written drafts. Chris Neuwirth and David Kaufer created a number of digital tools in the early 1980s, including *PREP Editor* and *Notes*, working with grant funding from U.S. Department of Education and the National Science Foundation (see, e.g., Neuwirth, Kaufer, Chimera, and Gillespie 1987; and Neuwirth, Kaufer, Chandhok, and Morris 1990).

Paul LeBlanc gave the C&W movement one of its taglines with the title of his 1993 book *Writing Teachers Writing Software*, naming a trend that continues today. As the rhetoric and composition movement matured and broadened its own research focus over the last forty years, the field's focus on the digital has similarly broadened to include scholarship beyond the classroom. Engagement in what was known early on as *humanities computing* and now as *digital humanities* is part of that expansion, with notable contributions by scholars representing the diversity of rhetoric and writing studies such as Ned O'Gorman, Dene Grigar, Stuart Moulthrop, and Dean Rehberger, to name but a few.

We argue that rhetoric and writing studies' recent attention to DH not only demonstrates the need for this collection to put scholars in conversation with one another but also suggests that there is much work to be done. One way to begin this work is to examine some ways the term *digital humanities* functions and how it can inform conversations in rhetoric studies. In *Debates in the Digital Humanities*, Matthew Kirschenbaum (2012) claims that the term *digital humanities* functions largely tactically. He argues: "To assert that digital humanities is a 'tactical' coinage is not simply to indulge in neopragmatic relativism. Rather, it is to insist on the reality of circumstances in which it is unabashedly deployed to get things done—'things' might include getting a faculty line or funding a staff position, establishing a curriculum, revamping a lab, or launching a [research] center" (415). Following Kirschenbaum's discussion, we argue that there are two ways that DH can be tactical for scholars in rhetoric studies, TPW, and technical communication. First, we argue that scholars may want to consider selectively redefining digital projects under the umbrella of DH in order to leverage funding, institutional recognition, and extrafield audiences. Second, we propose studying the DH job market as an example of how fields in crisis (literature and history) are responding to market pressures and, additionally, how rhetoric studies can leverage DH for additional hires.

First, Lisa Gerrard (1995) notes that the earliest informal meeting of the Computers and Writing conference at the University of Minnesota (in 1982) originated from Department of Education Funding for the Improvement of Postsecondary Education grant. Project principal investigators were tasked with developing a computer program for student authors called the Writing Aid and Author's Helper (WANDAH), an "integrated system, consisting of invention tools, revising tools, and a word-processing program—[it] was the first computer program to address the entire writing process" (279). The origin story of this project exemplifies many contemporary projects funded by the NEH ODH. However, the story of WANDAH is not one that has been translated into the recent field history of DH; rather, it remains under the disciplinary umbrella of C&W, absent from DH conversations. We argue that the absence of WANDAH from the DH literature has implications for C&W, especially as C&W leverages its field histories as the basis for external funding and resources. In this respect, rhetoric studies more broadly should look to C&W and past digital research as a digital field history that can—and should—be articulated beyond the discipline to the umbrella of DH.

Specifically, we cite the rise of external funding earmarked for DH through agencies such as the NEH ODH, the Andrew W. Mellon Foundation, the Joint Information Systems Committee, and the American Council of Learned Societies as evidence that scholars in our field can benefit from translating their research into the grant language of funding opportunities in DH. From 2008 to 2011 the NEH ODH alone funded 250 projects totaling $15,268,130. The Mellon Foundation, a private funding organization, "paid $30,870,567 to projects in 2010" in their Scholarly Communication and Information Technology category (Terra 2011). For example, scholars working in either rhetoric studies or C&W have received at least four NEW ODH Start-Up grants (Potts and Gossett 2012; Carter 2011; Ball, Eyman, and Gossett 2010; Hart-Davidson and Ridolfo 2008) and an NEH Digging into Data grant (Rehberger 2010). These funded projects include work on digital archives and repositories, software for field journals, computer-assisted hand-writing analysis, and research on remix and composing. We argue that it is important that researchers in rhetoric and writing studies continue to apply, compete for, and receive these grant awards. If we are represented in these awards, then we have the ability to serve as future reviewers and help determine the kinds of projects that are funded. If we sit out on either applying or reviewing, then we will lose representation in federal funding categories and, in doing so, forfeit resources and local institutional recognition.

Second, we urge faculty in rhetoric and composition to study job advertisements and institutional interest in DH as, we argue, an example of how some fields are responding to market pressures at the institutional level. While we do not think that DH as an area will scale widely enough in terms of available tenure track or alternative academic positions to offset the significant reserve army of labor created by the excessive output of Ph.D.s in literature and history, we do think that rhetoric and composition should closely follow and, at times, *tactically* participate, in the terminology of the DH job market. By *tactical participation*, we mean, for example, responding to commonplace terms in institutions: Is the administration responding to the term *digital humanities*? Is it possible, then, that this term may be used to argue for human-computer interaction (HCI)/user-centered design or digital rhetoric hires? For example, Alex Reid (2012) notes: "Perhaps [future] digital humanities specialists will function similarly to computers and writing specialists in rhetoric and composition, but it is also the case that virtually any doctoral program in rhetoric and composition would include at least one professor who could provide graduate students with curriculum in technology" (351). Tactically, how will programs negotiate the language of these position descriptions? What are the specific institutional affordances and disadvantages to labeling a position DH or C&W? These specific distinctions, we argue, will require our fields' future attention in the years to come.

Beyond the Tactical: Seeding New Conversations in Rhetoric and DH

In *Rhetoric and the Digital Humanities*, what we are most excited to see emerging in the work of our colleagues in rhetoric studies is a broader and deeper set of shared interests and intellectual commitments.

Part 1, "Interdisciplinary Connections," consists of seven chapters that define field connections between rhetoric studies and DH and address issues in speculative rhetoric, software studies, bibliometrics, digital publishing, cultural rhetorics, materiality, and race. In chapter 1, "Digital Humanities Now and the Possibilities of a Speculative Digital Rhetoric," Alexander Reid offers perspective on rhetoric studies' examination of discursive *networks*—assemblages of humans and machines—and the procedures that create textual artifacts. He argues that a rhetorical critique, in particular one that adopts a "speculative realist" viewpoint, can act as a check on the way DH scholarship is produced and the way it operates to (re)produce knowledge. In chapter 2, "Crossing State Lines: Rhetoric and Software Studies," James J. Brown Jr. argues that "software is one of the available means of persuasion," opening the way for source code texts to serve as primary sources in rhetorical analysis. In chapter 3, "Beyond Territorial Disputes: Toward a 'Disciplined Interdisciplinarity' in the Digital Humanities," Shannon Carter, Jennifer Jones, and Sunchai Hamcumpai investigate Charles Bazerman's term disciplined *interdisciplinarity* through the treatment of their *Remixing Rural Texas* NEH ODH–funded project. They discuss how their project "fostered DH situations that lead to new questions, new insights, new ways of making sense of the world and teaching the students within it." In chapter 4, "Cultural Rhetorics and the Digital Humanities: Toward Cultural Reflexivity in Digital Making," Jennifer Sano-Franchini uses the framework of her YouTube archive of East Asian blepharoplasty to provide a theoretical rationale for a DH grounded in cultural rhetorics, an emergent field concerned with the diversity of meaning and text-making practices that help sustain cultural identities. In chapter 5, "Digital Humanities Scholarship and Electronic Publication," Douglas Eyman and Cheryl Ball argue that publication and dissemination of digital scholarship relies on three critical forms of infrastructure—scholarly, social, and technical—and move from an infrastructural understanding of invention to examine the human and machine infrastructure necessary for born-digital publishing. In chapter 6, "The Metaphor and Materiality of Layers," Daniel Anderson and Jentery Sayers illuminate the extradimensional reasoning that goes on during the inventional work of born-digital multimodal artifacts. They offer scholars making digital media a framework and a vocabulary with which to examine "distance as a means of theorizing relations among presumably disparate fields: digital humanities, digital rhetoric, media studies, textual studies, and electronic literature," and they also begin a systematic account of the repertoire of digital rhetors. In chapter 7, "Modeling Rhetorical Disciplinarity: Mapping the Digital Network,"

Nathan Johnson offers an exploration of disparate fields. Transitioning to part 2, he stitches together scientometrics, information visualization, and sociology of knowledge to show how these factors influence the production of scholarship.

Part 2, "Research Methods and Methodology," consists of six chapters focused on qualitative and quantitative approaches to rhetoric studies and DH with a particular strength in the area of corpus-assisted research. In chapter 8, "Tactical and Strategic: Qualitative Approaches to the Digital Humanities," Brian McNely and Christa Teston focus on the nature of rhetorical action and writing in networked spaces, exploring qualitative research methods adapted to the task of studying digital rhetoric in action *in situ*. They argue that, in the time and space of networked environments, there are important methodological issues to consider when studying writing and rhetoric. In chapter 9, "Low Fidelity in High Definition: Speculations on Rhetorical Editions," Casey Boyle sketches a vision for preparing digital critical editions that builds on a rhetorical understanding of how texts are the beginnings of inventional processes. The implication is that, in digital spaces, critical editions of texts become locations for engagement in their own right; they provide shared digital spaces where values and interests are aligned but diverse interpretations and derivative uses can also coincide. In chapter 10, "The Trees within the Forest: Extracting, Coding, and Visualizing Subjective Data in Authorship Studies," Krista Kennedy and Seth Long tackle questions related to the treatment of digital texts as evidence of writing activity, where the object of inquiry is the author and authorship more generally. With sections on extracting, coding, and visualizing data, they offer a useful set of methods that can form the core of a study or be recruited to triangulate analysis of primary source materials.

With computation as the medium for analytic work, the second half of part 2 explores computational rhetorics. Now that rhetoric studies that examine thousands or millions of texts at a time are possible, how best can scholars take advantage of this emergent capacity? What does computational rhetoric promise, what might it threaten to obviate, and what new ethical dynamics should rhetoric scholars take into account? Chapters 11–13, "Genre and Automated Text Analysis: A Demonstration" by Roderick P. Hart, "At the Digital Frontier of Rhetoric Studies: An Overview of Tools and Methods for Computer-Aided Textual Analysis" by David Hoffman and Don Waisanen, and "Corpus-Assisted Analysis of Internet-Based Discourses: From Patterns to Rhetoric" by Nelya Koteyko, offer detailed accounts of computational methods tailored for rhetorical inquiry. In Hart's chapter, we see the way clusters and word adjacencies can be computationally read as the building blocks of genre. Hoffman and Waisanen demonstrate how textual analysis software might enhance rhetorical approaches to contemporary and historic public discourse. In Koteyko's chapter, we move to the field of "webometrics" to "combine the established methods of corpus linguistics developed specifically to search, sort, and retrieve patterns in vast textual repositories" as a means to advance engaged research.

Part 3, "Future Trajectories," is composed of ten short chapters and offers several paths for exploring the relation between rhetoric studies and DH. It includes topics related to departmental configurations, building programs and labs, archives, programming, and materiality.

In part 3, we see engagement develop as a key theme. Chapter 18, Jenny Rice and Jeff Rice's "Pop-Up Archives," explores the ways scholars in rhetoric studies might build archival thinking and practice with and in local communities as a way to scale the archival impulse in the ways we have seen peer production scale in participatory culture. Similarly, in chapter 16, "Tackling a Fundamental Problem: Using Digital Labs to Build Smarter Computing Cultures," Kevin Brooks, Chris Lindgren, and Matthew Warner address the challenges of leveraging computing as a means to build culture. Drawing on their multiyear efforts with an after-school procedural literacy curriculum, they draw on the work of Richard McKeon to discuss civic engagement and technoscientific complicity. Engagement within the academy but across disciplinary boundaries is also the focus of chapter 14, Jennifer Glaser and Laura R. Micciche's "Digitizing English," chapter 23, David Gruber's "New Materialism and a Rhetoric of Scientific Practice in the Digital Humanities," and chapter 15, Douglas Walls's "In/Between Programs: Forging a Curriculum between Rhetoric and the Digital Humanities." In particular, Glaser and Micciche and Walls examine how the landscape of English studies is shifting and discuss the ways DH can provide common ground for program and curriculum building among literature, language, and rhetoric and writing faculty. Gruber explores DH as an interdisciplinary space whose collaborative modes of scholarship and project orientation work to break down or break through disciplinary silos.

Chapter 19, Liza Potts's "Archive Experiences: A Vision for User-Centered Design in the Digital Humanities," chapter 21, Brian Ballentine's "Procedural Literacy and the Future of the Digital Humanities," and chapter 20, Karl Stolley's "MVC, Materiality, and the Magus: The Rhetoric of Source-Level Production," each work to broaden and deepen our understanding of writing practice in digital spaces. Ballentine's "procedural literacy" framework coins the name for new core knowledge for DH students, while Stolley's and Potts's work offers a glimpse at the range of contributions that digital rhetoricians can make to the development of interactive media and application systems.

Chapter 17, Tarez Samra Graban, Alexis Ramsey-Tobienne, and Whitney Myers's "In, Through, and About the Archive: What Digitization (Dis)Allows," and chapter 22, Elizabeth Losh's "Nowcasting/Futurecasting: Big Data, Prognostication, and the Rhetorics of Scale," each offer no less transformative visions enabled by computation. However, like Hart (chapter 11), these authors are careful to raise ethical considerations regarding the limits and potential consequences of computation, intended or otherwise, when it comes to matters of privacy, cultural heritage, and identity. What do the expanded affordances of digital spaces mean for the ethical dimensions of archives? Graban, Ramsey-Tobienne, and Myers raise this question in relation to important topics such as "digital repatriation," copyright, and levels of access as they intersect with cultural heritage issues such as right of representation. Losh offers a critical perspective on big data and the enthusiasm surrounding the promise of analytic procedures—including rhetorical analysis—not only to illuminate the past but also to frame the present in real time and forecast the future. But, rather than offer mere caution, she adds requirements to the emergent functional spec being compiled for big data analytics in DH by media theorists-cum-futurists such as Lev Manovich and Malcolm Gladwell. The result is a more rhetorical research agenda for DH.

While the debate about the relation between DH and pre-DH is ongoing and is the subject of other volumes, such as Matthew K. Gold's *Debates in the Digital Humanities* (2012), the chapters in *Rhetoric and the Digital Humanities* explore field connections between DH and rhetoric studies. As the editors of this collection, we take a capacious view of DH and rhetoric, recognizing the important work of scholars outside rhetoric in DH and the work of scholars in the allied areas of study associated with rhetoric: composition, writing studies, cultural rhetorics, C&W, HCI, parts of communication studies, and TPW. Our collection aims to provide a first step toward building interdisciplinary discussions between rhetoric studies and DH by defining shared research trajectories, methods, and projects between DH and the federation of rhetoric studies, composition, C&W, and areas of TPW. In the years ahead, we see the driving research questions behind the collection as future points of conversation and investigation:

- What is the relationship between rhetoric/cultural rhetorics/C&W/computational rhetorics/digital rhetoric and DH?
- What are some of the disciplinary/funding/collaborative challenges for scholars of rhetoric working in DH or for DH scholars using rhetorical methods? What is at stake in claiming one disciplinary identity over another?
- How might DH shape and redefine the relation of rhetoric studies to English studies?
- What are some of the emerging digital research and methodological connections common to rhetoric studies/C&W and DH?
- What research methods in rhetoric studies/C&W complement the work that is currently under way in DH? How might DH as a field benefit from qualitative approaches to rhetoric research? How might rhetoric scholars working with computers benefit from the disciplinary identity of DH?
- What are the opportunities for research collaboration between scholars of rhetoric studies and other disciplines now working under the umbrella of DH?
- What rhetorical questions/rhetoric studies are possible through big data and computational rhetorics?
- How might collaboration in DH prompt scholars in rhetoric studies to rethink their model for doing research?
- How do various project funding and labor models in DH speak to the experiences of scholars in rhetoric studies/C&W?
- How will DH change the way scholars in rhetoric studies/C&W approach research/collaboration/interdisciplinary conversations/teaching?
- How might collaboration within DH shape/affect/change specific field conversations in rhetoric studies?
- How might the intersection of DH and rhetoric studies influence English studies at the department and institutional levels?
- What is at stake, for rhetoric studies as a discipline, in not being a part of these larger interdisciplinary field conversations?
- How might DH challenge and shape existing notions of disciplinarity and/or the job market?

While by no means conclusive, we hope that *Rhetoric and the Digital Humanities* is a useful step toward answering many of these questions.

Note

1. For WPA-L, there were seven in 2008, two in 2009, one in 2010, nine in 2011, and thirty-four in 2012. there were none in 2008, none in 2009, one in 2010, four in 2011, and two in 2012.

References

Ball, Cheryl, Douglas Eyman, and Kathie Gossett. 2010. *Building a Better Back-End: Editor, Author, and Reader Tools for Scholarly Multimedia.* https://securegrants.neh.gov/PublicQuery/main.aspx?g=1&gn=HD-51088-10.

Burns, Hugh L. "Stimulating Rhetorical Invention in English Composition through Computer-Assisted Instruction." Ph.D. diss., University of Texas at Austin, 1979.

Carter, Shannon. 2011. Office of Digital Humanities. *Remixing Rural Texas: Local Texts, Global Context.* https://securegrants.neh.gov/PublicQuery/main.aspx?g=1&gn=HD-51398-11.

Gerrard, Lisa. 1995. "The Evolution of the Computers and Writing Conference." *Computers and Composition* 12.3:279–92.

Gold, Matthew K., ed. 2012. *Debates in the Digital Humanities.* Minneapolis: University of Minnesota Press.

Hart-Davidson, William, and Jim Ridolfo. 2008. *Archive 2.0: Imagining the Michigan State University Israelite Samaritan Scroll Collection.* https://securegrants.neh.gov/publicquery/main.aspx?f=1&gn=HD-50445-08.

Hockey, Susan. 2004. "The History of Humanities Computing." In *A Companion to the Digital Humanities*, ed. Susan Schreibman, Raymond Siemens, and John Unsworth, 3–19. Malden, MA: Blackwell.

Kirschenbaum, Matthew G. 2012. "Digital Humanities As/Is a Tactical Turn." In *Debates in the Digital Humanities*, ed. Matthew K. Gold, 415–28. Minneapolis: University of Minnesota Press.

LeBlanc, Paul J. 1993. *Writing Teachers Writing Software: Creating Our Place in the Electronic Age.* Advances in Computers and Composition Studies Series. Urbana, IL: National Council of Teachers of English.

Neuwirth, Christine, David Kaufer, Rick Chimera, and Terilyn Gillespie. 1987. "The Notes Program: A Hypertext Application for Writing from Source Texts." In *Proceedings of the ACM Conference on Hypertext (HYPERTEXT '87)*, 121–41. New York: ACM.

Neuwirth, Christine M., David S. Kaufer, Ravinder Chandhok, and James H. Morris. 1990. "Issues in the Design of Computer Support for Co-Authoring and Commenting." In *Proceedings of the 1990 ACM Conference on Computer-Supported Cooperative Work*, 183–95. ACM.

Potts, Liza, and Katherine Gossett. 2012. "Building an Open-Source Archive for Born-Digital Dissertations." NEH, Office of the Digital Humanities. https://securegrants.neh.gov/publicquery/main.aspx?f=1&gn=HD-51561-12.

Rehberger, Dean. 2010. *Digging into Image Data to Answer Authorship Related Questions.* NEH, Office of the Digital Humanities. https://securegrants.neh.gov/publicquery/main.aspx?f=1&gn=HJ-50001-10.

Reid, Alex. 2012. "Graduate Education and the Ethics of the Digital Humanities." In *Debates in the Digital Humanities*, ed. Matthew K. Gold, 350–67. Minneapolis: University of Minnesota Press.

Schreibman, Susan, Raymond George Siemens, and John Unsworth. 2004. "The Digital Humanities and Humanities Computing: An Introduction." In *A Companion to Digital Humanities*, ed. Susan Schreibman, Raymond George Siemens, and John Unsworth, xxiii–xxvii. Malden, MA: Blackwell.

Terra, Melissa. 2011. "Stats and the Digital Humanities." *Melissa Terras' Blog*, November 28. http://melissaterras.blogspot.com/2011/11/stats-and-digital -humanities.html.

## PART ONE

Interdisciplinary Connections

## ONE

Digital Humanities Now and the Possibilities of a Speculative Digital Rhetoric

ALEXANDER REID

Discussions of the digital humanities often encounter the problem of defining the field. There are some methods and areas of study that are clearly defined as digital humanities: these employ computers to study traditional objects of humanistic study, an area that was once called *humanities computing*. Other methods and areas bear a more ambiguous relation to digital humanities, such as media study and rhetoric and composition, which have long-standing practices of studying digital media and technologies that have paralleled those of humanities computing. Within rhetoric and composition, digital rhetoric faces identity challenges similar to those of the digital humanities as it potentially envelops work from various subdisciplines such as technical and professional communication, computers and writing, and new media rhetoric. Given the difficulties in defining either digital humanities or digital rhetoric, imagining how the two might relate in general terms generates a wide range of possibilities. The relation is further hampered by the now well-known troubled relation between rhetoric and the humanities. For more than a century, starting in English departments, the humanities have largely disassociated themselves from rhetoric. Some rhetoricians no longer consider themselves humanists; they are trained and work in communications departments and practice social scientific methods. There can be a fair amount of ill will and suspicion that must be overcome for digital rhetoricians and digital humanists to collaborate. This disagreement might be a relatively minor matter, to be settled locally, were it not intertwined with the problems that the humanities in general and the digital humanities in particular face. As has been widely discussed in both academic and mainstream discourses, the humanities are in an apparent state of crisis, with declining numbers of majors, fewer jobs for faculty, funding cuts, and a general questioning of their value in a system of higher education that is itself under attack. Digital humanities has been identified, rightly or wrongly, as a potential solution to this crisis. However, it seems unlikely that any new methodology, digital or otherwise, will solve this problem. Instead, the promise of the digital humanities lies in its potential to address the political, ethical, and rhetorical challenges of living in a digital age: a set of challenges that are not particularly addressed by the traditions of conventional digital humanities but that are at the core of digital rhetoric. This is not to suggest that rhetoricians have all the answers either. Rather, what is required is a rethinking of the humanities that accounts for technology and rhetoric in a new way.

In this brief chapter, I will propose one possible approach to this rethinking. While there are certainly many possibilities, my central argument is that any approach will need to identify and address the problem with modernity that Bruno Latour has elaborated in *We Have Never Been Modern* (1993) and elsewhere. This is not to suggest that we must all become Latourians; there may be other ways to address this concern. Instead, what I believe is crucial in Latour is the issue that has resulted in this particular kairotic moment that brings together a humanities in crisis, the digital humanities, and (digital) rhetoric. This issue, simply put, is the identification of cultural objects and practices as knowable only through a limited set of humanistic methods that are kept separate from the methods of mathematics and science. This identification has created the absolute divide between nature and culture: a definition that, for Latour, shapes the modern era. The humanities has, as a modern discipline, operated on the principle that scientific discourses and methods are appropriate only to matters of nature while cultural matters demand a separate set of methods and inquiries. The contemporary moment has put unrelenting pressures on that divide. The complaints raised about the digital humanities reflect those pressures as humanists reject the idea that human experience and aesthetic endeavors can be productively or legitimately explored by computational means. Digital rhetoricians face a related objection from those who view digital literacy as secondary to, and often disruptive of, a primary, humanistic (and print-based) literacy. Not coincidentally, thinkers in the speculative realist movement, such as Latour, have faced similar criticism for their willingness to consider the value of contemporary mathematics and science for addressing traditionally humanistic concerns. The traditional views in both rhetoric and the humanities share a faith in a human exceptionalism that must of necessity posit every new technology as a potential threat to the already existing human with his independent and self-contained capacities for thought, agency, and expression. On the other hand, digital humanities and digital rhetoric share (at least potentially) the speculative realist view that humans are not ontologically exceptional but rather participate openly in an environment that includes other nonhuman objects and blends nature and culture. (I put *potentially* in parentheses here as it is certainly possible to undertake digital work and hold on to a belief in human exceptionalism.) How is this step toward the nonhuman and away from the modernist nature/culture divide related to the perceived humanities in crisis? The easiest way to understand this relation is as a paradigm shift wherein scientific discoveries, the emergence of digital media, and the development of new global relations (i.e., all the trappings of the postindustrial world) have created new conditions for which traditional humanistic paradigms, built in the modern, industrial age, are no longer suited. I will focus primarily on Latour as one thinker who offers some insight into this issue. Latour's work has become increasingly well-known in digital rhetoric, so he offers a somewhat familiar starting point. However, I also want to situate him in relation to the larger philosophical movement of speculative realism and, thus, as one possible contributor to a speculative *rhetoric* that might develop.

What Is a Speculative Rhetoric?

Speculative rhetoric refers to the speculative realism movement in philosophy that has developed over the last decade. Briefly, speculative realists all acknowledge in one way or another the contemporary philosophical situation that Quentin Meillassoux (2008) terms *correlationism*: "the idea according to which we only ever have access to the correlation between thinking and being, and never to either term considered apart from the other" (7). That is, correlationists (following Kant) assert that humans can know the world only in relation to themselves. Correlationism sets up an important question for ontology. Given this apparent limit on knowledge, what can we say about being? Speculative realists offer different answers to this question, and this is not the occasion to attempt to account for them all, though I will momentarily take up one. Rhetoric has traditionally operated within the correlationist circle, concerning itself only with human symbolic behavior (or symbolic action, to use Burke's phrase). That said, it has also always dealt with the problems and opportunities that nonhumans—technologies in particular—pose for communication. That is, rhetoric has always recognized that symbolic behavior cannot be simply human. Nevertheless, rhetoric has imagined symbolic behavior as primarily human, as something that nonhumans might enhance or disrupt, but as something that is ultimately *of us* and *for us*. Indeed, in the absence of a divine explanation, symbolic behavior has been the central evidence of human ontological exceptionalism: that is, what makes humans unique is that they possess symbolic behavior as an ontological characteristic. A speculative rhetoric begins with recognizing that language is nonhuman. It is not "ours," though clearly humans have a powerful relation with language. As such, one must approach rhetorical relations as relations within nonhumans; this is where a speculative rhetoric begins, with an investigation of nonhumans.

Though there are many possible methods for undertaking this investigation, here I will focus on a Latourian approach. Meillassoux's correlationism can be encountered in a different register in Latour's critique of the modern split of culture from nature. By this, I mean to suggest not that Latour and Meillassoux are making the same argument but rather that there are resonances. As Latour points out, the modern world allows one to speak of natural, scientific knowledge, or of sociocultural knowledge, but not of both simultaneously. Correlationism applies equally to both natural and cultural objects, but in practice the indeterminacy of a text or a cultural practice is understood differently from the inscrutability of a natural object. As Latour writes: "In the eyes of our critics the ozone hole above our heads, the moral law in our hearts, the autonomous text, may each be of interest, but only separately. That a delicate shuttle should have woven together the heavens, industry, texts, souls and moral law—this remains uncanny, unthinkable, unseemly" (1993, 5). One of the effects of a Kantian correlationism has been to construct these different worlds: a natural world that is clearly not human and a social world that while also beyond us is closer to us, is produced by us, and, thus, might be understood differently as operating by a different set of laws. As the quote offered above suggests, for Latour rhetoric and discourse form a third space in the modern formulation where it is possible to speak of a system of signs or the text itself. This results in a postmodern condition composed of "a nature and a technology that are absolutely {softlinesleek; a society made up solely of false consciousness, simulacra and illusions; a discourse consisting only in meaning effects detached from everything; and this whole world of appearances keeps afloat other disconnected elements of networks that can be combined haphazardly by collage from all places and all times" (Latour 1993, 64–65). A Latourian speculative rhetoric then takes up the challenge of investigating a hybridized space that technology, nature, society, culture, and discourse commonly share.

References

Digital Humanities Now. 2012, "About." http://digitalhumanitiesnow.org/about/.

Galloway, Alexander. 2013. "The Poverty of Philosophy: Realism and Post-Fordism." *Critical Inquiry* 39.2: 347–66.

Grusin, Richard. 2013. "The Dark Side of the Digital Humanities—Part Two." *Thinking C21* blog, January 13; accessed January 18, 2014. http://www.c21uwm.com/2013/01/09/dark-side-of-the-digital-humanities-part-2.

Latour, Bruno. 1993. *We Have Never Been Modern*. Trans. Catherine Porter. Cambridge, MA: Harvard University Press.

———. 2010. "An Attempt at a 'Compositionist Manifesto.'" *New Literary History* 41.3:471–90.

Liu, Alan. 2012. "Where Is Cultural Criticism in the Digital Humanities?" In *Debates in the Digital Humanities,* ed. Matthew K. Gold, 490–506. Minneapolis: University of Minnesota Press. http://dhdebates.gc.cuny.edu/debates/text/20.

Meillassoux, Quentin. 2008. *After Finitude: An Essay on the Necessity of Contingency.* Trans. Ray Brassier. London: Continuum.

## TWO

Crossing State Lines: Rhetoric and Software Studies

JAMES J. BROWN JR.

In *Rhetoric and Reality* (1987), Jim Berlin claims textual production for rhetoric and argues that poetics is primarily concerned with interpretation. His history of twentieth-century writing instruction goes to great lengths to explain how theories of rhetoric and poetics are always intertwined at any historical moment. However, his primary goal is to "vindicate the position of writing instruction in the college curriculum" (1) and to refute the idea that the primary focus of English departments is the interpretation of literature. Berlin's work offered a necessary corrective to the often-marginalized field of rhetoric and composition, and it put into question the idea that literary interpretation is the core disciplinary concern of English. While things have certainly shifted since the publication of *Rhetoric and Reality*, the disciplinary lines traced by Berlin remain with us in various forms. In fact, a new version of this struggle is playing out as rhetoricians decide how or whether to engage with work in the digital humanities (DH). DH journals and conferences often focus on using computation to do literary analysis, leading rhetoricians to see the (sometimes) small tent of DH as excluding work in computers and writing, rhetorical theory, and composition studies.

DH's historical trajectories and its roots in "humanities

computing" have been covered in detail elsewhere, and it is important to note that DH's link to English departments is tied up with this complicated history (Kirschenbaum 2012). However, none of this changes the fact that the relation between DH and literary studies reminds rhetoricians of the battles fought by Berlin and others, leading scholars such as Alex Reid to respond to some of DH's more exclusionary impulses by suggesting that "rhetoricians in English Studies should be familiar with such shenanigans" (2011). Cheryl Ball has expressed similar concerns, suggesting that much work in DH has ignored scholarship in computers and writing: "It seems I always end up in sessions where 'DH' folks present on topics as if they've just discovered them. Digital dissertations aren't a new problem. Using discussion forums in your classes is not a new pedagogy. Getting tenure for digital work is not a new form of administrative harassment" (Croxall 2011).

In a Twitter conversation about this same issue, Ball suggested that "DH-as-lit" has too often tended to "hold their noses at [the] long history of rhet/comp research" (2012). While DH encompasses other disciplines such as information science and geography, there is little doubt that the tensions between literary studies and rhetoric and composition are influencing discussions about the disciplinary boundaries of DH.

The roots of this problem are deep, and many in rhetoric and composition seek to draw clean lines between the worlds of literary interpretation and rhetorical production. For instance, an influential essay by Erika Lindemann (1993) argues that literature does not belong in the rhetoric and composition classroom because literature-based courses focus on "consuming texts, not producing them" (313). Further, she insists that literary interpretation does not "connect literature with life," teaches style "not as language to emulate, but as language to appreciate," relies on the expert interpretations of teachers, and is too bound to the discipline of English to be of use to students as they move into other writing situations (314–15). This argument is often tied up with long-standing intradisciplinary battles. We all know the stories—it is an unshakable part of the history of English studies. It is a complex web of anxieties: the marginalization of composition by literature faculty, a shifting job market that reconfigures the influence of rhetoric and composition on the field, the concerns that those teaching literature do not see their work as being bound by disciplinary concerns, the calls to "break our bonds," and so on. This is difficult territory, and these questions touch raw nerves. However, the time has come to think differently about some of our terms: *literature, composition, production, interpretation, reading, writing*. The task, as I see it, is to develop theories and practices that meet the needs of the contemporary environment, the contemporary scholar, and the contemporary student, regardless of these difficult histories.[1]

That this debate is now playing out with regard to DH is troubling, but it also presents an opportunity for rhetoricians to engage differently with disciplinary divisions. Rhetoric studies can and does have a place in various strands of DH scholarship, but deep collaborations between rhetoric and composition and literary studies require that we cross state lines, letting go of our tendency to claim particular practices and assumptions in disciplinary turf wars. As I demonstrate here, the study of electronic literature is a particularly useful place to start given that it requires categories that move beyond separable notions of *interpretation* and *production*. In addition, software studies, an emerging set of methods and theories for analyzing software and code with the tools of the humanities, can help us see that the analysis of electronic literature (like the interpretation of any literary work) does not necessarily lead to, in Lindemann's terms, the "appreciation" of literature.

Reading and interacting with electronic literature reveals what Katherine Hayles (2008) calls *intermediatory dynamics*. For Hayles, *intermediation* means many things, but here I am most interested in how she uses the term to discuss human-machine collaborations. Intermediation involves "dynamic heterarchies" among humans and machines, complex relations between distributed cognitive systems, and recursive feedback loops that show us how humans and machines learn from one another. Intermediation provides a way of understanding both reading and writing as complex performances that never originate in any one place. By interacting with computational artifacts, we get a "feel for the algorithm" at work. We gain insight into how an object works and how it creates meaning, and we are reminded of the complexities of any interpretive effort. But the feedback loop works in the other direction as well. The machine learns from (and, for Hayles, *thinks about*) our interventions. These same loops affect our complex relations with writing tools, meaning that "humans engineer computers and computers reengineer humans in systems bound together by recursive feedback and feedforward loops" (48). The concept of intermediation accounts for the complexity of both reading and writing situations, and it connects meaning-making activities to an emergent network of humans and machines. What Hayles gives us is not only a way to read electronic literature but also a way to understand how technologies rewire us: "When a programmer/writer creates an executable file, the process reengineers the writer's perceptual and cognitive system as she works with the medium's possibilities. . . . [T]he programmer experiences creation as an active dynamic in which the computer plays a central role" (56).

Who or what is writing in these situations? Who or what is reading? These two categories are not of much use in attempts to understand the interaction between humans and computational machines. For this reason, electronic literature is precisely where we might start reimagining how rhetoricians and literary scholars can collaborate on DH research.

The following analysis embraces these intermediatory dynamics and connects rhetoric studies with work in DH by way of software studies. The work of scholars such as Ian Bogost, Katherine Hayles, Noah Wardrip-Fruin, and Matthew Fuller is showing us how software is a medium of inscription. As Wardrip-Fruin has argued, ubiquitous computing now means that understanding software is a crucial part of civic life: "In our society we are surrounded by software—from everyday Google searches to the high stakes of Diebold voting machines. We need to be prepared to engage software critically, accustomed to interpreting descriptions of processes, able to understand common pitfalls, and aware of what observing software's output reveals and conceals about its inner workings" (2009, 422).

Far from serving as the background of rhetorical situations, software is one of the available means of persuasion. In recognizing this, rhetoricians can play a part in important interdisciplinary conversations while building alliances with scholars in DH. My treatment of *Reagan Library* (1999), a work of electronic literature by Stuart Moulthrop that uses HTML and Javascript to dynamically generate narratives, builds a bridge between rhetoric and DH in three ways: it positions software studies as a rhetorical project, as a set of methods attuned to understanding how software is authored in response to particular situations and problems; it focuses on the arguments expressed by a literary artifact; and it examines that artifact by assuming the inability of cleanly separating questions of interpretation from questions of production.

The Expressive Processes of *Reagan Library*

Like many works of electronic literature, Moulthrop's *Reagan Library* asks interactors to piece together interlocking and overlapping narra-

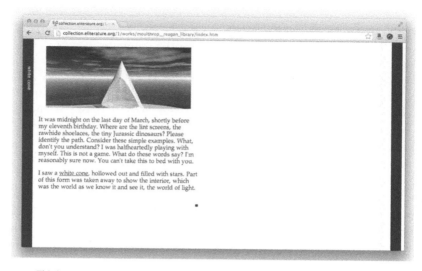

2.1. This is a screenshot of *Reagan Library*'s "White Cone" page. Notice that this is the first visit to this particular page, as indicated by the single (blue) dot in the lower-right-hand corner. At this point, the text is a series of incoherent sentences and phrases.

tives. This work features color-coded zones of narrative that include dynamically generated text and QuickTime VR panoramas. Each zone contains a different story, though the stories also overlap at various points (see fig. 2.1). For instance, a gray zone of the story features a stand-up comedian in psychotherapy, and a blue zone focuses on a deceased film director named Emily St. Cloud.[2] At one point, the stand-up comic makes direct reference to one of St. Cloud's films.

An interactor can navigate the narrative by clicking hyperlinks in either the text or the Quicktime panoramas. The narratives, as the title of the work suggests, all deal with recalling memories. For instance, the stand-up comedian, who has survived a plane crash and is severely burned, is using virtual reality in therapy sessions. Emily St. Cloud discusses previous films and a time capsule that she has buried. Each of these characters makes reference to objects or places that are represented in the Quicktime panoramas. As an interactor clicks through the piece, through hyperlinks in either the text or the panoramas, he or she moves among the different narratives and finds pages of mostly incoherent text. However, the longer one spends with *Reagan Library*, the more coherent the pages become. Text becomes less fragmentary, and interactors find that visiting a page four times completes its transformation. Small blocks in the corner of the screen tell interactors how many times they have visited a page, and with some experimentation they can begin to play *Reagan Library* as a game, trying to ensure that each page has reached maximum coherence.

As we will see, a closer look at *Reagan Library*'s software reveals that the piece is not only a series of narratives about the fraughtness of memory. It is also a set of computational processes that offers a commentary on technological memory and that expresses something about a particular historical moment. *Reagan Library* provides us with an argument about life in a computational world, circa 1999, and it does so by using what Wardrip-Fruin calls *expressive processing*. Wardrip-Fruin coins this term to describe two dimensions of computation. First, like others in software studies, he argues that computation is an expressive medium that can be used to make meaning. Thus, we can see *Reagan Library* as procedurally expressive, as using computation to make meaning. The second meaning of *expressive processing* addresses "what processes express in their design—which may not be visible to audiences" (2009, 4). Here, Wardrip-Fruin's work intersects with some of the concerns of critical code studies since it insists that a close analysis of the code itself can help uncover important aspects of its design and history. *Reagan Library* embodies this second meaning of *expressive processing* as well since it presents us with a window into the use of Javascript to track the state of a browsing session, a practice that was relatively new when *Reagan Library* was first released. By examining the code and the processes of Moulthrop's piece (it is important to note that these two things are distinct and that one need not have access to code to observe computational processes in action), we gain insight into the history of a computer language and into the ways *Reagan Library* uses software to make meaning. While Moulthrop has written a series of interlocking stories about memory, he has also written a piece of software, and scholars in software studies argue that understanding both these types of authorship is imperative when making sense of computational artifacts.

The value of something like *Reagan Library* is that it reveals some of its expressive processing as we interact with it. This means that interactors can gain some insights about *Reagan Library*'s procedural expressions before delving into its code, discovering that the work offers a commentary on Web-browsing technology and Javascript. For instance, one of the color-coded zones (the "red zone") provides tips to the reader about how to navigate the piece. By following these tips (some are red herrings), and by playing with this interface, an interactor learns a number of rules for traversing the work. One page in the "red zone" tells us: "Your shopping cart is not yet full." This clue, along with the small blocks in the corner of the screen, indicates that *Reagan Library* is tracking its reader.

When we dig beyond our surface interaction with *Reagan Library*, we learn that it uses Javascript to record information about the browsing session. *Reagan Library* was republished as part of the *Electronic Literature Collection, Volume 1,* and the CD-ROM that houses this collection provides access to Moulthrop's code. By examining the Javascript files on this disc, we gain further insight into how this work uses computation to achieve certain literary and rhetorical effects. A file called *rlscr. js* contains a series of functions, and a function within that file called *keepTrack* is of particular interest:

```
1 function keepTrack(place, fourState)
2
                                                                       {
3                                     if(fourState<3) fourState ++;
4         parent.frames[1].document.forms[0].elements[place].value = fourState;
5
                                                                       }
```

This function uses a variable called *fourState* to track how many times an interactor has visited each of the work's twenty-eight pages. Once a page is visited four times, the text reaches coherence. But we also learn from line 4 of the code reproduced above that the data tracking these page visits are sitting in a frame right behind the text we are reading. *Reagan Library* increments the fourState value on each visit to a page and then stores that value in a hidden table. Examining the keepTrack function helps us understand how the work tracks the state of a browsing session (keeping a record of how many times an interactor has visited each page). This "deep" reading also reveals that *Reagan Library* stores that information *right under our noses*. With the help of tools that are now standard in most browsers (such as Chrome's "Developer Tools"), we can now reveal that hidden frame relatively easily (see fig. 2.2).

By using these tools, we see that the HTML attribute *frameset* sets up two columns, one of which takes up 100 percent of the screen, and another of which is sitting behind this first. By changing that 100 percent value to 50 percent, we can change the interface of *Reagan Library* altogether, placing each page alongside a table called *tracker* that updates each time we click links. Once each cell in this table contains the num-

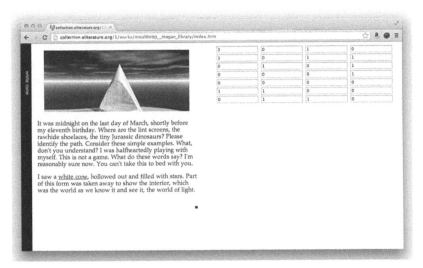

It was midnight on the last day of March, shortly before my eleventh birthday. Where are the lint screens, the rawhide shoelaces, the tiny Jurassic dinosaurs? Please identify the path. Consider these simple examples. What, don't you understand? I was halfheartedly playing with myself. This is not a game. What do these words say? I'm reasonably sure now. You can't take this to bed with you.

I saw a white cone, hollowed out and filled with stars. Part of this form was taken away to show the interior, which was the world as we know it and see it, the world of light.

2.2. This is a screenshot of *Reagan Library*'s "White Cone" page that has been manipulated using the Google Chrome browser's "Developer Tools." In a typical interaction with *Reagan Library*, the "tracker" table on the right-hand side of the page is hidden. By changing the column attributes, an interactor can reveal the table and see how many times each page has been viewed.

ber *3* (we can "cheat" by just typing a *3* into each cell), we have reached the completed version of *Reagan Library*, something the red zone of the work tells us is, in fact, possible: "You can end this." In fact, Moulthrop's introduction explains this as well: "By visiting all the places a sufficient number of times, you can bring the text to a final form. Yes, there is an end to it."

The various narratives presented in this piece comment on the fraughtness of memory, and the title of the piece suggests the same. But the software mirrors this idea, using expressive processes to make a procedural argument. In *Persuasive Games* (2010), Bogost coins the term *procedural rhetoric* to describe how rules (computational or otherwise) make arguments. Designers of procedural systems use rules to shape an interactive experience, and this is what *Reagan Library* does with its use of Javascript. By using computational procedures to make arguments about the state of browser technology in the late 1990s, Moulthrop's *Reagan Library* is an "expressive agent . . . that use[s] processes for expression rather than utility" (11). Works like this remind us that computational procedures can be used for more than just tool making—they can be deployed as an expressive and rhetorical medium. Taking advantage of this expressive power, *Reagan Library* links the browser's ability to *remember* to the characters' engagements with their own memories. While the keepTrack function affects how (or whether) the various narratives emerge, Moulthrop's quip about the "shopping cart" shows us that this is about more than just the dynamic generation of narrative fragments: keepTrack is a commentary on how code is used to track visitors to a Web page. While this is a commonplace notion to-day, *Reagan Library* was published in 1999, at a moment when the typi-cal Web surfer might not yet completely grasp the capabilities of Web browsers or Javascript. Like many works of electronic literature, *Reagan Library* uses computation to reflect on life in a computational world.[3]

Anyone interacting with *Reagan Library* is asked to link compu-tational function to literary meaning. We are asked to consider how the various objects of electronic life were constructed and composed, how that composition made use of computational technologies, and how our own interactions with the piece help make meaning possi-ble. When examining *Reagan Library* as both literature and software, it is not enough to consider, for instance, that the story's stand-up co-median is a burn victim working in psychotherapy. This information must, of course, be part of our interpretation of the piece. However, that information can also be linked to how and when computational procedures are revealing portions of the narratives.[4]

Crossing State Lines

One section of *Reagan Library* extends a warning to the interactor: "Links may cross state lines." This quip can be read in a number of ways. It might be telling us that links jump between the narratives, taking us among the four narrative zones. This reference to state lines also evokes movement through space as certain links actually cross over into different virtual spaces in the Quicktime panoramas. Each of these 3-D spaces has a different layout and houses different objects (though some objects do appear in more than one zone). One moves between these virtual spaces, or "states," by clicking *Reagan Library*'s various hyperlinks. Finally, this reference to state lines might also be a reference to the "state" of the browsing session. The Web runs on hypertext transfer protocol (HTTP), which is a stateless protocol. Any given click on a Web page is seen as an independent event by the server housing that page. The server makes no reference to prior clicks. However, software can be used to track the state of a browsing session, to keep track (or keepTrack) of what is in one's "shopping cart," or to remember whether one is logged in to Facebook. This is what Moulthrop has done with Javascript. As one traverses *Reagan Library*, each click is part of a monitored browsing session. Clicks are no longer "stateless," and this reference to state lines can be read as a pun on the tracking of an interactor's activities as he or she reads (or, better, *plays*) *Reagan Library*.

But my analysis is an attempt to use Moulthrop's quip in an additional way, as an opportunity to rethink the various state lines that we continue to draw between disciplinary practices. How might rhetoricians cross the state lines that have been drawn around DH, both from within and from without? There is little justification for leaving aside literary analysis as "just" interpretation, as "mere" appreciation, or as a disciplinary practice that has no connection to other reading and writing activities. Further, the act of literary interpretation need not be cut off from the concerns of writing or rhetorical analysis. My analysis of *Reagan Library*, which uses the theoretical tools of software studies to link surface experience to computational mechanism and to link literary meaning with rhetorical purpose, offers one example of how rhetoricians can look for productive ways to cross state lines. While this will require DH to commit to a bigger tent and to consider the tradition of scholarship on digital media in rhetoric and composition, it will also require rhetoricians to theorize the relation between production and interpretation. The willingness to separate these practices along disciplinary lines stands as a barrier to collaborations between rhetoric and DH, and scholars on both sides of this divide should be looking for ways to dissolve such barriers.

Electronic literature and software studies are particularly useful tools for rhetoricians interested in building bridges with other scholars in DH. As Katherine Hayles argues, electronic literature "revalues computational practice" (2008, 131), showing us that computer programs are more than tools, that they are *compositions* and sometimes even arguments. It shows us that new media technologies have opened up new modes of expression, and it opens up questions of composition and meaning making that reach beyond the concerns of any one academic discipline. Rhetoric should take up the concerns of software studies for any number of reasons, chief among them that computational artifacts are now an integral part of the available means of persuasion. But taking up software studies also presents us with a concrete way to cross state lines, to let go of disciplinary boundaries that hinder more than they help.

Analyzing an artifact such as *Reagan Library* with the critical tools of software studies demonstrates that the work of interpretation is not separate from the work of production. I have, as Stephen Ramsay reminds us, *deformed* the text not only with Chrome's developer tools but also with an interpretive algorithm that attempts to understand *Reagan Library*'s arguments about memory and computational life. While Ramsay's *Reading Machines: Towards an Algorithmic Criticism* is focused on the use of software to conduct literary interpretations across a large textual corpus, his discussion of algorithmic criticism is still helpful here. He finds the roots of such criticism in the *I Ching* and the Oulipo, arguing that such an interpretive strategy "calls attention to the always dissolving boundaries between creation and interpretation" (2011, 45). Any interpretive effort is an *authoring effort* in that it involves the crafting of an algorithm that one uses to make sense of an object. While much work in DH might use such algorithms to identify patterns in a literary archive, any critical reading is a productive event as readers write programs (they need not be *computer* programs) that they then test out in their attempt to make sense of an artifact. No interpretation without production; no production without interpretation.

My own algorithm involves linking *Reagan Library*'s use of Javascript to its narratives about the fraughtness of memory. It attempts to tell us something about this piece of software's historical moment and about Moulthrop's procedural argument. But, even without delving into the intricacies of Javascript or browser states, *Reagan Library* never allows us to imagine an interaction as confined to a passive realm of interpretation in which meaning is merely consumed. Any given performance of this work relies on an interaction between the reader and the computational machine, and each reading is unique owing to the dynamic way in which text is generated. This work invites the kind of intermediatory dynamics that Hayles describes, calling on the reader to play and, in the process, creating a compelling rhetorical and literary experience. An astute interactor will see that *Reagan Library* is saying something about life in a computational world, but such a reading requires an act of *writing* on the part of that interactor, an algorithm that deforms and remakes the text. It is this blurred boundary between production and interpretation that rhetoricians can embrace in their attempts to cross state lines.

Notes

1. Recent work indicates that the conversation is shifting. For instance, Emily Isaacs has presented a convincing case for using literature in certain

general education writing classes, arguing that "composition faculty need to put aside personal, professional, and even theoretical arguments against literary studies" (2009, 100). I would add only that the conversation will have to work in both directions and that literary scholars should be putting aside the same personal, professional, and theoretical biases against the field of rhetoric and composition. Given these arguments and others, perhaps we are ready to rethink this distinction between production and interpretation and to imagine how literary scholars and rhetoricians can work together. See also Richardson (2004), Bergmann and Baker (2006), Anderson (2007), Brady (2008), and Mattison and Elbow (2003).

2. In my attempts to make sense of Moulthrop's narrative threads and the computational function of *Reagan Library*, I am indebted to the work of Perla Sassón-Henry (2006), Adrian Miles (2004), and Katherine Hayles (2004).

3. In fact, in its very deterioration, *Reagan Library* opens up questions about life in a culture increasingly shaped by computation. Modern browsers do not allow interactors to click the links in the Quicktime panoramas. People engaging with this version of the work are forced to consider how software upgrades change or degrade texts and their ability to make meaning. Thankfully, Moulthrop has created an updated version, which allows us to experience a fully functional electronic text: https://panther file.uwm.edu/moulthro/hypertexts/rlx.

4. In the digital supplement to this chapter, Lauren Gottlieb-Miller, Margaret Hamper, and Richard Ness provide a more detailed account of *Reagan Library*'s expressive processes: http://jamesjbrownjr.net/rdh.

References

Anderson, J. H. 2007. *Integrating Literature and Writing Instruction: First-Year English, Humanities Core Courses, Seminars.* New York: Modern Language Association of America.

Ball, Cheryl E. 2012. "@rogerwhitson See, If DH-as-lit Didn't Hold Their Noses at Long History of Rhet/comp Research in This Area, There's *plenty* of Evid. #anvil." Microblog. *@s2ceball.* https://twitter.com/s2ceball/status/254262502907604993.

Bergmann, L. S., and E. M. Baker, eds. 2006. *Composition and/or Literature: The End(s) of Education.* Urbana, IL: NCTE.

Berlin, James A. 1987. *Rhetoric and Reality: Writing Instruction in American Colleges, 1900–1985.* Carbondale: Southern Illinois University Press.

Bogost, Ian. 2010. *Persuasive Games: The Expressive Power of Videogames.* Cambridge, MA: MIT Press.

Brady, L. 2008. "Retelling the Composition-Literature Story." *College English* 71.1:70–81.

Croxall, Brian. 2011. "Reporting from HASTAC 2011." *Chronicle of Higher Education*, ProfHacker, December 14. http://chronicle.com/blogs/profhacker/reporting-from-hastac-2011/37717#comment-387479756.

Hayles, N. Katherine. 2004. "Bodies of Texts, Bodies of Subjects." In *Memory Bites: History, Technology and Digital Culture*, ed. Lauren Rabinovitz and Abraham Geil, 257–82. Durham, NC: Duke University Press.

———. 2008. *Electronic Literature: New Horizons for the Literary*. Notre Dame, IN: University of Notre Dame Press.

Isaacs, E. 2009. "Teaching General Education Writing: Is There a Place for Literature?" *Pedagogy* 9.1:97–120.

Kirschenbaum, Matthew. 2012. "What Is Digital Humanities Doing in English Departments?" In *Debates in the Digital Humanities*, ed. Matthew K. Gold, 3–11. Minneapolis: University of Minnesota Press.

Lindemann, Erika. 1993. "Freshman Composition: No Place for Literature." *College English* 55.3:311–16.

Mattison, M., and P. Elbow. 2003. "A Comment on 'The Cultures of Literature and Composition: What Could Each Learn from the Other?'" *College English* 65.4:439–43.

Miles, Adrian. 2004. "Review of Stuart Moulthrop's 'Reagan's Library.'" *Hypertext.rmit.* http://hypertext.rmit.edu.au/essays/rl.

Moulthrop, Stuart. 1999. *Reagan Library*. http://collection.eliterature.org/1/works/moulthrop__reagan_library/index.htm.

Ramsay, Stephen. 2011. *Reading Machines: Toward an Algorithmic Criticism*. Urbana: University of Illinois Press.

Reid, Alex. 2011. "Digital Humanities Tactics." *Digital Digs*, June 17. http://www.alex-reid.net/2011/06/digital-humanities-tactics.html.

Richardson, M. 2004. "Who Killed Annabel Lee? Writing about Literature in the Composition Classroom." *College English* 66.3:278–93.

Sasson-Henry, Perla. 2006. "Borges' 'The Library of Babel' and Moulthrop's Cybertext 'Reagan Library' Revisited." *Rocky Mountain Review* 60.2. http://rmmla.wsu.edu/ereview/60.2/articles/sasson.asp.

Wardrip-Fruin, Noah. 2009. *Expressive Processing: Digital Fictions, Computer Games, and Software Studies*. Cambridge, MA: MIT Press.

## THREE

Beyond Territorial Disputes: Toward a "Disciplined Interdisciplinarity" in the Digital Humanities

SHANNON CARTER

JENNIFER JONES

SUNCHAI HAMCUMPAI

If we choose the path to disciplinarity of narrowing the acceptable data, method, or theory, we are in danger of misunderstanding or even distorting the processes, practices, and products of writing. Rather . . . we should choose a path that finds discipline in our questions and goals, allowing us to draw on the resources of many disciplines. CHARLES BAZERMAN

A near constant media presence in recent years, the digital humanities (DH) seem poised to either save the humanities or destroy them, depending on your perspective. We would like to think a successful rescue is under way, yet we are far more concerned with our discipline's contributions to those rescue efforts. In this chapter, we draw on what Charles Bazerman (2011) calls the "disciplined interdisciplinarity of writing studies" to suggest we concern ourselves first with DH's potential contributions to our field's key questions and goals. What do we want to know, as a discipline? What do we want to teach, as a discipline? How might DH help us reach these goals?

In his recent retrospective, Bazerman argues: "We

should choose a path that finds discipline in our questions and goals, allowing us to draw on the resources of many disciplines" (2011, 8). We suggest that DH offers rhetoric and composition rich avenues through which to "draw on the resources of many disciplines" to answer our field's key questions about writing and writers. However, not every approach to DH is equally compatible with these goals.

Where DH is framed as a territory to be colonized, for example, our discipline's contributions to DH seem limited, as are DH's potential contributions to our own disciplinary goals. Instead of making new knowledge in our field, approaching DH in this way lends itself to territorial disputes as we draw boundaries around what we claim as rhetoric and composition's key concerns and everything else. To determine citizenship and map territory, we are forced to look inward rather than forward, feeling compelled to stake our claim to questions increasingly present across DH, arguing that we were here first and that this is nothing new. Instead, we suggest, we might more productively draw from our strengths, the key questions that align us as a discipline, asking what other disciplines and resources might have to offer us in our attempts to understand and communicate how writing works. For us, this very disciplined interdisciplinarity (DI) is the promise of DH.

We begin by acknowledging the significant ways in which the territory identified in recent years by digital humanists (DHers) as "uncharted" (Rowe 2012) has, indeed, been inhabited by generations of rhetoric and compositionists, especially those in computers and writing. Next, we read these tensions emerging from territorial disputes through a lens provided by Bazerman's (DI). We suggest that metaphors more compatible with this approach are DH as situation (Alvarado 2012) and instrument. To illustrate, we conclude with an extended treatment of this concept through the concrete example of our current interdisciplinary project, *Remixing Rural Texas: Local Texts, Global Contexts (RRT)*, funded in part by a grant from the National Endowment for the Humanities Office of Digital Humanities.[1]

Our approach to *RRT* is framed by critical race theory and transnational studies, which makes it a particularly useful vehicle through which to explore these issues of territory and power (see Carter and Dent 2013). Basically, *RRT* is a visualization tool for archival research on local, underrepresented texts by writers from groups historically excluded from public spaces.[2] Thus, it treats *place* as a fluid, dynamic construct shaped by mobile and immobile actors, contributing to our discipline's growing knowledge base about how historically marginalized populations in underresourced, understudied areas can change our understanding of rhetoric's past.

The *RRT* prototype itself consists of two components: (1) a documentary about student activism for racial justice in a rural university town in Texas (1967–68), remixed almost entirely from archival materials, and (2) a data source annotation tool that foregrounds relevant geographic and temporal elements as well as the original context of all source materials. The project makes strategic use of oral history interviews for the recovery, interpretation, preservation, and delivery of forgotten, contested, or otherwise underrepresented stories about local activism for racial justice. Appropriately, then, we begin our reflections on DH as territory from the perspective of the colonized.

DH as Territory

Digital humanists often present the "territory" of DH as "uncharted" (Rowe 2012) or, at the very least, an isolated frontier recently populated by small settlements brought together under the "big tent" (Davidson 2013; Kirschenbaum 2010; Pannapacker 2011) clearly identified with the markings that represent the "right kind" of DHer (e.g., HASTAC [Humanities, Arts, Science, and Technology Alliance and Collaboratory]). Yet much of the territory claimed by DHers was inhabited by rhetoric and composition long before DH arrived. In her contribution to the much-cited TechRhet listserv thread "Are You a Digital Humanist?" (April 2010), Cheryl Ball puts it this way: "We're still the outliers there. And, yes, I relish a little in knowing that this field was DH before their 'DH' was ever born. And that we have a lot to offer. And that other fields are coming to realize that rhetoric is at the center of everything."

Indeed, we have been here for decades, filling our field's top journals and library shelves with research, scholarship, pedagogical tools, and professional guidelines to address the very issues only recently being raised by DHers. Yet rarely is our field's literature cited by DHers. In their hands, topics like tenure issues surrounding digital work, collaborative authorship (Spiro 2009), multimodal scholarship (McPherson 2009, 2012), and implications for the humanities have dominated DH conferences, journals, and middle-state venues like blogs and Twitter. Yet far too infrequently are those rhetoric and composition scholars asked to contribute to DH conversations on the very topics that made them seminal figures in our field. To return to the metaphor of DH as territory, we occupy a territory colonized by those unwilling or unable to recognize the history of the place that came before.

Extending the metaphor of territorial disputes still further, we realize that this cycle is a familiar one. America is "discovered" by explorers who then relocate those already there. Neighborhoods home to our nation's immigrants, poor, and minorities are gentrified, forcing families out of their own communities and erasing generations of history in the process. Those displaced by the new occupants are "invisible." The colonizers necessarily see not those they colonize but their "surroundings, themselves, . . . everything and anything except" those they oppress/occupy, "as though [they] have been surrounded by mirrors of hard, distorting glass" (Ellison 1952, 3).

As Ellison explains: "I am invisible, understand, simply because people refuse to see me" (1952, 3). Of course, the academy, regardless of the discipline, is largely a white middle-class enterprise. Our situation hardly mirrors anything close to that experienced by our nation's minorities, especially in the Jim Crow era. Even so, many of us in the discipline have felt invisible, as though DHers "refuse[d] to see" us.

Examples of this frustration as expressed across our discipline are plentiful, including the Techrhet thread "Are You a Digital Humanist?" (April 2010) and the town hall by the same name that took place at the Computers and Writing conference the following year. In an environment of dwindling resources, it is easy to understand why an approach to DH as territory and the resulting territorial disputes might dominate the conversation. However, we can no more ascribe intentionality to DH's inattention to our discipline than we can to the racism, sexism, or other inequities embedded in the very fabric of everyday American life (Bell 2004; Crenshaw 1995; Omi and Winant 1994; Williams 2010).

"The Eternal September of the digital humanities," Bethany Nowviskie explains, makes it commonplace for DH participants speaking on topics core to our discipline to ignore the extensive body of literature our field has produced. Not unlike many of our own "newer colleagues" in rhetoric and composition, "they think that all of this is new; and they think that the current scene is all there is" (Nowviskie 2010). Under circumstances like these, it seems not unreasonable to assume that a great deal of the most relevant scholarship will remain unaddressed. Though the DH-as-territory approach continues to dominate, increasingly present in these conversations are those who call for meaningful dialogue between DH and rhetoric and composition. A useful illustration of both these approaches can be found in the Association for Computers and the Humanities forum "What is the relationship of DH to Computers and Writing?" (Williams 2010). Prompted by the frustration caused by DHers appearing to ignore our field, a number of posters illustrate the territorial approach to DH. Yet woven throughout are posts expressing a very different approach: Mark Sample shares a program description for the MLA 2012 panel "Composing New Partnerships in the Digital Humanities," a roundtable specifically designed to "facilitate interactions between digital humanists and writing studies scholars" (Gold 2012); Jim Ridolfo (2011), lamenting the lack of cross-disciplinary examples between the two fields, insists that "both fields have something to gain from one another" and posts the CFP for the very volume you are holding in your hands as a venue for just these conversations. Similarly, Kathy Gossett (2011) insists on the need to work together: "Many of us have been working on the fringes of a 'fringe' field within English Dept for quite a while, and now, almost suddenly, we find that our area of study has become the 'hot topic,' yet our contributions to this scholarship are frequently not cited or ignored." The solution, she insists, is to "build bridges between DH and C&W . . . *rather than fighting over who said what first*" (emphasis added).

Indeed, the two areas have a great deal more in common than a dispute over common territory: a "shared history of marginalization," "shared focus on the sometimes unglamorous, hands-on activities such as writing, coding, teaching, and building" (Gold 2012), an interdisciplinary origin story, and a deep commitment to the pedagogical that is atypical elsewhere across the humanities. Yet, as Matthew Gold explains, many DHers are equally perplexed by the many rhetoric and composition folks who seem unable or unwilling to engage DHers. At MLA 2012, representatives from DH and rhetoric and composition came together to explore the potential for (and obstacles to) generative partnerships. "Given what we share," according to Gold, "it's surprising to me that so many *writing-studies scholars seem to misunderstand what DH is about*" (Gold 2012). In a roundtable that appeared at times not unlike a meeting of a zoning commission at Small Town USA City Council, representatives from both DH and rhetoric and composition began to engage in a series of bridge-building efforts increasingly visible across both disciplines.

We are encouraged by such efforts yet frustrated by the many challenges that remain, especially as DH continues to gain momentum everywhere and the status of rhetoric and composition remains firmly at the margins. We suggest that, rather than allow a territorial approach to dominate such conversations, we might more productively approach

DH as a vehicle for Bazerman's DI, "a perspective grounded in the disciplinary problematics of writing studies" (Bazerman 2011, 12) that draws from methods, theories, research, and interpretations of many disciplines.

DH as DI

"Writing is a complex activity," insists Bazerman (2011, 8), a fact accepted largely without argument throughout our discipline. It does not seem at all controversial to insist, as Bazerman does, that "an understanding of what writing is and does and how people learn to do it must draw on [the] hermeneutic and rhetorical disciplines of the humanities" (8). Yet we rarely do. Bronwyn Williams raises similar concerns, lamenting our discipline's reluctance to draw from the wealth of research coming from education and literacy studies, areas no less committed to understanding writing, writers, and how to teach writing and writers. "Because writing happens everywhere," says Williams, "we need to study it everywhere" (2010, 142). "Meaning is at the heart," says Bazerman, "but texts, language, materialities, society, minds, and histories are everywhere" (2011, 8).

The solution Bazerman offers those of us who study writing is to cross boundaries into disciplines without established traditions and methods for studying writing and writers. Indeed, the value of disciplinarity, he argues, is also the problem with disciplinarity: "The modern academy's distinctive disciplines . . . have created distance from other disciplines' ways of knowing and reformatted the phenomena they study as disciplinary objects" (2011, 10). In other words, we see in our research what the tools have been designed to find. Each discipline's "epistemologies, strategies, procedures, and literatures" (10) reveal some things and hide others. As Bazerman argues, we should be guided by "the complexity of our subject rather than the limits of a small range of methods" (10). Unfortunately, without crossing those boundaries we cannot know what we do not know, nor can we truly imagine what we cannot see. When approached as a *situation* rather than as a *territory*, DH makes that boundary crossing possible, productive, and generative.

DH as Situation

As Bazerman has noted: "As my interdisciplinary experiences distanced me from the conventional perspectives about writing, *I saw things dif-*

ferently and saw different things" (2011, 17 [emphasis added]). But there's no evidence that he had DH in mind when he wrote his retrospective. Rather, his goal was to offer some insight into the research methods he has developed in his thirty or so years as a leader in our field. However, DI seems to us infinitely applicable to DH. Indeed, DH can provide a vehicle for the very DI that Bazerman describes as "hard, but not impossible" (2011, 19). It also seems to require a different perspective on our field's relation to DH than the one we have seen most frequently represented on our profession's listservs and, to a lesser extent, at conferences. As a territory, DH can encourage us to define boundaries (ours/not ours) and criteria for membership/citizenship. Such attention to maintaining disciplinary boundaries makes it more difficult to cross them. Alternatively, insufficient attention paid to our core commitments as a field can make meaningful contributions all but impossible. Instead, we approach DH as a *situation* brought about through our interactions with DH as an *instrument.*

In making this claim we are, of course, evoking Rafael C. Alvarado's "The Digital Humanities Situation" (2012). Here, he identifies what he describes as a "territorial instinct" taking place across DH recently as DHers, their area increasingly popular and in demand, express an "anxiety of self-definition" (50), drawing boundaries, charting DH territory, and identifying the criteria for membership.

Yet such efforts are futile. DH cannot be defined by a discrete and agreed-on set of methods, epistemologies, and approaches because no such agreement exists. Indeed, DH is "neither in fact nor in principle a discipline" but rather what people who identify as DHers—those who "share a common bond as humanists" combined with "a shared interest in texts and the use of computational technologies to explore and understand them" (Alvarado 2012, 53, 51)—actually *do* to carry out the work that emerges from these shared interests.

In other words, territorial disputes cannot resolve the issue of "who's in and who's out" (see Ramsay 2011b) in DH. The criteria for DH citizenship cannot be determined nor the boundaries starkly drawn. Instead, Alvarado sees "the encounter with the digital representation itself" as the "center of gravity" for DH. He "calls this encounter the situation of digital representation, a stable but always-in-flux event space" (Alvarado 2012, 54).

We see a great deal of compatibility between Alvarado's approach to DH as a situation and Bazerman's articulation of DI. DH exists not in territory or in people but in the *situations* it enables. By way of illustration, we offer a concrete example of how, evoking Bazerman again, "interdisciplinary journeys in pursuit of understanding the multidimensionality of writing" (2011, 12) helped bring into being a DH situation.

A DH Situation

When Shannon first picked up Bazerman's article, she had been struggling with a seemingly insurmountable research problem that had all but stalled her second book project. This history of community writing in the decade surrounding desegregation in her rural university town depended on archival materials that were largely unavailable. This included interviews with community members that were for the most part available to researchers, but only through institutional access, making archived-memories evidence difficult to access, interpret, and, to be quite frank, trust. This is the nature of such work in understudied areas among underrepresented groups. Her goal was to understand how members of historically marginalized groups like African American students and community members in the Jim Crow South garnered rhetorical agency (see Carter 2012a, 2012b; Carter and Conrad 2012). Though our field has developed increasingly sophisticated methods, frameworks, and models for such complicated work, she continued to struggle with the particulars of this situation. She drew from a range of methods well represented in our discipline—including life history interviews (Brandt 2001; Duffy 2007), reliance on citizen and community archives in addition to university collections (Enoch 2008; Enoch and Glenn 2010; Glenn 2004; Gold 2008)—as well as theoretical frameworks like those provided by Michael Warner and Chantal Mouffe and models for feminist rhetorical inquiry like those provided by Jacqueline Jones Royster and Gesa Kirsch. Even so, she struggled. To pursue her research goals, she needed meaningful ways to capture that dynamic interplay through which texts and related literacy practices create meaning (Carter and Dent 2013). What she needed was a way to reconstruct and interpret local literacy scenes without succumbing to what Deborah Brandt and Katie Clinton refer to as the "limits of the local" or violating the principles of reciprocity, participation, and sustainability (Carter and Conrad 2012).

There was a need to create a *situation* in which different disciplines could come together with community members, archivists, and technology specialists to understand, preserve, interpret, and communicate something about this local phenomenon. What Shannon needed was the DH situation that Alvarado describes. In fact, it was "playful encounters with a digital representation" (Alvarado 2012, 54) that drew

Shannon most directly into DH in the first place (when she encountered a digital representation in remix culture that inspired *RRT*) and attracted her coauthors Jennifer and Sunchai and the other members of *RRT* project team soon thereafter. The DH instrument we built together helped create a series of situations that were, at once, interdisciplinary, generative, reciprocal, participatory, and sustainable, including archival development, oral history interviews, public programming, and two short documentaries that drew from and expanded on available archival materials to tell stories long invisible, absent from the collective memories and silenced.

Working together from our diverse interdisciplinary positions as a rhetorician (Shannon) and Ph.D. students specializing in film studies (Jennifer) and second-language acquisition (Sunchai), we spent a year remixing archival materials to circulate stories about local literacy scenes through which the agents involved circulated social justice. Though this project builds directly from Shannon's more traditional, print-based scholarship, the contributions the coauthors and the other members of our interdisciplinary team have made played key roles in both the interpretations of the literacy scenes themselves and the expansion of these local stories for broader audiences across the disciplines and throughout the community. In addition to Jennifer and Sunchai, our research team includes graduate students in political science (Kelly Dent) and history (Adam Sparks) as well as professional staff from the archives (Andrea Weddle) and multimedia services (David Moseley). The artifacts we bring together to tell these local stories emerge from a range of disciplines and other relevant contexts, but the people involved are equally "interdisciplinary" in both position and approach.

Bazerman identifies what he needed as "methods that forcefully captured the kinds of evidence [he] was looking for" (2011, 17). He sought those methods in other disciplines. We did too—by creating a new tool together and by interacting with the digital representation and learning from the event space it provided.

DH as Instrument

It is tempting to view the development of and encounters with digital tools as part of the territorial disputes noted earlier. Indeed, the tensions are not just across disciplines but, in fact, within DH itself. As Stephen Ramsay has famously argued: "If you aren't building, you aren't a digital humanist" (2011a). We would ask readers to set aside the recurring "hack versus yack" debates to consider instead how such tools function as a DH situation that, as Bazerman (2011) says of DI, "deepens inquiry and makes possible a more comprehensive understanding of one's objects of concern" (19). At the end of this section, we return to the debate between tools and builders to explore our discipline's (potentially) unique position on these tensions. After all, as Wendy H. Chun argued at the 2013 Modern Language Association convention: "Writing can be making as well, just as much as building tools can be" (see also Liu 2011, 2012; Mandell 2012; Ramsay 2011a). Similarly, Stephen Ramsay and Geoffrey Rockwell ask: "What happens when building takes the place of writing?" (2012, 83). Who better to ponder such questions than those of us who study texts as they mediate human activity?

More than anything else, *RRT* is an instrument that created the event space we needed to carry out our desired work. In this event space, we built short documentaries together by remixing archival materials previously scattered across the region into a narrative sequence about race relations in the decade after desegregation reached this rural university town in the Jim Crow South (see, e.g., Carter 2012b, 2013a). We screened these remixes on campus, in the community, and at professional conferences across a range of disciplines, including but not limited to rhetoric and composition.[3] As often as they were available, we included the activists and students featured in the remix among the panelists following each screening. More often than not, we have invited other former students (potentially) involved as our distinguished guests who, like so many others with whom we have worked in the event space DH has created, continue to inform our interpretations of these events and scenes and generously donate relevant artifacts to the university archives that had been previously unavailable to researchers and the community. We worked with archivists and community members to expand the Northeast Texas African American Collection in unprecedented ways, including dozens of oral histories we had conducted with area activists and former students who, while affecting the community in significant ways, had been all but erased from the historical record. The result is a data-source annotation tool that provides additional information layers for all archival materials included in the remix, revealing the original source context of all artifacts on playback alongside relevant information about creative rights. We built *RRT* because we needed a way to indicate the dynamic interplay connecting texts, objects, and people in the local literacy scenes we were investigating. The remix provided an opportunity to demonstrate the data-source annotation tool, featuring not only the original source context for all audio, video, and images included in the remix but also geographic (via Google Maps), temporal, and contextual elements muted or otherwise unavailable in the linear mode through which the video, like print-based texts, must be delivered. Despite the original intent of the DH instrument, the DH situation it enabled did not limit itself to the agenda of the principle investigator. In fact, it was enhanced on all sides by the interaction *through* the tool: with the university archivists, community members, historians, and other members of our profession.

In rhetoric and composition, we view writing simultaneously as a tool (how writing works/can work) and a theory. This is the DI that binds us. *RRT* has, indeed, forced those of us involved in its creation to see the world differently, or at least our corner of it, as Ramsay and Rockwell (2012) have argued is a fundamental goal of building a prototype. *RRT* argues for a particular interpretive frame, suggesting that the local literacy scenes under investigation (*a*) must not be limited to the local agents and objects involved and (*b*) are shaped by patterns of noise and information flow often beyond the control of any individual actors and in excess of any individual's capacity to comprehend and negotiate. Producing the *RRT* prototype was, indeed, a deliberate interpretive act (see also Galey and Ruecker 2010). We needed better access to the literacy scene, both in our study and as we present it in our research. *RRT* enabled new interpretations and new mechanisms for communicating the results with others. The resulting project is, itself, a mechanism for communicating that interpretation resulting from our study in ways that are contestable, defensible, and sustainable (see also Ramsay and Rockwell 2012).

In this way, it has been far more productive for us to understand DH as a situation brought into being through an encounter with a digital representation (DH as instrument) than as a territory to which one belongs (or does not belong). However, it can serve our discipline in sustainable ways only as long as we remain mindful of our field's core commitments and problematics. Though flexible enough to support a range of disciplinary, professional, and community goals, any instrument designed to benefit rhetoric and composition must be continually recalibrated for the DI that Bazerman advocates. As rhetoric and composition scholars navigate the DH situation that such an instrument makes possible, we should continually ask ourselves questions like these: What am I trying to learn from this about how writing works, how writers write, and how they learn to do it? What are the implications for writing instruction? (see Bazerman 2011, 19).

Conclusion

As Bazerman noted: "I am not asking to wish away the disciplines, but rather I am asking for a much harder task of rethinking the relation of disciplines to each other, respecting the accomplishments and perspectives of each, taking seriously especially the evidence each makes available, and then developing a disciplined account that makes sense of these multiple perspectives within an integrative discipline and finally developing new research questions and inquiries coming from integrated perspectives" (2011, 19). For us, the promise of DH is the promise it holds for crossing disciplinary boundaries in meaningful, purposeful, generative, and disruptive ways. The DH promise is the *situation* it creates for meaningful boundary crossings between the campus and the community, teaching and learning, preservation and interpretation, building and theorizing. We value disciplinary boundaries inasmuch as they foster quality, depth, and intellectual rigor. Our experiences with DH as what Todd Presner et al.'s "The Digital Humanities Manifesto 2.0" (2009, 2) calls "not a unified field but an array of convergent practices" have only strengthened our commitments to the disciplines with which we most identify: rhetoric and composition (Shannon), film studies (Jennifer), and teaching English as a foreign language (Sunchai).

The threat of DH, we believe, is carried not by DH itself but by the logic of scarcity that fuels an understanding of DH as *territory*. As a territory, DH suggests finite resources and, by extension, the necessity of ownership, property, limits, and credit. As a *situation*, on the other hand, it may be productively guided by a logic of abundance rather than one of scarcity, suggesting infinite resources and an infinitely generative potential. An "economy of abundance" is, of course, the way that Presner et al. (2009) characterize DH: "The overflowing bounty of the information age, an age where, though notions of humanistic research are everywhere under institutional pressure, there is (potentially) plenty for all. And, indeed, there is plenty to do" (Presner et al., 2009, 4).

The DH situation created by *RRT* has exposed us to this "overflowing bounty" and served our disciplinary interests in the process. Of course, Shannon's interests are shaped by the core commitments of rhetoric and composition and, more precisely, historically marginalized rhetors. Jennifer's, on the other hand, serve film studies, certainly through her scholarship on the auteur filmmaker Terrence Malick, but perhaps more obviously through the making of a documentary with Kelly Dent, another member of the *RRT* research team. This project on the state of feminism in today's society was inspired by a handful of oral history interviews collected for *RRT* and brings together existing oral histories with other archival materials, found footage, and native media. Sunchai's interests in second-language acquisition and extensive background in literacy studies have led him to a dissertation project that adapts a handful of oral history interviews collected for *RRT* for the teaching of English in a similarly rural community on the other side of the globe—in his home country of Thailand. For this, he will build an annotation framework that, much like the variation we built for *RRT*, links geographic, temporal, and similar contextual elements to the remix to provide what he calls the *horizontal domain* of second-language development.

In other words, *RRT* is generative. This is a tangible outgrowth of a DH that "implies," as Presner et al. (2009) insist, "the multi-purposing and multiple channeling of humanistic knowledge" where cocreation and curation are "central features" (4, 8). *RRT* was both curated and cocreated by an interdisciplinary team of academics, students, professionals, and community members. The coauthors represent a small portion of the projects emerging from *RRT*, and the possibilities for new research and creative projects seem endless. At its best, *RRT* fostered DH situations that lead to new questions, new insights, new ways of making sense of the world and teaching the students within it. This, it seems, is the promise of DH.

Notes

1. To access *RRT* and interact with the *RRT* prototype, visit the project site: http://faculty.tamuc.edu/RRT.
2. The *RRT* White Paper provides much useful information about the project (see Carter 2013b).
3. At CCCC 2013 in Las Vegas, *RRT*'s remixes on East Texas activism were featured in three different presentations (Carlos 2013; Carter, Carlos, Tave, and Page 2013; Carter, Dent, Cooper, Page, and Gold 2013) that brought activists featured in these documentaries to speak directly with members of our discipline about the public work of composition (see also Carter and Dent 2013).

References

Alvarado, Rafael C. 2012. "The Digital Humanities Situation." In *Debates in the Digital Humanities*, ed. Matthew K. Gold, 50–55. Minneapolis: University of Minnesota Press.

Ball, Cheryl E. 2010. "Re: [techrhet] Are You a Digital Humanist?" Letter, April 4.

Bazerman, Charles. 2011. "Standpoints: The Disciplined Interdisciplinarity of Writing Studies." *Research in the Teaching of English* 46.1:8–21.

Bell, Derrick A. 2004. *Silent Covenants: Brown v. Board of Education and the Unfulfilled Hopes for Racial Reform.* Oxford: Oxford University Press.

Brandt, Deborah. 2001. *Literacy in American Lives.* Cambridge: Cambridge University Press.

Brandt, Deborah, and Katie Clinton. 2002. "Limits of the Local: Expanding Perspectives on Literacy as a Social Practice." *Journal of Literacy Research* 34.3:337–56.

Carlos, John. 2013. "The Silent Protest: Open Hands, Closed Fists, and Composition's Political Turn." Featured session at the Conference on College Composition and Communication, Las Vegas, March 13.

Carter, Shannon. 2012a. "A Clear Channel." *Remixing Rural Texas: Local Texts, Global Contexts*, Converging Literacies Center (CliC), August 2. Video. http://www.youtube.com/watch?v=GXA4Yy7VbjE.

———. 2012b. "A Clear Channel: Circulating Resistance in a Rural University Town." *Community Literacy Journal* 7.1:111–33.

———. 2013a. "John Carlos: Before Mexico City." *Remixing Rural Texas: Local Texts, Global Contexts*, Converging Literacies Center (CliC), April 16. Video. http://www.youtube.com/watch?v=UlHPMrp6cGs.

———. 2013b. "White Paper: Remixing Rural Texas: Local Texts, Global Contexts." National Endowment for the Humanities, Office of Digital Humanities, grant no. HD-51398-11. https://securegrants.neh.gov/public query/main.aspx.

Carter, Shannon, John Carlos, Joe Tave, and Belford Page. 2013. "The Political Turn: Writing Democracy for the 21st Century." Paper presented at the Conference on College Composition and Communication, Las Vegas, March 12.

Carter, Shannon, John Carlos, Joe Tave, Belford Page, Jennifer Jones, and Kelly Dent. 2013. "Racing the Local, Locating Race: Rhetorical Historiography through the Digital Humanities." Panel discussion presented at the Conference on College Composition and Communication, Las Vegas, March 16.

Carter, Shannon, and Jim Conrad. 2012. "In Possession of Community: Towards a More Sustainable Local." *College Composition and Communication* 64.1:81–121.

Carter, Shannon, and Kelly Dent. 2013. "East Texas Activism (1966–68): Locating the Literacy Scene through the Digital Humanities." *College English* 76.2:152–70.

Carter, Shannon, Kelly Dent, Carleton Cooper, Belford Page, and Matthew Gold. "Racing the Local, Locating Race: Rhetorical Historiography through the Digital Humanities." Paper presented at the Conference on College Composition and Communication, Las Vegas, 2013.

Chun, Wendy H. 2013. "The Dark Side of Digital Humanities." *Thinking C21*, January 9. http://www.c21uwm.com/2013/01/09/the-dark-side-of-the -digital-humanities-part-1.

Crenshaw, Kimberlé. 1995. *Critical Race Theory: The Key Writings That Formed the Movement.* New York: New Press.

Davidson, Cathy. 2013. "Inside HigherEd: MLA's Big (Digital) Tent." *The Brain in a Digital Age Blog*, January 25. http://www.cathydavidson.com/2013/01/ inside-highered-mlas-big-digital-tent.

Duffy, John. 2007. *Writing from These Roots: Literacy in a Hmong-American Community.* Honolulu: University of Hawaii Press.

Ellison, Ralph. 1952. *Invisible Man.* New York: Random House.

Enoch, Jessica. 2008. *Refiguring Rhetorical Education: Women Teaching African American, Native American, and Chicano/a Students, 1865–1911.* Carbondale: Southern Illinois University Press.

Enoch, Jessica, and Cheryl Glenn. 2010. "Invigorating Historiographic Practices in Rhetoric and Composition Studies." In *Working in the Archives: Practical Research Methods for Rhetoric and Composition*, ed. Alexis E. Ramsey, Lisa Mastrangelo, and Barbara L'Eplattenier, 11–27. Carbondale: Southern Illinois University Press.

Galey, Alan, and Stan Ruecker. 2010. "How a Prototype Argues." *Literary and Linguistic Computing* 25.4:405–24.

Glenn, Cheryl. 2004. *Unspoken: A Rhetoric of Silence.* Carbondale: Southern Illinois University Press.

Gold, David. 2008. *Rhetoric at the Margins: Revising the History of Writing Instruction in American Colleges, 1873–1947.* Carbondale: Southern Illinois University Press.

Gold, Matthew K. 2012. "DH and Comp/Rhet: What We Share and What We Miss When We Share." *The Lapland Chronicles*, January 7. http://blog .mkgold.net/2012/01/07/dh-and-comprhet-what-we-share-and-what -we-miss-when-we-share.

Gossett, Kathy. 2011. Comment on George Williams, "What Is the Relationship of DH to Computers-&-Composition?" *Digital Humanities Questions and Answers*, December 21. http://digitalhumanities.org/answers/topic/ the-relationship-of-dh-to-computers-composition.

Kirschenbaum, Matthew. 2010. "What Is Digital Humanities and What's It Doing in English Departments?" *Association of Departments of English Bulletin* 150:55–61.

Liu, Alan. 2011 "The State of the Digital Humanities: A Report and a Critique." *Arts and Humanities in Higher Education* 11.1–2:8–41.

———. 2012. "Where Is Cultural Criticism in the Digital Humanities?" In *Debates in the Digital Humanities*, ed. Matthew K. Gold, 490–509. Minneapolis: University of Minnesota Press.

Mandell, Laura. 2012. "Does It Work? Where Theory and Technology Collide." *Initiative for the Digital Humanities, Media, and Culture's Commentpress*

(IDHMC). http://idhmc.tamu.edu/commentpress/does-it-work-where
-theory-and-technology-collude.

McPherson, Tara. 2009. "Introduction: Media Studies and the Digital Humanities." *Cinema Journal* 48.2:119–23.

———. 2012. "Why Are the Digital Humanities So White?" In *Debates in the Digital Humanities*, ed. Matthew K. Gold, 490–509. Minneapolis: University of Minnesota Press.

Nowviskie, Bethany. 2010. "Eternal September of the Digital Humanities." *nowviskie.org*, October 15. http://nowviskie.org/2010/eternal-september
-of-the-digital-humanities.

Omi, Michael, and Howard Winant. 1994. *Racial Formation in the United States: From the 1960s to the 1990s*. New York: Routledge.

Pannapacker, William. 2011. "Big Tent Digital Humanities: A View from the Edge, Part 1." *Chronicle of Higher Education*, July 31. http://chronicle.com/
article/Big-Tent-Digital-Humanities/128434.

Presner, Todd, et al. 2009. "The Digital Humanities Manifesto 2.0." UCLA Mellon Seminar in Digital Humanities. http://manifesto.humanities.ucla
.edu/2009/05/29/the-digital-humanities-manifesto-20.

Ramsay, Stephen. 2011. "On Building." *Stephenramsay.us*, January 11. http://
stephenramsay.us/text/2011/01/11/on-building.

———. 2011. "Who's In and Who's Out." *Stephenramsay.us*, January 8. http://
stephenramsay.us/text/2011/01/08/whos-in-and-whos-out.

Ramsay, Stephen, and Geoffrey Rockwell. 2012. "Developing Things: Notes toward an Epistemology of Building in the Digital Humanities." In *Debates in the Digital Humanities*, ed. Matthew K. Gold, 75–84. Minneapolis: University of Minnesota Press.

Ridolfo, Jim. 2011. Comment on George Williams, "What Is the Relationship of DH to Computers-&-Composition?" *Digital Humanities Questions and Answers*, December 21. http://digitalhumanities.org/answers/topic/
the-relationship-of-dh-to-computers-composition.

Rowe, Katherine. 2012. "Tri-College Digital Humanities: Studying How Liberal Arts Degrees Can Face the Future." *Technically Philly Blog*, September 12. http://technical.ly/philly/2012/09/12/tri-college-digital-humanities
-studying-how-liberal-arts-degrees-can-face-the-future-video.

Spiro, Lisa. 2009. "Collaborative Authorship in the Humanities." *Digital Scholarship in the Humanities Blog*, April 21. http://digitalscholarship
.wordpress.com/2009/04/21/collaborative-authorship-in-the-humanities.

Williams, Bronwyn T. 2010. "Seeking New Worlds: The Study of Writing beyond Our Classrooms." *College Composition and Communication* 62.1:127–46.

## FOUR

Cultural Rhetorics and the Digital Humanities: Toward Cultural Reflexivity in Digital Making

JENNIFER SANO-FRANCHINI

The work of both rhetoricians and digital humanists involves the representation of bodies. In this chapter, I introduce a culturally reflexive heuristic for multimodal analysis, production, and organization of bodies in digital texts with the hopes that such a heuristic will make clearer the complexity of representing embodied difference. This heuristic is derived from the findings of a study of representations of East Asian double eyelid surgery on YouTube. Grounded in the idea that rhetoric and digital humanities (DH) scholars may gain useful insights from the everyday practices of technology users and the ways in which they construct meaning, I analyzed approximately fifty videos and the comments that accompany them, paying attention to not only the videos but also the site interface through a cultural rhetorics framework. Through a brief description of this study and cultural rhetorics as it is deployed in my analysis, this chapter illustrates an approach that combines "hack" and "yack"—practice and theory—in fluid ways. Ultimately, I show how a cultural rhetorics approach to analyzing the discourse on double eyelid surgery can help us move toward greater cultural reflexivity in the kinds of digital making that take place across rhetoric and DH.

Producing artifacts in ways that are attentive to race, gender, sexuality, class, (dis)ability, and other kinds of difference is a long-standing challenge for makers who do not typically engage such issues through scholarship, activism, or other means. While there may still be those who purport that in the United States we live in a "postracial" society, many have argued that this is anything but the case. Just two years ago, *Sports Illustrated* published its annual swimsuit edition, this time featuring—alongside bikini-clad models—people of color as exotic props (Tatlow 2013). From Alexandra Wallace ranting about Asians in the UCLA library on YouTube ("ORIGINAL (FULL) Asians in the Library" 2011), to Twitter accounts like @OxfordAsians (Krause and Averett 2013), Michigan State University's Token Asian (@MSU_Asian_) (Redden 2012), and @OSU_Asian (Bloom 2012), to J. Crew "style guides" in which models "accessorize with brown kids" ("J. Crew's Bali Catalog Shoot" 2012), to name just a few examples, it is clear that many individuals and organizations are not thinking about race in reflexive or sophisticated ways. Organizations and individuals like the *Huffington Post* and other news sites, along with angryasianman.com, have been sure to point out the problems with such representations. Yet, as much as it is important to identify racist, sexist, and classist remarks and images, we should also be able to articulate why and how something is racist, sexist, or classist in ways that circumvent the shutting down of dialogue about structural inequality. An easy yet arguably more detrimental "solution" is to not engage such issues at all. Furthermore, while the kinds of artifacts produced within DH do not always feature images or textual representations of bodies raced, gendered, sexualized, classed, disabled, or otherwise different, we should consider the nonpresence of difference in critical ways—ways that acknowledge absence as not simply neutral.

Of course, I am not the first to bring DH's lack of engagement with cultural difference to attention. Besides the many Twitter users asking, Where are all the people of color? during DH (un)conferences, of note are McPherson's "Why Are the Digital Humanities So White?" (2012), which argues "that we desperately need to close the gap between [discussions of race, tools, and infrastructure]" (140). McPherson's argument echoes that of Selfe and Selfe's "The Politics of the Interface" (1994), wherein it is noted: "Computer interfaces . . . are . . . sites within which the ideological and material legacies of racism, sexism, and colonialism are continuously written and re-written" (484). Along similar lines, Liu (2012) argues that DH needs to engage cultural criticism, imploring: "To be an equal partner—rather than, again, just a *servant*—at the table, digital humanists will need to find ways to show that thinking critically about metadata, for instance, scales into thinking critically about power, finance, and other governance protocols of the world" (177). From another angle, Bailey (2011) explains: "The ways in which identities inform both theory and practice in the digital humanities have been largely overlooked." And initiatives such as Marta S. Rivera Monclova's Transformative Digital Humanities: Doing Race, Ethnicity, Gender, Sexuality and Class in DH (#TransformDH), which maintains a list of projects that "integrate cultural studies approaches (race, gender, class, LGBT, postcolonial, disability studies etc.) and the digital humanities" and Adeline Koh and Roopika Risam's Postcolonial Digital Humanities (#dhpoco) have called attention to these absences in a number of ways.

This chapter extends the work of McPherson, Selfe and Selfe, Liu, Bailey, Monclova, Koh, and Risam as it proceeds with the notion that DH needs more attention to the relation between cultural difference, identity, and digital production in ways that make clearer why such discussions are relevant not just to scholars of difference but also to digital humanists interested in access, visual production, methodology, audience, and language. Indeed, we need explicit scholarship—discussions surrounding the cultural meanings of DH work—because attention to identity has the potential to remind us of the structuring power that DH has. This is not to say that there have not been projects and initiatives that have engaged issues of race and culture for some time, including much of the work headed by MATRIX: Center for Digital Humanities and Social Sciences Online; Koh's Digitizing "Chinese Englishmen"; Alexander Gil's work on THATCamp Caribe; Roger Whitson and Miriam Posner's "Lynchings in Georgia, 1875–1930"; and the panels at the Modern Language Association's 2013 annual convention "Representing Race in the Digital Humanities" and "Accessing Race in the Digital Humanities." At the same time, the specific cultural issues that these projects have engaged are less often discussed within larger DH conversations; they tend to be partitioned off through the kind of "lenticular logics" that McPherson (2012) describes as "a way of seeing the world as discrete modules or nodes, a mode that suppresses relation and context": "As such, the lenticular also manages and controls complexity" (144). And, while Lisa Nakamura is often cited by digital humanists for her extensive body of work engaging issues of race and technology, she has also critiqued the ways in which DH tends to engage (or, rather, not engage) the complexities of culture:

"Digital humanities" boils down to using computers to do exactly the same silo-ed and intellectually buttoned down work that people did before. It is the opposite of expansive. But it's always easier to get money for equipment (ie computers to make a million concordances of literature that people don't even read anymore and sure as hell don't want to read lit-crit about) than it is to re-envision a field. People in this kind of digital humanities are very concerned with "preservation" in every sense of the word—preservation of the status quo, of themselves and their jobs, and of the methods and fields of the past. (Nakamura quoted in Bogost 2010)

Indeed, the case can be made that some of the projects listed above reinscribe hegemonic structures of knowledge production even as they purport to resist such structures. And, for some reason, less attention is paid to projects like the Centre for Organisational and Social Informatics' Trust and Technology Project, which, unlike many DH archives, "model[s] Indigenous community-oriented archival services" (Monash 2012). It is my argument here that cultural rhetorics provides a framework for interrogating such organizational structures and analyzing professional practices in ways that effectively attend to cultural difference and the situatedness of meaning as it is being produced.

What Is Cultural Rhetorics?

To clarify what I mean when I say *cultural rhetorics*, cultural rhetorics theorizes how rhetoric and culture are interconnected through a focus on the processes by which language, texts, and other discursive practices like performance, embodiment, and materiality create meaning. It is, therefore, not simply the rhetorics of race, nor is it cultural studies, critical race theory, cultural philosophy, or cultural studies of technology. It is not "minority" rhetorics, or "alternative" rhetorics. Cultural rhetorics is an interdisciplinary field of study, a scholarly practice, and a category for interpreting the world around us. Cultural rhetoricians draw from across disciplinary boundaries because diverse fields of study offer important insights about the relation between culture and knowledge. Moreover, cultural rhetorics is based on the premise that rhetoric has been and will always be a culturally located practice and study.[1] As Haas (2008) explains: "When formulating methodologies, cultural rhetoricians tend to . . . value local discourses, practices, and knowledges and experiential culturally-saturated knowledge through narrative, the body, performance, memory, etc." (10).

Cultural rhetoricians are, furthermore, concerned with a wide range of questions, including the following: What does a rhetorical approach to culture offer? What becomes visible when we think about culture and rhetorical and knowledge-making contributions? And, conversely, what becomes visible when we locate rhetorical situations as existing within cultural frames? How does culture order discourse? How do our intellectual genealogies inform and affect the work that we do? What kinds of texts that have not been traditionally accepted for study in the rhetorical tradition should be accounted for? What are the affordances of using the term *cultural rhetorics* as opposed to *rhetoric*? What are the cultural implications of our pedagogical practices? (See Powell 2012; and Haas 2007.) This list is intended not to be exhaustive or exclusive but to serve as a starting point for understanding cultural rhetorics as a field of study.

Some of the key goals of cultural rhetorics scholarship include exposing and disrupting dominant narratives, particularly those that do damage to historically marginalized cultures; building bridges, making connections, and coalitioning for sociopolitical change through teaching, language, and playing with the notion of academic discourse; making space for the work and voices of groups who have traditionally been silenced; and doing the intellectual work of renaming, reconceptualizing, and continually resituating the kind of work that rhetoricians can and should do. For example, in the most recent issue of *College Composition and Communication*, Powell's (2012) chair's address draws on Lee Maracle's definition of *theory*:

Among European scholars there is an alienated notion which maintains that theory is separate from story, and thus a different set of words are required to "prove" an idea rather than to "show" one. We [indigenous people] believe the proof of a thing or idea is in the doing. Doing requires some form of social interaction and thus, story, is the most persuasive and sensible way to present the accumulated thoughts and values of a people. . . . There is a story in every line of theory. The difference between us [indigenous] and European scholars is that we admit this, and present theory through story. (384)

Through this definition of *theory*, Powell suggests that we be attentive to the kinds of silencing that happens within the discipline and beyond as well as the implications for the bodies that inhabit them when we privilege particular forms of knowledge as more or less legitimate than others. This may mean that, rather than building the rhetorical tradition around Aristotle or Kenneth Burke, we start with American Indian or Asian American or working-class intellectual traditions because the very centering of particular theorists says something about whose intellectual traditions are valuable and whose are not.

Moreover, Haas has done significant work at the intersection of American Indian rhetorics and digital and visual rhetoric. In "Wampum as Hypertext" (2007), she discusses American Indian "wampum belts as hypertextual technologies—as wampum belts have extended human memories of inherited knowledges through interconnected, nonlinear designs and associative storage and retrieval methods— long before the 'discovery' of Western hypertext" (77), thus positioning "American Indians as the first known skilled multimedia workers and intellectuals in the Americas" (78). In this way, she offers a historiographic decolonial narrative that suggests that we "challenge the current dominant 'history' of hypertext [and] include non-Western intellectual traditions that existed prior to Bush's Memex" (82). And Walls (2008) provides a cogent argument for the inclusion of postcolonial theory in multimodal visual design in "Authentic Design." In this video, he compares *authentic* as a visual design trope in the signage of Mexican restaurants in Columbus, Ohio, to the rhetoric of colonialism. Drawing on the work of Victor Villanueva and David Spurr, he argues that visual design—and I would add information design as is done in DH—has significant implications for the people who are being signified as such texts have a role in creating and sustaining stereotypes and ideological dehumanization. He further nods to remix as having the potential to disrupt these types of tropes. In a collaborative manuscript, my coauthors and I push at this idea that is widespread in discussions of remix culture. Drawing on the work of Kimberly Christen, Michael Brown, and Boatema Boateng, alongside a historical analysis of Hawai'i Creole English and a rhetorical analysis of the Official Hawai'i Tourism Website (http://www.gohawaii.com), we show how the practice and idea of remix needs to be further interrogated to account for issues of cultural appropriation, settler colonialism, and ideological domination (see Sano-Franchini, Tasaka, and Ledbetter, in press). And Ridolfo, Hart-Davidson, and McLeod's (2011) work with the Samaritan "Archive 2.0" project has shown the limits of working with textual documents alone and the importance of working with cultural and community stakeholders in building digital repositories. All the projects and scholarship mentioned in this description of cultural rhetorics deal directly with the cultural implications of knowledge production. In other words, these projects are in some fashion concerned with the role of bodies—of people—in textual production. Such concerns are highly relevant to DH, whether in terms of academic structuring or of digital making. The section that follows provides a case study that uses a cultural rhetorics framework to not only do analysis but also build a heuristic for a more culturally reflexive approach to analyzing, producing, and organizing bodies in digital texts.

Case Study: Looking at Double Eyelid Surgery on YouTube

Between 2011 and 2013, I analyzed approximately fifty YouTube videos related to East Asian double eyelid surgery.[2] East Asian double eyelid surgery is a very common type of cosmetic surgical procedure among people of East Asian descent, one in which the surgeon makes an incision and/or stitches in the eyelid so that a fold forms, making the eye appear larger and rounder. Using search terms like *double eyelid surgery, Asian blepharoplasty, Asian plastic surgery, Asian cosmetic surgery, race plastic surgery,* and *ethnic plastic surgery,* I accessed videos in a wide range of genres, including mass media excerpts such as talk show segments and news clips, before and after slideshows, testimonials of those who had gotten the surgery, journals of healing and recovery, short lectures on surgical techniques, documentary film, and viewer response. In my analysis of these videos, I looked specifically at how people rationalized the decision to get—or not get—the surgery. The cross-cultural conversations that take place on YouTube provide a compelling look at how technological advancement in the realms of medicine, social media, and multimodal technologies affects the way people attach an array of meanings to raced, technologically modified bodies. Through these videos situated across the United States as well as in South Korea, Malaysia, Singapore, and Australia, I was able to see how cultural values about these bodies are articulated, negotiated, and sometimes realigned transnationally.[3]

On the basis of this research, I identified five tropes through which users supported, or critiqued, the decision to get the surgery: racialization,[4] emotionologization,[5] pragmatization, the split between nature and technology, and agency. These tropes function as rhetorical strategies that also communicate particular values—about beauty, success, and morality—across cultures. To very briefly describe each trope, *racialization* refers to the process by which people attach race to the decision to get double eyelid surgery, often marking the surgery as an indicator of internalized racism or self-hate on part of Asians and Asian Americans. For example, this is when people interpret the decision to get the surgery as a means to "erase the race." The trope of racialization is visible in the title "WTF VIDEO—Young Korean Girls Have Surgery to Look More White!!!" (2011) along with its description: "Young women all across Asia are getting plastic surgery on their faces and eyes in order to look less Asian!, but rather to look more white and westernized instead. (what a crying shame)." This video is tagged "strange," "weird," "crazy," "sad," so that YouTube users looking for strange, weird, crazy, or sad videos can find it. Another example of racialization can be found in an excerpt from *The Tyra Banks Show* that features a conversation between Tyra and Liz, a twenty-five-year-old Korean American woman who had recently gotten double eyelid surgery. In this clip, Tyra informs Liz that her decision to get double eyelid surgery is "not so much about necessarily just a droopy eye; it's also about wanting to look more Caucasian" ("Tyra Banks" 2008). Racialization is the most common trope seen across media excerpts as well as in online commentary, and issues of race are often implicated in the tropes that follow.

Emotionologization refers to how double eyelid surgery is considered a way to take control over one's emotional affect: many who get the surgery, as well as surgeons, talk about how it makes them appear more lively, less sleepy, more expressive, and, thus, prettier. For instance: "Fans of the surgery say it makes them look prettier, less angry and more awake" ("Surgery to Alter Your Ethnicity" 2011). And as twenty-year-old Heidi Liow explains: "I look angry and frowny all the time or I look worried or something like that and I think by opening my eyes up a bit more it makes me look happier, easily approachable" ("Surgery to Alter Your Ethnicity" 2011). Underlying such rationalizations are issues of race and beauty and how Asian bodies are read in the West through particular normative visual conceptions of emotions.

By *pragmatization*, I refer to how surgeons who offer and those who get double eyelid surgery give practical reasons for doing so. For example, some state that it is easier to apply makeup with double eyelids, or the supratarsal fold that is created through the surgery. In a CNN excerpt, the reporter narrates: "Many Asian women overseas have cosmetic surgery for a more Western look. But that's not the case for Jennifer; her reason was much more *practical*. 'It was always kind of hard being a little teenage girl wanting to go and try on makeup and stuff like that. It was always difficult to find somebody who can actually apply it correctly and make it look nice" ("Asian Plastic Surgery" 2007 [emphasis added]). This example also points to how beauty and makeup application conventions in the West leave particular people out. Others talk about how the surgery helps them save the extra time it would take to either apply makeup that looks good on eyes without the supra-tarsal fold or temporarily produce a supratarsal fold using glue or tape products on a daily basis. As Dr. Charles Lee explains on the *Tyra* show: "[Patients] usually come in because they get tired of [applying double eyelid tape] everyday" ("Tyra Banks" 2008).

The split between nature and technology is where natural bodies are distinguished from technological bodies, which are often seen as un-natural, unacceptable, and inappropriate. This trope is often deployed in critiques of the surgery that have religious undertones, for instance, the argument that, if God wanted things/us to be this way, he would have made it/us that way, an argument made in other instances where technology is used to modify what is natural, that is, cloning or abor-tion. There is a lot of discussion about how to achieve a natural look, and sometimes those who have gotten the surgery talk about how they still feel like themselves, as if to reassure others that having changed some aspect of their physical appearance has not led to a sudden change in their internal identities. For example, shutupjunie ("Why I Got Double Eyelid Surgery/FAQ" 2011) says: "I feel like myself. Like, I don't look in the mirror, I'm like [*does a double-take*], 'Who the hell is that??' I'm like, 'Oh, it's still Junie,' you know? . . . I don't feel like a dif-ferent person at all, I just feel like myself except more confident, and like, slightly prettier [*laugh*]."

Finally, by *agency*, I refer to how people often talk about cosmetic surgery as a means for social mobility and status, via career or marriage, a position based on the idea that more attractive people have more op-portunities. For instance, prior to her surgery, Heidi Liow confesses: "I feel insecure when I go into an interview. I think, 'Oh, maybe they won't pick me because I'm Asian. Maybe if I looked less Asian I'd feel more confident or something like that'" ("Surgery to Alter Your Ethnic-ity" 2011). She admits that she views her appearance as it is linked to race as a professional hindrance. And JuciShockwave comments on a video: "I can't hate, at lease [*sic*] she got the money to get this surgery. If it'll make her feel better about herself why not. . . . Too many idiots on the net saying shit like 'Looks dont matter' can kiss my ass, because it does. Looks for the most part will give you the job/man you want" ("NEVER PERFECT" 2007). Through the trope of agency, we are asked to consider the question, if technologies are available that allow people to change their destiny, why should they not take advantage of them?

If we understand the tropes listed above as rhetorical strategies through which values in relation to race and other kinds of embodied difference are articulated, I argue that such tropes can also help us think about how DH scholars and others who work with digital texts might make culturally reflexive decisions in moments of digital making. Such culturally reflexive decisions would be mindful of how cultural values are articulated in moments of rhetorical production; how embedded in such values are implications for access, power, authority, and privilege; and how complex histories and an array of meanings shape the way bodies are constructed and interpreted. For example, someone editing a video might use the tropes listed above to interrogate how textual and aural statements, visual framing, and music soundtracks position particular identities in problematic ways. While reviewing the videos, one might ask oneself:

RACIALIZATION

- What is the construction of race in this image/text/soundtrack/clip?
- Are particular races positioned as more or less moral than others?
- Are racialized bodies positioned as more or less efficient than others?
- Are particular racial identities being essentialized?
- Are particular racial identities being sexualized?

EMOTIONOLOGIZATION

- Are particular emotions or character traits being attached to particular bodies?
- Are particular emotions tied to particular goals?
- In what ways are preconceived notions about emotional states being problematized?
- Are particular emotional states tied to particular embodied identities?
- Are particular emotions cast as desirable?

PRAGMATIZATION

- Are particular bodies positioned as more or less practical than others?
- In what ways are stereotypes about practicality and use value being exploited or broken down?
- Are practical bodies depicted as a more efficient means toward particular goals?
- Is the use value of a person or persons depicted as desirable?

NATURAL VERSUS TECHNOLOGICALLY MODIFIED BODIES

- What is the distinction between the natural body and the technologically modified body?
- Are natural (or unnatural) bodies essentialized?
- Are naturally modified bodies positioned as more desirable than technologically modified bodies, and vice versa?

AGENCY
- Are particular bodies cast as agents of change?
- How are these bodies positioned in relation to other bodies?
- In what ways are stereotypes about bodies as agents of change being exploited/ broken down?
- In what ways are agentive bodies being essentialized?
- Are bodies that have agency cast as powerful and, thus, desirable?

Because the tropes listed above are visible not only in the videos themselves but also in the metadata that organize the videos, these sets of questions might also be used by a digital humanist curating video, or other kinds of digital texts, in thinking about how these texts are framed through metadata, whether via titling, tags, or other kinds of organizational methods. To do so, one might ask how these questions apply to particular "ways of knowing." For instance, what is the construction of race (or other kinds of identity) in this interface? That is, are particular ways of knowing positioned as more or less practical than others? Does the organizing structure or viewer interface of this archive privilege particular ways of reading?

Ultimately, the goal should be to produce not only more culturally reflexive digital texts but also more culturally cognizant writers and readers who are aware of and deliberate about the rhetorical strategies they are using. It is an understandable concern that a systematized heuristic for analyzing identity would risk problematic oversimplification, and I understand that this is a risk here. However, it is my hope that such a framework will work to *complicate* rather than *simplify* race, the way we understand bodies, and how we then construct meaning on the basis of those understandings. To be clear, this heuristic is intended to show that representing bodies is difficult work and that we should be thoughtful and reflexive if we are to do it well. It is, therefore, not useful to look to a digital text and simply say, Yes, race is being attached to bodies; therefore, there is a problem with this representation. In fact, such an approach may simply work to silence racist thinking. Rather, the point of this heuristic is to get people talking about identity and the various ways it is rhetorically constructed in a way that is reflexive and productive. In other words, the questions laid out above should not be reduced to easy yes/no, good/bad binaries but should be used as starting points for reflecting on the implications of how bodies are being represented while also thinking about questions of context, purpose, and audience. To treat culture reflexively means to understand that, when it comes to representing culture, there are no simple and easy answers; nothing is always right, and nothing is always wrong. Rather, representations come with multiple and sometimes conflicting implications for many different groups of people—people who are complicated and whose identities are entangled in webs of meaning.

Conclusion

Using a cultural rhetorics framework, I examined how text, image, sound, and metadata create meaning about raced bodies through five tropes—racialization, emotionologization, pragmatization, the split between nature and technology, and agency. Moreover, through this study, I deployed Maracle's definition of theory, exploring how users themselves do theoretical work through their participation in cross-cultural dialogue. Furthermore, I consider what these acts of knowledge production via the discourse surrounding East Asian double eyelid surgery can teach us about digital making. When we understand rhetoric as always located in culture, we must also acknowledge that white is not neutral and that absence is meaningful.

The heuristic presented above is not intended to be universally applicable; it is limited in that it is about a very specific kind of body modification, one that is embedded within specific histories and specific cultures. Thus, other tropes that articulate other cultural values can be found in other contexts. Rather, my hope is that this study will serve as an example for others to make similar heuristic guidelines for other kinds of cultural representation in other contexts. For instance, what data sets might we use to analyze the discourse on representations of other kinds of body modification such as tattoos, exercise, anorexia, or sex affirmation surgery, and is it useful to do so? How does this framework help us think about what we need to take into account when considering the embodied representation—or lack thereof—of difference via gender, class, sexuality, (dis)ability, age, and other identity markers? Many have studied digital cultures and online activities in a variety of ways, and I suggest that we look to such sites of everyday, cultural rhetorics for what they can teach us about doing DH.

As a Cultural Heritage Informatics graduate fellow at Michigan State University, one of the first lessons that the program's director, Ethan Watrall, taught me about DH is the notion of "building as a way of knowing." Both cultural rhetoricians and many DH scholars believe that making and knowing go hand in hand and that both are interested in everyday practices of knowledge production, beyond traditional forms of alphabetic textual production. Within DH, for instance, an understanding of the variety of ways that people work and make meaning has also opened up discussions of adjunct labor and the value of digital texts and projects, and cultural rhetorics is concerned with knowledge production as it happens not only within alphabetic texts but also via embodiment, language, orality, stories, materiality, technologies, and methodologies, as is visible in the range of work being done in American Indian rhetorics on wampum belts, khipu, and codices, to name just a few examples. A project that incorporates elements of cultural rhetorics and DH's attention to nonalphabetic forms of knowledge production is the Mukurtu project ("Cultural Protocols" 2012), a "free, mobile, open source platform built with indigenous communities to manage and share digital cultural heritage." Specifically, Mukurtu uses cultural protocols that allow users to "define a range of access levels for digital heritage objects and collections, from completely open to strictly controlled, for groups and individual members of [the] community," depending on the needs of the community. Through these cultural protocols, the project attends to the ways in which technological infrastructures work to shape the material realities of specific communities.

Both cultural rhetorics and DH also talk about collaborative forms of knowledge production, though how this collaboration takes shape varies. Digital humanists generally embrace multiauthored texts, crowdsourcing information, open access to information, and unconferences, wherein participants work together to build programs on the spot. In cultural rhetorics, collaboration is often emphasized in the form of community and alliance building. Cultural rhetorics also theorizes collaboration and its implications through the understanding that rhetoric is constellated and built through webs of relationality. Ríos (2013), for example, situates this relation through a lens of biocultural diversity, examining how land, bodies, language, and Native science intersect. Yet, while cultural rhetorics and DH have several shared concerns, there has been very little dialogue across the two fields. I would like to conclude by inviting scholars to do more intersectional work across cultural rhetorics and DH, whether collaborative or otherwise.

Notes

1. Parts of this section originally appeared in a seminar paper for Bill Hart-Davidson's "Research Methodologies" and Julie Lindquist's "American Cultural Rhetorics" graduate courses and later coauthored with the Cul-

tural Rhetorics Theory Lab in a handout titled "Cultural Rhetorics Startup Guide."

2. A longer and more detailed discussion of this study is available in Sano-Franchini (2013).

3. All videos were in English.

4. I use Omi and Winant's (1994) concept of racialization, "the extension of racial meaning to a previously racially unclassified relationship, social practice or group . . . an ideological process, an historically specific one" (14), to show how it is a rhetorical process by which racial categories and race-based connotations are attached to bodies, practices, and ideas through language and other signifiers.

5. I draw on Stearns and Stearns's (1985) definition of *emotionologization* as "the attitudes or standards that a society, or a definable group within a society, maintains toward basic emotions and their appropriate expression; ways that institutions reflect and encourage these attitudes in human conduct, e.g. courtship practices as expressing the valuation of affect in marriage, or personnel workshops as reflecting the valuation of anger in job relations" (813).

References

"Asian Plastic Surgery on CNN." 2007. YouTube video, 6:02, posted by "surgeryvide099," May 3. http://www.youtube.com/watch?v=OWOUyFOYR2E.

Bailey, Moya Z. 2011. "All the Digital Humanists Are White, All the Nerds Are Men, but Some of Us Are Brave." *Journal of Digital Humanities* 1.1. http://journalofdigitalhumanities.org/1-1/all-the-digital-humanists-are-white-all-the-nerds-are-men-but-some-of-us-are-brave-by-moya-z-bailey.

Bloom, Molly. 2012. "Ohio State Responds to 'Anti-Asian' Twitter Feed with Community Meeting." *StateImpact Ohio*, May 14. http://stateimpact.npr.org/ohio/2012/05/14/ohio-state-responds-to-anti-asian-twitter-feed-with-community-meeting.

Bogost, Ian. 2010. "The Turtlenecked Hairshirt: Fetid and Fragrant Futures for the Humanities." *Ian Bogost—Videogame Theory, Criticism, Design*, January 9. http://www.bogost.com/blog/the_turtlenecked_hairshirt.shtml.

"Cultural Protocols." 2012. Mukurtu CMS. http://www.mukurtu.org/node/28.

Haas, Angela. 2007. "Wampum as Hypertext: An American Indian Intellectual Tradition of Multimedia Theory and Practice." *Studies in American Indian Literatures* 19.4:77–100.

———. 2008. "A Rhetoric of Alliance: What American Indians Can Tell Us about Digital and Visual Rhetoric." Ph.D. diss., Michigan State University.

"J. Crew's Bali Catalog Shoot: Misguided?" 2012. *Huffington Post*, May 24. http://www.huffingtonpost.com/2012/05/24/j-crew-bali-catalog-style-guide_n_1541864.html.

Krause, Sean, and Nancy Averett. 2013. "Miami Student Accused of Racist Tweets against Asians; Students and Professors Call on University to Condemn." *Oxford Townie: The Grassroots Voice of Oxford, Ohio*, February 29. http://oxfordtownie.net/miami-student-accused-of-racist-tweets-against-asians-students-and-professors-call-on-university-to-condemn.

Liu, Alan. 2012. "Where Is Cultural Criticism in the Digital Humanities?" In *Debates in the Digital Humanities*, ed. Matthew K. Gold, 490–509. Minneapolis: University of Minnesota Press.

McPherson, Tara. 2012. "Why Are the Digital Humanities So White? or, Thinking the Histories of Race and Computation." In *Debates in the Digital Humanities*, ed. Matthew K. Gold, 139–60. Minneapolis: University of Minnesota Press.

Monash University Information Technology. 2012. "Trust and Technology Project." Monash University, Information Technology, Research in the Faculty of IT. http://infotech.monash.edu/research/about/centres/cosi/projects/trust.

Omi, Michael, and Howard Winant. 1994. *Racial Formation in the United States: From the 1960s to the 1990s*. New York: Routledge.

"ORIGINAL (FULL) Asians in the Library Ching Ching Ling Long Ting Tong Alexandra Wallace UCLA Student." 2012. YouTube video, 2:52, posted by "waxonwaxoff28," March 13. http://www.youtube.com/watch?v=AQQr3hUepZM.

Powell, Malea. 2012. "2012 CCCC Chair's Address: Stories Take Place: A Performance in One Act." *College Composition and Communication* 64.2:383–406.

Redden, Elizabeth. 2012. "'I'm Not Racist, But.'" *Inside Higher Ed*, October 16. http://www.insidehighered.com/news/2012/10/16/tensions-simmer-between-american-and-international-students.

Ridolfo, Jim, William Hart-Davidson, and Michael McLeod. 2011. "Archive 2.0: Imagining the Michigan State University Israelite Samaritan Scroll Collection as the Foundation for a Thriving Social Network." *Journal of Community Informatics* 7.3. http://ci-journal.net/index.php/ciej/article/view/754/757.

Ríos, Gabriela Raquel. 2013. "In Ixtli in Yollotl/A (Wise) Face a (Wise) Heart: Reclaiming Embodied Rhetorical Traditions of Anahuac and Tawantinsuyu." Ph.D. diss., Texas A&M University.

Sano-Franchini, Jennifer. 2013. "The Rhetorical Making of the Asian/Asian American Face: Reading and Writing Asian Eyelids." Ph.D. diss., Michigan State University.

Sano-Franchini, Jennifer, Robyn Tasaka, and Lehua Ledbetter. In press. "Toward a Reflexive Approach to Remix; or, What Hawai'i Creole English and Corporate Tourism Can Teach Us about Remix." In *Cultures of Copyright*, ed. Martine Rife and Dànielle DeVoss. New York: Peter Lang.

Selfe, Cynthia L., and Richard J. Selfe Jr. 1994. "The Politics of the Interface: Power and Its Exercise in Electronic Contact Zones." *College Composition and Communication* 45.4:480–504.

Stearns, Peter N., and Carol Z. Stearns. 1985. "Emotionology: Clarifying the History of Emotions and Emotional Standards." *American Historical Review* 90.4:813–36.

"Surgery to Alter Your Ethnicity (HUNGRY BEAST)." 2011. YouTube video, 5:23, posted by "abchungrybeast," April 6. http://www.youtube.com/watch?v=HZy_2-3tD-A.

Tatlow, Didi Kirsten. 2013. "Sports Illustrated's New Swimsuit Issue Rouses Ire over 'Ethnic Props.'" *International Herald Tribune: The Global Edition of the New York Times*, February 14. http://rendezvous.blogs.nytimes .com/2013/02/14/sports-illustrateds-new-swimsuit-issue-rouses-ire-over -ethnic-props/?_r=0.

"Tyra Banks—Asian Eyelid Surgery." 2008. YouTube video, 8:27, from the *Tyra* show, posted by "Flaw3dBeauty," January 9. http://www.youtube.com/watch?v=OOcSJSJWD60.

Walls, Douglas. 2008. "An 'A' Word Production: Authentic Design." *Kairos: A Journal of Rhetoric, Technology, and Pedagogy* 13.1. http://kairos.techno rhetoric.net/13.1/disputatio/walls.

"Why I Got Double Eyelid Surgery/FAQ." 2011. YouTube video, posted by "shutupjunie." http://www.youtube.com/watch?v=pCMR3-_T08U.

"WTF VIDEO—Young Korean Girls Have Surgery to Look More White!!!" 2011. YouTube video, 1:44, posted by "SirGrowalott."

## FIVE

Digital Humanities Scholarship and Electronic Publication

DOUGLAS EYMAN

CHERYL BALL

Discussing the creation of the Office of Digital Humanities (ODH) within the National Endowment for the Humanities (NEH), the director, Brett Bobley, explains that most digital humanities (DH) work funded by the NEH involves "collections of cultural heritage materials, which are one of the primary objects of study for researchers across all humanities disciplines. Books, newspapers, journals, paintings, music, film, audio, sculpture, and other materials form a primary dataset for study" (Bobley 2008, 1). What is missing in this description is the development of collections of new cultural materials that are "born digital"—that is, texts that are authored to use affordances of screen-based interactions and new media technologies and are neither digitizations of print-based materials nor reproducible in print forms. Following, what is also missing from the ODH description of DH texts is the development of methods and methodologies for both studying and producing these new forms. While ODH's intended corpus of DH materials has certainly expanded in the intervening years, the focus of many start-up grants funded by NEH are still primarily linguistic (e.g., language driven) instead of multimodal (e.g., linguistic, visual, spatial, aural, and/or gestural; see Cope and Kalantzis, 2000). As the realm of DH matures, we suspect that there will be a strong turn toward screen-based scholarship—what we are calling *scholarly multimedia* or *Web texts*—and suggest that digital rhetoric is well positioned to participate in and contribute to DH when it does so.

The term *digital rhetoric* is perhaps most simply defined as "the application of rhetorical theory (as analytic method or heuristic for production) to digital texts and performances" (Eyman, in press). In this chapter, we take up the relation between DH and screen-based scholarship as a form of digital rhetoric practice. One of the ways in which we can further the study of Web texts is to develop scholarly approaches that partake of the same digital rhetoric methods and practices as the works we study. To that end, we argue that DH scholarship that takes advantage of digital, networked media and platforms serves as an enactment of digital rhetoric practice. And, as we develop scholarly approaches and platforms that further these practices, it is important to pay attention to the affordances and constraints of these platforms and to carefully consider the intellectual, social, and technological support structures that need to be used in the construction and dissemination of scholarly multimedia work. In this chapter, we reflect on a DH project that we undertook as editors of *Kairos: A Journal of Rhetoric, Technology, and Pedagogy* to discuss how digital rhetoric informs the scholarly, social, and technological infrastructures of this Web-textual journal.

Publishing Web-Textual Scholarship: Digital Rhetoric and Infrastructure

In a recent review of four books about digital scholarship, Cheryl Ball (2010) notes that most books on this topic address the institutional or technological activity systems of print-based scholarship put online. There is no coherent body of scholarship that offers a sustained analysis of scholarly multimedia and its growing impact on digital scholarship in the humanities, although there are several journals that publish this kind of work. Readers familiar with *Kairos*, for instance, know that it is a peer-reviewed, independent, open-access journal that has been publishing screen-based, media-rich DH scholarship since 1996 (see http://kairos.technorhetoric.net). Since its first issue, the mission of *Kairos* has been to publish scholarship that examines digital and multimodal composing practices, promoting work that enacts its scholarly argument through rhetorical and innovative uses of new media. *Kairos* authors design their own Web texts, drawing on whatever technologies, genres, and media they need to enact their arguments. Underlying each design is a unique information architecture of file names, file types, and directories. Every Web text is different, and, as editors, we cannot know or dictate (for the most part) what these combinations might be, which means that our submission, copyediting, and publishing infrastructures must be flexible enough to work with whatever architecture an author creates. (However, there are certain technologies that, for preservation purposes we do not accept. If we cannot host a Web text on our server, we will not publish it. This is an infrastructural issue that will, despite its importance, fall outside the scope of what we are able to discuss in this chapter.)

Because the journal is independent and totally open access, it has no budget. This means that the editorial team has historically relied on in-kind donations (of servers, staff time, software, etc.) to fulfill its mission. In addition, the unique designs of Web-textual publications as well as the length of time the journal has been publishing have meant that the journal's staff has had to rely on creative hand-made social and technical infrastructures to support its editorial work flow and the unique design needs of Web texts. That is, everything *Kairos* does to publish an issue is done manually since its staff uses the same technologies that were available in 1996: e-mail, listservs, SFTP, and HTML editors. We have not had the time, technology, or funding to change our process in the intervening years. Only recently, and only in response to the DH project we discuss below, did we create a wiki to track some parts of our editorial work flow outside this hacked-together, low-tech system.

In 2010, after several years of brainstorming ways to build an editorial-management system that would help us automate our submission, review, and copyediting processes in ways that were suitable to the multimedia content that *Kairos* publishes, we realized that we could not continue to rely on volunteers to build and maintain such a massive system. So we applied for and received an NEH Digital Humanities Start-Up Grant (Level II, $50,000) to explore building scholarly multimedia plug-ins for open journal systems (OJS). OJS could automate our back-end work flows such as uploading and tracking submissions, initiating the review process, and tracking the copyediting process. It had a built-in user base of over ten thousand journals worldwide that might use or expand on our plug-in prototypes. It seemed an ideal avenue to explore because we would have a community to help support the software instead of a very small group of overworked English professors in primarily teaching-intensive faculty positions. A large part of our choosing OJS was based on the infrastructural support we hoped it could provide *Kairos* and the digital rhetoric community.

Based on our tenure as editor and publisher of *Kairos*, we offer a three-part framework to analyze the underlying structures that support DH work: (1) the importance of design as a rhetorical vehicle for scholarly argumentation; (2) the available means of assessment and peer review; and (3) questions of the sustainability of the scholarly work, regardless of form, in the rapidly evolving technological ecosystems of the Internet. We apply these scholarly, social, and technical infrastructural issues to our uptake of OJS for *Kairos*'s use. Although this chapter approaches infrastructure from the perspective of editors and publishers, this framework will be useful to DH scholars as they consider whether to engage with publication outlets that can support DH production, as opposed to reporting in traditional, primarily textual forms.

The Scholarly Infrastructure of Digital Scholarship: Design as Rhetoric

The first challenge for scholarly multimedia in the humanities is the rhetorical function of design in the presentation of digital work. Just as Buchanan (1985) argued for the necessity of a theory of rhetoric in design, we posit that there is a need for a more explicit theory of design as an integral element of digital rhetoric practice: design as rhetoric. For digital rhetoric, design is equivalent to style; thus, scholars must be concerned with understanding all the available elements of document design, including color, font choice, and layout as well as multimedia design possibilities including motion, interactivity, and appropriate use of media. Style in this sense is also an important quality in terms of a given text's use and usability. Bradley Dilger (2010) reminds us that, for rhetoric, "style is never optional, as the common sense opposition of style to substance wrongly indicates" (16). Rather, it is an integral element of all rhetorical communication, and the question is not whether we want style or substance but what kind of style we want to deploy as a component of substance.

The function of design as an enactment of rhetorical practice for digital scholarship is a relation that we have attempted to champion and promote in each issue of *Kairos*, and the work that we publish has helped demonstrate how meaning making need not be solely textual. As we continue to promote the idea that digital scholarship can and should make arguments through the design of the work itself, we call on authors to take up Anne Wysocki's (2004, 15) approach to composing texts in which their designs are overtly enacted through new media. In practical terms, engaging design as rhetorical practice means that digital humanists need to critically wield both rhetorical and aesthetic principles and bring together the particular design affordances of the *medium* of scholarly multimedia. The digital rhetorician (and, by extension, the DH scholar) must be able to work equally well with rhetoric, design, and code, if not alone, then in collaboration. Either way, academe's scholarly infrastructure—the ecosystems in which scholarship is an expected product of our reading, teaching, learning, and composing—must support design as much as it already supports content (as if content can ever be divorced from its form; see, e.g., Ball and Moeller 2008; Wysocki 2001).

At *Kairos*, as at several other online Web text journals in digital rhetoric, including *C&C Online* and *Vectors* and, more recently, *Enculturation* and *Harlot of the Arts*, design is treated as an equivalent form of argument to written content. Go to any of these journals' Web sites, and peruse the table of contents for a few minutes. It will not take long to discover how Web texts look like and draw on but function differently than linear scholarship (Ball 2004; Purdy and Walker 2010, 2012). Yet design as argument is mostly absent in DH journals such as *Digital Humanities Quarterly* or *Journal of Digital Humanities* (*JDH*). The Winter 2012 issue of *JDH*, on the visually stimulating methodology of topic modeling, is a great resource, but, within the journal's narrow-columned Wordpress template, the articles are primarily print-like. Screenshots capturing examples of topic modeling are included as small, in-line figures, but they are difficult to read because they are shrunk to fit a narrow column (see fig. 5.1). *JDH* is not a singular example here: illustrations do not make a print-like article into a Web text. Peruse most any online journal in DH, media studies, or game studies—fields whose missions *require* some form of multimedia as a corpus for close reading and, in some cases, production—and you will find only print-like articles talking *about* new media, not *with* and *through* new media. *Kairos*, on the other hand, is situated within a field built on researched practice, and authors do not have these same infrastructural constraints and are expected to highlight the visual and interactive designs as a main feature of the Web text (see fig. 5.2).

We mention *JDH*'s use of Wordpress not to denigrate that choice. Many other online journals use similar content-management systems, such as Drupal, CUNY Commons, MediaCommons, and OJS—and for good reasons relating to those fields' journals' scholarly (print-based)

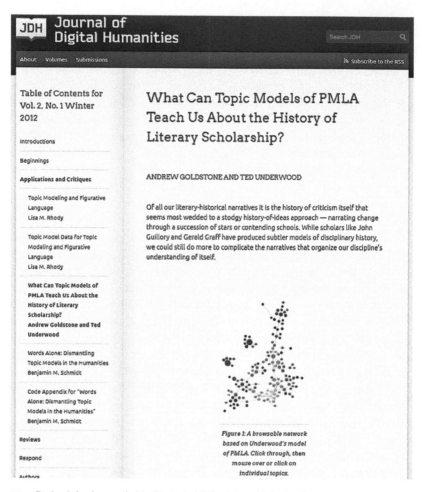

What Can Topic Models of PMLA Teach Us About the History of Literary Scholarship?

ANDREW GOLDSTONE AND TED UNDERWOOD

Of all our literary-historical narratives it is the history of criticism itself that seems most wedded to a stodgy history-of-ideas approach — narrating change through a succession of stars or contending schools. While scholars like John Guillory and Gerald Graff have produced subtler models of disciplinary history, we could still do more to complicate the narratives that organize our discipline's understanding of itself.

Figure 1: A browsable network based on Underwood's model of PMLA. Click through, then mouse over or click on individual topics.

5.1.   Design is backgrounded in this typical DH article published online.

values. But we do want to point out that, as Selfe and Selfe (1999) said, interfaces are political, and technical-infrastructural choices are based on scholarly infrastructural values. Wordpress, for instance, allows only certain kinds of media types to be embedded in its pages, and HTML (the primary medium basis of Web text construction) is not one of them. So, if a journal's technical infrastructure does not support scholarly multimedia as an equivalent rhetorical tool to linguistic content, then the scholarly infrastructure of that journal and its discipline is au-

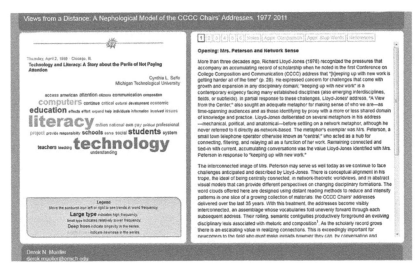

5.2. Design is foregrounded (through the interactive word clouds, screen left) in this typical Web text from *Kairos*.

tomatically constrained to valuing print-based, linguistic scholarship. Or worse, authors link out to their rich DH project from a print-like article they have written, effectively doubling (or tripling) their workload without ever getting credit for the original, designed work. This retroactive unmediation, which serves (to get digital projects to count within our traditional scholarly ecologies), performs what Gresham and Aftanas (2012) called the *second-shift work* of digital scholarly production. We argue that, until authors, editors, and publishers assume that design as argument can be a fundamental part of our scholarly infrastructure in DH, we will continue to see scholars shoehorn their screen-based projects (think large-scale DH projects like Hypercities, Writing Studies Tree, CompPileCritical Commons, etc.) into print-based, linear, traditional peer-reviewed articles so that designers can get institutional credit (Anderson and McPherson 2011; Godkin 2012). We at *Kairos* knew, for instance, that OJS was built to publish print-like scholarship and that it would be more work than a $50,000 grant could accommodate to make it suitable to hosting Web texts as a front-end, reader interface, so we focused on modifying. We did not want to ask authors to shoehorn their work into a print-like system. Instead, we hoped to modify OJS to use for our back-end, social and editorial processes, such as peer review, discussed next.

The Social Infrastructure of Digital Scholarship: Collaboration and Peer Review

The infrastructure of scholarly practice for DH work is primarily the responsibility of the scholars and publishers of that work; what we are calling the *social infrastructure* is the most difficult of the challenges facing the publication of digital scholarship because the outcomes are dependent on the reception and use of that work. Traditional notions of scholarship and the institutional practices that rely on them (academic recognition, particularly in the form of tenure and promotion) represent a status quo that does not align well with new practices. DH work tends to redefine and complicate what constitutes a scholarly work as well as what should count as scholarly work (see Schreibman, Mandell, and Olsen 2011; Purdy and Walker 2010). It also tends to be collaborative, which serves as an additional challenge to the humanities status quo, which valorizes the scholar as an individual contributor to knowledge in the field (Spiro 2012). One of the benefits of supporting the social infrastructures of digital scholarship is that it helps show the benefits of collaborative work, which has been a challenge for scholars who publish in traditional forms as well.

Social infrastructure, then, concerns both assessment and peer review of digital scholarship. We have noticed that DH practitioners at conferences such as the Humanities, Arts, Science, and Technology Alliance and Collaboratory and the Digital Media and Learning Competition are beginning to wrestle with the frictions that arise between traditional mechanisms for evaluating the quality of scholarly work and their limited applicability to the assessment of new media scholarship. Thus, we echo Fitzpatrick's (2011) call for additional venues and mechanisms for providing peer review for scholarly multimedia. Doing so need not look like a traditional journal. Indeed, there is a clear need for means of providing assessment for the tools built by digital humanists, the production of digitized and categorized data sets, and scholarly multimedia, and it is likely that the traditional structure and time-bound practices of the academic journal may not be the most appropriate framework for these new publication and review platforms. Newer journals such as the *Journal of Interactive Pedagogy and Technology* and *DHCommons*, established venues taking new directions such as *Enculturation* and *Basic Writing e-Journal*, and presses including C&C Digital Press, Sweetland Digital Rhetoric Collaborative, and the WAC

Clearinghouse are implementing this social infrastructure in measured ways through a variety of bootstrapped content-management systems.

At *Kairos*, the new platform we planned would merge the linear, double-anonymous model of traditional journals, replicated and automated in OJS, with the collaborative, multitiered model of *Kairos*'s partially open peer-review process. During the second tier of review (see "The *Kairos* Editorial Review Process," n.d.), editorial board members collaboratively review a Web text submission on a closed listserv. Any one of the fifty board members can participate over a four-week stretch of review. Most submissions receive feedback from at least five board members, but some receive more. One of the challenges that *Kairos* has faced over the years is a decreasing number of participants during editorial review, we suspect because of overloaded service commitments; reviewing, which takes place over three or four weeks, often gets reprioritized in our overloaded in-boxes since we know others are likely to take up the slack in this collaborative process. But *Kairos* prides itself on always providing a collaborative review, which simultaneously ensures rigor and helpful critique in this nonblind process. (Space does not allow us to justify here why it is pedagogically inappropriate and technologically impossible to anonymously review scholarly multimedia.)

So, in an effort to increase collaborative participation during editorial reviews, we wanted to add a synchronous review option to our OJS project. Ideally, we would continue to provide the social infrastructure of asynchronous discussion forums, as one feature of the *Kairos*-OJS codebase (as John Willinsky, the creator of OJS, referred to it during the 2011 Public Knowledge Conference). And we would provide a new feature to that social infrastructure by offering synchronous reviewing, made possible through individual navigation of submissions with annotation tools (sticky notes, highlighters, etc.), text-based chat, and "share" buttons so that other reviewers could see the markup on one reviewer's screen.

Whereas the editorial board listserv discussions of around fifty scholars tended to make more junior scholars shy at responding when they were unsure of their asynchronous audience, we wanted to revive the communal idea of the late 1990s' Thursday Night MOOs, as the TechRhet community that is *Kairos*'s primary audience base called them (John Walter, personal communication, July 10, 2012). The idea for this multimedia-based OJS review interface was that, whenever we had a submission ready for the board, the editors would post a notice for a review about a week in advance and then whoever could show up (drink in hand at that time of the evening if need be) would live-review the Web text for an hour. A week or two later, the editors would collate those responses with the asynchronous ones from the discussion forums and write a review letter to the author(s). The synchronicity of the so-called Thursday night review also meant that reviewers would have to do less transduction from nondiscursive elements such as images, navigation, and color into discursive elements for a written review when they could circle, highlight, and share their screens in a way the database could capture and export.

This last point was crucial for us as editor and publisher: we still use YahooGroups for most staff and editorial board work because it archives everything. But a good portion of the journal's work, especially with authors, is conducted through nonarchived e-mails. So our interest in migrating to OJS as a back-end for *Kairos* also lay in the fact that it would archive and preserve all our correspondence in a single place—a technical infrastructural issue not to be dismissed when one considers the amount of e-mail correspondence *Kairos* has produced in its nearly two decades of existence, given its one hundred staff and board members and alums and the nearly one thousand Web texts it has published.

Sustainability and the Technical Infrastructure of Digital Scholarship

The third issue in editing and publishing scholarly multimedia (and digital scholarship in general) is sustainability, which includes both access and maintenance. Because technologies and systems are in a state of constant evolution, it is critical to build and maintain sustainable platforms for the publication of DH work. Many DH scholars are working specifically on these issues of sustainability and preservation with regard to digital artifacts, and it behooves us to make sure that these concerns are addressed proactively in terms of publication. Sustainability has long been an important issue at *Kairos*, as evidenced by its status as the longest continuously running online journal in writing studies. Other journals in these areas have either stopped publishing or taken a significant hiatus (see, e.g., Tirrell's [2012] mapping of online rhetoric and composition journals that shows this stoppage). While it is beyond the scope of this chapter to present the full range of technical best practices and recommendations, we do want to call attention to a few technical infrastructure challenges that are particularly pressing for DH scholarship—each of which affects the long-term usability and sustainability of DH publishing venues. Some of these challenges include a reliance on proprietary software, the preservation of and access to obsolete formats, and citation rot.

The first of these challenges is the reliance on proprietary software formats. While there has been a championing of the use of open-source systems for DH work in general, many Web-textual forms and DH approaches rely on functionality that is not available via open-source systems. DH scholars are currently wrestling with the question of preserving and maintaining access to obsolete formats, and even in just the past decade we have seen a rapid shift in formats. As a case in point, one of the most innovative and compelling examples of new media scholarship that we have published in *Kairos*, Anne Wysocki's "A Bookling Monument" (2002), is no longer accessible in all current browsers because the version of Macromedia Director used to create it is no longer fully supported by the latest version of the Shockwave plugin needed to view the work; moreover, that plugin is not available for Linux-based systems. And, between 2006 and 2008, no Shockwave plugin was available for Macs either—which is emblematic of the difficulties of maintaining digital scholarship over multiple platforms and in formats that may change over time (in this case, changes in the platform were made when Adobe Systems bought Macromedia in 2005). Since there is no guarantee of stability, editors and publishers must push for greater use of open-source, sustainable, and flexible formats, an argument that Karl Stolley (2006, 2013), among others, has made repeatedly within the digital rhetoric literature. One of the problems, however, with pushing for open-source versus proprietary systems is that there is not always a good open-source alternative. For instance, "A Bookling Monument" could not be reproduced in current applications (although it would be possible to update it to work more efficiently with the latest version of Adobe Director/Shockwave, but that would require considerable time and energy and the purchase of fairly expensive software—none of which should become a requirement of scholarly production).

Another key issue for digital scholarship is the quotation and citation of other online works. We have found that almost every work that *Kairos* has published includes links or references to works that have since moved location or vanished entirely. In this case, the author does not have control over what happens to these external sources, so, unlike the issue of format, it is not a question of asking producers to make better or more informed choices about which sources to use; rather, this is an issue that needs to be addressed by publishers directly. In terms of technical infrastructure, we do have some options that can help alleviate this problem. Publishers can support and encourage the use of standardized systems that help track and monitor the location and status of both the works we publish and those that our authors cite by using systems like the International DOI Foundation's document object identifiers (DOIs), which function as "persistent interoperable identifiers for use on digital networks" (International DOI Foundation 2010). Because DOIs cost money, however, *Kairos* is limited in implementing them, but we have been pointing to versions of no-longer-extant works archived at the Internet Archive (archive.org) whenever possible (recent policy decisions mean that the archive is no longer a stable repository, unfortunately).

For both the proprietary or obsolete format problem and the ephemerality problem, metadata (defined as data about data) will solve some of these problems. We discovered this solution when completing a metadata mining project associated with our push to use OJS as a searchable database for *Kairos* Web texts (see Ball 2013). Metadata provides information about the contents, format, ownership, and publication of a digital work whether that work is still available or not. It also aids in accessibility and research; for instance, if Wysocki's (2002) "A Bookling Monument" Web text becomes inaccessible again owing to bitrot or plug-in failures, having a long scholarly and technical description, mimetype(s), and other types of metadata included as part of the Web text will allow readers and researchers to interact with the text in fundamentally more sustainable ways, even if not the way the author or editors originally intended. Inclusion of metadata should be an integral part of an author's invention and production process for digital works as well as a standard feature in the digital publishing process.

Building Support for DH Infrastructures: A Call to Action

While each of the three infrastructure areas discussed above affects all the stakeholders who produce and publish DH scholarship, the responsibilities for engaging and developing the foundations for effective production and dissemination reside with different actors for each form—creators of DH scholarship are most concerned with the scholarly infrastructure of rhetoric and design; editors and publishers are best situated to work on the technical infrastructure; and both creators and publishers need to focus on the social infrastructure challenges of these new forms of scholarly work.

Current economic trends affecting scholarly publishing and increasing development and funding of DH work seem to indicate that those of us who support digital rhetoric work find ourselves at an opportune moment to promote DH scholarship writ large. Thus, we end with a call to action with an outline of four key tasks that DH scholars and those who support them should undertake:

- DH scholars need to consider developing and publishing scholarly multimedia work that is effective and accessible—which means learning to deploy rhetoric, design, and code.
- Editors and publishers need to develop new publication and peer-review platforms for screen-based work—and they need to hold scholars to high standards of accessibility, usability, and sustainability.
- Both scholars and publishers need to pay attention to and effectively use technological infrastructure to ensure findability and accessibility of new media scholarship.
- All the stakeholders in DH need to educate their colleagues and administrators and push for broader acceptance of new scholarly forms.

Although our efforts at creating a version of OJS suitable to meet these challenges was ultimately unsuccessful (see Ball, Eyman, and Gossett, in press), our NEH start-up grant did allow us to discover that these are, indeed, key challenges and needs for a scholarly community engaged in DH publishing. If we can collectively continue to develop appropriate publication venues and educate those outside DH, we have an opportunity to fully support a wide range of innovative new forms of scholarship.

References

Anderson, Steve, and Tara McPherson. 2011. "Engaging Digital Scholarship: Thoughts on Evaluating Multimedia Scholarship." *Profession* 16:136–51.

Ball, Cheryl E. 2004. "Show, Not Tell: The Value of New Media Scholarship." *Computers and Composition* 21:403–25.

———. 2010. "Goldilocks and the Three (or Four) Digital Scholarship Books; or, Reconceptualizing a Role for Digital Media Scholarship in an Age of Digital Scholarship: A Review Webtext." *Kairos: A Journal of Rhetoric, Technology, and Pedagogy* 15.1. http://kairos.technorhetoric.net/15.1/reviews/ball/index.html.

————. 2013. "'Pirates of Metadata'; or, The True Adventures of How One Journal Editor and Fifteen Undergraduate Publishing Majors Survived a Harrowing Metadata-Mining Project." In *Common Ground at the Nexus of Information Literacy and Scholarly Communication*, ed. Stephanie Davis-Kahl and Merinda Kaye Hensley, 93–111.

Ball, Cheryl E., Douglas Eyman, and Kathie Gossett. In press. "Building a Better Back-End: Editor, Author, and Reader Tools for Scholarly Multimedia." NEH White Paper. Chicago: Association of College and Research Libraries.

Ball, Cheryl E., and Ryan M. Moeller. 2008. "Converging the ASS[umptions] between U and ME; or How new media can bridge the scholarly/creative split in English studies." *Computers and Composition Online*. http://www.bgsu.edu/cconline/convergence.

Bobley, Brett. 2008. "Why the Digital Humanities?" http://www.neh.gov/files/odh_why_the_digital_humanities.pdf.

Buchanan, Richard. 1985. "Declaration by Design: Rhetoric, Argument, and Demonstration in Design Practice." *Design Issues* 2.1:4–22.

Cope, Bill, and Mary Kalantzis. 2000. *Multiliteracies: Literacy Learning and the Design of Social Futures*. New York: Routledge.

Dilger, Bradley. 2010. "Beyond Star Flashes: The Elements of Web 2.0 Style." *Computers and Composition* 27:15–26.

Eyman, Douglas. In press. *Digital Rhetoric*. Ann Arbor: University of Michigan Press.

Fitzpatrick, Kathleen. 2011. *Planned Obsolescence: Publishing, Technology, and the Future of the Academy*. New York: New York University Press.

Godkin, Kevin. 2012. "Episode #2: On Tenterhooks, On the Tenure Track." 3620 Podcast, Annenberg School of Communication. http://podcast.asc.upenn.edu/2012/09/up-next-on-tenterhooks-on-the-tenure-track.

Gresham, Morgan, and Roxanne Kirkwood Aftanas. 2012. "Not Your Mother's Argument: The Second Shift and the New Work of Feminist Composing in a Digital World." In *The New Work of Composing*, ed. Debra Journet, Cheryl E. Ball, and Ryan Trauman. Logan: Utah State University Press, Computers and Composition Digital Press. http://ccdigitalpress.org/nwc/chapters/gresham-aftanas/welcome.html.

International DOI Foundation. 2010. "Digital Object Identifier System." http://www.doi.org.

"The *Kairos* Editorial Review Process." n.d. *Kairos: A Journal of Rhetoric, Technology, and Pedagogy*. http://kairos.technorhetoric.net/board.html#review.

Purdy, James P., and Joyce R. Walker. 2010. "Valuing Digital Scholarship: Exploring the Changing Realities of Intellectual Work." *Profession* 15:177–95.

————. 2012. "Scholarship on the Move: A Rhetorical Analysis of Scholarly Activity in Digital Spaces." In *New Work of Composing*, ed. Debra Journet, Cheryl Ball, and Ryan Trauman. Logan: Utah State University Press, Computers and Composition Digital Press. http://ccdigitalpress.org/nwc/chapters/purdy-walker.

Schreibman, Susan, Laura Mandell, and Stephen Olsen. 2011. "Evaluating Digital Scholarship." *Profession* 16:123–201.

Selfe, Cynthia, and Richard Selfe. 1999. "Politics of the Interface: Power and Is Exercise in Electronic Contact Zones." *College Composition and Communication* 45.4:480–504.

Spiro, Lisa. 2012. "'This Is Why We Fight': Defining the Values of the Digital Humanities." In *Debates in the Digital Humanities,* ed. Matthew K. Gold, 16–35. Minneapolis: University of Minnesota Press.

Stolley, Karl. 2006. "A Lo-Fi Manifesto." *Kairos: A Journal of Rhetoric, Technology, and Pedagogy* 12.3. http://kairos.technorhetoric.net/12.3/topoi/stolley/index.htm.

———. 2013. "In Search of Troublesome Digital Writing: A Meditation on Difficulty." Keynote address presented at the Computers and Writing conference. https://github.com/karlstolley/cwcon-keynote/wiki/Transcript.

Tirrell, Jeremy. 2012. "A Geographical History of Online Rhetoric and Composition Journals." *Kairos: A Journal of Rhetoric, Technology, and Pedagogy* 16.3. http://kairos.technorhetoric.net/16.3/topoi/tirrell/index.html.

Wysocki, Anne Frances. 2001. "Impossibly Distinct: on Form/Content and Word/Image in Two Pieces of Computer-Based Interactive Multimedia." *Computers and Composition* 18:137–62.

———. 2002. "A Bookling Monument." *Kairos: A Journal of Rhetoric, Technology, and Pedagogy* 7.3. http://kairos.technorhetoric.net/7.3/binder2.html?coverweb/wysocki/index.html.

———. 2004. "Opening New Media to Writing: Openings and Justifications." In *Writing New Media: Theory and Applications for Expanding the Teaching of Composition,* ed. Anne Wysocki, Johndan Johnson-Eilola, Cynthia Selfe, and Geoffrey Sirc, 1–41. Logan: Utah State University Press.

## SIX

The Metaphor and Materiality of Layers

DANIEL ANDERSON

JENTERY SAYERS

Can the metaphor and materiality of layers help explain the shifting relations between composing, the humanities, and digital culture? We can start answering this question by substituting the basic metaphor of layers for our usual sequential representations of reading and writing (e.g., linear text and numbered pages). Layers add verticality to our sense of composing. Each reading performs and even generates new versions of a text over time, but accumulated representations of those readings can be gathered, simultaneous, viewed through one another. And writing is layered, too, revision over revision, stratified over time. Really, the boundaries between versions are more like folds among piles of fabric or sedimentary layers in the material world (Anderson 2012), as are the boundaries between reading and writing, print and digital: the page in your hand is a physical leaf, analog yet layered over countless (often digital) material processes. As an artifact, this text is a composite, emerging through networked and circulating modes of production and distribution, performing what John Bryant calls "a dynamic coupling of book and computer screen" (Bryant 2002, 145), a series of digital/analog convergences all too frequently reduced to ostensibly flat, finished, and polished products on the screen or the page.

Figure 6.1 documents this chapter's first such conver-

6.1. Videos composed while writing this essay. *Source*: Daniel Anderson and Jentery Sayers, http://vimeo.com/channels/metaterials.

gence, represented by a screenshot of a Vimeo channel containing videos—perhaps best understood as process documentations—composed in concert with the chapter itself. The Vimeo channel (https://vimeo.com/channels/metaterials) includes screencasts excavating early Web materials and snapshots of this chapter's iterative composition. These videos feature visual and sonic strategies of layering, offering an alternative mode of engaging the ideas covered here, in this print volume. The videos mark histories of this text, and each marking is an inscription cast from the materials of composing, artifacts crystallized as agate, quartz, whatever granular substance might best account for tangible objects in the world. We examine several other such composites in this chapter: software, diskettes, text files, and graphic interfaces, among others. These artifacts and a granular attention to them evoke activities like collecting, stacking, erasing, and saving. When texts are understood this way, layers become aggregations of objects, parts, or entities. As they unfold through time, we are reminded of ongoing and recurrent events, of compilers gathering bits and granules over and over, never quite the same way twice.

That is, layers conjure for composing fluid, (dis)continuous circulations accumulating in time. Examining these processes through physical composites moves us toward exploring rhetorical ontologies, particularly those that trouble neat demarcations between process and product or the digital and the material. For our tracing here, such ontological inquiries correspond with terms like *snapshot, inscription*, and *commit*. Since these markings always involve processes, composites are put into motion, each emerging from and converging with other entities, calling for vocabularies of *branching* and *merging*. Layering thus becomes—at once—representation in space and recursive movement through time. At all points, it intersects knowing with doing, abstractions with particulars, and bodies with technologies.

Layers also elicit rhetorical and archaeological approaches featuring both the materiality of composing and the historicity of processes. Rather than treating media as finalized composites consumed by audiences, we uncover artifacts through antiquarian understandings (Ernst 2005, 588–89) of making, masonry, and excavation. Wolfgang Ernst remarks: "History is not just text, but the materialist emancipation of the object from an exclusive subjection to textual analysis" (589). From an antiquarian perspective, the object is not relegated to a product of scholarly interpretation. It instead resists human access; it is opaque. Memories form through selection, and collections as well as histories of making are constructed through this selective imagination. A challenge, then, is to talk about the spatiotemporal dimensions of composing without rendering them natural or obvious effects of a "binding historical narrative" (589) or a teleological sequence of events. We argue that layers afford precisely that opportunity for unpacking the ambiguous (dis)continuities, versions, and relational pressure points of composing.

Composing is (dis)continuous because it is perpetual reassembly, or—as Wendy Chun suggests—it is an act of inventing originals after the fact (Chun 2011, 24–25). In this chapter and elsewhere, all our sources are indeed re-sources (24–25), reconstructions of historical artifacts, materials, work flows, behaviors, and practices. These objects are collected from various component parts in circuit with tactile engagement: clicking, touching, sliding, and scrolling, enacting the embodied materiality of the digital, or what Alex Reid charts as the "exteriorization of the subject or the rhizomatic distribution of compositional processes" (Reid 2007, 24)—processes that materialize through multiple modes. Not only are objects and bodies involved, but so too are affect (Murray 2009), design practices, machine acts, and various instances of automagical compiling. These are actions and behaviors we can never remember perfectly (if we can remember them at all). At best, we have repositories with process documentation. More often, we have emulations, screen grabs, redundancies, and 404s. All our sources are re-sources (Reid 2007, 24–25), reconstructions of historical work flows, behaviors, and practices that we can perform again, embody, and repeat differently.

Through this chapter, we provide a sampling of artifacts and terms that engage new media as remnants and relics of a very recent past (the early 1990s forward). To be sure, the inventory is incomplete, and its articulation—at least here—is somewhat detached from the practice of making new media. With that inevitable quibble in mind, we repeatedly point to the video collection that corresponds with the making and versioning of this very text. In fact, we push the limits of intertextuality and material convergence, asking readers to see this text as layered, to commit to "the painful pleasures of fluid texts," and to at least entertain the possibility that rhetoric may be based "not on texts but on the distance between [them]" (Bryant 2002, 147, 143).

We also invite readers to consider this distance as a means of theorizing relations among presumably disparate fields: digital humanities, digital rhetoric, media studies, textual studies, and electronic literature, for example. Instead of clearly defining these fields or framing them as distinct formations, we suggest that the metaphor and materiality of layers together allow an array of practitioners to better understand how they produce, identify, and examine distance between texts. For instance, mapping and spatialization play out frequently as methodologies for implementing humanities work through digital modes. These methodologies tend to privilege homogeneous, flattened, and abstract representations. They are views, if you will, from above. And they produce distance between concepts, entities, or resources in order to express relations, flows, and patterns. Often, these relations are heterogeneous and stratified. They speak to a codified materiality anchored in texts, behaviors, and composing habits. But distances also afford layered relations, which frequently resist abstraction. They involve the overlaps and opacities of disciplines that rarely appear at scale.

The videos associated with this project trace attention to the digital ontologies and epistemologies articulated by the (at least) two-decade-old history of scholarship developed around the intersections of computers and composing. To be sure, these intersections span practices in digital humanities and digital rhetoric (often before either term gained traction in and around the academy). Further, our videos perform metaphors through the materiality of the screen, which—though flat—can exhibit the depths, opacities, and ambiguities of layered composition. In effect, the videos animate our sketch of terms and revise our artifact texts. They are somewhat outside the analytic cold of the well-critiqued text (Latour 2004), or so we hope. They foreground the transformative potentials of the digital while offering a somewhat cautionary tale. Is the tradition of transformative rhetoric about the digital an indication of its continued growth and its possibilities for affecting change? Or does our current celebration belie a long history of transformative rhetoric that has been subsumed beneath layers of disciplinary formations mostly resistant to change? Whatever the answers, both these questions attest to the need to further pursue modes that foreground composing through—and not just about—digital materials and networked culture. Perhaps, then, our emphasis on creative and scholarly communication is how we blur digital humanities, rhetoric, media studies, and their allied fields. This claim is not to suggest that these fields and their definitions do not matter. Rather, it is to suggest that, until they deliberately work across modalities and beyond the logics of print, these endeavors share a limited sense of the layered material practices of the digital.

Levels, Stacks, and Tracks

Exemplified by the interface of the contemporary image editor (e.g., Photoshop), screen-based, multimodal composing evokes a vocabulary of layers (Manovich 2001, 229). The ability to composite and separate multiple layers in a single graphics file instantiates both simultaneity and presence in software. Layers oppose sequentiality, suggesting instead the ability to frame, window-like, numerous items at the same time. As metaphor and material, the layer also casts presence as nuanced and adjustable through opacity sliders, filters, and other software behaviors. Composing an image lets authors turn either up or down the visual presence of a layer. We imagine a kind of negative capability as we bring multiple layers together, suspending one while arranging or adjusting another, producing and performing along a spectrum of representation and inscription.

Performing with software, we work with these layers to compose, creating artifacts as material gatherings accrue, strata-like, one after another. In figure 6.2, we spatialize layers as levels in a palette, as stacks of cards, or as bundles of tracks. Yet these representations are not simply

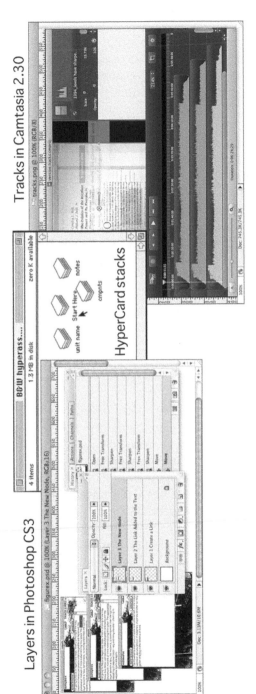

6.2. Layers in an image editor, icons for hypercard stacks, and levels in a video editor. *Source: Daniel Anderson and Jentery Sayers.*

spatial in character. As Niklas Luhmann notes of ontological systems, any structure or instance of stability can be temporalized, and the events or "operations of the system . . . disappear as soon as they appear, they vanish in the very process of emerging" (Luhmann 1993, 771). Elsewhere, Chun claims that memory is the primary characteristic of digital media, which compilers and software constantly refresh (Chun 2011, 154, 166). Consequently, the three instances of digital composing corresponding with figure 6.2 are best understood as modes of capture layered over the dynamics of making. In the HyperCard stacks we find machine and human merging through the shared language of event and object—onmouseup go next card. The image editor suggests structural strata in the levels of its layers palette. And the adjacent history palette links each of those concrete levels to a set of particular machine and operator actions—bring to front, send to back, align (Galloway 2006, 5). The video editor says space and time with its horizontal tracks stacked atop one another. It also automates the translation of this into that, of one image into the next, affording the impression of movement.

The spatial impulse is particularly visible when we excavate software from the 1990s, rife with diagrams and e-maps affording readers and writers an indexical sense of their position within a given computational system—on what card, page, or platform. Spatialized, hypertexts can be layered nodes, stacked, or flattened into tree-like or rhizomatic networks (Deleuze and Guattari 1987).

The spatial impulse (before and after the 1990s) often corresponds with information management and design, whereby people steer (hence *cyber*space) information as they are situated by and within a larger system. For Geoffrey Bowker and Susan Leigh Star, such systems appear whole or complete, though typically premised on mutually exclusive categories abiding by ostensibly consistent classificatory principles (Bowker and Star 1999, 11). Although they are individuated and chunked, the categories relate, overlap, and even cohere. And they are often naturalized (or rendered invisible) through file formats, operating systems, and metadata initiatives, enabling habits in composition, continuity across screens, consistency of design, and interoperability through standardization. The visualizations might seem homogeneous or flat, a flatness Bowker and Star would no doubt deem deceptive. But, comparable to library stacks, layers on a screen are expressed through sets of deep relations (e.g., between people, files, hard drives, and memory chips) and complex navigational and operational features (e.g., "Browse," "Copy," and "Map" tabs) that invite embodied actions such as discovery, annotation, illustration, sampling, and comparing

(Unsworth 2000). More than anything else, flatness corresponds with convenience, an interface that enables the collapse of distance and the illusion of immaterial behavior (Kirschenbaum 2008, 11).

These sets of deep relations and navigational features—not to mention their infrastructures and conventions—facilitate and shape acts of making without determining them. Jamie Skye Bianco's attention to "movements" proves insightful here. In "Composing and Compositing," Bianco understands movements as "a way to rethink theoretical and critical approaches to studies of contemporary digital and analogue cultural production," a metaphor that accounts for levels, nodes, or tracks since "each is particular but all are in a circuit of movement and speed relative to the constellation of objects and streams in the field" (Bianco 2007). For Bianco, the products and processes associated with layered artifacts evoke digital composing across time and space, sparking an exponential (and even excessive) growth of making and expression. One implication of this growth is that layers are difficult and arguably impossible to isolate. As re-sources, they are constantly slipping away and proliferating as new compositions surface. They are simultaneously at hand and receding, bound and fluid.

If cards, levels, and stacks suggest arrangements of materials in space, then tracks spatialize composing along both vertical and horizontal axes. While stacks necessarily engage questions of temporality (homogeneous or not), tracks provide a persuasive metaphor for the layered nature of time in digital/analog material convergences. Echoing Brian Eno, we might say tracks give texture to new media and composing (Eno 2004, 95). Pragmatically, they introduce concerns of tempo, sequence, and transition. Conceptually, they introduce what Andrew Pickering might call a *performative idiom* to complement the representational paradigms associated with spatialized objects. Tracks help us see that there is "a temporal pattern" to materiality (Pickering 1995, 147). However, the choice is never one of substituting a spatial scheme with a temporal or sequential model. Rather, tracks exist simultaneously as layers and sequences, implying a spatiotemporal composition. They are "material-conceptual" configurations (144) that render snippets of sound, images, and other media spatially in time (or temporally in space). Tracks also underscore how media become, or are perceived as, dynamic objects, tweening together frames, stills, clips, and other snapshots on a motion path, which can be situated above or below other paths performing comparable behaviors (see fig. 6.3).

To afford demarcation and arrangement, tracks are frequently labeled, numbered, and color-coded in a time line. Such description

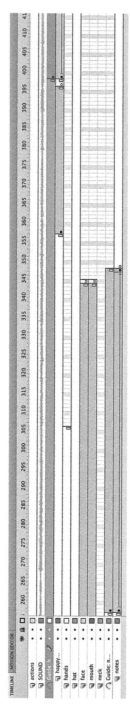

6.3.   Layers of a flash media object. *Source:* Daniel Anderson and Jentery Sayers.

allows authors to recall what each track does in a particular composition, especially when accumulating files, layers, and edits facilitates a forgetting (or a delegation of remembering to the machine) so often associated with "the digital age."

Inscription

As Matthew Kirschenbaum demonstrates in *Mechanisms* (2008), the digital is very much material, despite rhetorics and ideologies of cyberspace that suggest otherwise. The digital *rots*. It *decays*. It *degrades*. Verbs like these invite us to dig through digital materials, not just steer or surf them. The digital is at once smooth and striated. It is written to something, which is often eclipsed by the primacy or essentialism of the screen (Montfort 2004). As such, layers cannot be reduced to the functions of software or even metaphor. They are part of a larger ecology or system, including hardware, platforms, standards, and formats. Digging into them looks past screen immersion in order to better appreciate "how this becomes that" (Fuller 2007, 85) or "at becomes through" (Lanham 1993, 5), connecting us with the "material particulars" (Kirschenbaum 2008, 36) of storage technologies and inscriptive acts. For instance, in 1992, the display and performance of the Eastgate hypermedia novel *Uncle Buddy's Funhouse* are neatly imbricated with the stuff of five 3.5-inch diskettes, a twelve-page book, two cassette tapes, a twenty-four-centimeter box, Hypercard 2.0 (or later), 4.2 megs of free hard drive space, 2 megs or more of memory, and an Apple or Macintosh II (see fig. 6.4).

A bundle of analog and digital media, *Uncle Buddy* was pitched by Eastgate as a "Tarot deck," a stack of objects involving various behaviors, playback mechanisms, modes of inscription, and fidelities. Importantly, as the novel ages, it becomes increasingly hard to access, and its behaviors become difficult to run, enact, or emulate. A layer of its composition (or a granular entity within its compositional layers)—a cassette tape, a Hypercard file, a 3.5-inch floppy—thus asserts itself as inscribed, a relic, resistant, historically contingent, material. Its conditions of storage and playback (e.g., how it was written, through what formats and platforms, and to what drive) remind us that neither new media nor digital inscriptions are magically persistent, somehow outside time, infrastructure, and operation. In fact, through their distributed and layered instantiations, composites like *Uncle Buddy* remind us of the materiality of inscription as well as the boundaries and objects at play in the shifting dynamics of execution, compiling, and storage.

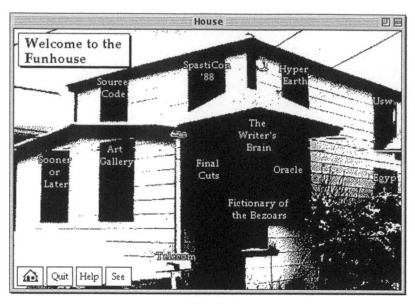

6.4. Screengrab of *Uncle Buddy's Phantom Funhouse. Source*: John McDaid and Eastgate, care of http://www.eastgate.com/catalog/Funhouse.html. Also Daniel Anderson and Jentery Sayers.

Snapshots and Commits

Of course, as inscriptions, layers mark history. They are indexical. They point to something, and they allow authors to follow the (data) trails of compositional practice, even if that practice never unfolds the same way twice. Pragmatically, then, layers evoke archaeological metaphors that invite us to look back and develop tracings particularly suited to the multiply instantiated lives of digital texts and writers.

Bruno Latour deploys a nice photo metaphor for such tracings or maps, offering a "zoom effect," a "framing activity" for grasping moving entities and creating a panorama (Latour 2005, 189). The picture is the product, a momentary capture or suspension of circulating entities comparable to pausing the machine actions of a video game (Galloway 2006, 12). These pauses "provide the only occasion to see the 'whole story' as a whole," and then, like a vacation snapshot receding as the family wagon pulls away from the gas station, the camera goes back into the travel bag. The pause is "added as so many new places dotting the flattened landscape we try to map" (Latour 2005, 189). As an act of framing, it is also a choice or what, in other contexts, might be called a *commit*.

In order to better understand the metaphor and materiality of a commit, compare this excerpt from *Git Basics* (Chacon 2009) with its corresponding visualization (fig. 6.5): "Git thinks of its data more like a set of snapshots of a mini filesystem. Every time you commit, or save the state of your project in Git, it basically takes a picture of what all your files look like at that moment and stores a reference to that snapshot. To be efficient, if files have not changed, Git doesn't store the file again—just a link to the previous identical file it has already stored." The image shows how the version control system, Git, captures the landscape of versions, files, and changes associated with any text or repository of texts. Zoomed out, the snapshot offers a panorama showing objects and traces of activity in the project's source tree. Comparable to the conventions of the Dublin Core Metadata Initiative, each commit (i.e., a state of the project) is attributed with a title, description, author, and time that collectively communicate change to people involved (or not) in a particular project. Again, a commit is a choice—a decision by authors to pause the work they are doing, document and describe the changes they have made, and frame a given project through a particular moment. Here, the zoom effect helps us better understand how commits both metaphorically and materially capture the inscription status and change histories of texts and how such momentary pauses are more like conscious decisions and reckonings than objective instances of frozen time. We need only zoom out another level in order to capture a new snapshot that might show an image from a book about

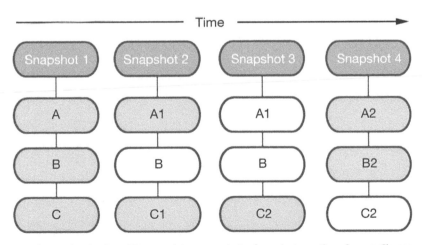

6.5.   Image showing how Git stores data as snapshots of a project over time. *Sources*: Chacon (2009); Git Basics (http://git-scm.com/book/en/Getting-Started-Git-Basics).

version control software in the frame together with artifacts from the early 1990s in a book about digital humanities and rhetoric.

Branching and Merging

Layers also help us understand how even metaphors have a materiality. Unlike the arboreal figure, version branching evokes simultaneity, spatially represented as akin to tracks, as in figure 6.6. Figure 6.6 depicts the movement of objects (codes, files) and activities (events, coding) across the branches of the project—the bug fix, for instance, branching and then merging with the master (*sic*) and development branches. We find movements through the branches, shifting materials and energies from one level to another. In Git, a branch is a line of action, inquiry, or development. And the mediations between branches are cast from and situated within materiality, what Graham Harman sometimes describes as an ether, flowing yet made of elements, "distinct bits, chips, beads, flakes, fragments, shards . . . [entities that] neither recede . . . nor flood us" (Harman 2005, 159). The boundaries, it seems, between

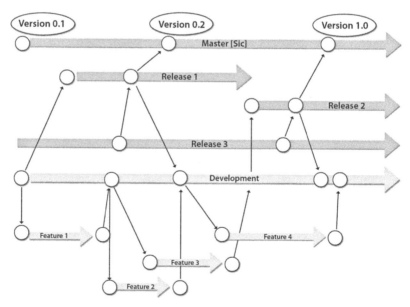

6.6.   Representation of project with branches developed with Git version control. *Source*: http://nss.github.com/slides/gitflow/images/gitflow_2.png.

branches, tracks, or layers are fluid yet distinct, linked yet (dis)continuous. Like audio tracks with varied volumes, they offer "an endless ring of overtones beneath and above [objects]" (160) that, switching now to Ian Bogost's description, "coalesce together and recede again" (Bogost 2012, 28), ultimately, at some level, resisting human access. In practice, "the experience of things can be characterized only by tracing the exhaust of their effects on the surrounding world and speculating about th[eir couplings]" (100).

Pictured as tracks or layers, branching and merging offer the flow of materials through time. Again, zooming metaphors reveal the mobius nature of these flows. Each node in figure 6.6, for instance, suggests a commit in the project, a snapshot. These inscriptions come together and recede as the project and its change history materialize over time. Here, merging calls forth the mixing metaphors of new media. In terms of layers, such merging is represented, as Manovich well describes, through the development of composites. Composites range from the particularities of stacked or merged layers in, say, a movie or an image editor to mixings wrought through the elemental materiality of new media "since a typical new media object is put together from elements that come from different sources" (Manovich 2001, 139). Any composition is a merging and a reissuing (Barthes 1991). Referencing Jacques Derrida's contention that, through citational practices, "two texts are transformed, deform each other, contaminate each other's content, tend at times to reject each other, or pass elliptically one into the other and become regenerated in the repetition, along the edges of an overcast seam" (Derrida 1981, quoted in Reid 2007, 134), Alex Reid notes that even a citational merging "remarks the territory of the text and its peripheral traces and returns back upon the previous text to rewrite that as well." Again, we have fluid boundaries as composites evoke layers that "maintain their heterogeneity while establishing relational points between one another." Even when layers are merged into composites, committing their arrangements and activities to a material inscription, "one can still uncover the edges between the grafts" (135).

Closing

Kenneth Goldsmith said John Cage said: "If something is boring after two minutes, try it for four. If still boring, then eight. Then sixteen. Then thirty-two. Eventually one discovers that it is not boring at all" (Allen 2013). The last moments in this document were composed in

Daniel Anderson @iamdan   10 Feb
RT @betajames: "In my class, they must plagiarize or
they will be penalized. . . ." #screenlit #elit theawl.com
/2013/02/an-int...

Details

6.7. A tweet by @betajames linking to an interview with Kenneth Goldsmith.
Source: James Shirmer.

concert with some of the videos in the Vimeo channel (https://vimeo
.com/channels/metaterials) associated with this chapter. Those pieces
are versions of this text. They evoke alternative modes of responding:
spending time with words, images, sounds, rewatching, immersing,
cross-reading. We can engage the videos through branching and merging. We can try to atomize and connect them, chart meanings or patterns, creating and examining distances as we bring them together with
this text in your hands. Moving through these materials, we discover
processes and products at every level as versions play out even in the
metaphors we string together to point at their composing—layer after
layer, like the burned edge of a leaf in our palm, curling in heat mag-
nified by convex glass hovering above the tissue of the two together,
receding as we zoom out (see fig. 6.7).

References

Allen, Mark. 2013. "Proudly Fraudulent: An Interview with MoMA's First Poet
    Laureate, Kenneth Goldsmith." *The Awl*, February 6. http://www.theawl
    .com/2013/02/an-interview-with-avant-garde-poet-kenneth-goldsmith.
Anderson, Daniel. 2012. "Sediment." Last modified December 12. http://
    vimeo.com/55546722.
Barthes, Roland. 1991. *S/Z*. Translated by Richard Miller. New York: Noonday.
Bianco, Jamie Skye. 2007. "FCJ-061 Composing and Compositing: Integrated
    Digital Writing and Academic Pedagogy." *Fibreculture* 10. http://ten
    .fibreculturejournal.org/fcj-061-composing-and-compositing-integrated
    -digital-writing-and-academic-pedagogy.
Bogost, Ian. 2012. *Alien Phenomenology; or, What It's Like to Be a Thing*. Minne-
    apolis: University of Minnesota Press.
Bowker, Geoffrey C., and Susan Leigh Star. 1999. *Sorting Things Out: Classifica-
    tion and Its Consequences*. Cambridge, MA: MIT Press.
Bryant, John. 2002. *The Fluid Text: A Theory of Revision and Editing for Book and
    Screen*. Ann Arbor: University of Michigan Press.
Chacon, Scott. 2009. *Pro Git*. http://git-scm.com/book.

Chun, Wendy Hui Kyong. 2011. *Programmed Visions: Software and Memory.* Cambridge, MA: MIT Press.

Deleuze, Gilles, and Félix Guattari. 1987. *A Thousand Plateaus: Capitalism and Schizophrenia.* Translated by Brian Massumi. Minneapolis: University of Minnesota Press.

Derrida, Jacques. 1981. *Dissemination.* Translated by Barbara Johnson. Chicago: University of Chicago Press.

Eno, Brian. 2004. "Ambient Music." In *Audio Culture: Readings in Modern Music,* ed. Christoph Cox and Daniel Warner, 94–97. New York: Continuum.

Ernst, Wolfgang. 2005. "Let There Be Irony: Cultural History and Media Archaeology in Parallel Lines." *Art History* 28.5:582–603.

Fuller, Matthew. 2007. *Media Ecologies: Materialist Energies in Art and Technoculture.* Cambridge, MA: MIT Press.

Galloway, Alexander. 2006. *Gaming: Essays on Algorithmic Culture.* Minneapolis: University of Minnesota Press.

Harman, Graham. 2005. *Guerilla Metaphysics.* Chicago: Open Court.

Kirschenbaum, Matthew. 2008. *Mechanisms: New Media and the Forensic Imagination.* Cambridge, MA: MIT Press.

Lanham, Richard A. 1993. *The Electronic Word: Democracy, Technology, and the Arts.* Chicago: University of Chicago Press.

Latour, Bruno. 2004. "Why Has Critique Run Out of Steam? From Matters of Fact to Matters of Concern." *Critical Inquiry* 30:225–48.

———. 2005. *Reassembling the Social: An Introduction to Actor-Network Theory.* Oxford: Oxford University Press.

Luhmann, Niklas. 1993. "Deconstruction as Second-Order Observing." *New Literary History* 24:763–82.

Manovich, Lev. 2001. *The Language of New Media.* Cambridge: MIT Press.

Montfort, Nick. 2004. "Continuous Paper: The Early Materiality and Workings of Electronic Literature." http://nickm.com/writing/essays/continuous _paper_mla.html.

Murray, Joddy. 2009. *Non-Discursive Rhetoric: Image and Affect in Multimodal Composition.* Albany: State University of New York Press.

Pickering, Andrew. 1995. *The Mangle of Practice: Time, Agency, and Science.* Chicago: University of Chicago Press.

Reid, Alex. 2007. *The Two Virtuals: New Media and Composition.* West Lafayette, IN: Parlor Press.

Unsworth, John. 2000. "Scholarly Primitives: What Methods Do Humanities Researchers Have in Common, and How Might Our Tools Reflect This?" http://people.lis.illinois.edu/~unsworth/Kings.5-00/primitives.html.

## SEVEN

Modeling Rhetorical Disciplinarity: Mapping the Digital Network

NATHAN JOHNSON

This chapter proposes factor mapping of humanistic research as a way to understand how institutions, academic lineage, citationality, and geography influence scholarship. Because factor mapping requires a large collection of information, the chapter also encourages the development of an open source database as a collaborative project. Therefore, the remainder of the chapter outlines a typology of data that can be used to generate factor maps for generating models specific to humanistic research.

In February 2012, the *New York Times* ran an article describing how Target uses consumer information from numerous databases to predict and control how their customers purchase products (Duhigg 2012). One of the more memorable examples involved Target sending coupons for pregnancy items to a teen's house. The father contacted Target, furious that his teen daughter was being targeted for a potential pregnancy. It was only later that the father found out that his daughter was already pregnant and that Target had used her buying patterns to deduce the upcoming birth before she had told anyone. The overall narrative of the story seems to be that, given enough data, which is not difficult in the era of big data, knowledge can be archived into a world brain and future actions can be easily predicted. This idea has not gone unnoticed within contemporary scholarship, as network scientists and scholars use similar backgrounded assumptions to organize their research. Increasingly, big data and the related data visualizations are becoming popular arguments of the twenty-first-century world.

Scholars have already built this concept into their research, lines of work that have been recently popularized by the network guru Albert-Lázló Barabási's *Linked* (Barbasi 2003). Frequently, especially in the hard and social sciences, research is analyzed as though it were a linked set of objects in the world. For example, the well-known Eigenfactor Project maps and evaluates scholarship through network analysis (West, Bergstrom, Althouse, Rosvall, and Bergstrom 2012). Eigenfactor, like many other bibliometric projects, begins from the assumption that scholarship consists of a process in which "ideas are built upon ideas, models upon models, verifications upon prior verifications." Scholarship, according to Eigenfactor's working theory, is a straightforward unit that can be measured and that adds to a generative understanding of all knowledge.

That is not a criticism of Eigenfactor or other bibliometric network research. These types of models are designed to measure, predict, and control scholarship, and network researchers are careful about describing the limitations of such a theoretical approach. In particular, bibliometricians and scientometricians are especially aware of and sensitive about the limitations of their approach as a means to predict and control (MacRoberts and MacRoberts 2010). Eigenfactor does what it was designed do to well: measure scholarship.

Yet bibliometric modeling techniques also provide an opportunity for digital humanists to participate in research arguments that are gaining institutional hold for important stakeholders. Eigenfactor visualizes how convergences of institutions, technologies, and people enmesh with published academic research. And, instead of interpreting bibliometric models as a measurement of scholarship, they could be interpreted as models of the powerful dynamics influencing academic work. For instance, bibliometric factor models of scholarship provide rich visualizations depicting which institutions have more control over the types of research that are produced. Factor models with bibliometric indicators generate influential rhetorics, and digital humanists could be enriching them by developing them while simultaneously reinterpreting their theoretical foundations.

Identifying Factors of Influence

Factor mapping is a method of using relations between normalized research data in combination with mathematical formulas to generate information graphics that synthesize and argue with large amounts of data. The technique and its variants have become more popular as data storage and collection have become cheaper in the computer age.

Numerous factors influence the production of written scholarship. For instance, writing spaces contain cues that end up in the text of final drafts by influencing the ideas that become inscribed on the page. These factors cannot all be taken into account, so it is necessary to select a subset of data that would be valuable for humanistic inquiry. Unfortunately for humanities scholarship, but fortunately for digital humanists working with factor maps, very little work has been done to map existing humanities scholarship, and this provides many possibilities for future work. While bibliometricians have developed tools for factor mapping, these tools have been largely developed for a social science audience. Humanities research has its own distinct challenges, and, below, I discuss how to adapt and apply these tools while also discussing how their application speaks to broader humanities research interests.

Currently, advances in computing have changed the research environment. The world is being archived digitally at an astounding rate. These new types of data are alluring for humanists because they capture parts of the human condition in unprecedented ways. Yet the traditional humanistic methods fall short when trying to make sense of the new data. Several prominent digital humanists have outlined some techniques to help with the problem (Kirschenbaum 2007a, 2007b; Moretti 2005), and, given the vastness and depth of the issue, many more solutions would be useful. Factor-mapping techniques provide some solutions to this data problem, especially when adapted for the values and concerns of the digital humanities.

To select the necessary data for visualization, factor mapping requires the consolidated efforts of digital humanists across universities because the amount of data that would need to be collected is vast. Yet, because so many factors influence scholarship, collecting information for all possible factors and realities is a huge undertaking and theoretically implausible. Some factors are local and fairly unique to each individual. For example, an individual researcher's personal belongings are fairly contained to one locality, influencing the work of one person. Some factors are more global, share characteristics across research spaces, and are standardized through academic information infrastructure. For instance, database vendors of journals standardize, classify, and normalize research papers. These infrastructural and globalized papers are disseminated across institutions via licensing contracts and database technology. The normalization process builds consistency, or globalization, into some factors involved with the making of scholarship. This local/global difference provides a heuristic for factor mapping, one particularly well explained by information infrastructural theory.

Information infrastructural theory suggests that information is embodied in globalized and standardized technologies that instantiate and project the values of history onto the present (Bowker, Baker, Millerand, and Ribes 2007). Infrastructural components are cemented at specific historical points called *reverse salients* (Hughes 1983) and become key influencers of social interaction. Because the historically important points are difficult to reverse, the values that undergird construction of infrastructure during the creation of reverse salients stabilize the infrastructure, which then influences how people, information, and technology interact in the present. Scholarship has an infrastructural background, standardizing, classifying, and providing resistance and feedback to the work of academe. Thus, global infrastructural components provide prime data for factor modeling.

Research journal databases are only one infrastructural component in a large regime of technologies in the scholarly information infrastructure (Borgman 2007). Other research factors are standardized, classified, normalized—infrastructured—through a variety of institutions, spaces, times, and places. Modeling these factors provides the data that can then be used to visualize and reimagine how scholarship is influenced by a wide range of factors. The four factors outlined below provide a base foundation for factor mapping the academic information infrastructure of the humanities.

Benefits and Limitations of Factor Mapping

Factor mapping is only one technique for better understanding academic literature using newer digital technologies. As a methodology that relies on digital databases that can be reused to understand humanities literature, it belongs within the tool kit of digital humanities methods.

Similar methods have been used successfully in other disciplines. Yet humanists have been largely reluctant to engage in the practice of factor mapping, largely for two reasons: (1) when used in combination with academic scholarship, it generates numerical values for scholarship that can be used in the tenure and promotion process; (2) it reduces the complexity of the literary work. Both these are correct, but the tenor of the criticism should be reconsidered.

In regards to generating numerical values that influence tenure and promotion practices, critics usually are suspicious of the idea because some scholarship numbers could be used to deny tenure. Yet the factors for denying tenure are frequently much more complex and fuzzy than publication or citation counts. Scholars who are hesitant to adopt numerical values as a way to bargain for tenure and promotion are giving up one of the more powerful argumentative rhetorics of the twenty-first century—the use of mathematics to support argument. Complaints about using numbers related to academic scholarship seem to frequently be misguided. They are not so much about the use of numerical value to prove the value of scholarship; rather, they seem to be an epiphenomenon of an us/them binary. That is, complaints about using something like an h-index to help guide the tenure and promotion process are often lodged at a stasis that sees scholar and department, school, and university at odds with each other. If this is the case, the issue runs much deeper than the use of numbers and factor mapping as arguments for granting tenure and promotion. Factor maps neither alleviate nor worsen the process of healthy institutions.

Second, critics of factor analysis and citation analysis have complained that the procedure reduces the complexity and value of texts. This is true, but there is no method of interpretation or data analysis that could ever exhaust the complexity of research. Factor analysis simply provides one tool for better understanding the complexity that is celebrated by humanists. In other words, it provides new appreciations of the work of literature but does not seek to ever fully explain it. It does so by generating visualizations that contribute to perspectives that would not otherwise exist. Consider the following analogy. If a person were lost, would you suggest that it is not a good idea to use a map of the area to navigate the terrain because a two-dimensional map could not adequately represent the area it purports to represents? That is, it will not point out the shops, restaurants, and people one is likely to meet on a journey. Or would it be wise to use the map because it provides one more tool that would otherwise be unavailable to help understand the richness of the terrain? Factor analysis provides a way to understand scholarship that scholars should not dismiss simply because it has consequences. The act of dismissing factor and citation analysis has consequences as well.

One of the major benefits of using this approach is that it participates in one the most powerful languages organizing scholarship today: quantitative measurement. Grants, funding, scholarships, and reviews are influenced frequently by the novelty, insight, and richness of research. To use factor analysis is to use methods that have stronger currency with many audiences. Factor mapping is a powerful rhetoric that can help validate research in the eyes of audiences that are interested in the metaphors and tools that science uses. It does not exhaust research value, it hints at one facet of it.

Factor 1: Institution

Institutions, such as publishers, government departments, universities, and other funding organizations, often significantly influence who has access to resources, and this shapes published literature. As an example, a previous factor-mapping study has shown a relation between publication counts and institutional prestige from past decades (Börner, Penumarthy, Meiss, and Ke 2006). The studies show that institutions like universities become significant force factors for the type and quality of scholarship. For example, Börner, Penumarthy, Meiss, and Ke used an institutional approach to analyze whether increased availability of the Internet in the last several decades made the scholarly publication process more democratic (i.e., could authors publish without the support of a major institution?). They found that, contrary to expectations, it was actually more difficult for independent scholars to publish research. They hypothesized that the reason for this was that increased information available on the Web increases the likelihood that scholars will rely more on existing peer networks. In this case, that meant the entrenchment of older academic networks. In that study, mapping institutions to publication data yielded significant information about how scholarship continues to be primarily shaped by past institutional configurations.

For reasons like those demonstrated in the Börner, Penumarthy, Meiss, and Ke study, visualizing relations between types of publication and the organizations that support or do not support those types provides a new lens for understanding scholarship. Without mapping the institutions, common sense might suggest that older institutions are less powerful today, losing influence to smaller, disruptive organizations and people. Because many humanists study historical institutions, mapping institutional information adds nuance to research for existing humanities work. For example, the Mapping Texts project at the University of North Texas uses institutional data about newspaper publishers, mapping geographic data in combination with publication information related to newspapers (Torget, Mihalcea, Christensen, and McGhee, n.d.). By doing this, the project provides a visualization depicting the growth of powerful newspapers in a specific geographic region over time. As the Torget, Mihalcea, Christensen, and McGhee study shows, systematically taking institutions into account to understand literature has the ability to show other literary influences, too. Notably, this type of analysis is not able to determine causation, but it does point to abnormalities that are otherwise not part of modern sensibilities. Humanists are well trained to interpret what factor mapping can say about scholarship.

Factor 2: Citation Patterns and Quotation Grafting

Citation patterns are a popular factor among information scientists for identifying systemic patterns in scholarship, and they have extensive potential for digital humanists interested in using sources that are typically secondary as primary research. Bibliometrics and citation analysis have much to offer as an exploratory for digital humanists. Those factors, as well as others, can be used to create visualizations of disciplinarity that can enrich the humanistic interpretation of texts.

For instance, the h-index is an indicator that is frequently used to generate a ranking value for a scholar based on the number of papers written and the number of citations to each paper. The creator of the h-index describes the process of generating a scholar's h-value as follows: "[A] scientist has index h if h of his/her N_p papers have at least h citations each, and the other ($N_p - h$) papers have no more than h citations each" (Hirsch 2005, 1). This generates values that are large for individuals with many published papers and many citations. While this number may not be a good indicator of academic value, it can be an effective tool for visualizing the embeddedness of writers who are better known and central to a field. This can be done by creating visual nodes that have a size in ratio to an h-index number representing the work of specific individuals. Visual vectors can also be calculated using h-index values. When humanists do the work of interpreting the what and how of bibliometrics indicators, they can generate powerful analysis that clearly benefits their scholarship. For example, one of the reasons that citation pattern analysis has not yet caught on in humanities scholarship is that no one has identified best methods for figuring out what a humanities citation is or could possibly mean. For instance, large block quotes are analyzed in unique ways in humanities literature. *No one has figured out how to analyze these types of quotations with citation analysis.*

Bibliometric indicators not only consist of citations and impact factors; they can also be any quantitative data derived from texts, such as standardized publication data, textual descriptors/subject headings, and footnote frequencies. If there is text involved, likely a bibliometrics indicator can be used to better understand humanities data through modeling. Some of these indicators, like topic modeling, have already been widely used in the digital humanities (Graham, Weingart, and Milligan, n.d.). Others still need to be developed. For example, the h-index could be refashioned to identify individuals who frequently appear within personal correspondences or academic Twitter streams. The revised h-index would indicate individuals in society who are appearing frequently in publication. Mapping this revised h-index would provide a new way to understand a literary text. By comapping influential individuals to institutions through a revised h-index, it would be possible to have a better understanding of the individuals publicly appearing and representing specific institutions.

Similar bibliometric alteration techniques can be used in many other ways, such as in the following examples. Cocitation analysis has been used widely to identify families of scholarship in academic literature (Osareh 2011). Assuming that coauthors are roughly interested in similar topics, pairing coauthorship and considering frequency of coauthorship is a powerful method for generating visual maps of disciplines. These kinds of techniques are more accessible to humanists than before. Google's popularization of using n-grams (Google 2012b) to identify patterns and academic interest in topic modeling (Graham, Weingart, and Milligan, n.d.) has made bibliometrics approaches and data more accessible to humanities scholars.

Factor 3: Location

Location can be one of the most significant indicators for factor analysis because institutions, publications, and people are materially bound by place. Even during a time that has witnessed an upsurge in globalized communication practices, place matters (Graham 2004). Location makes a difference because, even though it is possible to communicate more globally than ever before, the geography of the past constrains modern communication practices. For instance, recall that Börner, Penumarthy, Meiss, and Ke (2006) found that academic communication among scholars actually depends more on older lines of communication now than it did in the past. They hypothesized that the reason for this was because, when inundated with nearly unlimited access to information, scholars tend to rely on older peer networks to select which scholarship is the most important to read. In their study, they found that today it is actually more difficult for unaffiliated scholars or scholars at smaller institutions to become part of a larger academic community, simply because they do not have access to the institutional communication channels that scholars at large institutions have. These institutions were all megaliths situated in specific geographies. Place is intimately bound to human communication and social change.

Even if there were changes in the ways that institutions are related to geography, shifting the relation between institutions and place, place can still be used as a significant mapping factor. Urban sociologists find that cities are still important loci for productive output in societies (Neff 2005). When people physically live close to each other, it creates a hotbed of innovation that is unique to the location and time. Community gathering places like restaurants, shops, museums, libraries, and universities depend on the physical capital of people living together in shared locations. When people physically commune, they communicate in ways that are unique in the way they produce ideas, products, literature, or scholarship. These patterns can be illustrated through factor mapping.

Because places differ from each other, factor analysis is useful for identifying hotbeds of specific types of literature or ways of thinking. It is also useful for identifying the movement of ideas from one place to another. This is important because it provides a sense of influential communication channels and ideas that are stickier than others. This has relevance to both the scholarship of rhetoric and the study of rhetoric. Ideas from rhetoric scholarship can be traced from place to place, and the analysis simultaneously highlights the relations between place, ideas, and people.

As with institutions, many good geographic resources allow data points for geography to be easily used in mass. Perhaps the most forgiving geocoding software is available through Google's Map API (Google 2012a). Many of the primary sources used for humanistic research are already rich with location information that can be quantitatively recorded and organized for factor mapping. Place matters. An important next step is collaboratively collecting data to show how place matters.

Factor 4: Metadata Factors: Venues, Subjects, and Dates

Metadata provide some of the most innovative information available for factor analysis. It is information that is a related epiphenomenon of literature and scholarship. Current practices in publishing generate a huge amount of metadata related to publication. Most recognizably, each type of scholarship contains information on publishers that is captured as metadata. Journal articles are associated with specific journals, specific journals used specific style guides and editorial strategies, volumes, numbers, pages, and so on. Archival materials have metadata about provenance associated with them. All these types of data have become digitally available for mining in the digital age. Each has the potential to answer questions that can help highlight something new about existing texts. Full text mining of texts is widely possible for many modern and archival materials.

Frequently, scholars shudder at the thought of using this type of data analysis, considering it to be a type of bean counting. Yet it is useful for helping to better understand the practice of scholarship, which is never confined to what ends up on the written page, and can help highlight scholarship in new ways. For instance, by looking at page counts in publications in a set of a publisher's books, scholars can identify whether page frequency is going up or down or fluctuating in a recurrent way, perhaps seasonally, or how increasing numbers of citations may indicate less reading on the part of scholars (*Emerging Configurations of Knowledge Expression* 2012). Once these data have been collected and visualized, digital humanists are then able to interpret the reasons for metadata patterns. Factor mapping may start with (or include) bean counting, but the metadata allow much better questions than we could ask previously. And, as previously suggested, humanists can offer new types of rich interpretation (Kirschenbaum 2007a, 2007b; Moretti 2005).

Even though full-text analysis is possible for humanistic interpretation, perhaps some of the richest types of metadata for factor-mapping projects are the subject headings, classifications, descriptors, and keywords associated with primary and secondary texts. This type of information is frequently generated by human interpretation, usually by librarians or indexers who are hired specifically to interpret the nature of books. Because of this added human dimension, subject headings are a particularly interesting way to approach large sets of data. Interpretation at the classification level by librarians and reinterpretation by humanists at the publication level make the work of the digital humanities rife with research possibilities and new ways of knowing.

The research outcome of a theory and methodology of factor analysis is to use data that exist about humanities texts and scholarship to create visualizations to better understand factors of influence within existing and upcoming humanities scholarship. The method has the potential to identify unconsidered factors significantly influencing how institutions, geography, friendship links, or a number of other factors shape texts. To some extent, scholars already suspect and hypothesize these hidden influences in the production of their ideas. Creating data maps to help analyze these influences is useful for suggesting new lines of research and new types of collaboration between scholars. It is an important job of the digital humanities to use new tools to highlight this influence. A first step, then, is to begin collaborations that work to make relevant data available to aid the questions of digital humanists.

References

Barabási, Albert-László. 2003. *Linked: How Everything Is Connected to Everything Else and What It Means.* New York: Plume.

Borgman, Christine L. 2007. *Scholarship in the Digital Age: Information, Infrastructure, and the Internet.* Cambridge, MA: MIT Press.

Börner, Katy, Shashikant Penumarthy, Mark Meiss, and Weimao Ke. 2006. "Mapping the Diffusion of Scholarly Knowledge among Major U.S. Research Institutions." *Scientometrics* 68.3:415–26.

Bowker, Geoffrey C., Karen Baker, Florence Millerand, and David Ribes. 2010. "Towards Information Infrastructure Studies: Ways of Knowing in a Networked Environment." In *International Handbook of Internet Research*, ed. Jeremy Hunsinger, Lisbeth Klastrup, and Matthew Allen, 97–117. New York: Springer.

Duhigg, Charles. 2012. "How Companies Learn Your Secrets." *New York Times*, February 16. http://www.nytimes.com/2012/02/19/magazine/shopping -habits.html.

Emerging Configurations of Knowledge Expression. 2012. YouTube video, 56:03, from a recording of a lecture in Vancouver, BC, posted by "UBC." November 13. https://www.youtube.com/watch?v=Dl3qNQ-qY54.

Google. 2012a. "Google Maps Developer Documentation—Google Maps API— Google Developers." *Google Developers.* Last modified December 17.

———. 2012b. "Google Ngram Viewer." *Google Books Ngram Viewer.* http://
books.google.com/ngrams. https://developers.google.com/maps/
documentation.

Graham, Shawn, Scott Weingart, and Ian Milligan. n.d. "Getting Started
with Topic Modeling and MALLET." *Programming Historian.* http://
programminghistorian.org/lessons/topic-modeling-and-mallet.

Graham, Stephen. 2004. *The Cybercities Reader.* London: Routledge.

Hirsch, Jorge E. 2005. "An Index to Quantify an Individual's Scientific Research Output." *Proceedings of the National Academy of Sciences of the United
States of America* 102.46:16569–72.

Hughes, Thomas Parke. 1983. *Networks of Power: Electrification in Western Society, 1880–1930.* Baltimore: Johns Hopkins University Press.

Kirschenbaum, Matthew G. 2007a. *Mechanisms: New Media and the Forensic
Imagination.* Cambridge, MA: MIT Press.

———. 2007b. "The Remaking of Reading: Data Mining and the Digital
Humanities." In *The National Science Foundation Symposium on Next
Generation of Data Mining and Cyber-Enabled Discovery for Innovation,
Baltimore, MD.* http://www.cs.umbc.edu/~hillol/NGDM07/abstracts/
talks/MKirschenbaum.pdf.

MacRoberts, M. H., and B. R. MacRoberts. 2010. "Problems of Citation Analysis: A Study of Uncited and Seldom-Cited Influences." *Journal of the American Society for Information Science and Technology* 61.1:1–12.

Moretti, Franco. 2005. *Graphs, Maps, Trees: Abstract Models for Literary History.*
London: Verso.

Neff, Gina. 2005. "The Changing Place of Cultural Production: The Location
of Social Networks in a Digital Media Industry." *Annals of the American
Academy of Political and Social Science* 597.1:134.

Osareh, Farideh. 2011. "Bibliometrics, Citation Analysis and Co-Citation
Analysis: A Review of Literature I." *Libri* 46.3:149–58.

Torget, Andrew J., Rada Mihalcea, Jon Christensen, and Geoff McGhee. n.d.
"Mapping Texts: Combining Text-Mining and Geo-Visualization to
Unlock the Research Potential of Historical Newspapers." White Paper.
Denton: University of North Texas. http://mappingtexts.org.

West, Jevin D., Carl T. Bergstrom, Ben Althouse, Martin Rosvall, and Ted C.
Bergstrom. 2012. "Well-formed.eigenfactor.org? Citation Patterns."
Eigenfactor.org. http://well-formed.eigenfactor.org/radial.html.

## PART TWO

Research Methods and Methodology

## EIGHT

Tactical and Strategic: Qualitative Approaches to the Digital Humanities

BRIAN MCNELY

CHRISTA TESTON

Like other contributors to this volume, we have a broad, interdisciplinary perspective concerning the study of humanism and rhetoric. Our work draws from traditions of qualitative inquiry in rhetoric and the social sciences around our overarching interest: relations between methodological strategies, attendant framing theories, and tactical implementations of fieldwork and analysis that help us explore the nuances of lived (digital) experience. We are interested, therefore, in adapting and extending qualitative inquiry to studies of rhetoric and the digital humanities (DH). Given the wide range of potential approaches to research practices in this emerging confluence of academic and professional fields, our work in this chapter is necessarily limited; however, by providing examples from our fieldwork, we hope that this chapter will act as a touchstone for further discussions and explorations of the strategies and tactics we might deploy in empirical studies of rhetoric and DH.

What are the differences between *tactics* and *strategies* in rhetorically informed qualitative research methodologies, and why should they matter to digital humanists? Though broad considerations of tactics and strategies have been explored across a wide range of pursuits—from the ancient military planning of Sun Tzu (2005) through contemporary invocations of de Certeau (1984)—we see tactics and strategies as a way into broader discussions of research methods and methodologies exploring how people act with technologies (Kaptelinin and Nardi 2006). Clay Spinuzzi defines the differences between methods and methodologies succinctly: "A *method* is a way of investigating phenomena; a *methodology* is the theory, philosophy, heuristics, aims, and values that underlie, motivate, and guide the method" (2003, 7). We see a parallel relation between tactics and strategies: methods are *tactical*, sometimes involving kairotic adjustments in a given research context. Methodologies, on the other hand, are *strategic*: they carry and inculcate specific and layered epistemologies that shape one's approach to an object of study. As funding and institutional support for projects in DH have developed, we see a strong temptation for researchers to use emerging technologies in largely tactical ways—appending the "digital" or digital tools to extant (often pre-digital) strategies. Project Bamboo, funded by the Mellon Foundation, is an apt example of the temptations available to DH scholars. The collection of digital research tools available at the Project Bamboo Web site offers several tactical implementations. But rhetorically informed digital humanists should proceed with caution— *doing* DH is not as simple as choosing a digital tool and then combining that tool and tactic with a given methodological approach; indeed, a given tactic may be at odds with one's strategy.

We invite researchers, therefore, to begin by considering strategies that account for the complexities of articulating "the digital" with humanistic research. We surely must attend to tactics in DH, but we argue that such tactics should be meaningfully and reflexively configured to broader *strategies* of research. Effective tactics, then, must begin with a clearly articulated strategy, for choosing tactics that support broader strategies might help alleviate some of the tensions DH researchers experience when negotiating their theoretical dispositions alongside a desire to conduct data-driven investigations. Empirical researchers in rhetoric and writing have much to offer DH in this regard; scholars in the field have long explored reflexive empirical approaches to situated writing and rhetorical practice (see, e.g., Kirsch and Sullivan 1992; Mortensen and Kirsch 1996; and MacNealy 1999). We are interested in finding strategies that help us explore and better understand the complexity of lived (digital) experience and using those strategies to direct and shape tactical fieldwork and analysis. As we describe below, a global focus on strategies allows us to be tactically agile at the local level, choosing fieldwork and analytic methods because they are productively articulated with our methodological strategies. We describe these moves through examples from our research. First, we discuss a study of transmedia storytelling by using tactical visual research methods as part of a more traditional ethnographic strategy. We then discuss a collaborative investigation of a publicly available, online corpus of FDA deliberations; tactically, a doppelgänger coding schema was used as part of a broader strategy of analytic transparency. We conclude with a brief discussion of the implications of our work and of the potential for future studies.

Qualitative Inquiry and Lived Digital Experience

The empirical, field-based study of rhetorical and humanistic pursuits is necessarily enmeshed in complex assemblages of material culture and activity. Even mundane digital practices involve a host of nondigital technologies in concrete sociocultural contexts. Since at least the late 1970s (Emig 1979; Faigley and Witte 1981), scholars in writing and rhetoric have been interested in how systemic material contexts, social histories, and generic expectations (Miller 1984) both enable and constrain writing and rhetorical work. This early and ongoing interest in the situatedness of writing—the embodied, sensory, and material contexts of everyday rhetorical practice—has resulted in several tactics for tracing and analyzing situational variables in situ; this disciplinary tradition has the potential to enrich DH. Our own work draws on many of these traditions as we have attempted to research and represent some of the complexity of lived experience through both digital and nondigital writing and rhetorics (McNely 2011, 2012, 2013; Teston 2009, 2012a; McNely, Teston, Cox, Olorunda, and Dunker 2010; McNely, Gestwicki, Geims, and Burke 2013; Teston and McNely 2013). In this section, we describe the overarching methodologies and framing theories that have informed our work and contributed to the research strategies guiding our tactics.

Shipka's (2011) recent work foregrounds the need for scholars of writing to be mindful of how we use the term *technology* and how we approach the products of digital rhetorics. In emerging DH scholarship, this perspective is especially trenchant. Drawing on Prior (2009), Shipka argues that writing studies has moved away from explorations of processes and contexts, tending instead to see writing "as a noun rather than a verb, and to privilege the analyses of static texts" (2011, 13). In contrast, Shipka is interested in studying mediated actions within the often messy social and historical contexts of everyday life. Like Shipka, we are interested in "tracing the processes by which texts are produced, circulated, received, responded to, used, misused, and transformed, [because in so doing] we are able to examine the complex interplay of the digital and analog, of the human and nonhuman, and of technologies, both new and not so new" (30). In order to effectively deploy such an approach, we need context-sensitive theories coupled with appropriate field methodologies; our work has effectively drawn from both writing, activity, and genre research (WAGR) and grounded theory (GT) to do so.

Methodologically, much of our respective empirical work takes the form of ethnographies or systematic qualitative case studies, and, theoretically, WAGR and GT perspectives often guide such studies. WAGR is a relatively recent coinage for the body of work synthesizing scholarship in rhetorical genre studies (Bawarshi and Reiff 2010) and cultural-historical activity theory (Russell 1997a, 1997b, 2009; Spinuzzi 2003, 2004, 2008, 2010). In WAGR approaches, genres are not only typified, tool-mediated responses to recurrent problems in situated (and often overlapping) activity systems; they are also ways of knowing and being in the world (Russell 2009, 43). Rhetorical genres and the ways they are used in everyday practice—in assemblages of sociocultural artifacts and often nondigital materiality—thus have powerful epistemic and ontological functions. Genre knowledge, in this view, mediates everyday practice, powerfully and materially shaping intersubjective human relations (Russell 2009, 45). Such relations can be observed, documented, and explored, in part, through attention to the artifact and genre ecologies that people use repeatedly in their everyday work, which necessitates particular methodological strategies (Spinuzzi 2003; Bødker and Nylandsted Klokmose 2011). As a methodology and mode of deep theorizing (Lillis 2008), ethnography is especially well suited to WAGR investigations of writing and rhetorical practice (see McNely, Gestwicki, Geims, and Burke 2013).

GT approaches to data collection and analysis involve the constant comparison of inductively derived codes and categories. Theories are generated (vs. verified) from emerging codes and categories. Integral to this methodological approach is the continual pushing and pulling apart of boundaries between codes. Initial observations are made by conducting what Glaser and Strauss (1967) call *open coding*, or the opening up of inquiry (Strauss 1987). Theoretical memoing is also a key tactic in GT approaches. According to Strauss, theoretical memos have an "indispensable function in discovering, developing, and formulating a grounded theory" (1987, 109). Once codes become somewhat stable and fixed, researchers move toward dimensionalization of codes and, ultimately, selective coding. Trends and outliers are noted during these practices, and theory building begins once certain salient aspects of the data are explored in greater detail. Core categories are made more apparent during selective coding. Essentially, GT approaches are a way to account for embodied, sensory, and material contexts of everyday practices such that theories about those practices are built from the sites themselves.

Ethnography and systematic qualitative case study research are effective methodologies for exploring the kinds of complex mediated actions and processes that Shipka (2011) argues are essential to seeing writing (and broader rhetorical practice) as a verb rather than a noun. Yet these methodologies do not become truly strategic until they are carefully articulated with an appropriate theoretical frame (see Smagorinsky 2008). In this way, it is ethnography deployed from a WAGR perspective, for example, that forms a strong *strategy* for qualitative inquiry into—and understanding of—participant practice in rhetorical and humanistic pursuits. In our own research strategies, a premium is placed on reflexive implementation: global strategies, reflexive by design, foster local tactical agility in fieldwork and analysis. In the next section, we describe how WAGR- and GT-informed strategies of qualitative inquiry afford certain tactics and limit others; understanding tactical possibilities and limitations, we argue, is crucial in both developing and executing an effective qualitative research strategy.

Strategies, Then Tactics

Strategies developed from global, reflexive methodologies of qualitative inquiry articulated (joined) with nuanced theoretical frameworks for understanding rhetorical and humanistic pursuits position researchers to better evaluate and deploy fieldwork and analytic tactics. For example, ethnographic work taking a WAGR perspective necessitates fieldwork methods that explore not only the *what* and *why* of lived (digital) experience but also the *how* and *when*. Engeström argues: "Mediation by tools and signs is not merely a psychological idea. It is an idea that breaks down the Cartesian walls that isolate the individual mind from the culture and society" (1999, 29). Because human beings act with tools and signs in purposeful, historically conditioned ways, a focus on mediation sees artifacts and tools as inseparable from human activity

(Engeström 1999). This strategic perspective clearly has tactical implications: What are appropriate methods for studying complex mediation? What tactics are effective in the analysis of mediated action? And is DH, at root, not a new conceptualization of humanistic mediation? Supported by well-articulated methodological and theoretical perspectives, we can choose tactics that are relationally configured to our overall strategies.

This affords a certain tactical promiscuity—we are better positioned to structure an array of appropriate local methods to support the overarching strategy we have developed. Bazerman (1997) argues that research using multiple methods (tactics of triangulation) "holds much promise for drawing humanities' understandings of the workings of language into relation with the social sciences' understandings of human relations, behavior, and consciousness" (23). One form of fieldwork or analysis—one tactical approach to a given object of study—cannot be expected to carry the weight of inquiry; instead, multiple methods guided by a reflexive global strategy provide nuance to our understandings of DH concerns. Concomitant with this tactical agility is the need to recognize when certain methods of fieldwork or analysis—no matter how popular or how strongly tied to the agendas of certain funding venues—may not be appropriately articulated with one's global strategy.

Finally, well-articulated research strategies should be rigorously reflexive. Stated another way, strategies of qualitative inquiry in DH will certainly frame fieldwork and analytic tactics, but they do not simultaneously circumscribe a priori assumptions or perspectives. Such strategies are ways of *looking* and *being with* participants and their work rather than ways of *seeing*. Brown (2011, 204) argues that seeing in fieldwork is a kind of disinterested awareness—a distancing of the researcher from participants and their everyday contexts. Looking, on the hand, involves granular scrutiny, the adoption of a participant's perspective (as much as possible), and deep engagement with one's object of study. Reflexive strategies enable tactical adjustments for looking, understanding, analyzing, and representing participant knowledges.

Strategies, Then Tactics in Practice

In this section, we provide details on how we have made tactical decisions in fieldwork and analysis, commensurate with our qualitative strategies. First, we describe the use of visual research methods in an ethnographic study of transmedia storytelling to support a WAGR-inspired investigation of artifact and genre ecologies. We then describe how a doppelgänger coding schema facilitated analytic transparency. Through both cases, we illustrate how (1) local fieldwork and analytic tactics are relationally configured to broader strategies of qualitative inquiry and (2) qualitative methodologies can be productively deployed in empirical research in DH.

Using Visual Research Methods to Explore Transmedia Storytelling

Transmedia storytelling—an emergent narrative form leveraging interwoven artifacts, genres, and delivery channels to distribute coherent, large-scale productions—has garnered increasing attention since the early years of the twenty-first century. A popular approach in the entertainment industry (particularly in television, film, and gaming), transmedia storytelling pulls together multiple, tightly interconnected narrative and performative genres—digital and nondigital. McNely (Hashimov and McNely 2012) led an ethnographic study of transmedia work among an undergraduate team over the course of a full academic year, exploring how an interdisciplinary group of writers, artists, graphic designers, and audio and video engineers actually *do* the work of creating complex transmedia narratives. Much of the current scholarship on transmedia storytelling is primarily hermeneutic—exploring what transmedia stories *mean* to audiences, for example (see Jenkins 2008; and Long 2010). Our study thus offered a complementary approach grounded in the lived experience of participant practice, through an ethnographic strategy framed by WAGR.

Tactically, we used several different methods of fieldwork over the course of the project. For example, we relied heavily on traditional ethnographic approaches: we conducted over sixty hours of fieldwork across forty-two site visits, producing over sixty thousand words of field notes and analytic memos; we conducted semistructured interviews with twenty-two participants; we recorded audio of group interactions and informal interviews; and we collected an array of participant-produced written and designed artifacts, from storyboard sketches to completed narratives. Following the work of scholars in visual anthropology and sociology (Banks 2001; Pink 2007; Mitchell 2011; Spencer 2011), we also made extensive use of video and photography as ways of looking, understanding, and representing participant experience—we composed almost three hundred photographs and twenty-one videos. Tactical visual fieldwork supported our overall strategy and worked to aid our explorations of how, when, and why team members used an array of artifacts and genres to mediate everyday actions within their activity system and with overlapping activity systems (university stakeholders, a community partner, and broader public audiences).

Scholars in anthropology and sociology have used visual methods of empirical research for decades, but they are rarely used in studies of writing and rhetoric. Brown sees photographic fieldwork as a way of visualizing the object of social research: "[Photographic fieldwork seeks] to fix visually the fleeting and transient in the swirl of events. But it also seeks to capture and describe the event as event, exhibiting connections and distinctions which have hitherto lain hidden or cannot be as well expressed in writing" (2011, 204). Indeed, visual methods can uncover tacit knowing and understanding among participants, particularly when researcher-produced images are used with participants in a process known as *photoelicitation* (Lapenta 2011). For example, we used photography to document, analyze, and represent the artifacts and technologies that participants used in the course of their work—individually and collaboratively. We were able to use these images to make the familiar strange; during both informal and semistructured interviews, we often showed participants the images we had composed, asking them to describe their artifact ecologies (Bødker and Nylandsted Klokmose 2011) while recounting the details of their work practices. As Lapenta (2011, 201) notes, photoelicitation is a nondirective method of researcher-participant collaboration; such tactics helped us better develop understandings of our participants' mediated actions.

Given our global, WAGR-inspired strategy, visual research methods are relationally configured tactics that aid documentation, analysis, and representation of embodied, situated practices in rich social contexts. Photography and video are ways of making visible and then collaboratively exploring what participants often take for granted—the mundane, everyday contexts of their writing and rhetorical work.

In figure 8.1, for example, we can see two of our research participants storyboarding an interactive graphic that they would develop together over several weeks. The photograph represents an aspect of collaborative experience for these participants, but it also creates opportunities for discussions of writing and participant situatedness. We were able to show participants the photograph as a way of eliciting reflection on their collaborative work, and, more importantly, we gained

8.1. Collaborative storyboarding.

granular insights into how Jenna (left) used her notebook to mediate this task and others.

In this way, visual tactics are far more than merely illustrative; they serve the overarching strategy as ways of detailed looking, as means for intersubjective understanding, and as moves toward more fully representing participant experience. And, while individual photographs or videos are useful, employing these tactics over time and across a series of writing and collaborative events deepened our understanding and representation of participant practice. In figure 8.2, we see Jenna working individually, sketching details she would later incorporate into the user interface of the interactive graphic.

Figures 8.1 and 8.2 (and other photographs—see the digital companion to this volume: www.press.uchicago.edu/sites/rdh/) helped us assemble documentation about the artifact and genre ecologies essential to Jenna's role as a graphic designer in the collaborative transmedia story. In just these two figures we can see the importance of Jenna's coffee cup, her reliance on sketching and traditional note making, and her use of Web-based graphics and photo-editing software. And, while the present discussion focuses on just one participant, our tactical fieldwork extends across the full development team, helping us explore the complex, collaborative, interdisciplinary work of transmedia storytelling.

8.2. Jenna sketching user interface elements.

How Did You Get There? Using Doppelgänger Coding Schemas to Explore Deliberation

Researchers in DH continue to grapple with the tension between data-driven scholarship and scholarship that takes on a decidedly critical or theoretical stance early in their research (see Hall 2012; Scheinfeldt 2012). Hall argues: "Without such reflexive critical thinking and theories many of those whose work forms part of this computational turn find it difficult to articulate exactly what the point of what they are doing is" (2012, 128). One possible way to resolve this tension between data-driven research and predominantly critical, theoretical approaches is to embrace research tactics that are in service of a strategy affording analytic transparency. The conundrum that Hall seems to acknowledge is, How might DH researchers surface that sweet spot between raw data and explaining that data through the lens of preexisting theories? Conversely, how do researchers avoid sacrificing a critical theoretical stance when developing data-driven scholarship? Takayoshi, Tomlinson, and Castillo argue: "Leaving the relationship between epistemological positions, experience, and research invisible leads inevitably to the reinscription of unexamined biases" (2012, 97; see also Naples 2003).

These methodological conundrums are not necessarily unique to digital humanists. Researchers in the humanities and social sciences have long struggled with how to avoid the premature assumption of theoretical garb. How might we wade around in the complexity of large swaths of data to allow constructs' definitions to emerge locally instead of being deployed a priori? How do we do this rigorously? And how do we accomplish this when many of our study sites are not accessible because of issues related to confidentiality or privacy (Teston 2012b)?

We explicate a tactical method that could be adopted by researchers who are similarly concerned with how to strike a balance between data-driven approaches and critical theoretical approaches and are, perhaps, hamstrung by the complexities of research site and participant access. In response to these methodological complexities, a research team that included Teston deployed a doppelgänger coding schema as a tactical way to achieve analytic transparency, in keeping with an overarching GT approach to data collection and analysis. This tactic allowed the surfacing and subsequent reviewability of analytic choices.

In order to explore how a controversial, end-stage breast cancer drug, Avastin, came to be approved by the FDA under an accelerated process, only to have approval rescinded three years later, this research team investigated a large corpus of textual and video data wherein debates about Avastin persisted (see Teston and Graham 2012; Teston, et al., in press). While FDA deliberations about Avastin's risks and benefits occurred prior to our team's work, more than twenty hours of video data and hundreds of pages of transcribed deliberations, public policy documents, popular press articles, and patient testimony exist online. After several weeks of data collection, each of the team's five members began open coding of the data using qualitative data-analysis software (NVivo 9). During our weekly research meetings, and in our regular theoretical memos, it quickly became clear that we were being swayed by our theoretical predispositions as we attempted to capture the complexity of these deliberations. Where we saw issues associated with expertise, we longed to invoke Collins and Evans (2009); where we saw uncertainties, we longed to invoke stasis theory; where we saw genre in deliberators' arguments, we longed to invoke Toulmin's (2003) argumentative model. Yet we had not even finished coding all the data sources.

In an exchange between two of the team's researchers via theoretical memoing, we acknowledged that we could not theoretically unsee what it was we saw. But we could be intellectually honest about it. In order to do so, we began to theorize about how a kind of foil, or doppelgänger coding schema, might surface the theoretical and analytic moves we made along the way. This schema might not necessarily be enacted or used, but it provided a space where we could posit the potentiality of the codes we, in that moment at least, had sought to shed or shrink (via the "pushing out and pulling in" characteristic of GT approaches [see Farkas and Haas 2012, 93]). Many qualitative data-analysis software systems allow exploration of alternative coding schemes without abandoning progress afforded by other schemes. This doppelgänger coding schema can act as a series of confessional codes and categories that allow the research team to indulge the theoretical critical dispositions we feel inclined to follow while maintaining an alternative, theory-free coding schema that is as locally responsive as possible. The doppelgänger coding schema gave our research team an analytic space where methodological forks in the road could be mapped.

At the least, using data-analysis software to enact doppelgänger coding schemas may be analytically heuristic. That is, considering foil codes, and actually conducting a small-scale selective coding exercise with those foil codes, may yield new insights, constructs, and theories that capture the complexity associated with a certain site or set of practices. Such tactics might be seen as a modification of Glaser and Strauss's (1967) dimensionalization process. Developing a doppelgänger coding schema is one way for researchers to explain how they arrived, theoretically, in the places they arrived. Such tactics facilitate the tracing of analytic decisionmaking, allowing the researcher to strategically remain data-driven without sacrificing theoretical rigor.

Implications for Future Work

In this chapter, we have stressed the importance of well-articulated and relationally configured strategies and tactics of qualitative research in rhetoric and DH. By thinking about our modes of inquiry in terms of strategies and tactics (as parallel to empirical methodologies and methods), we argue for attention to the important and complex relations between overarching strategies, concomitant (potentially tacit) framing theories, and tactical implementations of fieldwork and analysis for exploring the nuances of lived (digital) experience. By providing examples from our own studies, we have illustrated some of the ways in which tactical fieldwork and analysis can be relationally configured to reflexive global strategies.

But our work here should be seen as a jumping-off point to novel, creative articulations of strategies and tactics in the empirical study of rhetoric and DH. These are exciting times for the field, but we urge scholars to resist purely tactical temptations; by beginning with strategies that are sensitive and responsive to both digital and nondigital practice, we can choose appropriate and meaningful tactics for carrying out fieldwork and analysis. In doing so, qualitative inquiry in DH will remain grounded in participant experience.

References

Banks, Marcus. 2001. *Visual Methods in Social Research*. London: Sage.

Bawarshi, A., and M. J. Reiff. 2010. *Genre: An Introduction to History, Theory, Research, and Pedagogy*. West Lafayette, IN: Parlor.

Bazerman, Charles. 1997. "The Life of Genre in the Classroom." In *Genre and Writing: Issues, Arguments, Alternatives*, ed. Wendy Bishop and Hans Ostrom, 19–26. Portsmouth, NH: Boynton/Cook.

Bødker, S., and C. Nylandsted Klokmose. 2011. "The Human-Artifact Model: An Activity Theoretical Approach to Artifact Ecologies." *Human-Computer Interaction* 26:315–71.

Brown, Roger. 2011. "Photography as Process, Documentary Photographing as Discourse." In *Visual Research Methods in the Social Sciences: Awakening Visions*, ed. Stephen Spencer, 199–224. New York: Routledge.

Collins, H., and R. Evans. 2009. *Rethinking Expertise*. Chicago: University of Chicago Press.

de Certeau, Michel. 1984. *The Practice of Everyday Life*. Berkeley and Los Angeles: University of California Press.

Emig, Janet. 1979. *The Composing Processes of Twelfth Graders*. Urbana, IL: NCTE.

Engeström, Yrjö. 1999. "Activity Theory and Individual and Social Transformation." In *Perspectives on Activity Theory*, ed. Yrjö Engeström, Reijo Miettinen, and Raija-Lenna Punamäki, 19–38. Cambridge: Cambridge University Press.

Faigley, L., and S. Witte. 1981. "Analyzing Revision." *College Composition and Communication* 32.4:400–414.

Farkas, K., and C. Haas. 2012. "A Grounded Theory Approach for Studying Writing and Literacy." In *Practicing Research in Writing Studies: Reflexive and Ethically Responsible Research*, ed. Katrina M. Powell and Pamela Takayoshi, 81–96. New York: Hampton.

Glaser, B. G., and A. L. Strauss. 1967. *The Discovery of Grounded Theory: Strategies for Qualitative Research*. Chicago: Aldine Transaction.

Hall, Gary. 2012. "Has Critical Theory Run Out of Time for Data-Driven Scholarship?" In *Debates in the Digital Humanities*, ed. Matthew K. Gold, 127–32. Minneapolis: University of Minnesota Press.

Hashimov, E., and B. McNely. 2012. "Left to Their Own Devices: Ad Hoc Genres in the Design of Transmedia Narratives." In *SIGDOC '12: Proceedings of the 30th Annual Conference on Design of Communication*, 251–59. New York: ACM.

Jenkins, Henry. 2008. *Convergence Culture: Where Old and New Media Collide.* 2nd ed. New York: New York University Press.

Kaptelinin, V., and B. Nardi. 2006. *Acting with Technology: Activity Theory and Interaction Design.* Cambridge, MA: MIT Press.

Kirsch, G., and P. Sullivan. 1992. *Methods and Methodology in Composition Research.* Carbondale: Southern Illinois University Press.

Lapenta, Francesco. 2011. "Some Theoretical and Methodological Views on Photo-Elicitation." In *The Sage Handbook of Visual Research Methods,* ed. Eric Margolis and Luc Pauwels, 201–13. Thousand Oaks, CA: Sage.

Lillis, Theresa. 2008. "Ethnography as Method, Methodology, and 'Deep Theorizing': Closing the Gap between Text and Context in Academic Writing Research." *Written Communication* 25.3:353–88.

Long, Geoffrey. 2010. "How to Ride a Lion: A Call for a Higher Transmedia Criticism." *Convergence Culture Consortium,* March. http://www.convergenceculture.org/research/c3-transmediacriticism-full-public.pdf.

MacNealy, Mary Sue. 1999. *Strategies for Empirical Research in Writing.* New York: Allyn & Bacon.

McNely, Brian. 2011. "Sociotechnical Notemaking: Short-Form to Long-Form Writing Practices." *Present Tense: A Journal of Rhetoric and Society* 2.1. http://www.presenttensejournal.org/volume-2/sociotechnical-notemaking-short-form-to-long-form-writing-practices.

———. 2012. "Shaping Organizational Image-Power through Images: Case Histories of Instagram." In *Proceedings of the IEEE International Professional Communication Conference.* Lexington, KY: IEEE. http://ieeexplore.ieee.org/xpl/login.jsp?tp=&arnumber=6408624&tag=1.

———. 2013. "Exploring Lived Experience through Ambient Research Methods." In *Advancing Research Methods with New Technologies,* ed. Natalie Sappleton, 250–56. Hershey, PA: IGI Global.

McNely, Brian, Christa B. Teston, Garret Cox, Bolutife Olorunda, and Noah DUnker. 2010. "Digital Publics and Participatory Education." *Digital Culture and Education* 2.2:152–71.

McNely, Brian, Paul Gestwicki, Bridget Gelms, and Ann Burke. 2013. "Spaces and Surfaces of Invention: A Visual Ethnography of Game Development." *Enculturation* 15. http://www.enculturation.net/visual-ethnography.

Miller, Carolyn. 1984. "Genre as Social Action." *Quarterly Journal of Speech* 70:151–67.

Mitchell, Claudia. 2011. *Doing Visual Research.* Thousand Oaks, CA: Sage.

Mortensen, P., and G. Kirsch. 1996. *Ethics and Representation in Qualitative Studies of Literacy.* Urbana, IL: NCTE.

Naples, Nancy A. 2003. *Feminism and Method: Ethnography, Discourse Analysis, and Activist Research.* New York: Routledge.

Pink, Sarah. 2007. *Doing Visual Ethnography: Images, Media and Representation in Research.* 2nd ed. Thousand Oaks, CA: Sage.

Prior, Paul. 2009. "From Speech Genres to Mediated Multimodal Genre Systems: Bakhtin, Voloshinov, and the Question of Writing." In *Genre in a Changing World*, ed. Charles Bazerman, Adair Bonini, and Debora Figueiredo, 17–34. Fort Collins, CO: WAC Clearinghouse/Parlor.

Russell, David. 1997a. "Rethinking Genre in School and Society: An Activity Theory Analysis." *Written Communication* 14.4:504–54.

———. 1997b. "Writing and Genre in Higher Education and Workplaces: A Review of Studies That Use Cultural-Historical Activity Theory." *Mind, Culture, and Activity* 4.4:224–37.

———. 2009. "Uses of Activity Theory in Written Communication Research." In *Learning and Expanding with Activity Theory*, ed. Annalisa Sannino, Harry Daniels, and Kris D. Gutiérrez, 40–52. Cambridge: Cambridge University Press.

Scheinfeldt, Tom. 2012. "Sunset for Ideology, Sunrise for Methodology?" In *Debates in the Digital Humanities*, ed. Matthew K. Gold, 124–26. Minneapolis: University of Minnesota Press.

Shipka, Jody. 2011. *Toward a Composition Made Whole*. Pittsburgh, PA: Pittsburgh University Press.

Smagorinsky, Peter. 2008. "The Methods Section as Conceptual Epicenter in Constructing Social Science Research Reports." *Written Communication* 25.3:389–411.

Spencer, Stephen. 2011. *Visual Research Methods in the Social Sciences: Awakening Visions*. New York: Routledge.

Spinuzzi, Clay. 2003. *Tracing Genres through Organizations*. Cambridge, MA: MIT Press.

———. 2004. "Four Ways to Investigate Assemblages of Texts: Genre Sets, Systems, Repertoires, and Ecologies." In *SIGDOC '04: Proceedings of the 22nd Annual Conference on Design of Communication*, 110–16. Memphis: ACM.

———. 2008. *Network: Theorizing Knowledge Work in Telecommunications*. Cambridge: Cambridge University Press.

———. 2010. "Secret Sauce and Snake Oil: Writing Monthly Reports in a Highly Contingent Environment." *Written Communication* 27.4:363–409.

Strauss, Anselm. 1987. *Qualitative Analysis for Social Scientists*. Cambridge: Cambridge University Press.

Takayoshi, P., E. Tomlinson, and J. Castillo. 2012. "The Construction of Research Problems and Methods." In *Practicing Research in Writing Studies: Reflexive and Ethically Responsible Research*, ed. Katrina M. Powell and Pamela Takayoshi, 97–121. Kresskill: Hampton.

Teston, Christa. 2009. "A Grounded Investigation of Genred Guidelines in Cancer Care Deliberations." *Written Communication* 26.3:320–40.

———. 2012a. "Considering Confidentiality in Research Design: Developing Heuristics to Chart the Un-Chartable." In *Practicing Research in Writing Studies: Reflexive and Ethically Responsible Research*, ed. Katrina M. Powell and Pamela Takayoshi, 307–30. Cresskill: Hampton.

————. 2012b. "Moving from Artifact to Action: A Grounded Investigation of Visual Displays of Evidence during Medical Deliberations." *Technical Communication Quarterly* 21.3:187–209.

Teston, C., and S. S. Graham. 2012. "Stasis Theory and Meaningful Public Participation in Pharmaceutical Policy-Making." *Present Tense: A Journal of Rhetoric and Society* 2.2. http://www.presenttensejournal.org/volume-2/ stasis-theory-and-meaningful-public-participation-in-pharmaceutical -policy-making.

Teston, C., and B. McNely. 2013. "Undergraduate Research as Collaborative Knowledge Work." In *The New Digital Scholar: Exploring and Enriching the Research and Writing Practices of NextGen Students*, ed. Randall McClure and James P. Purdy, 213–34. Medford, NJ: ASIST.

Teston, C., S. S. Graham, R. Baldwinson, A. Li, J. Swift, et al. In press. "Definitional Multiplicity: Negotiating 'Clinical Benefit' in the FDA's Avastin Hearing." *Journal of Medical Humanities*.

Toulmin, Stephen. 2003. *The Uses of Argument*. Cambridge: Cambridge University Press.

Tzu, Sun. 2005. *The Art of War*. Translated by Ralph D. Saywer. New York: Basic.

## NINE

Low Fidelity in High Definition: Speculations on Rhetorical Editions

CASEY BOYLE

It is much easier to try one's hand at many things than to concentrate one's powers on one thing. QUINTILIAN

Many of the earliest projects in digital humanities (DH), particularly those associated with literary scholarship, were projects that preserved, digitized, and networked canonical texts as digital editions.[1] Such work holds some importance for rhetoric scholars, but preservation is seldom, if ever, our primary aim. This is not to say that rhetoric scholarship finds itself unmoored from texts. If anything, scholars in rhetoric host fewer disagreements about their canonical texts as evidenced by a largely—not wholly—uncontested foundation of Isocrates, Gorgias, Aristotle, Cicero, Quintilian, and many others from antiquity and beyond. That said, research in rhetoric does not hold the same *fidelity* to its texts as does traditional literary scholarship. Different notions of fidelity persist between traditional literary study, which places more importance on textual authenticity, and rhetoric scholarship, which pays its attention to textual effects. Put in another way, as rhetoricians we are not as interested in what a text *is* as we are in what a text *does*. What seems like a slight difference in approach makes all the difference for how rhetoric scholars might develop digital editions of our texts. This chapter will introduce some initial methodological differences between what we have seen in DH dealing with *critical editions* and what rhetoricians might seek as features and goals for *rhetorical editions*.

Before teasing out the different methodologies informing our approaches to digital editions, we can establish a productive, if little discussed, commonplace between DH and rhetoric (and its related fields). In addition to similar investments in multidisciplinarity, collaboration, and a broad notion of techne, the two fields also share a repeated critique in which critics charge the two as unfaithful to a traditional understanding of the humanities. In particular, critics lament the rise of DH methods and DH's affinities with corporate culture (and products) as yet one more neoliberal commercialization of humanities research and curricula, as yet one more example of a general corporate takeover of the university whose relentless advance forces teachers and researchers to become entrepreneurs. Instead of arguing against this position, I encourage us to accept it in ways similar to how Jeff Nealon counters similar claims of the "corporate university." Briefly, Nealon responds to the charge that the university (by extension DH and rhetoric) is too corporate with a counterintuitive suggestion that "in many ways *the corporate university isn't corporate enough*" (2012, 124). That is, unlike private-sector corporate takeovers, whose goals often include streamlining connections between customer and creative talent (students, researchers, and teachers in our case), corporate takeover in the university operates differently by investing in the institution's middle management (expanding administration and its programs). Nealon also notes that one shortcoming with today's humanities is not that we fail to resist capitalistic practices, like those germane to high finance, but that the humanities fail in not embracing the practices inherent to those institutions. Interestingly, he proposes that the humanities imitate high finance by adopting its use of futures markets or *speculation* as among its primary practices. That is, a humanities based around *speculation*—alongside its long tradition in teaching close and critical thinking—would provide the discipline license to work in ways that DH and rhetoric are uniquely equipped to do: to project and build knowledge and not simply interpret it. To invent as a way of knowing. With speculation in mind as an implicit and explicit practice, what follows is an attempt to extend DH methods for *critical editions* to what we might call a *rhetorical edition*.

Concerning the Critical Edition

Efforts to digitize primary materials, reaching their intensity in the 1990s and the first decade of the twenty-first century, constitute what Todd Presner has called the *first wave* of DH scholarship (Pressner, n.d.). This initial wave helped organize disparate practitioners of the nascent field around some shared problems for creating the *critical edition*, my loose designation for projects that organize textual materials as a single structured corpus. Encountering the limitations of using basic markup languages, such as HTML, for translating printed texts to digital texts, these researchers began to formulate best practices for editing printed texts for electronic delivery by collectively posing a series of questions. Namely: What affordances do electronic environments offer critical editions (Proud 1989)? How do these tools change scholarship (Unsworth 1996)? Should there be common encoding practices across projects (Burnard 1988)? What do these editions look like (Finneran 1996)? What concerns should we pay to aesthetic and usability factors when creating these texts (Shillingsburg 1996)? Such questions have even led many scholars to propose the alternative terms of *archive, collection,* or even *library* to better describe how digital editions function (Price 2007, 2009).

These questions begin to get at key differences to account for when considering rhetorical texts. One difference is that rhetorical texts are more explicitly situated in and as conversations than are literary texts. This is not to say that literature and its methods are without the conversations of intertextuality, allusion, and tradition. As we will see in the next few passages, these interactions are central to the production, study, and teaching of literature and become important considerations when developing digital editions. Many rhetorical texts, however, are themselves assumed to be collections, practical guides, and manuals and, as such, are better understood as relays of cultural and practical knowledge. Rhetorical texts offered by Isocrates, Aristotle, Cicero, Quintilian, Augustine, and Boethius include not only the exercises, reflections, proclamations, and histories of the times and cultures from which they emerged but also explicit attempts to carry forward those of prior generations. The notion of relay, then, becomes more important in that it does not assume the same forms of authorship or originality that we find in more distinct literary forms. In fact, it is these more particular notions of authorship and originality that we find shaping many of the digital editions of literary works.

The rise of digital methods created two movements in editing that affected how editors conceived of and developed critical editions, particularly for literary texts. Outlining these two movements, Peter Shillingsburg (2010) argued that digital textual editing was initially restorative, making the goal for a textual editor to correct the text in question to a version as close as possible to an author's original intention. The Spenser Archive (http://spenserarchive.org) serves as an emblematic example in that its goal is to faithfully scan and digitally preserve all extant sources of Edmund Spenser's *Faerie Queene* to better enable textual, bibliographic, and critical scholars to generate reproducible accounts of its textual conditions. According to its Web site: "[The archive will] contain the fully edited text of the *Collected Works*, which will be richly marked up to enable readers to examine textual features and scholarly materials in ways not possible with a print edition. The *Archive* will also contain facsimiles of original materials, including scans of each textual variant."

The second movement in digital editions moves away from striving to attain a text that was faithful to an author's intention and toward accounting for those wider conditions in which texts were produced and initially received. In this version, the editor seeks to include as many of the materials surrounding the production of the text available. Such efforts can be seen in projects like the Walt Whitman Archive (http://www.whitmanarchive.org). Its Web site proclaims that "[Whitman's] many notebooks, manuscript fragments, prose essays, letters, and voluminous journalistic articles all offer key cultural and biographical contexts for his poetry" and that the archive's purpose is to "incorporate as much of this material as possible, drawing on the resources of libraries and collections from around the United States and around the world."

While Shillingsburg's overview attempts to make distinctions between two different aims for critical editions, it becomes clear that the editions differ only in degree, not in kind. That is, both share similar desires for *fidelity*. In the first, the fidelity sought is an author's intention and, in the second, an accurate account of the text's time, culture, and reception. While each engages the construction of a corpus differently, each aims to interpret what a text *is*. Thus, we find that an ongoing, pressing concern for literary digitization projects is to maintain fidelity to primary and related materials by drawing boundaries between what is included as important to the text and excluding those things not important to a text. The adherence to fidelity, then, guides the methods through which the projects unfold, but the number of texts and their digitized forms have other effects as well.

The scope of the material involved and our increasing facility with digitization projects move toward requiring a revision to the notions of fidelity that shape how we develop digital editions. Stephen Ramsay recently challenged this fidelity in proposing "algorithmic criticism" (computer-assisted literary criticism), a call for humanists to "create tools—practical, instrumental, verifiable mechanisms—that enable critical engagement, interpretation, conversation, and contemplation" (2011, x). For Ramsay, algorithmic criticism leverages computational constraints to substantiate critical reading methods. Relying on digitally encoded texts, as we see proliferating in digital editions, Ramsay works to develop the concept of *deformation* as a set of algorithmic protocols that experiment with a distinct text through enumerations, cross-references, and alternate arrangements to better determine what that corpus *is*. In this way, we can consider deformation as an interpretive exercise not dissimilar to mathematical topology, whose study of a geometric shape is undertaken by twisting, folding, stretching, and squeezing that shape to determine its limits. However, against a reluctant humanities that still "speak[s] of 'faithfulness' to a text, of 'flawed' or 'misguided' readings," Ramsay suggests: "Our fear of breaking faith with the text may need to give way to a renewed faith in the capacity of subjective engagement for liberating the potentialities of meaning" (2011, 56–57). These algorithmic programs, he proposes, performed on the internal structures of the text, would allow for new possibilities for interpretation.

An ongoing allegiance to interpretation, one partially expressed by Ramsay, has recently led Jeff Rice to question DH's "we always interpret; the question for the digital humanities is *if we only interpret*" (2013, 376). Working from a rhetorical orientation, Rice makes a compelling case for "suggestion" as an enthymeme-based practice that understands and traces texts (e.g., the technical image) as always part of a wider network. Rice's argument pushes DH to reconsider the hermeneutic practices that guide its activities, a logic that underlies *critical editions*. I do not wish to counter Ramsay, but, following Rice's lead, I am inclined to expand Ramsay's notion of infidelity. That is, while Ramsay sees in digital texts an affordance for different interpretations using algorithmic criticism, he resists moving beyond distinct, predetermined texts. We witness this hesitation early in his argument where he explicitly seeks methods to produce a generative reading without falling prey to a rhetorical sophism that would seek to use a performative notion of invention (2011, 16). While Ramsay is not exactly against invention—as shown in his turn toward Alfred Jarry and pataphysics—he makes sure to safeguard the distinct text as something to be reread and to be returned to.

In addition to critical editions and tactics like algorithmic criticism that we might encounter in DH—tactics that hold a fidelity to texts and interpretation—a rhetorical approach to the same problems would embrace invention and avoid the definitive, closed, or fixed. Further, unlike the deformation for which Ramsay advocates or something like Jerome McGann's (2011) idea of radiant textuality, a rhetorical edition could not presume the same kind of stable center from which texts and readings emanate and to which readings return. Instead, a rhetorical edition would be compelled to ask the question, In what ways do secondary texts and tertiary responses influence a reinvention of a primary text(s)? Thus, the goal for any rhetorical edition would be not solely to faithfully capture and preserve but also to provide environments that re/construct texts as dynamic situations, confusing the primary, secondary, and tertiary. In the next section, I explain these concerns inherent for rhetorical texts and begin to speculate on what a rhetorical edition might do.

The Situation concerning Rhetorical Texts

Quintilian presents a good problem for digital editions and a great opportunity for developing rhetorical editions. Marcus Fabius Quintilianus, Roman rhetorician and teacher, composed the *Institutio Oratoria* (*IO*)—a twelve-volume rhetorical training manual—to educate its student "from the cradle to the grave." In addition to the inherent exhaustiveness that works well with networked and digital logics, Quintilian makes a good case for a rhetorical edition in that he is not thought to be terribly original. As many scholars have argued, most notably James Murphy (1987), the practices for which Quintilian advocates can be found first in prior Greek sources. Not unlike that of any other writer from antiquity, Quintilian's project is at once a collection of previous attitudes, sayings, and systems as much as it is an attempt to codify something new.

Speaking toward historicity, we can recall that Quintilian was among the earliest and most comprehensive advocates for the importance of establishing lifelong education, the need for engaging civic responsibilities, and the necessity of preserving cultural knowledge. Considering the widely shared value of these interconnected practices, a digital edition of Quintilian would have to respond to many different humanities fields as his work serves as a touchstone for multiple disciplines, including rhetoric studies, education, comparative literature, and classics. In addition to its disciplinary reach, the history of *IO* as a text is extensive as it slips in and out of obscurity for hundreds of years at a time, as Michael Winterbottom (1967) has surveyed. Lee Honeycutt (2012) also adds that, according to "[Donald] Stewart, between 1470 and 1600, there were 118 editions of Quintilian's treatise produced in Italy, France, Switzerland, Belgium, Holland, and Germany." In addition to the multiple printings, *IO* also boasts five English translations, creating several textual bases from which scholarship and other commentary has responded. So *IO* shares many of the same issues of the literary texts we discussed above. However, as each version persisted for some extended duration of time, each version can be thought to have created entirely different situations in which responses also circulated and produced the need for further translations and adaptations, literally reconstituting and multiplying what *IO is*.

Quintilian is also a source to whom much work had been misattributed. What is now referred to as *(Pseudo) Quintilian* is a set of declamations (practice orations) that circulated for more than a century before scholars finally decided to no longer consider them Quintilian's work (Ellis 1911). Despite the later realization, much scholarship continues to maintain strong connections between the two, as evidenced by a journal's recent special issue devoted to attending to these texts with a collection of international responses (see "International Project" 2011).

Because Quintilian's work is largely predisciplinary and occupies a vital intersection of humanities study, a digital edition project offers an opportunity to blur the boundaries between scholar and general public by foregrounding the lasting conversations concerning Quintilian's work that emerge in scholarship and, today, even in social media. As any search on Twitter will show, in any given moment multiple quotes attributed to Quintilian circulate and are redistributed on social media and Web sites, all contributing to a living corpus. Scholars and nonscholars alike could benefit from an edition that is inclusive of these varying textual forms not necessarily as marginalia but as the growth of the corpus we consider to be Quintilian. Such an edition would provide scholars and the general public a site to extend and participate in conversations on education, civic engagement, and cultural preservation.

Thus, what a rhetorical edition of Quintilian's *IO* would seek is not an accurate portrait of Quintilian or even an exhaustive account of *his* text. In fact, asking what *IO is* might be a rhetorical question, asked for effect rather than for response. Extending Ramsay's notion of what deformation and an algorithmic criticism might contribute to textual analysis, a rhetorical edition would demonstrate that such deformation is actually performed by an ever-expanding corpus as much as it is something we might do to a *single* text and its responses. Instead, what a rhetorical edition would seek is not Quintilian but, perhaps, a *Quintilianism*. This would be an isolated set of attributes expressed through relations between texts that we might ascribe as Quintilian, but not as one we would need to understand, in any absolute sense, *as* Quintilian. How might a misattributed quote in social media be thought of as also Quintilian? An appropriation? How might the very relations of texts preceding, concurring, and responding to Quintilian be consistent with other types of relations for other authors? For instance, how might an education theorist like Lev Vygotsky or John Dewey be shown to exhibit the same kinds of attributes that Quintilian expresses? To pursue these questions, the next section lays out some preliminary steps toward what this rhetorical edition might attempt to do.

The Quintilian Project as a Rhetorical Edition

The chief purpose for a rhetorical edition would be to consider, as one corpus, the evolving relations between primary texts, secondary scholarship, and tertiary commentary. As noted above, most collections gathered as critical editions focus on primary texts and subordinate those materials related to the production and reception of those primary texts. A rhetorical edition would widen that focus and create a resource that dynamically incorporates connections to the primary text(s) as primary to the text. In the remainder of this chapter, I briefly outline the early development and future plans for *The Quintilian Project*, a long-term collaborative project whose ultimate goals include building a rhetorical edition of Quintilian's *IO* and developing open-source software that can be used for other well-encoded texts.[2]

In terms of traditional scholarship, *The Quintilian Project* aims to offer an environment for responding to Quintilian's foundational texts by compiling all the English translations alongside secondary scholarship. This rhetorical edition would offer scholars a unique vantage point from which to visualize how Quintilian is taken up over time, determine which passages are cited most frequently, and discover which translations instigate the most responses. The underlying project, the software architecture for a rhetorical edition, will have an even greater effect throughout humanities fields as the interface and its software could contribute to standards for how we put our primary texts in conversations with its responses (via databases and/or emerging social communication networks) and, possibly, help problematize canonicity.

First and foremost, the project builds on previous attempts to create digital editions of Quintilian, the *Perseus Digital Library Project* (http://www.perseus.tufts.edu) and *Quintilian's Institutes of Oratory* (http://rhetoric.eserver.org/quintilian). In the former, Quintilian and *IO* are one part of a much more vast attempt to digitize and provide original Greek and Latin texts and translations of many classical texts. The *Perseus* Quintilian provides Harold Butler's 1920 English translation as well as the Latin text in an open-source XML file that adheres to TEI2 structures. Building on open-source materials adheres to best editorial practices as well as exemplifying the kind of ethic a rhetorical edition requires.

The other existing digital edition of *IO* is a static HTML-structured text of Shelby Watson's 1856 English translation of *IO* (http://eserver.org/rhetoric/quintilian/preface.html). This edition was built by Lee Honeycutt, who also provided helpful commentary, and, because of the HTML structure, it allows for an easy search and find feature to engage the text. These initial attempts to create digital editions of Quintilian are good, concrete examples for the evolution of digital editions in general. In addition to correcting and updating these open-source texts, team members are—at the time of this chapter's drafting—in the process of scanning three additional English translations and their Latin texts, performing optical character recognition, and encoding those digital text files into TEI5 markup.

While the current online editions make available translations of *IO*, neither allows for the dynamic relations that our speculation for a rhetorical edition seeks to create. As the project responds to and builds on prior projects concerning Quintilian's work, it also seeks to adopt and extend open-source tools for citation identification and extraction. As digitally based Web resources have become ubiquitous in the form of Web sites, databases, and digital surrogates, *The Quintilian Project* seeks to advance the digital edition genre by exploring the ways citation information and related texts can be rendered dynamic through discrete time-based representations. That is, how might a temporally capable text situate textual relations visually? Scholarly conversations occur asynchronously and incessantly. For instance, we might imagine researchers encountering *IO* as collaborators whose editing and commenting on a single line of text might unfold differently: one in a scholarly article, one in the process of editing a digital annotation, and one via Twitter. The project aims to provide those researchers an interface to combine these three citations and deploy them in time-lapse form. How could we turn back the conversation comment by comment to explore the evolution of understanding of that single line of text when the scholars are not actually talking to one another in the same medium or even at the same time—but are still in conversation? While each medium allows one to roll back conversations, a rhetorical edition would be able to roll back conversations simultaneously for comparative purposes.

Our rhetorical edition would seek to trace the way a corpus not only coalesced as a body of text but also spread into other texts not typically considered as primary or even secondary (or even as text). These other texts—tertiary commentary—might be reading notes on a blog or even the isolated quote circulating on social media sites. As *The Quintilian Project* attempts to develop a rhetorical edition, it aims to explore this possibility by marrying advances in digital editions, annotation technologies, topic modeling, and data mining of bibliographic citations to develop an interface to serve as a reproducible, cross-medium dynamic scholarly resource. Toward this end, it looks to build on recent advancements in data mining, text citation, and bibliographic extraction to expand the boundaries of digital editions through the development of a digital edition that is dynamic and inventive. As can be seen in the wireframe (a proposed interface), the "text" becomes understood as a distributed but connected corpus of relations (fig. 9.1).

Admittedly, the initial wireframe sketch is wanting in proper UI design, with particular concerns for accessibility and function, not to mention aesthetics. However, I include it here to aid our speculation for what a rhetorical edition aims to do. As shown in the wireframe, the primary text (on the left) serves as one node among others, wherein selections of any portion of the text will call up additional texts. While the wireframe's current view establishes the "primary" text as the dominate window, the eventual interface would allow any of the panels to be relatively resized, allowing a reader to focus on any one interaction while allowing the others (including the primary text) to recede into the background.

In addition to the interplay between primary texts, secondary texts, and tertiary commentary, another important function of our rhetorical edition would be dynamic visualizations for interactions between the texts. In the upper-right-hand corner, these functions would seek to create a visualization of the relations between the texts. Simple vi-

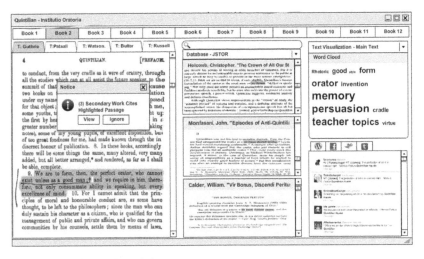

9.1.   The Quintilian Project wireframe.

sualization like word clouds, word trees, and network graphs would visually render relations that occur within and between different kinds of texts. Going back to our opening reference to high finance's futures markets and practices in speculation, the interface and these visualizations can help determine the "stock" of particular instances of Quintilian. Which translations have the most currency? What are the exchange rates between the versions of Quintilian? In this way, this rhetorical edition would create a Quintilian economy where a passage being "bought" and "sold" determines its value, not its interpretive or hermeneutic status. No one asks what a dollar means or what it is, but we often ask what a dollar can buy. A rhetorical edition could provide for a similar kind of market analysis.

The Quintilian Project aims to be more than a resource for studying Quintilian. While it will use Quintilian's work and its subsequent scholarship as its test case, any well-encoded text could serve as the primary text for the eventual application and interface. The project's overriding goal is to create reconfigurable software that any scholar can adapt to explore the dynamic relations between primary texts, secondary scholarship, and, eventually, tertiary commentary. Quintilian serves as a useful test case since his work has long affected the Western tradition—through education, civic engagement, and cultural preservation—and its continued impact will allow for a myriad of test cases for citation matching and extraction. In addition, the conservative pace of *IO*'s secondary scholarship (as opposed to, for example, the more frenetic pace of scholarship on Shakespeare or James Joyce) allows the team a reasonable challenge for the project's planning and pilot stage. In addition to the application's affect on Quintilian, it can also help reconfigure our notions of canonicity. Since a rhetorical edition and its underlying architecture would allow for us to postpone strict definitions of a corpus or even a canon in favor of speculation, in an economic sense we might accelerate canon re-formation by creating an environment for many non-Western rhetorical texts to be traced outside the value structures of a Western tradition of humanities that is based around meaning and interpretation. Taken together, these practices would invent rhetorical orientations to texts from which we would ask not what a text is but what a text can do.

Notes

1. While examples we can identify are numerous, a few enduring projects would include the *Walt Whitman Archive*, the *Rossetti Archive*, the *Women Writers Project*, and the *Spenser Archive*.
2. *The Quintilian Project* is a collaboration between researchers at the University of Utah and Maryland's Institute for Technology in the Humanities. Initial team members include the author, Alison Regan (Utah), James G. Smith (Maryland), Jennifer Gulliano (Maryland), and Travis Brown (Maryland). The project has funding proposals currently under review and plans for further development beyond those proposals.

References

Burnard, Lou. 1988. "Report of Workshop on Text Encoding Guidelines." *Literary and Linguistic Computing* 3.2:131–33.

Ellis, Robinson. 1911. *The Tenth Declamation of (Pseudo) Quintilian: A Lecture Delivered in the Hall of Corpus Christi College . . . May 11, 1911, by Robinson Ellis [Being a Translation of the Tenth Declamation]*. London and Oxford: Henry Frowde.

Finneran, Richard J. 1996. *The Literary Text in the Digital Age*. Ann Arbor: University of Michigan Press.

Honeycutt, Lee. 2012. "The History of the Text." *Quintilian's Institutes of Oratory*. http://rhetoric.eserver.org/quintilian/history.html.

"An International Project on the Pseudo-Quintilianic *Declamationes maiores*." Special issue, *Rhetorica: A Journal of the History of Rhetoric* 29.3 (Summer 2011).

McGann, Jerome. 2001. *Radiant Textuality: Literature After the World Wide Web*. New York: Palgrave MacMillan.

Murphy, James J. 1987. *Quintilian: On the Teaching of Speaking and Writing*. Carbondale: Southern Illinois University Press.

Nealon, Jeffery. 2012. *Post-Postmodernism; or, The Cultural Logic of Just-in-Time Capitalism*. Stanford, CA: Stanford University Press.

Presner, Todd. n.d. "Digital Humanities 2.0: A Report on Knowledge." *Connexions*. http://cnx.org/content/m34246/1.6/?format=pdf.

Price, Richard M. 2007. "Electronic Scholarly Editions." In *The Blackwell Companion to Digital Literary Study*, ed. Susan Schreibman and Ray Siemens, 434–50. Oxford: Blackwell.

———. 2009. "Edition, Project, Database, Archive, Thematic Research Collection: What's in a Name?" *Digital Humanities Quarterly* 3.3. http://www.digitalhumanities.org/dhq/vol/3/3/000053/000053.html.

Proud, Judith K. 1989. *The Oxford Text Archive*. London: British Library Research and Development Report.

Ramsay, Steven. 2011. *Reading Machines: Towards an Algorithmic Criticism*. Chicago: University of Illinois Press.

Rice, Jeff. 2013. "Occupying the Digital Humanities." *College English* 75.4:360–78.

Shillingsburg, Peter. 1996. *Scholarly Editing in the Computer Age*. Ann Arbor: University of Michigan Press.

———. 2010. "How Literary Works Exist: Implied, Represented, and Interpreted." In *Text and Genre in Reconstruction: Effects of Digitalization on Ideas, Behaviors, Products and Institutions*, ed. Willard McCarty, 163–80. Cambridge: Open Book.

Unsworth, John. 1996. "Electronic Scholarship; or, Scholarly Publishing and the Public." *Journal of Scholarly Publishing* 28.1:3–12.

Winterbottom, Michael. 1967. "Fifteenth-Century Manuscripts of Quintilian." *Classical Quarterly* 17:339–69.

## TEN

The Trees within the Forest: Extracting, Coding, and Visualizing Subjective Data in Authorship Studies

KRISTA KENNEDY

SETH LONG

Authorship studies, or the study of practical and theoretical dimensions of writerly labor, intellectual property ownership, and cultural constructions of the author, is a vital subfield of rhetoric and writing studies. It also intersects with communication studies and legal scholarship on copyright as well as with subfields of English studies that include the history of the book and literary criticism and history (Porter 1996; Woodmansee and Jaszi 1994). In the decades since the Conference on College Composition and Communication Intellectual Property Caucus was first convened by Andrea Lunsford in 1994, scholars in this topical area have increasingly turned toward digital matters, including file sharing (Porter and DeVoss 2006; Logie 2006; Reyman 2009), authorship of metadata (Reyman 2013), pedagogical issues in digital environments (Ridolfo and Rife 2011; Ritter 2005; Walker 2011; Westbrook 2011), academic publishing (Galin and Latchaw 2010; Fitzpatrick 2011), and robot-written texts (Kennedy 2009) as well as student attitudes toward and rights regarding digital intellectual property ownership (Herrington 2010; Lunsford, Fishman, and Liew 2013), among other areas. Rhetoricians in particular have devoted attention to issues of power and authorial agency in discrete textual contexts (Campbell 2005; Lunsford 1999; Howard 1999). The subfield continues to grow at a healthy rate, and calls for additional research include Charles Bazerman's assertion that one of writing studies' central concerns is further study of "the emergent historical picture of writing practices, genres, systems of circulation, and related institutions and social systems" (2002, 36). From the ecommunication studies side of rhetorical studies, Karlyn Kohrs Campbell calls for "synthetic, complex views of authorship as articulation, of the power of form as it emerges in texts of all sorts, of the roles of audiences in appropriating and re-interpreting texts when they emerge and through time, and of the links of all these to the cultural context, material and symbolic, in which discourse circulates" (2005, 8).

The methods and mores of the digital humanities have much to offer scholars of authorship and intellectual property. Cynthia Selfe's (1988) early work reminds us that digital work has been integrated into English (and, by extension, writing) departments for more than two decades now. In his examination of the intersections of digital humanities and English departments, Matthew Kirschenbaum (2012) points out that, since the 1980s, a broad variety of literary studies have incorporated digital methods in textual analysis, production of digital facsimiles, and corpus linguistics studies. Researchers are also harnessing and studying social media of all sorts as well as mining data from digitization projects such as Google Books. Data abound, and scholars of the written word in all its permutations are making good use of them.

We urge authorship scholars to continue this work through data-driven studies of authorship and authorial labor processes. In his response to Franco Moretti's *Graphs, Maps, Trees* (2005), Cosma Shalizi argues that a "materialist theory of literary form will ultimately . . . concern itself with the organic processes of reading and composition" and that "the way to do this is through empirical study of readers and writers" (2011, 128). In other words, while the study of authorship has benefited from traditional methods, it need not be limited to conclusions drawn exclusively from theoretical analysis, subjective intuition, and textual interpretation. One prominent example is the ongoing work of Howard and Jamieson's Citation Project, which demonstrates that data-driven study of composing processes can only enhance the already-rich discussions occurring in the field.

The methodologies discussed in this chapter enable researchers to test their theories against verifiable, replicable data. Distant reading (see Moretti 2013) of broad corpuses can help develop a more complex view that is simply not possible to attain at a smaller scale. This work ensures that an emergent theory does not simply reflect a locally observed phenomenon but rather provides a robust description of how rhetorical aspects of authorship operate at a larger scale. Hypotheses concerning circulation, composing processes, distributed collaboration, or the legitimation of disciplinary authority can all benefit from large textual data sets. In particular, studies of collaborative compositional labor and its theoretical implications have much to gain by employing these methods. Such investigations involve extracting the traces of a text's compositional growth: capturing, sorting, and coding the initial data, mining them for patterns, and interpreting the results with the goal of understanding the time-elapsed construction of a digitized or born-digital text.

We focus here on the problems of analyzing large collaborative projects such as wikis, but many types and sizes of collaborative texts are ripe for this sort of analysis. While wikis remain the standard for large-scale, radically collaborative projects, collaboration occurs in diverse digital forms. Writers collaborate in Word documents, of course, but they also use Facebook Notes and Google Docs to develop position statements for professional organizations and Flickr Sets to document worldwide protests.[1] The tool development logs of piratical file-sharing communities contain histories of community-built digital archives (Lewis 2013). Version control systems such as Git or Subversion trace changesets, or iterative development histories of live digital projects. All these forms (and many others) contain metadata that may be mined for research purposes.

In this chapter, we sketch the basic stages of such research and provide an overview of digital tools that are applicable to each research stage. Since we assume that these studies will be undertaken by humanists working with variable, smaller budgets rather than large grants, we point to common desktop applications and open-source tools. We categorize these tools according to levels of expertise: basic, moderate, complex. (See the digital version of this chapter for this information: www.press.uchicago.edu/sites/rdh/.) Digital humanities researchers with minimal coding experience need not shy away from this sort of work; there are suitable applications for every level of expertise, although some may be more powerful than others.

Our focus is on manageably sized data sets that require hand-coding of subjective elements. Moretti's literary trees represent millions of individual texts, such as those found in *Wikipedia*, but studying discrete texts within larger ecologies allows us to view each one as its own tree, its own complex body of interconnected and situated data that allows us to reconstruct authorial processes. Throughout our discussion, we provide, as an example, analysis from Kennedy's ongoing comparative study of authorship in the 1728 *Chambers' Cyclopaedia* and *Wikipedia*, to which Long has contributed as a research assistant. *Wikipedia* in particular presents the challenges of a huge textual corpus built by hundreds of thousands of editors over multiple years. While all readers may not find it comparable to the texts they would like to study, *Wikipedia* is a useful example because its 4,151,386 current articles likely represent the outside limits of a site of study for textual scholars. It is often difficult to scale up from examples according to one's own needs but not necessarily equally difficult to scale down.

Extracting Data

Strategic sample selection and management are the first steps toward developing a successful data-driven study. As numerous Internet scholars have noted, the dynamic nature of live digital artifacts often means that working with digital texts is rather like trying to hit a moving target. The version you read today may very well not be the version that is there tomorrow. Cheryl Geisler (2004, 43) suggests that in some contexts the *version* of a text or page may be the most effective segment of analysis a researcher uses for her coding. This is particularly true with *Wikipedia*, where constant edits mean that a text can move through several iterations while one reads. Consequently, it is vital to preserve the study data in a static environment, either by downloading or through another means of stable data capture. Many systems provide procedures for extracting data: wikis and GoogleDocs both preserve revision and discussion histories, and *Wikipedia* renders its downloadable in multiple "dump" formats (Wikipedia:Database download). Both Git and Subversion produce downloadable changesets. Digital community materials may require membership or access permissions through a sysadmin but are likely available. On occasion, downloaded files may not preserve information in the format required for one's research objectives. Kennedy downloaded edit and discussion histories for individual *Wikipedia* articles but elected to use screen capture software for the articles themselves since the placement of elements such as images, captions, and sidebars was an important part of her data. When capturing multiple iterations of a single artifact, it is essential to develop a careful file-naming structure that clearly accounts for each data capture's date and time.

A Note on Ethics

Subject privacy is an important factor in ethical decisions concerning data capture and should be determined by the nature of the artifact and the community culture. The Association of Internet Researchers (2012, 7) guidelines on ethics point to variable community norms as a central consideration for researchers, along with fundamental human subjects research principles of minimizing harm and attending to the contextual expectations writers may have for reasonable privacy. In our example, *Wikipedia* is a freely available site whose central purpose involves providing free access to every single person on the planet who wishes to participate or just simply read (Lih 2009, 1). Moreover, its interface produces a transparent document that is published in real time and purposefully leaves all levels of the work open to scrutiny through the History and Talk pages. Participants with sufficient digital literacy to contribute to the project typically understand that they are working in public and that anyone else might come along and read their notes, revert their edits, or simply add to the page. The Wikipedian community is also well aware of the numerous media articles and scholarly studies that examine its policies, procedures, and product ("Wikipedia:Wikipedia in the media"). Consequently, Kennedy treated Wikipedian texts as public texts and preserved the community norms of pseudonym use in her data.

Managing Data

Raw data sets will need to be trimmed to a manageable size, and appropriate methods of selection will depend on the specific needs of your initial research questions. You may choose to select *relevant text* or "passages of your [data] that express a distinct idea related to your research concerns" (Auerbach and Silverstein 2003, 46) and focus your analysis exclusively on them. Geisler (2004, 17–18) details multiple methods of sampling, including convenience sampling, focused on convenient data; typical case sampling, which concentrates on a typical subject, object, or situation; best case sampling; criterion-based sampling; stratified sampling, which ensures inclusion of existing variations; and random sampling. Our example study used a criterion-based sample based on topics in *Chambers'* taxonomy of knowledge that had also retained comparable cultural meaning in the twenty-first century and had, thus, been given comparable *Wikipedia* entries. After the associated article pages, edit histories, talk pages, and contributor pages were captured, we moved on to coding this bounded but still ample amount of textual data.

Coding Data

The goal of coding is to convert textual or otherwise nonnumerical information into a form that can be analyzed quantitatively. More importantly, coding makes evident the orientations and methods that have guided a research project and through which the data are interpreted (Smagorinsky 2008, 399). In *Analyzing Streams of Language*, Giesler (2004) provides a detailed breakdown of coding processes that directly apply to research in rhetoric, composition, and other language-based disciplines. Her rich description deserves direct consideration, but we summarize it here in three steps. First, data are segmented into units of analysis, the precise nature of which depends on the phenomenon a researcher wants to study. Second, a coding scheme is created to arrange the different *types* of segments that exist in the data. Third, each segment type is assigned one (and only one) label that differentiates it from the other segment types. For example, the *Wikipedia* study focused on wiki entries' *edit histories*, which preserved every change made to a page since its inception. The edit histories demonstrate, among other things, whether editors' composition processes center on the contribution of original text or instead focus on tasks that are more curatorial in nature, such as including or deleting facts, tweaking links, making sure that images meet community intellectual property guidelines, and the like. To get a clearer picture of the types of writing deployed, Kennedy's segment of analysis was, therefore, the *edit*.

The initial review revealed general patterns of edit *types* or tasks appearing in the histories—from altering vandalism to adding images. Kennedy developed a grounded coding schema based on the tasks demonstrated in the data set. While the schema included original terminology based on the activities we found being performed, it also drew from common terminology developed by other *Wikipedia* researchers. For example, Kennedy retained vandalism typologies from previous studies by Viégas, Wattenberg, and Dave (2004) and Priedhorsky et al. (2007). After these precoding steps were complete, we began coding individual edits first for editor type (human or robot) and then for task type.

Hand-coding is a labor-intensive process: reading and categorizing the thousands of edits in each *Wikipedia* article took between one and three minutes per edit. While the coding process itself is not particularly difficult, it is certainly time consuming, and a research assistant is valuable to the process. Working with a single research assistant, Kennedy was able to code the complete edit histories of multiple *Wikipedia* pages in a couple of months. However, collaborative coding also requires more time up-front for "norming" to ensure that each coder knows how to apply the schema properly. Although our coding scheme was carefully detailed, not all edits mapped clearly or unproblematically onto a single code. Coding is, of course, a partially subjective process, but, when more than one coder is involved, it must be a *consistently* subjective one. Norming ensures that most judgments will be the same, thus maintaining the integrity of the coded data. Smagorinsky (2008, 401–2) recommends initial training followed by asking the assistant to code 15 percent of the previously coded data. If the assistant codes 80 percent of that data identically, she is deemed to be sufficiently normed. However, Smagorinsky also writes that perhaps the best collaborative coding practice is to be truly *collaborative*, that is, to code in proximity and to have face-to-face discussions whenever questions arise.

Researchers are likely familiar with prominent, costly software packages for qualitative and quantitative analysis such as NVivo and SPSS. Happily, there are also a number of easily accessible, low-cost or free tools that handle most functions required for basic coding. We have found it useful to take a "Pareto" view of big data studies—the idea that 80 percent of what humanities researchers need to do good quantitative work can be found in 20 percent of the possible computing capabilities available to more advanced researchers (Harris, Rouse, and Bergeron 2010). In other words, even basic programs and program capabilities go a long way in aiding digital humanities work. Information on applicable basic desktop applications and open access programs is available in the digital version of this chapter (www.press.uchicago.edu/sites/rdh/), along with screencasts.

Visualizing Data

There are a variety of avenues for interpreting results, including steps as simple as sorting Excel columns by type. One of the most useful options is data visualization, which can be a powerful tool for making data workable. Of course, data visualization—data-viz—is nothing new. The simplest pie chart is a data visualization; so are bar charts, lines on a Cartesian plane, and the more recently popularized word clouds. Whenever quantifiable information can be represented fairly in graphic form, data visualization is an option. In some cases—for example, Google mapping projects (Tirrell 2012)—visualizations and data results are one and the same. In both cases, data *visualization* is central to data *interpretation*, which, as Lang and Baehr (2012, 189) note, often necessitates a return to the data to look for corroborating visual patterns—an iterative process, one that leads to discovery. Without this transformative step of rendering text visual, certain trends and patterns may go unnoticed, hidden within the textual or numerical aggregate. This visual analysis may remain textual, as in the case of collation programs, or the researcher may generate nontextual data visualizations such as graphs or network maps. (See the digital edition of this chapter for example visualizations.)

Derek Mueller (2012) demonstrates the importance of visual discovery in his study of the "long tail" of author citations, which analyzed works cited entries from every article published in the journal *College Composition and Communication* between 1987 and 2011, for a total of 16,726 entries. His method included separating multiple-author entries and single-author entries in order to "smooth" the raw works cited data into a comprehensive single-author list, which he counted and graphed. Exploring this citation list in graph form, Mueller discovered that, although the *most cited* scholars were few in number, *most of the citations* referenced an eclectic mix of many different scholars. "The long tail,"[2] he writes, "shows how an abstract visual model potentially elicits new insights and, with its descriptive acuity, raises new questions" (209). However, the ubiquity of this phenomenon remained hidden until researchers like Mueller began to visualize aggregated data with graphing tools. Visualization of data fosters interpretation and allows patterns to be detected—and patterns, as Franco Moretti bluntly puts it, tell us that "something needs to be explained" (2005, 39).

There are many data-mining and visualization tools available for humanities researchers to deploy in their search for explanations, and we detail three in the digital version of this chapter. Data-viz tools allow researchers to discover these patterns quickly, easily, and accurately. They should, thus, hold a vital position in the toolkit of any researcher who wants to work with data sets and/or quantitative methods.

Conclusion

In this chapter, we have argued that theories of rhetoric and writing can benefit from a focus on the material, organic processes of authorship. We have also argued that an important method for studying authorial processes is a quantitative, data-driven inquiry into those qualitative processes. The ease with which texts can be digitized—and the ubiquity of born-digital texts—means that researchers almost always have sufficient data to trace the evolution of discrete texts as well as to unearth patterns in textual genres. Collaboratively written digital texts, such as the wiki entries we have discussed here, are particularly suitable for data-driven study because it is often possible to capture each rhetorical and stylistic move made by the writers involved, no matter how granular. It is precisely these writerly moves and practices that reveal the authorial life of the writer within the text as well as the development life of the document. That in itself is enough, but these quantitative stories in turn provide us with grounded ways of thinking about larger questions of performance, agency, and power—the larger questions of the discipline.

Tools

<> Coding Analysis Toolkit (CAT): http://cat.ucsur.pitt.edu
<> DeDoose: http://www.dedoose.com/AboutUs
<> Digital Research Tools Wiki: http://dirt.projectbamboo.org
<> Gephi: https://gephi.org
<> Juxta: http://www.juxtasoftware.org
<> Natural Language Toolkit: http://nltk.org
<> Pressure.to: http://www.pressure.to/qda

Recommended Resources on Qualitative and Textual Data

Auerbach, Carl F., and Louise B. Silverstein. 2003. *Qualitative Data: An Introduction to Coding and Analysis*. New York: New York University Press.
Bazerman, Charles, and Paul Prior. 2004. *What Writing Does and How It Does It: An Introduction to Analyzing Texts and Textual Practices*. Mahwah, NJ: Erlbaum.

Giesler, Cheryl. 2004. *Analyzing Streams of Language: Twelve Steps to the Systematic Coding of Text, Talk, and Other Verbal Data.* New York: Pearson Longman.

Priedhorsky, Reid, et al. 2007. "Creating, Destroying, and Restoring Value in Wikipedia." In *Proc GROUP 2007*, 259–68, New York: ACM.

Saldana, Johnny. 2009. *The Coding Manual for Qualitative Researchers.* Los Angeles: Sage.

Notes

1. See Feinberg's (2012) coordinated documentation of the worldwide protests against the incarceration of the transgender activist CeCe McDonald.

2. This long tail is a naturally occurring phenomenon across different domains, from economics to citations in scholarly journals (Anderson 2004).

References

Anderson, Chris. 2004. "The Long Tail." *Wired* 12.10. Last modified October. http://www.wired.com/wired/archive/12.10/tail.html.

Association of Internet Researchers. 2012. "Ethical Decision-Making and Internet Research: Version 2.0." http://aoir.org/documents/ethics-guide.

Auerbach, Carl F., and Louise B. Silverstein. 2003. *Qualitative Data: An Introduction to Coding and Analysis.* New York: New York University Press.

Bazerman, Charles. 2002. "The Case for Writing Studies as a Major Discipline." In *Rhetoric and Composition as Intellectual Work*, ed. Gary Olson, 32–38. Carbondale: Southern Illinois University Press.

Campbell, Karlyn Kohrs. 2005. "Agency: Promiscuous and Protean." *Communication and Critical/Cultural Studies* 2.1:1–19.

Feinberg, Leslie. 2012. "This Is What Solidarity Looks Like!" http://www.flickr.com/photos/transgenderwarrior/sets/72157631752126345.

Fitzpatrick, Kathleen. 2011. *Planned Obsolescence: Publishing, Technology, and the Future of the Academy.* New York: New York University Press.

Galin, Jeff, and Joan Latchaw. 2010. "From Incentive to Stewardship: The Shifting Discourse of Academic Publishing." *Computers and Composition* 27.3:211–24.

Giesler, Cheryl. 2004. *Analyzing Streams of Language: Twelve Steps to the Systematic Coding of Text, Talk, and Other Verbal Data.* New York: Pearson Longman.

Harris, Trevor M., L. Jesse Rouse, and Susan Bergeron. 2010. "The Geospatial Semantic Web, Pareto GIS, and the Humanities." In *The Spatial Humanities: GIS and the Future of Humanities Scholarship*, ed. David J. Bodenhamer, John Corrigan, and Trevor M. Harris, 124–42. Bloomington: Indiana University Press.

Herrington, Tyanna. 2010. *Intellectual Property on Campus: Students' Rights and Responsibilities*. Carbondale: Southern Illinois University Press.

Howard, Rebecca Moore. 1999. *Standing in the Shadow of Giants: Plagiarists, Authors, Collaborators*. Santa Barbara, CA: Praeger.

Howard, Rebecca Moore, Tanya K. Rodrigue, and Tricia C. Serviss. 2010. "Writing from Sources, Writing from Sentences." *Writing and Pedagogy* 2.2:177–92.

Kennedy, Krista. 2009. "Textual Machinery: Authorial Agency and Bot-Written Texts in Wikipedia." In *The Responsibilities of Rhetoric: Proceedings of the 2008 Rhetoric Society of America Conference*, ed. Michelle Smith and Barbara Warnick, 303–9. Long Grove, IL: Waveland.

Kirschenbaum, Matthew. 2012. "What Is Digital Humanities and What's It Doing in English Departments?" In *Debates in the Digital Humanities*, ed. Matthew K. Gold, 3–11. Minneapolis: University of Minnesota Press, 2012.

Lang, Susan, and Craig Baehr. 2012. "Data Mining: A Hybrid Methodology for Complex and Dynamic Research." *College Composition and Communication* 64.1:172–94.

Lewis, Justin. 2013. "The Piratical *Ethos*: Textual Activity and Intellectual Property in Digital Writing Environments." Ph.D. diss., Syracuse University.

Lih, Andrew. 2009. *The Wikipedia Revolution: How a Bunch of Nobodies Created the World's Greatest Encyclopedia*. New York: Hyperion.

Logie, John. 2006. *Peers, Pirates, and Persuasion: Rhetoric in the Peer-to-Peer Debates*. Lafayette, IN: Parlor.

Lunsford, Andrea Abernethy. 1999. "Rhetoric, Feminism, and the Politics of Textual Ownership." *College English* 61.5:529–44.

Lunsford, Andrea, Jenn Fishman, and Warren Liew. 2013. "College Writing, Identification, and the Production of Intellectual Property: Voices from the Stanford Study of Writing." *College English* 75.5:470–92.

Moretti, Franco. 2005. *Graphs, Maps, Trees: Abstract Models for Literary History*. London: Verso.

———. 2013. *Distant Reading*. Brooklyn: Verso.

Mueller, Derek. 2012. "Grasping Rhetoric and Composition by Its Long Tail: What Graphs Can Tell Us about the Field's Changing Shape." *College Composition and Communication* 64.1:195–223.

Porter, James E. 1996. "Author." In *Encyclopedia of Rhetoric and Composition: Communication from Ancient Times to the Information Age*, ed. Theresa Enos, 54–56. New York: Garland.

Porter, James, and Danielle Nicole DeVoss. 2006. "Why Napster Matters to Writing: Filesharing as a New Ethic of Digital Delivery." *Computers and Composition* 23:178–210.

Reyman, Jessica. 2009. *The Rhetoric of Intellectual Property: Copyright Law and the Regulation of Digital Culture*. New York: Routledge.

———. 2013. "User Data on the Social Web: Authorship, Agency, and Appropriation." In "Western Cultures of Intellectual Property," ed. Rebecca Moore

Howard and Krista Kennedy, special issue, *College English* 75.5:513–33. http://www.ncte.org/library/NCTEFiles/Resources/Journals/CE/0755 -may2013/CE0755User.pdf.

Ridolfo, Jim, and Martine Courant Rife. 2011. "Rhetorical Velocity and Copyright: A Case Study on Strategies of Rhetorical Delivery." In *Copy(write): Intellectual Property in the Writing Classroom*, Martine Courant Rife, Shaun Slattery, and Danielle Nicole DeVoss, 223–43. Fort Collins, CO: WAC Clearinghouse/Parlor.

Ritter, Kelly. 2005. "The Economics of Authorship: Online Paper Mills, Student Writers, and First-Year Composition." *College Composition and Communication* 56.4:601–31.

Selfe, Cynthia. 1988. "Computers in English Departments: The Rhetoric of Technopower." *ADE Bulletin* 90:63–67. http://www.mla.org/adefl _bulletin_c_ade_90_63&from=adefl_bulletin_t_ade90_0.

Shalizi, Cosma. 2011. "Graphs, Trees, Materialism, Fishing." In *Reading Graphs, Maps, Trees: Critical Responses to Franco Moretti*, ed. Jonathan Goodwin and John Holbo, 115–39. Lafayette, IN: Parlor.

Smagorinsky, Peter. 2008. "The Methods Section as Conceptual Epicenter in Constructing Social Science Research Reports." *Written Communication* 25:389–411.

Tirrell, Jeremy. 2012. "A Geographical History of Online Rhetoric and Composition Journals." *Kairos* 16.3. http://kairos.technorhetoric.net/16.3/topoi/ tirrell/index.html.

Viégas, Fernanda B., Martin Wattenberg, and Kushal Dave. 2004. "Studying Cooperation and Conflict between Authors with *history flow* Visualizations." *CHI* 6.1:575–82. http://alumni.media.mit.edu/~fviegas/papers/ history_flow.pdf.

Walker, Janice R. 2011. "Copy-Rights and Copy-Wrong: Intellectual Property in the Classroom Revisited." In *Copy(write): Intellectual Property in the Writing Classroom*, ed. Martine Courant Rife, Shaun Slattery, and Danielle Nicole DeVoss, 205–22. Fort Collins, CO: WAC Clearinghouse/Parlor.

Westbrook, Steve. 2011. "What We Talk about When We Talk about Fair Use: Conversations on Writing Pedagogy, New Media, and Copyright Law." In *Copy(write): Intellectual Property in the Writing Classroom*, ed. Martine Courant Rife, Shaun Slattery, and Danielle Nicole DeVoss, 159–77. Fort Collins, CO: WAC Clearinghouse/Parlor, 2011.

Woodmansee, Martha, and Peter Jaszi. 1994. *The Construction of Authorship: Textual Appropriation in Law and Literature*. Durham, NC: Duke University Press.

## ELEVEN

Genre and Automated Text Analysis: A Demonstration

RODERICK P. HART

This chapter is about three old things—argument, genre, and narrative—and one new thing: automated text analysis. The chapter provides (1) an overview of why computer-based studies are important, (2) a discussion of the controversies they engender, (3) an example of one such operationalization, and (4) thoughts about how such studies can benefit rhetoric scholarship. Throughout, however, I will be haunted by the words of the novelist John Barth (1966, 61), who once opined: "[The computer] could not act on a hunch or brilliant impulse; it had no intuitions or exaltations; it could request but not yearn; indicate, but not insinuate or exhort; command but not care. It had no sense of style or grasp of the ineffable; its correlations were exact, but its metaphors wretched; it could play chess, but not poker." Chastening though Barth's remarks are, I believe that computers can help us understand poker, a game deliciously linked to the rhetorical arts.

My work in this area sprang from my experience as an English major in the late 1960s, when I came under the sway of New Criticism, at the time a radical thing. New Criticism encouraged text centricity, paying less homage to an author's intentions, to the historical facts surrounding a text, or to readers' presumed responses to it. Although John Crowe Ransom of Vanderbilt was the father of New Criticism, Yale University became its epicenter, drawing on the talents of Robert Penn Warren, Rene Wellek, Monroe Beardsley, William K. Wimsatt, Cleanth Brooks, and others. While I matriculated at a more modest institution seventy-six miles to the west, I too embraced New Criticism, although my interests were more practical than aesthetic. As a result, Richard Weaver, Kenneth Burke, and Richard Ohmann became my guides.

I found New Criticism liberating. It let me treat the literary object on its own terms, not weighed down by the author's majesty or received notions of literary excellence. For a twenty-year-old in the 1960s that was heady stuff. But then came Sputnik, the rise of the social sciences, the invention of data processing, and the Vietnam War. All four had consequences for me. The result has been my career, an ongoing attempt to apply quantitative methods to rhetorical discourse. But the principles of New Criticism—be patient with the text, look for patterns within it, attend to linguistic proportions—never left me. With the rise of the digital humanities, one hears anew the urgings of Wimsatt and Wellek to go beyond the individual case and see what mysteries corpora may hold.

This chapter looks specifically at genre, what Northrop Frye (1957, 13) famously called that "alien and unpronounceable thing" undergirding criticism. There is much folklore connected to genre—poems are emancipatory, novels voyeuristic—but little empirical evidence for such claims. There have been three notable exceptions, however. The sociolinguist Douglas Biber has toiled in this vineyard for many years and recently penned a masterful work, *Register, Genre, and Style*, that asks basic questions about language forms (Biber and Conrad 2009). Franco Moretti (2005), in his Literary Laboratory at Stanford University, is also engaged in what he terms *distant reading* of texts, although he is rather narrowly concerned with plot development. Neither Biber nor Moretti has expressly examined rhetorical matters, but Carnegie-Mellon's David Kaufer has done so, patiently tracking distinctive patterns via his DocuScope project (http://www.cmu.edu/hss/english/research/docuscope.html).

My own work (Hart 1984; Hart 2000; Hart, Childers, and Lind 2013) has used a specific computer program, DICTION (www.dicitonsoftware.com), to study political works. My efforts have been guided by four assumptions: (1) people use words to do things; (2) they use them in varying proportions; (3) audiences react to these deployments cognitively, socially, and emotionally; and (4) they are guided by implicit understandings of rhetorical form when doing so. In what follows, I will show how these assumptions can be operationalized with computer assistance and how they prompt new questions. But first let us reflect on the machine that, according to John Barth, knows nothing of poker.

Computer-Assisted Text Analysis

When computers were first introduced to the humanities, the possibilities seemed endless: concordances of great literary works; authorship studies to discover how many Shakespeares were housed in Shakespeare; stylistic maps tracking the arc of Western thought; lexicographies following the migration of words from culture to culture. All such studies have been done and many to good effect. Too often, however, the computer has been treated "almost exclusively as an enumerator" (Raben 1991, 342) rather than as a springboard to theory. Computers have been judged best suited to performing "dumb tasks" repeatedly (Auerbach 2012), but computers should do more than reduce drudgery, says Willard McCarty (2012); they must add new ideas as well. Scholars must also combine "humble" work with rich interpretations, says Ray Siemens (2002). With the Internet now providing a treasure trove of "born-digital" materials, says Lev Manovich (2012), we must demand that computer-using scholars offer up larger and better ideas.

Perhaps because it is so new, automated text analysis has resulted in two kinds of imbalance. The *positivistic overreaction* argues that scale (Smith 2012) is computation's main bounty—all of Faulkner in a nanosecond. A second correlate treats the computer as an agency for mere hypothesis testing (Hockey 2000), an assumption that treats texts as linear, complete, and independent of a reception community. Assumptions like these, says Susan Wittig (1977), turn words into numbers efficiently but too often forsake the text itself. So, for example, one often finds social scientists, in their rush to get on with the model building, failing to provide textual exemplars in their content analyses, as if heuristic redemption of their findings were unimportant.

The *humanistic overreaction* is different. Whereas the positivists exclude the ineluctable from their inquiries, computer-using literary scholars embrace it too thoroughly by looking for "meaningful astonishment" (Ramsay 2012, 10). To be sure, we must go beyond the "mechanistic, reductive, and literal uses of computer studies" and search for great questions (Drucker 2012, 86), but answers are still important. Humanistic methods "are necessarily probabilistic rather than deterministic," and each reading of a text may produce a "new" text (Drucker

2012, 86, 88), but, like all human phenomena, texts respond to the laws of central tendency. In other words, quantification performed too casually must be avoided, but so too must textual anarchy. A law of parsimony must guide research in this area.

Rhetoric scholars can escape such excesses by remembering that the text is made for someone living somewhere at some moment in time. Rhetoric is a text in bondage to an audience, making it a preeminently sociological phenomenon. As a result, undertaking a study to map "the language common to very large populations" (Olsen 1993, 313) makes special sense in rhetoric studies since the vagaries of textual circulation frustrate all notions of a unitary text. As students of public argument, rhetoric scholars study "meaning systems" (Olsen 1993) shared in "a large, multivariate space" (Kaufer and Hariman 2008, 491). In such a space, knowing what was said is important, but knowing what was not said is important as well. Given the availability of large corpuses, the unsaid is now knowable. It is comparatively easy, for example, to compare a given locution to a data bank of other locutions to discover what has been hidden in public by a given author. Similarly, because the "tone of a text may be as influential as its substantive content" (Young and Soroka 2012, 205), and because tone is inevitably a contrastive phenomenon—it seems more "this" than "that"—we must understand people's rhetorical histories to explain their reactions to discourse. Computers can help in that regard.

Genre and Computer-Based Studies

The computer brings granularity to textual studies (Karlgren, Sahlgren, Olsson, Espinoza, and Hamfors 2012), helping a scholar go beyond simple dichotomies (good/bad, happy/sad) when describing a text. The computer-using scholar can now examine multiple texts simultaneously, using the semantic web to shed light on their properties. Because computer programs like DICTION attack a text from forty or fifty different angles simultaneously, each reading becomes a separate reading but also a mutually implicative reading, telling the user when a text conforms to, or deviates from, a set of norms. While traditional critics can—by dint of studied intelligence—also bring rhetorical history to bear on their inquiries, the computer increments that history easily when passing over a corpus.

That brings us to genre, what Miller (1984, 159) calls "typified rhetorical actions based in recurrent situations." When computers were still in their infancy, E. D. Hirsch (1965, 76) declared: "All understanding of verbal meaning is necessarily genre-bound." But that is not to say that genre is easy to understand since, according to Askehave (1999), texts have "official" (genre-bound) purposes but also "hidden" (speaker-defined) purposes. So, for example, a news report may tell an interesting tale, but its author also wants it to be believed and not treated as fantasy. For these reasons, says Bawarshi (2000), the "genre function" precedes the speech act, constraining both what will be said and how it will be heard. He notes, for example, that, while both obituaries and eulogies feature death, the former is a "civic" document announcing that death to strangers and the latter a personal, often spiritual remembrance of a beloved individual.

Because genres feature structural regularities, they become central to rhetorical theory. Orlikowski and Yates (1994) note that "genre repertoires" build up over time in a social grouping and, thus, help define its cultural expectations. So, for example, humanists "read" their papers at scholarly conventions—privileging the wording of ideas—while social scientists present less scripted talks, signaling scientists' always unfinished thinking. Genres are "typified social actions," says Devitt (2000), that trap large social understandings in the smallness of the text.

Because genres inhabit a complex universe, they are necessarily intertextual, say Briggs and Bautnan (1992, 147); they all "leak." So, for example, any good politician can deliver a Memorial Day address, but the wiliest of them will use that occasion to position their next piece of legislation. Because a text "participates in genres that it rejects as well as those it accepts," says Devitt (2000, 700), rhetoric is often rife with "internal heterogeneity and feature-blending" (Hyland 2002, 123). Poststructuralists are talented at noticing such effects (Perloff 1989), but social scientists do so as well. Douglas Biber (2004), for example, has used multidimensional scaling to tease out the matrix of rhetorical decisions manifested in a given corpus, a task that the World Wide Web has clearly complicated (Mehler, Sharoff, and Santini 2010). The Internet has produced myriad new genre—the blog, for example, and the tweet. As a result, the ink-stained wretch at the local editorial desk must now interact online with those good folks who had previously been gray and lifeless—news consumers, that is. Within that transformation lies not only a new genre but also a new set of power relations in the media space.

Given the importance of genre, can automated text analysis help us understand it better? Are generic markers distinctive enough for a computer to notice? Can we track the "often implicit design decisions" writers make (Ishizaki and Kaufer 2012, 276) and, thereby, say something fresh about the rhetorical universe? While some scholars have performed the former—definitional—function (Argamon et al. 2007; Stein and Eissen 2008), the latter—conceptual—function has been forsaken too often. While some scholars hold out hope for automated genre classification (Petrenz and Webber 2011), it will take considerably more theorizing to make such a project viable. Let us consider a modest effort in that direction.

Studying Genre via DICTION

I present here a thought experiment, not a full-blown piece of research. My hope is to show how automated text analysis can go beyond mere counting and become heuristic, even inveigling. Such approaches, I believe, call our attention to things we did not know and, worse, to things we thought we knew but did not. Because genres are composed of a "loose confederation" of common elements that interact in complex ways (Paltridge 1995), they inevitably invite surprise when arrayed side by side, a task that computers can deftly perform. Computers invite us to ask, How do I really know what I think I know? As a result, they often become an occasion for humility.

The program I use, DICTION, is but one of many tools available for doing what some people call *sentiment analysis* (Liu 2012). But DICTION is concerned with far more than simple (often simplistic) treatments of human emotions. As a rhetorical tool, it is also concerned with argument and values, with disposition and style, with tone and texture. As a rhetorical tool, it helps clarify inventional resources—where ideas come from—as well as their ultimate destination—the text as understood.

DICTION was written in Java (for both PCs and MACs) and uses some ten thousand search words apportioned across thirty-three word lists or dictionaries. It includes several calculated variables as well.[1] None of the search terms is duplicated in these lists, giving the user an unusually rich understanding of a text. The program also produces five master variables by combining (after standardization) the subaltern variables. These master variables include *certainty* (indicating the resoluteness of a text), *optimism* (the endorsement of some person, group, or experience), *activity* (movement, change, or the implementation of ideas), *realism* (words describing tangible, everyday matters), and *commonality* (language highlighting a group's values and commitments).

In essence, DICTION uses lexical layering to account for tone, something that becomes more identifiable when word families are comingled. The great charge against programs like DICTION is that they violate context, the text as created. While true, that is not to say that the text as created is the text as received. "Context," that is, vanishes the moment it comes into existence because readers "infect" the text by perceiving it selectively. Audiences are "gist processors," say Brainerd and Reyna (1993), taking what they need from a text and leaving the rest behind. They become the victims of "spreading activation," argue Boynton and Lodge (1994), overwhelmed by the sudden associations a text triggers. In other words, context may be far less important to an in-the-moment reader than to an after-the-fact analyst. Thus, while DICTION cannot distinguish between a sentence like "the dog bit the man" and "the man bit the dog," it notices the topical similarities between the sentences despite the differential sequencing of the relevant word families.

By "stepping away" from a text and tracking only its word families, DICTION "makes the text strange," as the phenomenologist might say, something that readers themselves are unlikely to do. And DICTION goes further, noting how a given text compares to the larger rhetorical universe, which, in DICTION's case, now contains some fifty thousand previously analyzed texts. That functionality lets a scholar compare a passage to some forty different genres, including speeches, news coverage, advertisements, citizen commentary, religious sermons, corporate reports, theater scripts, television drama, novels, poetry, etc. DICTION makes corpus a central component of rhetoric study.

Still, DICTION is imperfect. For one thing, it makes an assumption of mathematical transposition by supposing that audiences depend on human understandings of proportionality when responding to a text. It also makes an assumption of psychological additivity by presuming that words increase in importance as they increase in number, a linearity that can overlook the importance of infrequently used words. And it makes an assumption of semantic independence by taking words out of context, thereby violating the text-as-received. Elsewhere (Hart, Childers, and Lind, 2013), I have provided responses to each of these criticisms, ultimately concluding that, like all scholarly methods from factor analysis to postcolonial deconstruction, DICTION walls things out even as it walls things in. Such is the nature of scholarship, of the human condition.

Ultimately, DICTION's value is best judged by what it teaches us. Accordingly, let us experiment a bit by assuming that we know nothing about rhetorical genre, that we have just arrived in Earth's atmosphere. Let us assume further that we have only two measuring sticks at our command, one describing the strength of a given statement (what DICTION calls *certainty*) and the other its storytelling capacity (referred to here as *narrative force*). While many other factors inhabit the world of words, these two are surely ubiquitous. Most of us recognize, for example, when we have landed in church—the volume is higher and the arguments clearer; questions tend to waft away in church. But one also hears stories in church, stories describing people and their lives, and that humanizes the experience. Strong arguments, great stories—this is church for many believers.

But how to test that hypothesis? Let us begin with *certainty*, a variable derived from the work of general semanticists like Alfred Korzybski, S. I. Hayakawa, and Wendell Johnson who studied the effects of rigid language on people's day-to-day interactions.[2] In making the *certainty* calculation, DICTION tabulates eight subscores, four of which increase an expression's firmness and four that make it more tentative. After being reduced to Z-scores and combined, an overall *certainty* quotient is obtained. The additive variables include the following:

- *Tenacity*: All uses of the verb *to be* (*is, am, will*), three definitive verb forms (*has, must, do*) and their variants and contractions (*he'll, they've, isn't*).
- *Leveling*: Words used to ignore individual differences, including totalizing terms (*everybody, anyone, each*), adverbs of permanence (*always, completely, inevitably*), and resolute adjectives (*unconditional, consummate, absolute*).
- *Collectives*: Singular nouns reflecting categorical modes of thought, including social groupings (*crowd, choir, team*), task groups (*army, congress, staff*), and geographic entities (*county, world, kingdom*).
- *Insistence*: A measure of code restriction whereby all nouns or noun-derived adjectives occurring three or more times are identified, after which they are folded into this equation:

(number of eligible words $\times$ sum of their occurrences) $\div$ 10.[3]

Subtracted from this complex of variables are four others that make a text more provisional:

- *Numerical terms*: Specifying terms detracting from a statement's universality. Integers are treated as individual "words," as are those in lexical format (*one, ten-*

fold, hundred). Also included are numerical operators (*subtract, divide, multiply*) and quantitative topics (*digitize, tally, mathematics*).

- *Ambivalence*: Words expressing hesitation, including hedges (*allegedly, perhaps, might*), approximations (*almost, vague, somewhere*), and terms of confusion (*baffled, puzzling, hesitate*) or mystery (*dilemma, guess, seems*).
- *Self-reference*: All first-person references (*I, I'd, I'll, I'm, I've, me, mine, my, myself*) that index the locus of action within the speaker, not in the world at large.
- *Variety*: A measure analogous to Wendell Johnson's (1946) type-token ratio (different words divided by total words), with a high score indicating a speaker's preference for precise, molecular statements.

For the purposes of this exercise, *certainty* becomes my measure of argument, although there are surely many more ways of describing same. Similarly, *narrative force* becomes my way of getting at the "aesthetic" dimensions of rhetoric. For Ricoeur (1980), narrative time is a time of being with others; it is social time. If *certainty* is designed to settle things, stories tend to unsettle them, giving rhetoric a propulsive force, and encouraging readers to join in the action. For Bruner (1991), texts that have "narrative necessity" are motivating—characters are well rendered, people's motivations and actions made plausible. For Fisher (1984), narrative contrasts with the "rational world paradigm" by bringing reason and imagination together in a pleasing confection.

When computing *narrative force*, I reason thusly: narratives involve (1) vivid descriptions of (2) people's (3) activities at some particular (4) time and (5) place. Narratives are more than this of course—plot, characterization, motivations, etc.—but they are rarely less than this. Operationally, I ask DICTION to standardize the following variables prior to their being combined in a single measure:

- *Embellishment*: A selective ratio of adjectives to verbs giving a passage descriptive, psychological texture.
- *Motion*: Terms connoting movement (*bustle, jog, lurch*), physical processes (*circulate, revolve, twist*), journeys (*barnstorm, jaunt, wandering*), speed (*nimble, zip, whistle-stop*), and modes of transit (*ride, fly, glide*).
- *Human interest*: People give narrative its capacity for identification. Included are personal pronouns (*he, ourselves, them*), family members and relations (*cousin, wife, grandchild*), and generic terms (*friend, baby, persons*).
- *Temporal terms*: Words specifying literal (*century, instant, midmorning*) or metaphoric (*lingering, seniority, nowadays*) time. Also included are calendrical (*autumn, year-round, weekend*), elliptical (*spontaneously, postpone, transitional*), and judgmental (*premature, obsolete, punctual*) terms.

· *Spatial terms*: General geographic references (*abroad, locale, outdoors*) and specific ones (*Ceylon, Kuwait, Poland*). Also included are political locations (*county, municipality, ward*), points on the compass (*east, southwest*) and globe (*latitude, coastal, border*), as well as terms of scale (*kilometer, map, spacious*) and quality (*vacant, out-of-the-way, disoriented*).

Hemingway would surely be put off by this reduction of narrative, and Martin Luther King Jr. would be left speechless. But the strength of automated text analysis lies not in its nuance but in its functionality. Is it possible that these two measures alone could tell us something important about rhetoric? For me, at least, it is.

The measures outlined above were applied to some sixteen thousand contemporary texts spanning the rhetorical universe. They included moral commentary (religious sermons and social movement remarks), political discourse (speeches, ads, debates), news reports (both print and broadcast), fictional texts (novels, sitcoms, theater scripts), informal conversation (phone calls and Internet chat), scholarly essays (from both the humanities and the social sciences), commercial persuasion (television/magazine ads and public relations releases), and technical reports (financial and legal documents).

Tests run on the data (see fig. 11.1) find massive statistical differences among these genres, and the patterns obtained are sensible.[4] As one might have predicted, figure 11.1 displays the common literary/rhetorical divide, with lower *certainty* scores pointing to a more "readerly sensibility" (e.g., fictional texts) that provides room for—indeed, invites—the reader's participation. The classically rhetorical venues, in contrast—public discourse and moral commentary—are more "writerly" in orientation: the speakers know what they know and entreat their audiences to know it as well. As McCarthy, Graesser, and McNamara (2006) might have guessed, the technical reports are quite linear, their power coming from the embellishment they fail to provide ("just the facts") and from their understatement ("draw your own conclusions"). And, given the arcane vocabularies of the academy, it is not surprising to find scholarly essays all by themselves in quadrant 3—resistant to metanarratives, studies in incompletion.

These findings are not shocking unless one remembers that they were unearthed by a machine. Figure 11.1 shows quite different bids for authority—the forceful statesman versus the innocent dramatist, the reporter offering conclusions, the lawyer avoiding them. Stereotypes abound here but also subtlety. There is much that we can learn from such approaches, as in the following:

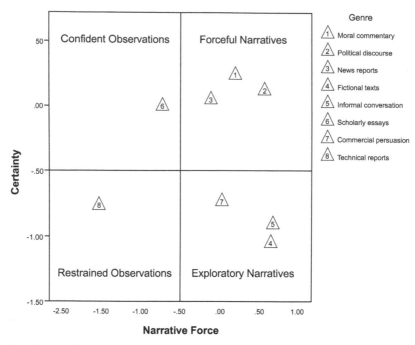

11.1. Rhetorical genre via certainty and narrative force.

- *Explaining rhetorical trajectories*: The novelist is in it for the long run, holding back on argument and waiting for the well-wrought narrative to have its eventual impact. The social movement leader has no time for indirection: the crisis is nigh, and the audience must be moved to action now.
- *Tracing rhetorical ontologies*: Figure 11.1 finds both Mazda commercials and F. Scott Fitzgerald occupying the same rhetorical space. Surely this is obscene. But, as Dégh (1985) reports, there is "magic for sale" in popular advertising. The drama of ring-around-the-collar is a shy little drama, but it is drama nonetheless—everyday innocence, the imminent crisis, the happy denouement. Not Shakespearean tragedies perhaps, but they carry us along.
- *Identifying long-standing tensions*: Quadrant 2 finds both preachers and politicians, an unholy alliance. We find Thomas à Becket here and also Bishop Daniel Jenky, who once compared Barack Obama to Joseph Stalin. Church and state do battle constantly—over immanence and transcendence—and both expect to be believed. An old story, this.
- *Explaining rhetorical antimonies*: Esimaje (2012) found more noun compounds in academic prose, more idioms in political speech. Idioms work better, pointing to

richer cultural narratives, as we see in figure 11.1. The scholar abjures such stuff, aghast at the thought of dalliance, while the politician looks back in wonder: What is it, exactly, the scholars are saying?

· *Identifying verbal shortcomings*: Gottschall (2012) observes that evolution still has legion detractors. After so many years of grand science, how is that possible? Evolution, Gotschall replies, is a tale without agency, while the God story is not only a story but also a powerful one (high *certainty*, high *narrative force*).

· *Mapping unmapped territories*: Quadrant 4 finds traditional fiction and informal conversation joined at the hip. That explains the power of drama—the human conversation done magnificently—but it also explains the gossipers in the break room regaling one another at lunch with stories of their witless boss. Narrative is us.

· *Documenting the undocumented*: Subsidiary analysis finds financial reports deploying less *certainty* than legal documents. That is the difference between lawyers and accountants. Too, philosophers use more *certainty* than social scientists; the former are tempted by the unknowable, the latter humbled by it.[5]

· *Charting rhetorical evolution*: Political campaign speeches use more narrative language than do policy speeches emanating from the Oval Office. The former have also become more narrational over the years.[6] The result is a quadrennial ritual: chickens in everyone's pot, blue skies galore. As a result, political cynicism now enwraps us.

· *Accounting for the popular*: Television news broadcasts create richer political narratives than do newspapers, and televised product ads are far sexier than magazine ads.[7] Television, the people's medium, draws us in with narrative. In a similar vein, news coverage of climate change has become more histrionic in recent years, less technical and more brocaded (Kirilenko and Stepchenkova 2012). Narrative. Who can resist it?

None of the data presented here are definitive, but they are suggestive. Such research uses a machine, but that research need not be mechanical. Ideally, it should lead one to wondering, What does it mean that social movement and church leaders are rhetorical neighbors? It means that they are often rivalrous—right to life comes to mind—because they speak the same language but in a different dialect. For that same reason, they can be powerful allies, as we saw in the civil rights movement. Both speakers tell a story with panache but have a different attitude toward ultimacy. Lived experience goads the social activist, eternal possibilities the preacher. That a computer can tease out such conformities may not be a grand thing, but it is a surely an intriguing thing.

Conclusion

Ishizaki and Kaufer (2012, 290) have established a daunting challenge for automated text analysis: to "capture the deep intuitions of the native speaker," to explain what we know but cannot articulate. Genre may prove central to such understandings. People, like computers, respond to structures. Both notice regularities in the world but often do so when their expectations have been violated—when expected structures cannot be found. In some cases, as when a sermon goes on too long, people become frustrated. At other times, as with a clever play on words, they are surprised, delighted. When making such observations, people use genre and their rhetorical data banks to make sense of the world. Asking a computer to simulate such experiences seems not an artificial but a natural thing to do.

New Criticism, the bold intellectual experiment of the 1950s, fell into disrepute when the postmodernists entered the academy twenty years later. This latter tribe rejected the orderliness and implicit positivism of the New Critics as well as their reverence for the accomplished text. The postmodernists made things more complicated because they found so much confusion in literature—texts with surfaces, texts with contradictions, texts with hidden hegemonies and ironies, texts without foundational truths, texts fragmented and decentered, texts endlessly reflexive.

Postmodernism admits to no binaries, but computers, alas, know only ones and zeroes. So can New Criticism be resurrected? I believe that it can but only if we ask the kinds of provocative questions Wimsatt and Wellek asked fifty years ago. They and their colleagues inquired into the how of discourse, and they were normativists at heart, understanding the particular by way of the general. And so they would be pleased by the rise of the digital humanities, its asking of new questions. They would be surprised, I suppose, that English professors can now use computers, but they would not be scandalized by it. They were people of ideas, these New Critics, and they asked fine questions. So should we all. If it takes a computer to bring these questions to the surface, that seems but a small scandal. It is time for a new New Criticism.

Notes

1.   DICTION also lets scholars build their own dictionaries for specialized purposes. A user can construct up to thirty such dictionaries (of up to

two hundred words each in length), which DICTION will then use in its search routines.

2. For more on this movement, see the Web site of the Institute of General Semantics: http://www.generalsemantics.org.

3. By default, DICTION extrapolates (or reduces) all passages submitted to it to a five-hundred-word standard, thereby allowing different users to compare their results no matter what sort of passages have been submitted to the program.

4. For *certainty* across genre: moral commentary = 0.2425, political discourse = 0.1231, news reports = 0.0496, fictional texts = −1.0483, informal conversation = −0.9041, scholarly essays = 0.0029, commercial persuasion = −0.7365, and technical reports = −0.7578, $F[7, 15720]$ = 248.264, $p < .000$. For *narrative force* across genre: moral commentary = 0.1100, political discourse = 0.5345, news reports = −0.1316, fictional texts = 0.5776, informal conversation = 0.4236, scholarly essays = −0.8052, commercial persuasion = −0.1037, and technical reports = −1.6474, $F[7, 15720]$ = 418.933, $p < .000$.

5. For *certainty* in technical documents: financial reports = −1.4484, legal documents = −0.0148, $F[1, 162]$ = 29.396, $p < .000$. For *certainty* in scholarship: social science scholarship = −0.8907, humanities scholarship = −0.7692, philosophical essays = 0.5031, $F[2, 299]$ = 59.100, $p < .000$.

6. For *narrative force* by subgenre: television political ads = 0.3169, political debates = 0.2266, campaign speeches = 0.7387, policy speeches = 0.4671, $F[3, 4173]$ = 75.864. For *narrative force* by era: campaign speeches in 1948–60 = 0.5570, campaign speeches in 1964–76 = 0.6637, campaign speeches in 1980–92 = 0.7508, campaign speeches in 1996–2000 = 0.9262, $F[3, 2353]$ = 23.996.

7. For *narrative force* in journalism: print reporting = −0.1842, television news = 0.3314, $F[1, 8526]$ = 435.559. For *narrative force* in advertising: television ads = 0.7345, magazine ads = −0.1268, $F[2, 201]$ = 16.930.

References

Argamon, Shlomo, Casey Whitelaw, Paul Chase, Sobhan Raj Hota, Navendu Garg, and Shlomo Levitan. 2007. "Stylistic Text Classification Using Functional Lexical Features." *Journal of the American Society for Information Science and Technology* 58.6 802–22.

Askehave, Inger. 1999. "Communicative Purpose as Genre Determinant." *Hermes—Journal of Linguistics* 23:13–23.

Auerbach, David. 2012. "Quantitative Methods in Literary Criticism: Franco Moretti and Brian Vickers." *Waggish*, February 20. http://www.waggish .org/2012/quantitative-methods-in-literary-criticism-franco-moretti -and-brian-vickers.

Barth, John. 1966. *Giles Goat-Boy*. New York: Doubleday.

Bawarshi, Anis. 2000. "The Genre Function." *College English* 62.3:335–60.

Biber, Douglas. 2004. "Conversation Text Types: A Multi-Dimensional Analysis." Paper presented at the seventh Journées Internationales d'Analyse Statistique des Données Textuelles, Louvain-la-Neuve, Belgium, March 10–12.

Biber, Douglas, and Susan Conrad. 2009. *Register, Genre, and Style.* New York: Cambridge University Press.

Boynton, G. R., and Milton Lodge. 1994. "Voters' Images of Candidates." In *Presidential Campaigns and American Self-Image,* ed. Arthur H. Miller and Bruce E. Gronbeck, 176–89. Boulder, CO: Westview.

Brainerd, Charles J., and Valerie F. Reyna. 1993. "Memory Independence and Memory Interference in Cognitive Development." *Psychological Review* 100:42–67.

Briggs, Charles L., and Richard Bautnan. 1992. "Genre, Intertextuality, and Social Power." *Journal of Linguistic Anthropology* 2.2:131–72.

Bruner, Jerome. 1991. "The Narrative Construction of Reality." *Critical Inquiry* 18.1:1–21.

Dégh, Linda. 1985. *American Folklore and the Mass Media.* Bloomington: Indiana University Press.

Devitt, Amy J. 2000. "Integrating Rhetorical and Literary Theories of Genre." *College English* 62.6:696–718.

Drucker, Johanna. 2012. "Humanistic Theory and Digital Scholarship." In *Debates in the Digital Humanities,* ed. Matthew K. Gold, 85–95. Minneapolis: University of Minnesota Press.

Esimaje, Alexandra Uzoaku. 2012. "Register Variation and the Multi-Word Item." *Theory and Practice in Language Studies* 2.1:97–104.

Fisher, Walter. 1984. "Narration as a Human Communication Paradigm: The Case of Public Moral Argument." *Communication Monographs* 51:1–22.

Frye, Northrop. 1957. *Anatomy of Criticism.* Princeton, NJ: Princeton University Press.

Gottschall, Jonathan. 2012. *The Storytelling Animal: How Stories Make Us Human.* Boston: Houghton Mifflin.

Hart, Roderick P. 1984. *Verbal Style and the Presidency: A Computer-Based Analysis.* New York: Academic.

———. 2000. *Campaign Talk: Why Elections Are Good for Us.* Princeton, NJ: Princeton University Press.

Hart, Roderick P., Jay P. Childers, and Colene J. Lind. 2013. *Political Tone: How Leaders Talk and Why.* Chicago: University of Chicago Press.

Hirsch, E. D. 1965. *Validity in Interpretation.* New Haven, CT: Yale University Press.

Hockey, Susan. 2000. *Electronic Texts in the Humanities.* Oxford: Oxford University Press.

Hyland, Ken. 2002. "Genre: Language, Context, and Literacy." *Annual Review of Applied Linguistics* 22:113–35.

Ishizaki, Suguru, and David Kaufer. 2012. "Computer-Aided Rhetorical Analysis." In *Applied Natural Language Processing: Identification, Investigation, and Resolution*, ed. Philip M. McCarthy and Chutima Boonthum-Denecke, 276–97. Hershey, PA: Information Science Reference.

Johnson, Wendell. 1946. *People in Quandaries: The Semantics of Personal Adjustment*. New York: Harper.

Karlgren, Jussi, Magnus Sahlgren, Fredrik Olsson, Fredrik Espinoza, and Ola Hamfors. 2012. "Usefulness of Sentiment Analysis." In *Advances in Information Retrieval: 34th European Conference on IR Research, ECIR 2012, Barcelona, Spain, April 1–5, 2012, Proceedings*, ed. Ricardo Baeza-Yates, Arjen P. de Vries, Hugo Zaragoza, B. Barla Cambazoglu, Vanessa Murdock, Ronny Lempel, and Fabrizio Silvestri, 426–35. Berlin: Springer.

Kaufer, David, and Robert Hariman. 2008. "Discriminating Political Styles as Genres: A Corpus Study Exploring Hariman's Theory of Political Style." *Text and Talk* 28.4:475–500.

Kirilenko, Andrei P., and Svetlana O. Stepchenkova. 2012. "Climate Change Discourse in the Mass Media: Application of Computer-Assisted Content Analysis." *Journal of Environmental Studies and Sciences* 2:178–91.

Liu, B. 2012. *Sentiment Analysis and Opinion Mining*. San Rafael, CA: Morgan & Claypool.

Manovich, Lev. 2012. "Trending: The Promises and the Challenges of Big Social Data." In *Debates in the Digital Humanities*, ed. Matthew K. Gold, 460–75. Minneapolis: University of Minnesota Press.

McCarthy, Philip M., Arthur C. Graesser, and Danielle S. McNamara. 2006. "Distinguishing Genre Using Coh-Metrix Indices of Cohesion." Paper presented at the Sixteenth Annual Meeting of the Society for Text and Discourse, Minneapolis, MN, July 13–15.

McCarty, Willard. 2012. "A Telescope for the Mind?" In *Debates in the Digital Humanities*, ed. Matthew K. Gold, 113–23. Minneapolis: University of Minnesota Press.

Mehler, Alexander, Serge Sharoff, and Marina Santini, eds. 2010. *Genres on the Web: Computational Models and Empirical Studies*. London: Springer.

Miller, Carolyn R. 1984. "Genre as Social Action." *Quarterly Journal of Speech* 70:151–67.

Moretti, Franco. 2005. *Graphs, Maps, Trees: Abstract Models for a Literary History*. New York: Verso.

Olsen, Mark. 1993. "Signs, Symbols, and Discourses: A New Direction for Computer-Aided Literature Studies." *Computers and the Humanities* 27:309–14.

Orlikowski, Wanda J., and JoAnne Yates. 1994. "Genre Repertoire: The Structuring of Communicative Practices in Organizations." *Administrative Science Quarterly* 39.4:541–74.

Paltridge, Brian. 1995. "Working with Genre: A Pragmatic Perspective." *Journal of Pragmatics* 24:393–406.

Perloff, Marjorie, ed. 1989. *Postmodern Genres*. Norman: University of Oklahoma Press.

Petrenz, Philipp, and Bonnie Webber. 2011. "Stable Classification of Text Genres." *Computational Linguistics* 37.2:385–93.

Raben, Joseph. 1991. "Humanities Computing 25 Years Later." *Computers and the Humanities* 25:341–50.

Ramsay, Stephen J. 2012. "Textual Behavior in the Human Male." Paper presented at the inaugural symposium of the Institute of the Humanities and Global Cultures, Charlottesville, VA, November 9.

Ricoeur, Paul. 1980. "Narrative Time." *Critical Inquiry* 7.1:169–90.

Siemens, Raymond G. 2002. "A New Computer-Assisted Literary Criticism?" *Computers and the Humanities* 36:259–67.

Smith, Kathleen. 2012. "Q&A with Brett Bobley, Director of the NEH's Office of Digital Humanities." *HASTAC*, February 1. http://hastac.org/node/1934.

Stein, Benno, and S. Meyer zu Eissen. 2008. "Retrieval Models for Genre Classification." *Scandinavian Journal of Information Systems* 20.1):93–119.

Wittig, Susan. 1977. "The Computer and the Concept of Text." *Computers and the Humanities* 11:211–15.

Young, Lori, and Stuart Soroka. 2012. "Affective News: The Automated Coding of Sentiment in Political Texts." *Political Communication* 29:205–31.

## TWELVE

At the Digital Frontier of Rhetoric Studies: An Overview of Tools and Methods for Computer-Aided Textual Analysis

DAVID HOFFMAN

DON WAISANEN

Over the last few decades a sizable arsenal of "textual analysis" software has become available to scholars and researchers who work with language. NVivo, Wordstat, Linguistic Inquiry and Word Count (LIWC), DICTION, and Concordance are some examples of such textual analysis software packages. While this software has been most commonly used in the analysis of open-ended survey questions and transcribed interviews, it can also be used in the analysis of "naturally occurring" public discourse that has traditionally been the domain of rhetorical criticism, such as political speeches and pamphlets, newspaper editorials, and blogs. Although one software package, DICTION, is designed to be an aid to rhetorical criticism, on the whole computer-assisted analysis is a rare thing in the pages of mainstream rhetorical criticism journals such as the *Quarterly Journal of Speech*, the *Rhetoric Society Quarterly*, and *Rhetoric and Public Affairs*.

This chapter will explore the uses and limitations of textual analysis software in the criticism of contemporary and historical rhetoric. Rather than trying to cover every existing software program—which would be a hopeless task, doomed to be dated before it was even printed—we discuss four broad functions that current programs perform and that future programs are likely to perform. We explore the capacities of the major textual analysis software packages, review published studies in which they have been used, and identify how these tools relate to other projects in the digital humanities writ large, with the goal of providing a number of suggestions concerning how textual analysis software might enhance rhetorical approaches to historical and contemporary public discourse.

Four Functions of Textual Analysis Programs

Textual analysis software comes in a variety of forms. Some software packages, like DICTION and Concordance, are built for very specific and limited purposes. Others, like NVivo and QDA Miner's Wordstat, are multifunctional, seeking to be the only software packages that their users will ever need in the course of research. These large, multifunctional packages incorporate tools that are designed for qualitative data management and automated textual analysis. Although many researchers use programs like N-Vivo primarily for data management, we will not comment on such features as they fall outside the range of this chapter's focus on using software for rhetorical criticism. We will also leave aside stylometric programs like Signature and the Java Graphical Authorship Attribution Program, which are designed primarily to determine the authorship of texts.

Our survey of extant textual analysis packages suggests that they have four broad functions. First, they can generate basic statistics about a text, such as word count, average sentence length, number of adjectives, the Gunning Fog Index (a basic measure of readability based on sentence length and number of complex words), and a host of others. Second, they can create indexes and concordances, quickly locating every instance of a word or word combination in a text or set of texts, cataloging and presenting them in context. Third, they can use dictionaries, either preprogrammed or user generated, to rate texts on a host of qualitative variables. DICTION, for instance, can score texts on their "certainty, activity, optimism, realism, and commonality" variables relative to other texts, using built-in dictionaries. Fourth, they can do cluster analyses, using sophisticated algorithms to determine the most important concepts in a given text or group of texts and how they are related to each other. In the following sections we will discuss how each of these functions has been used in published work.

Basic Textual Statistics

A variety of basic computational outputs are available for computer-aided rhetorical studies, such as findings about the frequency of a given term or the average word length. Outputs of statistical information can range from charts or tables to visualizations that juxtapose smaller and larger terms on the basis of their frequency, as in the program Wordle. Figure 12.1 shows a Wordle "cloud" graphic derived from a simple word-frequency analysis of Lincoln's Gettysburg Address. Throughout this chapter, we insert outputs derived from an analysis of Lincoln's speeches to facilitate comparisons between textual analysis programs and their various functions.

Basic textual statistics make simple but substantiated generalizations. Such generalizations can have a large practical impact in research and scholarship. One example of how this can work comes from the field of classical rhetoric. The loose group of fifth-century BC Greek thinkers known as the Sophists has long been associated with the beginning of formal rhetorical studies. Although the term *sophist*

12.1. The Gettysburg Address in "cloud" form: a mash-up of the Gettysburg Address. Word size represents word frequency.

has generally been used in a derisory sense for most of the last two and a half millennia, the surviving fragments of actual Sophists—such as Protagoras, Gorgias, Lysias, Antiphon, and Isocrates—reveal thinkers who were sophisticated (pun intended) and challenging, if sometimes highly skeptical about all truth claims. In the early 1980s, in works like G. B. Kerferd's *The Sophistic Movement* (1981), efforts to rehabilitate the Sophists in their true character began in classical studies. Such efforts were also made by those who studied rhetoric in speech communication and English departments and who saw in the Sophists a glimmer of a "postmodern"-flavored alternative to the Aristotelian orientation that had dominated thought about classical rhetoric in the previous generation. In the *Philosophy and Rhetoric* article "Toward a Sophistic Definition of Rhetoric," John Poulakos (1983) attempted to rethink the meaning of rhetoric from a sophistic perspective. Poulakos's sophistic perspective on rhetoric was challenged by Edward Schiappa in a series of articles and chapters (Schiappa 1990a, 1990b, 1991a, 1991b, 1992), touching off a heated debate, and, ultimately, changing accepted ideas about the relation between rhetoric and the Sophists.

Underpinning Schiappa's criticism of Poulakos's work was the contention that the actual Greek word for *rhetoric* did not appear in any Greek text before Plato in the first half of the fourth century BC, considerably after the Sophists' period. The claim was supported by a search of the *Thesaurus linguae graecae*, an early database of extant Greek literature. The debates touched off by Schiappa's challenge are typical of the kind of disputes that follow from the type of generalization made possible by simple textual statistics. For example, simply because no surviving text contains the word *rhetoric*, does that mean that it was not used anywhere? Even if *rhetoric* was not in use as a term, does that mean that the concept of rhetoric was not in play? On the other hand, if, as Schiappa claimed, Plato actually coined the term *rhetoric* in the fourth century, is that not a meaningful moment in the history of rhetoric?

The next generation of scholars learned the lesson of how powerful claims backed by exhaustive database searches could be and integrated these techniques into their work using the next generation of textual analysis tools. The Perseus Digital Library is a full, but not exhaustive, online collection of ancient Greek and Roman texts, together with some other materials like artworks. The site has textual analysis tools with the capacity to produce statistics about word frequencies across all major classical authors. In past published work, Hoffman has used this function of the Perseus Digital Library to make claims about the evolution of some key terms in the technical vocabulary of ancient Greek rhetoric, namely, *logos* and *eikos* (see Hoffman 2003, 2008a, 2008b). Such work demonstrated that *logos* began its life as the verb *legein*, with the original sense of "to gather," as in "to gather firewood," and was transformed, largely in early philosophical discourse, into the noun *logos*, which can be understood to mean "a gathering or collection of words and phrases—a composition." *Eikos* began life as a verb that meant "to be similar" and evolved into a participle that meant "similar to what is expected or likely." "By-author" and "by-text" term frequencies can allow researchers in any field to see where and when particular keywords began to be used. The ability to locate all keyword usages provides a foundation for an analysis of how purposes and meanings change over time, to which informed speculation about the forces that drove changes in meaning can be added.

Few, if any, programs currently offer *only* basic textual statistics. But they are accessible in most textual analysis packages, and the basics are often even provided by word-processing programs. Textual statistics typically form one component of more sophisticated approaches to computer-aided textual analysis. LICW, in addition to employing a dictionary-based approach, uses basic counts of words over six letters long, the number of personal pronouns, and counts of "function words," among other features, to make assessments of the complexity and emotional tone of a given text's rhetoric.

Indexes and Concordances

The creation of indexes and condordances constitutes a second function of computer-aided textual analysis. Traditionally referring to alphabetical lists of key terms contained within a text, "a concordance derives its power for analysis from the fact that it allows us to see every place in a text where a particular word is used, and so to detect patterns of usage" (McCarty 2007, "The Concordance," par. 2). Although Google searches of e-books can produce a very basic sort of concordance, some textual analysis software packages make it far easier to produce and manipulate concordances. The primary function of the program Concordance, for instance, is to index all words in texts and produce concordances. One output of such programs is a "keywords in context" display (see table 12.1).

Indexing and concordancing software may assist in finding and managing keywords in context but very much leaves these processes in the researcher's hands. For instance, to group similar terms together,

Table 12.1 The word *nation* in the Gettysburg Address

on this continent a new	nation,	conceived in liberty and dedicated
civil war testing whether that	nation	or any nation so conceived
whether that nation or any	nation	so conceived and so dedicated
gave their lives that that	nation	might live. It is altogether
died in vain, that this	nation	under God shall have a

Note: This is an example of the sort of "keywords in context" output than can be produced by Concordance and similar indexing software.

potential search words typically need to be inputted manually. In constructing a concordance of key terms, such *lemmatization* describes an author's grouping of certain close words under a single category, as in the words *go* and *goes* (McCarty 2007).

Researchers have used Concordance and similar programs to enhance content-analysis procedures by ensuring their accuracy and thoroughness and to cut down on the tedious human labor involved. Hansen and Benoit (2002) used Concordance to generate an exhaustive list of issues in all presidential television advertising between 1952 and 2000, as part of a project to track how closely issues in television ads are associated with public priorities (at least as revealed through opinion polls). Using this methodology, the researchers were able to produce a table comparing public priorities with the issues addressed in George H. W. Bush and Michael Dukakis's campaign ads in 1988 (see table 12.1). Where the numbers in the column "Public" represent the percentage of the public that thought the issue was "important," the numbers in the columns "Bush" and "Dukakis" represent the number of mentions of the issue in the advertising sample.

The methodology used to produce this table has some limitations, but it does open up some interesting avenues for "rhetoric and reality" types of studies. On the limitations side, the percentage of the public thinking an issue is important is not strictly comparable to the number of mentions by a candidate. Also, the way in which the advertising was sampled does not take into account that some ads about specific issues might have run more frequently on television than other ads. The first, but not the second, limitation is addressed when Hansen and Benoit move to a comparison of the rank ordering of priorities between candidates and the public. A similar use of Concordance in content analysis is made by Potnis (2010), who analyzed data from e-Government Readiness Assessments.

In general, Concordance is a powerful tool for finding discrete bits of content that can be manually classified by researchers. Yet dictionary-

Table 12.2 1988 Public policy priorities and issues addressed

	Public	Dukakis	Bush
Budget deficit	12	12	9
Economy (general)	12	5	11
Drugs	11	26	13
Unemployment	9	30	13
War/international	9	26	54
Poverty	7	1	0

Source: Hansen and Benoit (2002), table 4.

based textual analysis programs, treated in the next section, remove a need for the manual classification of content.

Dictionary Comparisons

Dictionary comparison programs constitute a third area for computer-aided rhetorical criticism. These programs use preconstructed dictionaries to assess the degree to which particular qualities are present in texts. The degree to which a given text expresses anger, for instance, might be assessed on the basis of how many of its words match a dictionary of "angry words." LIWC allows researchers to determine "the degree any text uses positive or negative emotions, self-references, causal words, and 70 other language dimensions" (http://www.liwc .net/#, par. 1) while also allowing scholars the ability to construct their own dictionaries (for a detailed comparison of LIWC with other programs, see Pennebaker, Mehl and Niederhoffer 2003).

One of the best examples of this type of software is DICTION, mentioned above, which uses preprogrammed dictionaries to make assessments of verbal style and linguistic habits (Hart 2001). Through approximately three decades of iterations and updates, current DICTION software compares a text or group of texts with thirty-five variable averages constructed from an extensive database of texts collected from public discourse. Vigorously championed by its creator, Roderick Hart, in *Verbal Style and the Presidency* (1984) and ensuing works like *Campaign Talk* (2000), DICTION has been employed in a large number political discourse studies, including Ballotti and Kaid (2000), Crew and Lewis (2011), and Hart and Lind (2010). It has also been used to examine discursive trends in education (Graddy 2004), diplomacy (Bashor 2004), religion (Eidenmuller 2002), management (Finkelstein 1997), and even stand-up comedy (Waisanen 2011a, 2011b, in press).

Figure 12.2 presents a chart based on DICTION results comparing

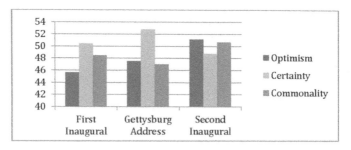

12.2. A DICTION-based comparison of three speeches by Lincoln: A comparison of Lincoln's First Inaugural, Gettysburg Address, and Second Inaugural in terms of optimism, certainty, and commonality. Note that the normal range for these DICTION scores is typically between 46 and 56.

Lincoln's First Inaugural, Gettysburg Address, and Second Inaugural using three of its five master variables: *optimism, certainty,* and *commonality.* According to DICTION, Lincoln gets steadily more optimistic as he moves through this set of speeches; however, his certainty peaks at Gettysburg even as he uses language with less commonality than in either of his inaugurals.

Through such outputs, dictionary programs provide researchers with the ability to do efficient comparative work both within and between texts. These programs make arithmetic judgments that can be a valuable supplement to contextualist claims (Hart 2000) and have an "ability to deal with great quantities of verbal information" that is useful in a "culture and era supersaturated with political messages" (Hart 1985, 103). But moving beyond—while also incorporating—basic statistical techniques, the comparisons between a text or texts and preloaded dictionaries move researchers from descriptive to more analytic and conceptual findings. By using dictionaries, one can gain an understanding of how common or deviant a text's language is in comparison with other texts, letting a researcher "quickly distinguish between idiosyncratic and normative behavior" (Hart and Lind 2010, 357).

To cite several telling examples of the types of claims that can be supported by dictionary comparisons, studies have showed how the presidential candidate Bob Dole's declaration of being the "most optimistic man in America" belied how he "used less verbal optimism in his campaign speeches than any Republican since Tom Dewey with one exception" (Hart 2000, 4). A speech by John F. Kennedy—which much of the American press described as quite typical—was actually "massively uncharacteristic": "Kennedy was much more pragmatic on this occasion than he normally was" (Hart 1985, 124). Furthermore, a comparison of President Carter's inaugural address with his State of the Union speech showed that the speeches were in many respects not similar, contrary to press accounts (Hart 1984, 240–41).

Dictionary software searches for what it is designed to search for, no less and no more (Hart and Daughton 2005, 168). Although a wide variety of dictionary-based programs for textual analysis are available— Wordstat has a list of ten that can be imported, including the whole of LIWC—if the dictionaries are not designed to answer the questions a researcher is interested in, they may not be valuable. For instance, if a scholar wanted to get an analysis of how much medical terminology was used in a set of speeches, DICTION would not be helpful—unless a dictionary specific to that purpose were constructed by the researcher. At the same time, not all dictionaries may be equal in terms of their validity. Although established programs like LIWC and DICTION have gone through decades of refinement, researchers are well advised to scrutinize the lists of search terms employed by dictionary programs to make sure that they are suitable for their purposes. Overall, like the other functions outlined in this chapter, dictionary comparisons can be used as a central or merely supplemental method for rhetorical work.

Cluster Analyses

While dictionary-based programs can rate and compare texts with reference to various qualities like optimism and certainty, they do not have the capacity to tell researchers how the actual *locations* of various terms relate and link with other terms. For such an approach, one needs to turn to cluster analysis programs, which can provide both written and more advanced visual outputs. These programs, such as NVivo, Wordstat, T-Lab, and Catpac, have the capacity to discover relations between key terms within and across texts. Where Concordance can give one an instance-by-instance view of how a key term is used, cluster analysis gives the researcher a statistically driven overview of what terms tend to be collocated with each other throughout a text.

One major use of cluster analysis programs has been to conduct *frame analyses* across large sets of texts. Yan Tian and Concetta Stewart (2005) used Catpac to analyze 332 *CNN* and 408 *BBC* reports about the SARS outbreak in 2003. With the aid of Catpac, the researchers were able to identify seven clusters of associated terms in the *CNN* reports and six in the *BBC* reports. The tables in which they reported their results are reproduced in tables 12.3 and 12.4.

Table 12.3 Clusters from the CNN text

Cluster number	Cluster theme	Keywords
1	Beijing	Beijing, millions, last, and cases
2	Public health	Disease, health, SARS WHO, Hong Kong, people
3	Symptoms, statistics, and effects on travel	Symptoms, patient, virus, outbreak, officials, reported, China, travel, number
4	Chinese government	Chinese, Taiwan, first, full, government
5	Toronto	Story, Toronto
6	Economic impact	Case, countries, death, hit, Yen, down, higher
7	Treatment and control	World, control, city, hospital, Singapore, infected, spread

Source: Tian and Stewart (2005), table 1.

Table 12.4 Clusters from the BBC text

Cluster number	Cluster theme	Keywords
1	Public health	Affected, public, country, death, authorities
2	World	Canada, Asia, world, countries
3	Singapore	Quarantine, Singapore, spread
4	China and Toronto	Beijing, China's, Chinese, government, reported, far, officials, patients, Toronto, city, hospital, number
5	Hong Kong and WHO	Cases, Hong Kong, people, WHO, SARS, virus
6	Outbreak and impacts	Disease, China, infected, illness, outbreak, first, health, died, travel

Source: Tian and Stewart (2005), table 2.

By comparing the two sets of clusters, the researchers were able to make a number of general observations about how the two networks framed the SARS outbreak. They observed that, while both networks focused on the impact of the outbreak on the travel industry, *CNN* reported on the situation in Taiwan far more frequently than did the *BBC*. Other instances of cluster analysis include Stewart, Gil-Egui, Tian, and Pileggi (2006) and Stephen (1999), who used the WordStat program in a similar manner.

Conclusion

Although the usefulness of textual analysis programs in rhetorical studies should be obvious from the examples discussed above, it is still relatively rare for those engaged in rhetorical criticism to make use of the tools they provide. There is, to our knowledge, at present no systematic treatment of how to use these tools in rhetorical scholarship. We have conducted this analysis to aid researchers and students in making intelligent choices about the appropriate place of textual analysis software in their work.

Although the potential contribution of textual analysis programs is great, certain global limitations of the available processes should be noted. One limitation is that, although these programs can compare large numbers of texts, *any capacity to understand context-related meanings must come from the human reader.* For example, there is no program that you could plug a transcript of *The Colbert Report* into that could, by itself, tell you that Colbert is a parody of a conservative pundit. A researcher could conduct a comparison between Colbert and an actual conservative pundit that could identify some of the parodic features between the two—but the initial idea that a parody was intended would need to come from the researcher. This inability to understand texts in context is likely to remain a limitation of computer-assisted textual analysis in the foreseeable future.

A second global limitation of these programs is that, although they allow some of the semantic features of text to be analyzed at an unprecedented scale, they are unable to deal with features of style and meaning that depend on sentence-level syntax. Although some stylometric programs, such as Signature, can register an author's tendency to use certain grammatical patterns, they cannot make any guess about the specific *meanings* that audiences may infer from such articulations. For example, consider the following three sentences:

1. Once upon a time, far, far, away, in a kingdom by the sea, there lived a handsome young prince.

2. In a far, far away kingdom by the sea, there lived a handsome young prince, once upon a time.

3. Once upon a kingdom, by the young prince, there lived a handsome time, in a far, far, away sea.

A human reader with sufficient cultural background can easily recognize the first sentence as a traditional, if somewhat clichéd, introduction to a fairy tale. The second sentence is the introduction to a fairy tale that is trying to be somewhat fresh while still alluding to the traditional formula. The third sentence is pure nonsense. Yet all three sentences contain exactly the same words and are grammatically correct. They differ only in syntax. Dictionary and clustering programs would find the same keywords in roughly the same proximity, with basic textual statistics unaffected. We do not know of any program that can analyze sense and style at the sentence level in all their syntax-dependent glory. No program could pick up the difference between

Ask not what your country can do for you, but what you can do for your country

and

Ask not what you can do for your country, but what your country can do for you.

Even in the area of semantics, where these programs generally excel, they can leave the researcher with a rather flattened view of the world. The statistical observation that Lincoln tends to use the words *constitution* and *government* in proximity to each other does not provide a "street-level" view of a passage like the following: "This country, with its institutions, belongs to the people who inhabit it. Whenever they shall grow weary of the existing Government, they can exercise their constitutional right of amending it, or their revolutionary right to dismember or overthrow it" (Lincoln, First Inaugural). In computer-aided textual analysis one is given a view equivalent to that of a recognizance satellite that strains to make out any features that are smaller than a meter in size—useful for detecting large-scale patterns, but not the proper instrument to photograph a fine painting. These tools are emphatically not a substitute for close reading.

Although these programs might be characterized as less than intelligent in some ways, they are superhuman in others. This kind of work sits on a nexus between quantitative and qualitative inquiry, holding the possibility of both bridging methodological divides and adding to researchers' repertoires. Overall, we find that computer-aided textual analysis can contribute to the study of rhetoric in at least three ways. (1) Programs that produce textual statistics and concordances can help us map the synchronic and diachronic distribution of ideographs and memes in a way that would fulfill many of the aspirations of Michael McGee's (1980) seminal article "The 'Ideograph,'" which were hitherto unrealizable. Huge numbers of texts can be analyzed to discover how the meaning and usage of key terms like *liberalism* and *conservatism* have changed over time and how catchphrases and choice bits of jargon—*paradigm shift*, for instance—have spread. (2) Programs like Diction and LIWC can do objective and systematic comparisons of broad features of textual style and tone. (3) Cluster analyses are useful in large-scale studies of framing.

These tools for textual analysis might be useful across a broader range of digital humanities efforts than are covered in detail here. Dictionary-based software might complement efforts to map the "literary genome" that result in charts showing stylistic and thematic similarities (Jockers 2012). Rather than generating information about the overall relatedness of works, dictionary-based textual analysis could show how works in a particular literary corpus stack up against each other in terms of specific qualities: optimism, introversion, passion, and others. This would enable researchers to ask questions like, Who was the angriest author of the nineteenth century? in addition to, Which author is most typical of nineteenth century literature?

Furthermore, there is no reason that such techniques should be confined to literature. They could be equally well applied in philosophy and history or in more professional applications. Systematic key-term analysis aided by programs like Concordance could provide further depth by showing how particular concepts—whether key terms of a disciplinary lexicon or the "ideography" of a political speech—have shifted in meaning according to the time and place in which they were used. Finally, cluster analysis techniques can point out recurring sets of terms in literature, philosophy, and history just as well as in contemporary public discourse. The Department of Homeland Security even recently began a program to use several textual analysis techniques, including LIWC, to identify which terrorist groups are the most dangerous (Dempsey 2011). There is no doubt that they might also be used for happier purposes.

It should be remembered that one of the most ardent humanities scholars, Kenneth Burke, assigned a role for statistical procedures and associational clusterings in works of rhetorical criticism. He admonished critics to trace words and images across a range of works and to look for "what goes with what" and "what is vs. what" (1974, 20, 69). While the scholar's ability to read and reflexively interpret texts from a close perspective should always remain central to rhetorical studies, it is also clear from our foregoing survey that computers can do much to supplement and forge new paths of inquiry for twenty-first-century discourse analysis.

References

Ballotti, John, and Lynda Lee Kaid. 2000. "Examining Verbal Style in Presidential Campaign Spots." *Communication Studies* 51:258–73.

Bashor, Harold. 2004. "Content Analysis of Short, Structured Texts: The Need for Multifaceted Strategies." *Journal of Diplomatic Language* 1:1–13.

Burke, Kenneth. 1974. *The Philosophy of Literary Form.* Berkeley and Los Angeles: University of California Press.

Crew, Robert E., and Christopher Lewis. 2011. "Verbal Style, Gubernatorial Strategies, and Legislative Success." *Political Psychology* 32:623–42.

Dempsey, Paul. 2011. "A War of Words." *Engineering and Technology* 6:64–66.

Eidenmuller, Michael E. 2002. "American Evangelicalism, Democracy, and Civic Piety: A Computer-Based Stylistic Analysis of Promise Keepers' Stadium Event and Washington D.C. Rally Discourses." *Journal of Communication and Religion* 25:64–85.

Finkelstein, Sydney. 1997. "Interindustry Merger Patterns and Resource Dependence: A Replication and Extension of Pfeffer (1972)." *Strategic Management Journal* 18:787–810.

Graddy, Duane B. 2004. "Gender and Online Discourse in the Principles of Economics." *Journal of Asynchronous Learning Networks* 8:3–14.

Hansen, Glenn J., and William L. Benoit. 2002. "Presidential Television Advertising and Public Policy Priorities, 1952–2000." *Communication Studies* 53:284–96.

Hart, Roderick P. 1984. *Verbal Style and the Presidency: A Computer-Based Analysis.* New York: Academic.

———. 1985. "Systematic Analysis of Political Discourse: The Development of DICTION." In *Political Communication Yearbook: 1984,* ed. Keith R. Sanders, Lynda Lee Kaid, and Dan Nimmo, 97–134. Carbondale: Southern Illinois University Press.

———. 2000. *Campaign Talk: Why Elections Are Good for Us.* Princeton, NJ: Princeton University Press.

———. 2001. "Redeveloping DICTION: Theoretical Considerations." In *Theory, Method and Practice of Computer Content Analysis,* ed. Mark D. West, 43–60. Westport, CT: Ablex.

Hart, Roderick P., and Suzanne M. Daughton. 2005. *Modern Rhetorical Criticism.* Boston: Allyn & Bacon.

Hart, Roderick P., and Colene J. Lind. 2010. "Words and Their Ways in Campaign '08." *American Behavioral Scientist* 54:355–81.

Hoffman, David C. 2003. "*Logos* as Composition." *Rhetoric Society Quarterly* 33:27–53.

———. 2008a. "Concerning *Eikos*: Social Expectation and Verisimilitude in Early Attic Rhetoric." *Rhetorica* 26:1–29.

———. 2008b. "Murder in Sophistopolis: Paradox and *Eikos* in the *First Tetralogy*." *Argumentation and Advocacy* 45:1–20.

Jockers, Matthew. 2012. "Computing and Visualizing the 19th-Century Literary Genome." http://www.matthewjockers.net/2012/07/20/computing-and-visualizing-the-19th-century-literary-genome.

Kerferd, G. B. 1981. *The Sophistic Movement.* Cambridge: Cambridge University Press.

McCarty, William. 2007. "AV1000: Fundamentals of the Digital Humanities: The Basics of Concording." http://www.cch.kcl.ac.uk/legacy/teaching/av1000/textanalysis/concord.html.

McGee, Michael Calvin. 1980. "The 'Ideograph': A Link between Rhetoric and Ideology." *Quarterly Journal of Speech* 66:1–16.

Pennebaker, James W., Matthias R. Mehl, and Kate G. Niederhoffer. 2003. "Psychological Aspects of Natural Language Use: Our Words, Our Selves." *Annual Reviews of Psychology* 54:547–77.

Potnis, Devendra D. 2010. "Measuring e-Governance as an Innovation in the Public Sector." *Government Information Quarterly* 27:41–48.

Poulakos, John. 1983. "Toward a Sophistic Definition of Rhetoric." *Philosophy and Rhetoric* 16:35–48.

Schiappa, Edward. 1990a. "History and Neo-Sophistic Criticism: A Reply to Poulakos." *Philosophy and Rhetoric* 23: 307–15.

———. 1990b. "Neo-Sophistic Rhetorical Criticism or the Historical Reconstruction of Sophistic Doctrines?" *Philosophy and Rhetoric* 23:192–217.

———. 1991a. *Protagoras and Logos: A Study in Greek Philosophy and Rhetoric.* Columbia: University of South Carolina Press.

———. 1991b. "Sophistic Rhetoric: Oasis or Mirage?" *Rhetoric Review* 10: 5–18.

———. 1992. "*Rhetorike*: What's in a Name? Toward a Revised History of Early Greek Rhetorical Theory." *Quarterly Journal of Speech* 78:1–15.

Stephen, Timothy. 1999. "Computer-Assisted Concept Analysis of HCR's First 25 Years." *Human Communication Research* 25:498–513.

Stewart, Concetta M., Gisela Gil-Egui, Yan Tian, and Mariri Innes Pileggi. 2006. "Framing the Digital Divide: A Comparison of US and EU Policy Documents." *New Media Society* 8:731–50.

Tian, Yan, and Concetta M. Stewart. 2005. "Framing the SARS Crisis: A Computer-Assisted Text Analysis of CNN and BBC Online News Reports of SARS." *Asian Journal of Communication* 15:289–301.

Waisanen, Don J. 2011a. "Jokes Inviting More Than Laughter . . . Joan Rivers's Political-Rhetorical Worldview." *Comedy Studies* 2:139–50.

———. 2011b. "Satirical Visions with Public Consequence? Dennis Miller's Ranting Rhetorical Persona." *American Communication Journal* 13:24–44.

———. In press. "Standing-Up to the Politics of Comedy." In *The Language of Public Affairs: Computational Research with DICTION*, ed. Roderick P. Hart. Hershey, PA: IGI Global.

## THIRTEEN

Corpus-Assisted Analysis of Internet-Based Discourses: From Patterns to Rhetoric

NELYA KOTEYKO

The emergence of Internet-based tools that enable selecting, storing, organizing, and analyzing data has opened up whole new areas for research in the humanities and social sciences and led to the reconsideration of attendant methodological arsenals (Thurlow and Mroczek 2011). An in-depth analysis of Internet-based data, however, does not mean discarding "older" methods. On the contrary, it is increasingly recognized that we need to combine novel methods with tried and tested techniques if we want to study the multifaceted nature of online discourses. This chapter explores some of the key methodological challenges and opportunities in researching discourses on the Internet, placing emphasis on the view of discourse as situated action, where text production and interpretation are seen as first and foremost social processes.

At present, scholars of digital rhetoric can choose from a variety of data-aggregation tools, such as search engines, RSS feeds, and recommendation systems that allow selecting texts of interest from the constantly changing online archive. However, although there are software packages that can quickly process patterns across this universe of texts and other data formats, these are often of little value for scholars of rhetoric owing to the decontextualized nature of results. By contrast, research in the tradition of corpus-assisted discourse studies have been grappling with the issues of context and meaning for some time now (Partington 2010) and have developed qualitative and quantitative techniques that can assist enquiries within the framework of digital rhetoric. Here, I therefore want to discuss how we can systematically retrieve Internet-based data and then use text analysis and data-visualization tools to establish both macro- and micropatterns of language use for specific projects within the framework of rhetorical studies in public understanding of science.

Background: Rhetorical Studies in Public Understanding of Science

According to Gross (1996), rhetoric has the following roles in the public understanding of science: as a theory for analyzing public understanding and as an activity aimed at creating it, through a forum where both scientists and the lay public can equally participate in the creation of science. Referring to the analytic role of rhetoric, Gross then distinguishes between two primary models in public understanding of science: the *deficit model* and the *contextual model* (see also Wynne 1991). The deficit model, akin to the conduit model of communication (Reddy 1979), portrays communication as a one-way flow from scientists to a passive public that is assumed to be already persuaded of the value of science. The contextual model, by contrast, is symmetrical and implies an active public: "It requires a rhetoric of reconstruction in which public understanding is the joint creation of scientific and local knowledge" (Gross 1995, 6). Here, rhetorical analysis plays a major role, shifting the focus from the examination of a scientific field to the situated study of the public understanding. Within this model, then, an understanding of audiences' cultural, political, and socioeconomic conditions, along with their ability to use technological resources, is a prerequisite.

Such understanding is increasingly necessary for public engagement with science research in our age of digital communication technologies. Previous studies show that new realities of the online information environment—such as science journalism and a reliance of audiences on blogs and other online sources for information about scientific issues, the politics of search engines, as well as the growing influence of social media networks—all have an increasing impact on the relation between the science community and the public and require further in-depth analysis (Brossard and Scheufele 2013). In principle, the Internet as a rhetorical context provides the public with the opportunity to form public opinion, engage with developments in science and policy, and contest elite messages (Hauser 2007). Discussions on Internet-based platforms enable spaces for rhetorical invention, and creative uses of language that often occur on the Web might foster discussion or even deliberation, although they also can "just as easily foreclose sustained, deeper engagement" (Thurlow and Mroczek 2011, 4). In the study of online science communication, Gross's contextual model therefore invites us to focus on the users and the uses of emerging forms of media rather than technologies themselves (MacKenzie and Wajcman 1999).

Scholars following in Gross's steps have examined different sites and modes of interaction between scientific and lay knowledges, focusing on various rhetorical devices such as metaphor and metonymy (for a detailed review, see Condit, Lynch, and Winderman 2012). In contrast to studies under the general rubric of frame analysis and analyses of public perceptions, this research adheres to a "broadened view of public participation" and the role of metaphors in it (Russill 2011, 117). Here, metaphor is viewed from the perspective of its creative capacity, its potential to spark dialogue and collaboration, and its importance for "illuminating and challenging a wider array of institutionalised and epistemic value commitments" than mere expressions of policy support or criticism (Russill 2011, 117). To provide a few examples, Ratto (2006) looks at the use of metaphors in the description of the Human Genome Project, demonstrating the paramount role of these rhetorical devices in the "strategic alliances" (32) between the key stakeholders. Jordan (2004) analyses how the interactions of medical and popular discourses lead to the view of body as a malleable, "plastic" object. The rhetorical properties of metaphors are also explored with regard to the communication of environmental issues by Valiverronen and Hellsten (2002) and Ungar (2007), the latter emphasizing the importance of metaphors derived from the popular culture in climate change communication. Koteyko (2009) examines how the voice of science is appropriated in the advertising discourse of functional foods producers through the metaphoric descriptions of the immune system on their Web sites.

In the domain of public engagement with climate science, the majority of research has been done on discourses in traditional media (but see O'Neill and Boykoff 2011; and Jaspal, Nerlich, and Koteyko, in press). Some of the recent studies have focused on an emerging new language in the English-speaking mass media, policy, and scientific discourses, evident through the use of such word combinations as, for instance, *carbon market, carbon footprint, carbon diet,* and *carbon criminal* (Nerlich 2012; Nerlich and Koteyko 2009). These lexical compounds are coined by the same mechanism where the elliptical use of the noun *carbon* (from *carbon dioxide* or *carbon emission*) is combined with other nouns from a variety of domains (e.g., *carbon emissions* plus *criminal activity: carbon criminal*). As can be seen from these examples, many of these combinations are metaphoric in nature, and as such they can be examined as communication tools used by different discursive actors. From the participatory perspective (Eden 1996), analysis of these compounds can illuminate the moral, ethical, and cultural dimensions of the climate change issue. The rest of this chapter provides an overview of insights provided by data-driven approaches to analyzing the use of these creative word combinations on the Internet, detailed in Koteyko, Thelwall, and Nerlich (2010) and Koteyko (2010).

Methodological Concepts and Tools

The studies outlined below demonstrate how we can combine the established methods of corpus linguistics developed specifically to search, sort, and retrieve patterns in vast textual repositories with more recent techniques employed in the field of webometrics, which, as its basic form, relies on statistics mined from search engines and individual Web sites.

Corpus linguistics combines quantitative methods based on frequencies and word distribution with data-visualization techniques that allow qualitative analysis and offers the analyst such tools as retrieval of clusters (or "lexical bundles"), retrieval of lexis adjacent to a search term within a predefined span (collocates), and concordances (giving a preview of the textual environment so that patterns surrounding the search term can be identified visually). Concordances in corpus linguistic software programs such as Antconc (Anthony 2005) or the Wordsmith Tools (Scott 2011) allow for the visual identification of textual patterns surrounding the search term (e.g., collocates carrying negative or positive evaluation), as well as sorting and resorting of the cotext, and in this way provide the analyst with additional perspectives that are not normally available without programming input and modifications of search functions. The semantic associations revealed through such concordance analysis can be used to establish lexical profiles of culturally and sociologically important words (Stubbs 1996; Koteyko 2010). When applied in the study of carbon compounds, such profiles will allow examining the interplay between the microlevel of linguistic choice and "the social processes of climate change conceptualisation i.e. what it is and how its causes and consequences, and the planned responses to it, are constructed" (Pettenger 2007, 2).

In contrast to an earlier focus on lexicography and language teaching, methods of corpus linguistics are now increasingly applied to study discourses (Baker et al. 2008), an approach referred to as *corpus-assisted discourse analysis* (Partington 2010). The important feature of this framework is attention to context—both the situational parameters and the broader sociocultural and political context in which texts making up corpora are embedded. Proponents of this approach therefore work with special purpose corpora—collections of texts interrelated via a common theme and/or discourse type rather than multigeneric corpora designed to be representative of language as a whole.

Webometics was developed to support research into Web-based phenomena from a quantitative perspective "using techniques that are not specific to one field of study" (Thelwall 2009, 6) and to analyze, inter alia, Web site content, search engine data, and URLs. In the field of public engagement with science, webometric techniques can be used to gain evidence about the nature and extent of public participation in science-related online discussions. Search engine data such as text abstracts and corresponding URLs can be stored together and analyzed via concordances and the "view text" functions of corpus linguistic software to inform compilation of special purpose corpora (e.g., a corpus of science journalism blogs and reader responses or a corpus of reader comments provided at online newspaper platforms [see Koteyko, Jaspal, and Nerlich 2013]). Combined with information about social actors and their linguistic choices, such analysis can begin establishing an initial picture of how the "joint creation of scientific and local knowledge" envisioned by Gross takes place in online spaces.

Overall, the combination of corpus-assisted discourse analysis and webometrics allows the analyst to make sure that the following levels are addressed: textual (analysis of cotext by generating concordances and collocates), aspects of human-computer interaction (statistics from Web sites and search engines using webometric techniques), and broader situational and social parameters addressed at the corpus compilation stage (attention to common topics, temporal aspects, information about audience and text producers).

Corpus-Assisted Analysis of Internet-Based Discourses on Climate Change Mitigation

In this section I present two sets of practical analyses demonstrating how the combination of analytic tools described above can be employed to carry out a historic/diachronic inquiry into the use of selected key terms from the beginning of the Web as well as to perform a systematic synchronic analysis to reveal a plethora of value commitments accompanying their use in blog discussions.[1]

A starting point for both studies is a collection of RSS (Really Simple Syndication) feeds—a format that provides the latest content updates for specific Web sites to their subscribers. The RSS scanning method was used to generate a large collection of recent online texts (82,049 feeds) with the help of the purpose-built RSS-collection and -processing software Mozdeh (Thelwall, Prabowo, and Fairclough 2006). This convenience sample (there is no single systematic register from which to select randomly) consists of daily updates from a wide range of blogs, news sites, and other sources throughout 2007 (Koteyko 2010). A list of compounds was isolated from word clusters generated from this RSS collection with the help of the AntConc software (Anthony 2005). The list was further studied by the project members to identify metaphoric compounds.

Studying Developments over Time

In the first study, the focus was on providing a chronological overview of the use of the compounds by compiling a database of contexts where they had been used since the beginning of the Web. The data was collected using the date-specific search function of the AltaVista Advanced Search interface for dates between 1990 and November 2008. AltaVista was selected because its advanced search facility allows results to be limited to a certain time period. The contexts of occurrence were traced by downloading the relevant sites' URLs, titles, and abstracts (the descriptions reported by the search engine), which were then run through the concordancer to reveal lexis adjacent to carbon compounds.

The longitudinal study revealed two patterns in the use of the compounds over time. First, the number of uses rose rapidly from 2000 on, peaking around the end of 2007 and the beginning of 2008. Second, it became possible to trace which compounds were the oldest and which began to be used only recently. Here, a tendency to cluster according to the time period and semantic set was observed. Thus, compounds headed by the lexis from the sphere of finance, such as *carbon tax, carbon trading, carbon allowance, carbon management, carbon saving*, and *carbon accounting*, appeared to be the "oldest" compounds as they started to be used between the early 1990s and 1999. Since the early 1990s, the economics of climate change has been a central issue in policymaking at the international level, and carbon compounds represent some of the lexical devices used to describe and conceptualize the transformation of environmental objects into market-based products.

The majority of middle-range (used between 1999 and 2005) compounds, such as *carbon footprint, carbon lifestyle, carbon calorie, carbon diet*, and *carbon challenge*, can be grouped under the label *lifestyle solutions* centered on calculating individual and collective impacts. Compounds that began to be used only from 2005 on are headed by the emotional and evaluative lexis, signaling what some observers call *climate change fatigue* (e.g., Ward 2008). These include such word combinations as *carbon morality, carbon crusade, carbon dictatorship*, and *carbon indulgence* (for further detail, see Koteyko, Thelwall, and Nerlich 2010).

Data collected from search engines (text abstracts and URLs) can be used to identify key institutional actors using the terms in the period under study. First, abstracts can be examined for the presence of names and themes (who is quoted or referred to) as concordances can be extended up to four lines to provide access to the textual surrounding of the search term. Next, the URL analysis can also reveal organizations and/or geographic locations behind the text of the abstract. For example, the contexts in which the "early" compounds were used before 1999 show little diversity as the URLs predominantly come from UK and US government organization reports and news reports, whereas later compounds appear to be used by a variety of institutional Web sites, blogs, and news pages.

In addition to establishing the chronological trends, one can focus on the distribution of key terms on specific Web sites. Thus, in Koteyko, Thelwall, and Nerlich 2010, analysis of the first twenty most frequently used domains revealed that some of the Web sites contained whole clusters of semantically related compounds rather than high frequencies of individual ones, pointing to the role of compounds in structuring arguments. The use of carbon compounds from only one semantic group can be indicative of the organization's position and function within climate change discourse. For example, government Web sites such as http://www.publications.parliament.uk were found to contain a range of finance- and lifestyle-related compounds but no recent metaphoric coinages such as *carbon morality* or *carbon crusade*, whereas blogging sites were found to use a mix of compounds from all these groups. This is the case when absences can be just as revealing as high frequency of use because the government Web sites without a single use of evaluative compounds did not offer online spaces for public participation, such as discussion boards or comment pages.

The techniques outlined above are useful at the initial stages of analysis and can provide "quick, indicative results" (Thelwall 2009, 6) as the combination of pages from a variety of online sources enables access to a broad spectrum of contemporary discussion. They can help establishing the general trends in the online use of selected terms, which in turn can inform the research design of a subsequent qualitative study.

A Synchronic Analysis of Internet-Based Discussions

The second study used the complete list of compounds extracted from RSS feeds as a starting point to build a special purpose corpus of online posts (predominantly updates from blogs) on the theme of climate change science and policy in 2007. The interactive features of blogs allow extensive opportunities for collaborative content creation, resulting in an continuously updated online archive of discussions where different voices can be heard and analyzed, often in real time. From this perspective, blogs are arguably one of the best media with which to study the issues of justice, morality, and uncertainty in relation to climate change and global warming (Koteyko 2010).

This time corpus linguistic techniques were used to examine semantic associations entertained by the compounds in the texts of RSS feeds (by identifying patterns in adjacent lexis). Whereas similar associations signal agreement among members of a discourse community, contrasting associations would indicate instances of debate, negotiation, or contestation. For example, some of the concordances generated for finance-related compounds showed that they were being used in the company of neutral to positive lexical items (*summit, report, debit,* and *evaluate*) and, therefore, were likely to promote consensus. At the same time, however, concordances of such compounds as *carbon tax, carbon credit,* and *carbon offsetting* also displayed negative semantic associations. The pejorative use of *carbon offsetting,* for example, reflects the debate over the commodification of carbon emissions and ethical implications, as indicated by such adjacent words and phrases as *backlash, hilarious parody, guilt-free,* and so on.

Additionally, we can see here a creative coinage of the new compound *carbon debit* used alongside the already institutionalized *carbon credit*: "The reason we sell Carbon Debits is simple—we want to take away the pathetic excuse of Carbon Credits from those liberals who hide their shame filled lives behind money-bought lunacy" (Koteyko 2010, 663). Similarly, middle-range compounds headed by the lifestyle-related lexis are used in both positive and negative contexts. Whereas finance-related compounds had helped conceptualize the corporate and government carbon-trading initiatives, the lifestyle carbon compounds are used to describe more local and/or individual attempts to deal with climate change, thereby providing a window into practical actions and action situations valued within public participation frameworks (Eden 1996). The positive instances of use retrieved from our corpus were often part of stories detailing individual efforts to reduce carbon emissions. Here, metaphoric compounds are coined and used as part of a collaborative search for solutions in the form of lifestyle choices (e.g., *low carbon living* may involve *carbon dieting* and using a *carbon calculator*). However, the pejorative uses display instances of blame and point to the moralization of discourses on individual mitigation initiatives. In such cases production of carbon dioxide is portrayed as something one should be ashamed of, whereas the efforts to lower one's carbon footprint become a way of showing that one is a good person (the uses of *carbon criminal* and *carbon champion/hero* reflect conceptualizations of these limited options).

The last but perhaps most interesting group of compounds appears to be recruited by online actors to present arguments in moral and religious terms by alluding to the notions of guilt and salvation. The main difference between these compounds and those from two earlier groups is that they are headed by lexical items that can carry evaluation on their own (e.g., *carbon sinner*) and are used to furnish various value arguments regarding climate science and policy. For example, carbon offsets and carbon credits are described as *carbon indulgences* in reference to the medieval practice of selling indulgences to sinners to absolve their sins. In the modern version, purchasers, that is, *carbon sinners*, are absolved from the need to cut down their carbon emissions: "I began this series of critiques of the greenhouse fearmongers with an evocation of the papal indulgences of the Middle Ages as precursors of the '*carbon credits*'—ready relief for carbon sinners, burdened, because all humans exhale carbon, with original sin" (Koteyko 2010, 667).

Other compounds, such as *carbon morality*, are used to refer to the moralizing tones and emphasis on restraint seeping through the textual surrounding of some of the lifestyle-related compounds. The compound *carbon guilt* is used in similar contexts to criticize the moral framing of the climate change issue according to which one should feel personal responsibility for high energy consumption. These novel creations, some of which had not entered either the dictionaries or the print media at the time of analysis, can be seen as a confirmation of the fact that climate change debate was expanding beyond the narrow circle of scientists, policymakers, and journalists.

The rhetorical effects will, of course, depend on who is using the compounds, and the study of semantic associations should be followed by the analysis of specific contexts characterizing the online uses. Nerlich and Koteyko (2009), for example, have examined the multiple meanings of the compound *carbon indulgence* in online newspapers and blogs, revealing divergent voices, including reactions to the official messages about climate change. The study of metaphoric compounds as nodes for different arguments can help us establish a more complex and multifaceted picture of how collaborative meaning creation takes place in online spaces.

Concluding Remarks

Studies in the rhetorical tradition have demonstrated how metaphors can be adapted to suit various argumentative purposes, changing meanings across different contexts and over time. This chapter has outlined how a combination of tools from corpus linguistics and webometrics that allow learning about specific texts and their life on the Web can help reveal some of these processes as well as point to instances that warrant further attention in relation to the use of metaphors online. Those pursuing rhetorical studies of public engagement with science, as well as digital humanities scholars more broadly, will therefore benefit from using the corpus linguistic techniques outlined here as a guide to popular topics, creative verbal/conceptual entities, and evaluative tendencies in large collections of text.

The analysis first established how the carbon compounds started to be used in online media in the early 1990s, gained popularity after 2000, and reached a peak in usage in 2008. Next, the concordance-driven approach provided an opportunity for a systematic analysis of the varied contexts in which these metaphoric coinages were used during the more limited time period of one year. Both studies capitalize on the potential of metaphors as a versatile tool to communicate different approaches to, values in relation to, and attitudes to the complex and urgent problem of climate change and, therefore, also promote public participation.

Thus, the patterns of language use around already institutionalized compounds such as *carbon offsetting* and *carbon footprint* helped reveal instances where these metaphors enable and promote a collective search for meaning as well as reveal loci of contestation and disagreement. In other instances, we observed a creative coinage of new compounds. In these more recent word combinations, the head nouns were found to harbor allusions to cultural/religious themes in order to express a critical stance toward a variety of objects and scientific and policy processes: the market-based strategies of carbon offsetting and trading, the increasing politicization of climate change issue, as well as the moralization of carbon reduction activities.

Grounded in discourse analysis, the approaches outlined above recognize that, whether face-to-face or digitally mediated, acts of communication have material consequence and that language plays a crucial role in establishing social norms. This means acknowledging that online discourses about scientific advancements and policy solutions have the potential to marginalize certain groups as the Internet is embedded in the long-standing economic and cultural structures.

The analytic tools discussed here hold future promise for examining online media and blog reactions to environment-related events and the interrelation between the two media. Compared to studies that use opinion surveys relying on recollections of feelings and activities in relation to media coverage of science, studying online activities provides a more situated picture of engagement with science and policy news. Additionally, the immediate availability of data enables scholars to examine popular responses to events as they occur and not long after they have been superseded by other events in the fast-flowing world of online news, discussions, and comments.

Notes

I would like to thank Professor Brigitte Nerlich and Professor Mike Thelwall for their valuable comments on earlier versions of this chapter. Funding from the Economic and Social Research Council, grant no. RES-062-23-1256, is gratefully acknowledged.

1.   A keyword-based study is necessarily limited and will miss texts that do not contain the terms of interest.

References

Anthony, L. 2005. "AntConc: Design and Development of a Freeware Corpus Analysis Toolkit for the Technical Writing Classroom." *Proceedings of Professional Communication Conference*, 729–37. New York: IEEE Xplore.

Baker, P., C. Gabrielatos, M. Khosravinik, M. Krzyzanowski, T. McEnery, and R. Wodak. 2008. "A Useful Methodological Synergy? Combining Critical Discourse Analysis and Corpus Linguistics to Examine Discourses of Refugees and Asylum Seekers in the UK Press." *Discourse and Society* 19.3:273–306.

Brossard, D., and D. A. Scheufele. 2013. "Science, New Media and the Public." *Science* 339.6115:40–41.

Condit, C., J. Lynch, and E. Winderman. 2012. "Recent Rhetorical Studies in Public Understanding of Science: Multiple Purposes and Strengths." *Public Understanding of Science* 21:386–400.

Eden, S. 1996. "Public Participation in Environmental Policy: Considering Scientific, Counter-Scientific and Non-Scientific Contributions." *Public Understanding of Science* 5:183–204.

Gross, Alan G. 1996. *The Rhetoric of Science*. Cambridge, MA: Harvard University Press.

Hauser, Gerald A. 2007. "Vernacular Discourse and the Epistemic Dimension of Public Opinion." *Communication Theory* 17.4:333–39.

Jaspal, R., B. Nerlich, and N. Koteyko. In press. "Contesting Science by Appealing to Its Norms: Readers Discuss Climate Science in the *Daily Mail*." *Science Communication*.

Jordan, J. 2004. "The Rhetorical Limits of the 'Plastic Body.'" *Quarterly Journal of Speech* 90.3:327–58.

Koteyko, N. 2009. "'I am a very happy, lucky lady, and I am full of Vitality!' Online Promotional Strategies of Probiotic Yoghurt Producers." *Critical Discourse Studies* 6.2:111–25.

———. 2010. "Mining the Internet for Linguistic and Social Data: An Analysis of 'Carbon Compounds' in Web Feeds." *Discourse and Society* 21.6:655–74.

Koteyko, N., R. Jaspal, and B. Nerlich. 2013. "Climate Change and 'Climategate' in Online Reader Comments: A Mixed Methods Study." *Geographical Journal* 179.1:74–86.

Koteyko, N., M. Thelwall, and B. Nerlich. 2010. "From Carbon Markets to Carbon Morality: Creative Compounds as Framing Devices in Online Discourses on Climate Change Mitigation." *Science Communication* 32.1:25–54.

MacKenzie, D., and J. Wajcman, eds. 1999. *The Social Shaping of Technology*. Buckingham: Open University Press.

Nerlich, B. 2012. "'Low Carbon' Metals, Markets and Metaphors: The Creation of Economic Expectations about Climate Change Mitigation." *Climatic Change* 110:31–51.

Nerlich, B., and N. Koteyko. 2009. "Compounds, Creativity and Complexity in Climate Change Communication: The Case of 'Carbon Indulgences.'" *Global Environmental Change* 19:345–53.

O'Neill, S., and M. Boykoff. 2011. "The Role of New Media in Engaging the Public with Climate Change." In *Engaging the Public with Climate Change: Communication and Behaviour Change*, ed. L. Whitmarsh, S. J. O'Neill, and I. Lorenzoni, 234–51. London: Earthscan.

Partington, A. 2010. "Modern Diachronic Corpus-Assisted Discourse Studies (MD-CADS) on UK Newspapers: An Overview of the Project." *Corpora* 52:83–108.

Pettenger, Mary E. 2007. *The Social Construction of Climate Change: Power, Knowledge, Norms, Discourses*. Aldershot: Ashgate.

Ratto, M. 2006. "Foundations and Profiles: Splicing Metaphors in Genetic Databases and Biobanks." *Public Understanding of Science* 15.1:31–53.

Reddy, M. J. 1979. "The Conduit Metaphor: A Case of Frame Conflict in Our Language about Language." In *Metaphor and Thought*, ed. A. Ortony, 284–310. Cambridge: Cambridge University Press.

Russill, C. 2011. "Temporal Metaphor in Abrupt Climate Change Communication: An Initial Effort at Clarification." In *Social, Economic and Political Aspects of Climate Change*, ed. W. L. Filho, 113–33. Berlin: Springer.

Scott, M. 2011. *WordSmith Tools Version 6 Lexical Analysis Software*. Liverpool.

Stubbs, M. 1996. *Text and Corpus Analysis: Computer-Assisted Studies of Language and Culture*. Oxford: Blackwell.

Thelwall, M. 2009. *Introduction to Webometrics: Quantitative Web Research for the Social Sciences*. San Rafael, CA: Morgan & Claypool.

Thelwall, M., R. Prabowo, and R. Fairclough. 2006. "Are Raw RSS Feeds Suitable for Broad Issue Scanning? A Science Concern Case Study." *Journal of the American Society for Information Science and Technology* 57.12:1644–54.

Thurlow, C., and K. Mroczek. 2011. *Digital Discourse: Language in the New Media*. New York: Oxford University Press.

Ungar, S. 2007. Public Scares: Changing the Issue Culture. In *Creating a Climate for Change: Communicating Climate Change and Facilitating Social Change*, ed. S. Moser and L. Dilling, 81–88. Cambridge: Cambridge University Press.

Väliverronen, E., and I. Hellsten. 2002. "From 'Burning Library' to 'Green Medicine': The Role of Metaphors in Communicating Biodiversity." *Science Communication* 24:229–45.

Ward, B. 2008. *2008's Year-long Fall-Off in Climate Coverage: Tracking the Trends, and the Reasons behind Them*. Yale Forum on Climate Change and the Media. http://www.yaleclimatemediaforum.org.

Wynne, B. 1991. "Knowledges in Context." *Science, Technology and Human Values* 16.1:111–21.

## PART THREE

Future Trajectories

## FOURTEEN

Digitizing English

JENNIFER GLASER

LAURA R. MICCICHE

In 2011–12, we team-taught and curated a year-long grad-uate course and lecture series focused on the digital hu-manities (DH), accessible at ropesuc.wordpress.com (the password for the Schedule page is "ropes"). Neither of us claimed DH as an area of expertise or even a niche area of scholarship, but we both felt that students should know how academics and creative thinkers of all sorts are doing digitality. We came to the course from our training in, re-spectively, American literature and rhetoric and composi-tion. Again and again, we found ourselves on uncertain ground—what content to include? speakers to invite? as-signments to require? issues to emphasize? Not very of-ten do either of us direct a graduate seminar in areas to which we ourselves are relative newcomers. We came to view our neophyte status as a valuable standpoint from which to imagine how our own work might be trans-formed in light of DH and to recognize the following tru-isms embedded in our students' frequent resistance to DH as a framework for meaning making in the twenty-first century:

- In general, in our English Department, and in the programs where our doctoral students earned their M.F.A.s and M.A.s, print is still largely treated as the default medium—a kind of in-visible nonmedium—through which texts are consumed, pro-duced, and delivered.

- Digital knowledge-making practices are viewed as peripheral to idea generation and composing even as most writers use word processors to draft and social media while composing.
- The stable, solitary "writer" figure stubbornly persists as the most credible manifestation of the author function.
- Collaboration is approached suspiciously because it is perceived as a threat to one's "real" work.

These beliefs reveal more about the failures of English departments to deal with changing realities than they do the quality of students who participated in our seminar. As a field, we ought to do better; we ought to be readying our students to imagine themselves in radically transformed work environments. Digitizing the English department, by which we mean applying principles of innovation, collaboration, and creativity learned through DH theory and practice, can help us move toward this goal. Not a magical antidote, DH represents a realistic and viable future for a field mourning a primarily textual past. It also recuperates rhetorical study within English departments. Through its emphasis on the rhetoric of design, theory and practice, orality and argumentation (as captured in wide-circulation online videos), and research methods like data visualization and close/distant reading, DH explicitly values the rhetorical dimensions of meaning making. In turn, rhetoric figures as much more than the stuff of required writing classes in English departments; it expands "the humanities' longstanding commitment to scholarly interpretation, informed research, structured argument, and dialogue within communities of practice" (Burdick, Drucker, Lunenfeld, Presner, and Schnapp 2012, 16).

The linguistic turn that continues to organize the approach to literary and cultural theory no longer makes sense in the densely mediated visual and material environment inhabited by most students and professors. Theoretical paradigms are changing, but theory within English departments, on the whole, is not keeping pace. In this context, theory is typically approached as content applied to texts—whether print, digital, filmic, embodied, or otherwise. This limited-application mode helps contextualize the difficulty of importing theoretical models that are not exclusively committed to explaining a text's meanings, ambiguities, uses, and ideological functions. Indeed, resistance to nonliterary theory in English departments helps explain why new materialism and other theories that bring materiality to the fore (i.e., actor-network theory, affect theory, DH, and material feminism) have been slow to infiltrate English curricula even as these ideas have been in circulation for more than ten years in one form or another.

Also fundamental to the conservative cast of English departments is a distinctly narrow idea of what scholarship is and can be, particularly in literary studies. Like many programs in the humanities, the English department is structured around an outdated model of expertise that discourages faculty members from straying outside a narrow period and methodological approach or conceiving of the audience for their work in anything but the most insular terms. And insularity breeds delusions of influence. N. Katherine Hayles points out that "the open secret about humanities print publications is their extremely low subscription rates and, beyond this, the shockingly small rate at which articles are cited (and presumably read)" (2012, 3). The same is true for most academic books—a fact made patently clear by the economic duress under which many academic presses currently labor (Brown, Griffiths, and Rascoff 2007). Nonetheless, despite the limited audience for academic print publication and the increasing difficulty experienced by junior faculty in publishing conventional, dissertation-based monographs with academic presses, the expectations for credentialing and tenure within the academy primarily focus on traditional print publications (i.e., Fitzpatrick 2011; and Jaschik 2009). Despite the increasing ubiquity of digital journals and presses, the popularity of academic and literary blogs, and projects like Anvil Academic, "a new press that aims to bring scholarly rigor to publishing digital projects," digital forms of publication scarcely permeate how the English department conceives of itself and, not surprisingly, how its members imagine an audience for their work (Koh 2012). This cleaving to outmoded ideas of expertise and address limits the viability of the English department and the humanities in the wider world.

Unfortunately, many of us communicate these narrow ideas about the appropriate audience for academic work to graduate students by suggesting that they write for an audience of specialists and submit work to academic journals, publications, and conferences exclusively, rarely suggesting more widely read and distributed outlets for intellectual work. In effect, we train students in our own image for jobs that are becoming increasingly rare. Michael Bérubé, a former president of the Modern Language Association, recently pointed out that graduate programs in English are currently doing little to address the exigencies of the academic job market and the inability of most graduates to attain tenure-track employment (Patton 2012). Graduate curricula, often organized by genre, time period, or author, remain largely stagnant, doing little to reflect shifts in how knowledge is organized and disseminated in the wider world or prepare students for the kinds of jobs they might get after obtaining their degrees. We believe that the theory and practice of DH—particularly its focus on collaboration, innovation, and forms of media that include and exceed print—can open up new vistas for graduate students and faculty alike.

The issue of how we train our students is intimately linked to a number of larger questions of identity. How does the humanities contribute to culture and to public conversations about learning, thinking, communicating, feeling, and meaning-making activities in general? Who constitutes the audience for our work beyond colleagues working in the same areas? Can we make ourselves indispensable to creative activity of all kinds both within and beyond the university? How might English departments borrow from the ideology and conceptual apparatus of DH—not to mention its focus on materiality—to become more explicitly relevant to twenty-first-century language practices, analyses, and studies, the likes of which are commonly encountered in the *New York Times Magazine*, *Slate*, and *The Daily Show with Jon Stewart*, among other popular venues?

Taking these questions as a jumping-off point for some recommendations aimed at digitizing English, we offer remarks organized into the following overlapping categories: *thinking with dh*; *creating collaboratives*; *reorganizing english*; and *going public*.

Thinking with DH

Digitizing English should take a number of forms, not all of which necessitate that teachers and students read, create, and share digital work, though we enthusiastically endorse such efforts. We have realized through our immersion in DH that the *mind-set*, or way of seeing the present and envisioning the future, communicated through this work can be just as potentially transformative as the practices. In other words, thinking like DH practitioners and theorists is a significant part of what we mean by *digitizing English*. For example, such thinking has led us to understand *work* as *belonging to* a community rather than to a single author, a view that makes it possible to conceive knowledge making and teaching as curatorial and distributed. In practical terms, this means that academic labor and its purposes can be conceived differently. Collaborative writing and teaching, for example, represent forms of distributed labor that build networks of scholars and that, in turn, have the potential to generate surprising and valuable collectives (more on this idea below). In a different register, the curatorial dimensions of creative and critical work are exuberantly evident in the work of online archivists like Charles Bernstein, Kenneth Goldsmith, and Craig Dworkin. Bernstein, along with Al Filreis and Michael S. Hennessey, curates PennSound, the largest collection of Web-based audio poetry recordings, all of which are available for free download. PennSound (and, earlier, the Electronic Poetry Center at the State University of New York at Buffalo) marries the work of a traditional scholarly archive to a more radical aesthetic and curatorial project—serving a global community of poets, critics, and teachers while also inventing new audiences for poetry who can engage it as a performative art rather than one that exists exclusively on the page. Projects like PennSound advertise the possibility of moving art and critical practice beyond the walls of the university—a point made clear to our students when Bernstein and Goldsmith visited our course to discuss their curatorial practices.

Creating Collaboratives

DH scholars make very clear the importance of institutionalizing collaboratives, or what Alan Liu calls working in "the seams of the academy" (2009, 21). Liu uses this unassuming description to refer to the centers he has helped build at the University of California, Santa Barbara. He describes the cross-departmental collaboration emerging from these centers as a way to build distributed intellectual collectives: "The idea is not to build strength in new intellectual areas by exiling the best minds into inter-, meta-, or para-organizational entities located outside departments. Instead, the goal is to build up thick nodes of people . . . inside a particular department; then link by elective affinity with similar nodes forming in other departments" (2009, 24). He is not talking about the duplication of relations within departments, which often exert a provincial model of ownership over knowledge. He wants to amplify intellectual and technological resources; make membership bigger, not smaller; more inclusive, not less; more of a quest for new knowledges, not codification of knowledge through the conservative effects of disciplinarity. The implication is that, among other things, research becomes more varied and methodological diversity becomes absolutely crucial in the drive to develop what Liu calls a *global humanities* that explicitly minimizes affiliation and increases relational nodes and creative thinking across sites of knowledge making. Scholars like Liu are showing us that disciplinary "pollution" is creating a paradigm shift in the knowledge economy. Purity, exclusivity, and isolationism are sacred heteronormative dreams that lead us back to ourselves, to reproduction, to necessary exclusions and illusions.

Our university, the University of Cincinnati, has begun to help faculty work in the seams by institutionalizing collaboratives through an initiative called UC Forward, spear-headed by the provost's office, aimed at driving innovation both within the university and beyond it. One goal is to aggressively confront the changed environments and conditions in which students will presumably find themselves on graduation. The initiative funds transdisciplinary collaborative projects that bring together a network of faculty who focus on compelling questions, experiential learning, and grounded research. In effect, UC Forward recognizes that knowledge is "iterative, cumulative, and collaborative" (UCLA Mellon Seminar 2011, 7). If we were to take this idea to heart, we might consider training scholars to work with other purveyors of culture and entertainment—from librarians and archivists to museum curators, filmmakers, and graphic designers. This push to extend knowledge work outside traditional boundaries might extend to how we develop and implement curricula as well. Organizing English areas or tracks around doing things, such as archiving, writing for publics, or participating in human rights activism, offers one way of reenvisioning our departments.

Reorganizing English

DH as ideology and practice can help us challenge what counts as English in at least two ways. First, it provides inspiration for revising English so that it rotates not around literary production and reception but around practices of making. One possible model, for example, could be organized around writing practices. This focus would make possible multidirectional, cross-sectional relations between and among subfields, all of which cohere around writing in one way or another. To foreground writing relations among English department members is to make powerful our collective emotional and intellectual attachments to language, its transcription, diversity, and effects. It is also to organize collectives around an *activity*—writing—rather than around subject matter, methods, or theory. Speaking of *writing practices* instead of discrete areas like *literature, creative writing,* or *cultural studies* insists on our entanglements with one another rather than suppressing them in the continual struggle for a fair take of diminishing resources. It also subverts the division between production, associated with rhetorical studies, and consumption, linked to literary studies, that has long plagued English department workings.

Another potential way to reorganize English is to foreground media that include and exceed print, prodding scholars to think more deeply about the connection between medium and materiality in their own work and, thereby, making it harder to take technologies of text making for granted. In their introduction to the conference "New Materialisms and Digital Culture," Jussi Parikka and Milla Tiainen contend that new approaches to digital media ask us to think beyond traditional notions of medium. They suggest that, "instead of being only something that in a Kantian manner prevents access to the world of the real or material, or things [Brown 2010, 51] . . . , the medium itself becomes a material assemblage." Rather than seeing the world as coherent through "symbolic, signifying structures, or representations," new materialists foreground "a network of concrete, material, physical and physiological apparatuses and their interconnections" (Parikka and Tiainen 2010). Focusing on the ways in which technology circumscribes our utterances and practices of signification would allow scholars in English to get beyond the domesticated views of language and textuality that undergird traditional literary theory and the widely used resources that support it. For example, the online pedagogical resource *Introductory Guide to Critical Theory* (Felluga 2002), which has received over ten million hits since its inception, is organized by the following familiar categories: *gender and sex, Marxism, narratology, new historicism, postmodernism*, and *psychoanalysis* (for a similar breakdown, see Richter 2000; Tyson 2006; and Waugh 2006). The remarkable similarity from one volume to the next gives an idea of how theory, both literary and critical (often conflated), is regularly conceptualized and taught within university settings. This limited context for engaging with theory no doubt characterizes a mind-set about the work of English departments that has relevance to DH and its uptake. A focus on new materialism would push scholars to transcend these tired categories and open their work to theories of matter, affect, and embodiment that have long held sway in other disciplines.

In addition, an expanded view of materiality would make indisputable the fact that *digital* is not synonymous with *immaterial*. While the seeming ephemerality of cloud computing and data storage tends to provoke a general sense that digitality is nowhere and everywhere, Lisa

Nakamura (2012) made clear that real bodies guide virtual experiences, a painfully obvious point in her analyses of the hate speech pervasive to gaming environments. To paraphrase N. Katherine Hayles, digitality does indeed have a body, and it is time for textual and rhetorical studies within English departments to start paying better attention to this reality. We can no longer justify bracketing digital media in favor of doing English in what ultimately amounts to a rarified way.

A second challenge to English as traditionally organized, and related to the above, is that DH offers an exigence for departments to theorize beyond the imagined divide between scholars and practitioners, researchers and creative writers. In a provocative list of recommendations to English departments on his Web site, Alan Liu argues: "The assumptions that divide, and unite, 'literary interpretation' and 'creative writing' in a literature department should be rethought in a larger social context that privileges over both poles of that binary such goals as 'innovation,' 'collaboration,' and 'entertainment'" (Liu 2008). English departments have long witnessed the collision precisely between these long-cherished ideas about the role of the artist and the scholar as well as their binary oppositions. Embracing new media forces us to challenge this exhausted opposition, pushing both creative writers and scholars to historicize their own practices and recognize that "the Age of Print is passing, and the assumptions, presuppositions, and practices associated with it are now becoming visible as media-specific practices rather than the largely invisible status quo" (Hayles 2012, 2). For starters, English departments need to embrace recent trends in literary scholarship that capitalize on this gradual recognition and position literature in a manner with equal resonance for academic and creative writers. Work in the sociology of literature, such as James English's *The Economy of Prestige* (2005) and Mark McGurl's *The Program Era* (2009), focus on print culture but do so in a way that historicizes and destabilizes reified notions of literary and cultural value while illuminating the mutually constitutive relationship between writers and literary taste makers.

At the same time, scholars and creatives should collaborate on projects that marry their mutual interests. The Stanford Storytelling Project, for example, envisions its role as using new media to join scholars and students in the humanities and arts. The project is described as "a new arts program at Stanford University that explores how we live in and through stories and how we can use them to change our lives." For the last four years, it has sponsored workshops, courses, a student journal, and a radio program/podcast that "brings together stories that deepen our understanding of single, common human experiences—fighting, giving, lying, forgiveness—all drawn from the experiences and research of the Stanford community" (http://www.stanford.edu/group/storytelling/cgi-bin/joomla, "About Us"). Recent broadcasts have focused on the experiences of student veterans at Stanford and the state of living in between one place or condition and another, and the program has given grants to undergraduates who want to research oral histories or translate their written research into audio narratives.

Going Public

The concept of the commons animates discussions about the future of the humanities in a variety of disciplines. Yet, until recently, English departments have participated in this conversation only in the constipated vernacular of the culture wars and the canon debates. DH—and particularly its blurring of the line between academic and public contexts—offers a way of crafting a public voice for the humanities that could lead to collective action. A number of public humanities programs are using DH as an inspiration to participate in social justice and advocacy as well as archival activity with a social purpose. The University of Iowa's Center for Public Humanities in a Digital World explicitly draws its mission from DH and the idea that scholars in the humanities are well equipped to describe and understand the role of the subject in the age of new media. The center's goal is "to create an energetic community of multidisciplinary scholars, including current digital artists and scholars, University of Iowa faculty members and graduate students who seek to develop digital expertise, and newly hired colleagues with expertise in the digital humanities and interests in publicly engaged scholarship" (http://www.uiowa.edu/~phdw/vision.html). In order to support this mission, they fund hiring initiatives, faculty seed grants, a public DH center, lectures and symposia, and collaborative work with local secondary schools and cultural institutions. By thinking about the digital as always already public in fundamental ways, such centers are advocating for humanities scholars to participate in wider cultural debates. What is happening at Iowa is not an anomaly; similar programs have emerged at Brown University, Yale University, and Portland State University. We believe that a widespread embrace of efforts to link the humanities and digital media can construct new and evolving sites of relevance for humanities research, an outcome that is crucial for the future of the humanities.

Our collaboration—teaching the DH course, organizing a tandem lecture series, and writing this meditation on doing digitality—has functioned as a metaexercise in reenvisioning our roles in the English department and our relation to the work we do. Perhaps more importantly, our students began to do the same, as was evident in the work they produced for the course. We close with brief descriptions of select student projects that give us a hopeful glimpse of a digitized English:

- Digital installation using video with voice-over exploring the role of technology in the Occupy movement.
- Prezi focused on the intersection of materiality and genre in graphic or sequential narratives.
- Hand-coded poems that displayed the semantic richness of coding as a vehicle for lyrical language.
- Multimedia presentation demonstrating how writing students can create an online archive to house diverse materials—photos, text, audio, video, handwritten, scanned texts, cartoons, etc.—related to a larger project.
- Photoshopped images exploring one student's experiences with prosopagnosia, or face blindness, and aimed at analyzing the limitations of a heavily visually mediated environment.
- Digital book trailer for a student's short story collection that unpacked the conventions of the genre and positioned trailers as operating at the intersection of aesthetics, book and Web publishing, and constructions of readers and authors.

References

Brown, Bill. 2010. "Materiality." In *Critical Terms for Media Studies*, ed. W. J. T. Mitchell and Mark B. N. Hansen, 49–63. Chicago: University of Chicago Press.

Brown, Laura, Rebbeca Griffiths, and Matthew Rascoff. 2007. "University Publishing in a Digital Age." *Journal of Electronic Publishing* 10.3. doi: 10.3998/3336451.0010.301.

Burdick, Anne, Johanna Drucker, Peter Lunenfeld, Todd Presner, and Jeffrey Schnapp. 2012. *Digital Humanities*. Cambridge, MA: MIT Press.

English, James. 2005. *The Economy of Prestige: Prizes, Awards, and the Circulation of Cultural Value*. Cambridge, MA: Harvard University Press.

Felluga, Dino. 2002. *Introductory Guide to Critical Theory*. www.purdue.edu/guidetotheory/introduction.

Fitzpatrick, Kathleen. 2011. *Planned Obsolescence: Publishing, Technology, and the Future of the Academy*. New York: New York University Press.

Hayles, N. Katherine. 2012. *How We Think: Digital Media and Technogenesis*. Chicago: University of Chicago Press.

Jaschik, Scott. 2009. "Tenure in the Digital Age." *Inside Higher Ed*, March 26. http://www.insidehighered.com/news/2009/05/26/digital.

Koh, Adeline. 2012. "A ProfHacker TweetChat with Anvil Academic: Presenting Digital Work for Promotion and Tenure." *Chronicle of Higher Education*, October 8. http://chronicle.com/blogs/profhacker/a-profhacker -tweetchat-with-anvil-academic-presenting-digital-work-for-promotion -and-tenure/43202.

Liu, Alan. 2008. "Suggestions for a 21st Century English Department." http:// liu.english.ucsb.edu/suggestions-for-a-21st-century-english-department.

———. 2009. "Digital Humanities and Academic Change." *English Language Notes* 47.1:17–35.

McGurl, Mark. 2009. *The Program Era: Postwar Fiction and the Rise of Creative Writing*. Cambridge, MA: Harvard University Press.

Nakamura, Lisa. 2012. "Flag as Inappropriate: Racism, Sexism, and Homophobia in Online Games." Lecture presented at the University of Cincinnati.

Parikka, Jussi, and Milla Tiainen. 2010. "What Is New Materialism?—Opening Words." June 23. http://machinology.blogspot.com/2010/06/what-is-new -materialism-opening-words.html.

Patton, Stacey. 2012. "MLA President Offers a Sobering Critique of Graduate Education in the Humanities." *Chronicle of Higher Education*, December 6. http://chronicle.com/article/A-Stark-Appraisal-of-Graduate/136171.

Richter, David H. 2000. *Falling into Theory: Conflicting Views on Reading Literature*. 2nd ed. Boston: Bedford/St. Martin's.

Tyson, Lois. 2006. *Critical Theory Today: A User-Friendly Guide*. 2nd ed. New York: Routledge.

UCLA Mellon Seminar. 2011. "The Digital Humanities Manifesto 2.0." August 25. http://www.humanitiesblast.com/manifesto/Manifesto_V2.pdf.

Waugh, Patricia. 2006. *Literary Theory and Criticism: An Oxford Guide*. Oxford: Oxford University Press.

## FIFTEEN

In/Between Programs: Forging a Curriculum between Rhetoric and the Digital Humanities

DOUGLAS WALLS

In February of 2012, the director of programs for my home department, the Department of Writing and Rhetoric at the University of Central Florida, asked me to participate in a multidisciplinary summer workshop to propose and build a cross-department undergraduate minor in digital humanities (DH).[1] I had recently finished working with colleagues in the Department of Writing and Rhetoric on our proposal for a B.A. major in writing and rhetoric. I was excited for the opportunity to help build alliances with other departments on campus; however, I was also aware of the challenges that can temper that excitement. As someone with a multidisciplinary background,[2] I am sensitive to the genuine differences between fields that can often be overlooked in designing curriculum. The Department of Writing and Rhetoric is a small unit in terms of research faculty and has existed only since 2010, while the Center for Digital Humanities and the English Department are established units within the college. Additionally, both the Department of History and the School of Visual Arts and Design were invited to be part of the DH minor initiative. Given the large number of institutional actors involved, how would the initiative benefit each participating unit within the university? Would the minor be good for our department, or would we trade our own valuable time and resources to an initiative that would not help our own mission? Would we lose minors to this new program and, therefore, funding? These are the questions I faced when I was asked to assess our potential contributions to the proposed minor. Others may face these questions in the field of rhetoric and writing studies when strategizing participation in DH initiatives.

In my own case example, I begin with the most troubling question offered to me during the development of the DH minor: Should our flagship course, "Writing in Digital Environments," be categorized as a theory or a tools course? "Writing in Digital Environments" was one of the most suitable classes that the Department of Writing and Rhetoric could offer to the new minor. The committee had decided that each new course offering in the proposed minor would have one or the other designation. The implication for the course being categorized as theory is that there is less time for students to practice with digital tools. While I understood the "building things" aspect of the course to be at the core of the DH ethos (Stephen Ramsay quoted in Gold 2012, x), the class "Writing in Digital Environments" is more importantly about the rhetorical concept of praxis (theory and action) and gnosis (critical interpretation) where we both *theorize* and then *make* digital things. The goal is to re*theorize* the work of making new things in a tight recursive process. Rhetoricians may read the course goals and objectives as expanding the scope of where and how rhetoric matters. But this was not true for other colleagues. While I certainly knew where the class fit in the writing and rhetoric major, I was taken aback at how I was being asked by scholars outside my own discipline to categorize our flagship course offering. I was worried about how in a DH curriculum these same goals and objectives break the way that the DH are ordered, at least in our minor, and disrupt expectations. Was I involved in a shared value of curricular production between rhetoric and DH? Or was I wrong in thinking that our rhetoric and writing courses converge with DH?

Histories of Alliances

There are many stories and more questions about rhetoric and DH, but one question seems most important to answer before a curriculum designer can decide on the relative purposes of theories, tools, and learning for digital humanists and rhetoricians. Who are we?[3] What is rhetoric? What is/are DH? These are questions that are asked by many in our own departments, and they may be questions asked by administrations seeking to eliminate units without adequate answers. Not that there needs to be a single answer, but we must have answers. So, if I begin with a story about rhetoric as opposed to DH, and I locate that conversation in the twentieth century as opposed to the fifth century BCE, it is not because I think that is the only place to start. I choose to begin with the twentieth century because that is where tensions in pedagogical mission and curriculum design are happening for rhetoric, something that might sound familiar to those in DH. I begin by asking questions that rhetoric has continually asked itself. What role should rhetoric play in the lives of students? How do we teach both praxis and gnosis of textual and oral performances?

Mailloux (2000), for example, begins his story of rhetoric by connecting how and why the disciplines of English and speech drew on rhetoric in the early twentieth century. He points to the creation of the National Council of Teachers of English, founded in 1911 as a response to the Modern Language Association of America's emerging "preoccupation" with research (Mailloux 2000, 6). By 1915, however, speech and autonomous speech departments had called for a separateness from English departments—not rhetoric, mind you—claiming methodological basis, not pedagogy, for the rationale. The study of speech was seen as a scientific pursuit, whereas the study of English was an interpretive art. Mailloux points out, however, that in the early part of the twentieth century some speech teachers decided to ally with more scientific disciplines because of their sense of subordination to other colleagues in English departments. It was not, however, that they abandoned rhetoric. They still taught public speaking. Rhetoric was the go-between.

This did not settle the issues involved in the speech/writing or science/humanities discussions, however. According to George and Trimbur (1999, 682), in its bylaws and constitution the Conference on College Composition and Communication (CCCC) of 1952 sought "to unite teachers of college composition and communication." In 1962 the outgoing CCCC chair, Francis E. Bowman, declared: "[The] 'communication' battle is over'" (George and Trimbur 1999, 682). This declaration coincided roughly with the publishing of three rhetorical texts that located rhetoric study as an act of hermeneutic interpretation over scientific knowledge making (Mailloux 2000). Rhetoric, it seems, had come back to the fold and now held court over scientific episteme at least in the interpretive realm.

Rather than becoming its own department, rhetoric ended up being nested with others, namely, English literature, with its emphasis on critical consumption of texts, and communication, with its focus on quantifiable methods. There was even more ebb and flow of rhetoric past the 1960s. To be sure, rhetoric has moved back and forth between science and the hermeneutic, between qualitative and quantitative, and between productive and interpretive methodologies. It has made homes in stand-alone programs, English programs, technical writing and communication, speech communication, and communication programs, but, in each of these disciplines, it also holds on to mandates dependent on undergraduate teaching missions.[4] It has depended on alliances. Rhetoric has been able to be research productive with a number of important journals by being nested. So how can a field with so many different and changing methodologies and objects of inquiry be so disciplinarily promiscuous and still remain stable enough to gather resources?

Rhetoric has been able to survive, at least through most of the twentieth century and into the twenty-first, as a direct result of two educational imperatives. First, as an undergraduate mandate, rhetoric has never gone away because someone has always thought that young people should be able to speak and write better. Second, and deeply related to the first point, someone has had to produce professors who theorize about and teach undergraduates how to speak and/or write better not in *their* class exclusively but in other contexts (Phelps 1988; Berlin 2003). These two needs have been what has sustained rhetoric in many institutions where it might otherwise have died. What can be said of this is that, despite the ebb and flow of research methodology popularity, what institutions have always valued about rhetoric has been its educational mission to improve the praxis and gnosis of textual and oral production. These have been rhetoric's killer apps, if you will, and they have allowed the discipline the flexibility to move back and forth in its research methodologies. They have also been useful in building alliances with other departments and administration (Berlin 2003; Bloom 1998).

Forging Digital Trade Routes and Rhetoric of Alliance

What I am attempting to forge, to craft, and to make with this chapter is a new sort of stance for rhetoric and DH based on mutual need. I think we are all at a point where both DH and rhetoric need to change and adapt by understanding the connectedness that we share both in terms of research and in terms of curriculum design. So when encountering questions like, Does this class belong in theory or tools? we need language that does not privilege one position over another. Rather, we seek to offer benefit in the exchange of stories, ideas, theories, tools, and pedagogies. I draw on a rhetoric of alliance to position DH and rhetoric as distinct entities that need to align with each other to create language that makes one potential "path" of exchange, one based on mutual respect rather than privileging.[5] I place this conversation with other "intellectual trade routes" efforts from Native scholars like Robert Warrior and Angela Haas wherein, as Haas states, the "reciprocal exchange of intellectual goods" (2008b, 97) is valued because it can be combined to make new forms of knowledge beneficial to all parties involved (see also Warrior 2005).

When I was asked the question about the positioning of a writing in digital environments class within the DH minor, I needed more language to exchange and build up relations or, as I am calling it here, *forge digital trade routes* with other departments interested in DH. I mean to forge digital trade routs here not only in the sense of moving forward but also in the sense of making *things* like paths and tools.[6] Powell positions rhetoric of alliance as a lens that Native peoples have used to respond to adaptation by examining their relation to change. Rhetoric of alliance is a Native American stance about rhetorical production of relations in the face of disruptive change (Powell 2004). A rhetoric of alliance is a language that helped Native people adapt their traditions for survival in a rapidly changing world by honoring, understanding, and respecting one another's beliefs and histories. It is not—and this is key—subordination or privileging of one belief system over another. As Powell claims: "We don't have to believe one another's beliefs, but we do have to acknowledge their importance, understand them as real, and respect/honor them in our dealings with one another" (2004, 42). A rhetoric of alliance is how we make digital trade routes. How we make connections. How we understand and position each other. How we can build things like curriculum or tools together rather than as competitors. I envision digital trade routes as making connections between rhetoric and DH not only in terms of the digital but also in terms of process, especially how we decide to offer those things to each other rather than to compete with each other. At the University of Central Florida, philosophy, history, English, digital media and arts, and rhetoric and writing all needed to band together to create the DH minor, but more can be done, and more conversations can happen, to ensure that mutual interests are served.

In essence, a rhetoric of alliance allows me to locate my conversation along a different trajectory about the relation between DH and rhetoric. I want to move away, at least in structure, from some previous conversations between DH and digital rhetoric where digital rhetoricians must affirm or deny "being" a digital humanist, such as happened at the 2011 Computers and Writing Conference town hall panel that asked, "Are you a digital humanist?" (Ball et al. 2011), or the subsequent 2012 Computers and Writing conference panel that affirmed, "Why yes, we are digital humanists!" (Gold et al. 2012), or substantial conversations that have taken place between scholars on the subject (Reid 2012). Not because those conversations are not productive, interesting, or important; I think that they can be important to other digital rhetoricians. However, I think that they have little to contribute to DH[7] and that they do little to address the curricular questions like the one asked of me. Belongingness conversations, useful as they may be, did not help me make decisions about my department's contributions to the university's DH minor or how to explain those contributions better to my fellow professors from other departments. A rhetoric of alliance like the one I am attempting to build here is "a new language, one that doesn't convince us of our unutterable and ongoing differences, one that doesn't force us to see one another as competitors," particularly in terms of institutional resources. So, taking Powell's advice and leadership, I seek here to make a rhetoric of alliance, a new language that is "respectful and reciprocal" between rhetoric and DH as well as one that acknowledges, as Powell puts it, "the degree to which we need one another . . . in order to survive and flourish" (2004, 41). So, while I focus here on pedagogy and curricular design, these are but two of many routes to be made. My hope is that, in the future, more routes are made between rhetoric and DH to create things like minors and majors together, building and articulating on what has already happened. I am not the first to see such possibilities, as I hope to show.

Theories and Tools or Praxis and Gnosis

It is not surprising to me to see quotes from computers and writing folks like Cynthia Selfe being used by Matthew Kirschenbaum (2012) to open up the first chapter of *Debates in the Digital Humanities* by way of explaining Selfe's (1988) use of the term *rhetoric of technopower*. Nor am I surprised to see rhetoric scholars like Alex Reid (2012) making smart arguments about the education and professional development of teaching assistants in the DH moment. Rhetoric has for some time had to think about how the digital transforms rhetorical practices not only in terms of production and reflection but also in terms of differing methodologies and digital technologies. The digital has already disrupted how we in rhetoric do things in terms of theory, practice, and interpretation.

If we look to work in DH on pedagogy, we can also see rhetoric scholars strongly represented. Bjork, for example, shows how both quantitative and qualitative methods can be deployed to make things in first year writing classrooms claiming that, "composition studies is moving toward digital humanities even as it moves away from the material humanities, or that the humanities, in becoming digital, have moved toward composition studies" (2012, 98).[8] In Bjork's case students make things through both qualitative and interpretive work and quantitative work. He goes on to describe how the creation of a multimedia text engages in deeply rhetorical concerns about delivery such as intellectual property, fair use, and the public domain (2012, 105) as well as engaging issues of textual appropriation in digital environments. As he describes the assignment, it is both productive and analytic. He adds to this a deeply quantitative project with roots in humanities computing and electronic text analysis. He has his students engage in electronic textual analysis by comparing a variety of features between a smaller corpus and a much larger one. For example, he has students do a feature comparison of "Shel Silverstein's children's books and his writings for adults" (2012, 114) that produces statistical counts of frequency and word variation. The numerical data of linguistic frequency are then interpreted. In each case, students are making and experimenting, making and theorizing.

Melanie Kill also strikes a similar balance, if not between qualitative and qualitative, then between production and analysis. Unlike Bjork's description of specific assignments, Kill's focus is on the use of projects that already involve and support digital rhetorical thinking through one particular Web site: *Wikipedia*. By asking students to engage with *Wikipedia*, she engages her students in "complex collaborative composing processes with civic-minded goals and public audiences." Rhetoric becomes a way to guide her students through both the "collaborative nature of knowledge-making" and the "skill in learning and working collaboratively" (2012, 390). Here, Kill is embracing not only a pedagogy that encourages production as both a theory and a practice but also a pedagogy and a politics that are deeply contingent and deeply collaborative in understanding texts, in other words, the praxis and gnosis of making things. Work like Kill's and Bjork's asks us to position theory and tools as highly integrated and in complex ways. They offer routes at the classroom level to help us think in new ways about praxis and gnosis. We must continue this work at the curricular level by listening, theorizing, and building together.

Future Needs, Future Fields, Future Trade

What I have tried to do here is describe a possible alliance between rhetoric studies and DH. That we have much more in common than we might suspect will surely not come as a surprise to those reading this volume. I am drawn to Powell's advice to make a rhetoric of alliance that is "respectful and reciprocal." In particular, we should not compete. We have much to learn from each other if we use the right language—language that respects our histories—and if we seek to add value to each other's conversations rather than to take resources from each other or to bend others to our way of doing things. With the chapter I have tried to offer a gift from rhetoric's disciplinary history of tensions between praxis and gnosis and how those tensions have played out in terms of educational mission in the twentieth century. I offer it not as instruction but as a gift. It is yours now; make of it what you will.[9]

None of this is to say that the road will be smooth. Clearly, there are still tensions in the digital rhetoric community (see Ball et al. 2011) as well as among those who have fought long and hard to develop a sense and body of digital pedagogy scholarship in rhetoric and want DH pedagogy to move beyond singular anecdotal examples (Ball 2103). I suspect, however, that there are many who want and are eager to engage DH's ability to transform pedagogy itself (Whitson 2013) and contend that to see research and pedagogy as competing relations is a false dichotomy (Hirsch 2012). Tensions manifest themselves and come to the forefront in projects that ask us to design curriculum (see Glaser and Micciche, in this volume).[10] If there is a language and a value that rhetoric and DH hold for undergraduate education, I think that it revolves around using theories to make things and around theorizing the things we make in robust ways.

If rhetoric and composition studies and DH listen to each other, we can help each other not only in understanding tensions between praxis and gnosis but also in making many curricular decisions. I am not sure what the killer app for DH is in undergraduate education yet, beyond something as basic as "the kids like technology!" I am sure the path to making one goes through praxis and gnosis. There are many chunks of DH that seem determined to develop one and to do so in a robust way. Despite that, Hirsch points out that pedagogy or teaching is frequently bracketed to "the almost systematic relegation of the word 'teaching' (or its synonyms) to the status of afterthought, tacked-on to a statement about the digital humanities after the word 'research' (or its synonyms), often in parentheses" (Hirsch 2012, 5), yet many of the projects that make their way to places like the *New York Times*, *Nature*, the *Boston Globe*, the *Chronicle of Higher Education*, and *Inside Higher Ed*—the stuff of nest big thing–ness (Gold 2012)—are projects that are public-outreach centered and deeply pedagogically focused. If DH has yet to settle on its own type of contribution to pedagogical work, I am encouraged to think that it will be collaborative and help undergraduates make things for themselves and their publics.

As a newcomer to DH, I suspect that the problem of whether to use the singular or the plural in connection with DH, as in "What is (or are) the 'digital humanities'?" (Kirschenbaum 2012, 431), along with other conversations about the size of DH's metaphoric tent, makes figuring out DH's pedagogical killer app more difficult. As Glaser and Micciche (in this volume) point, deep-seated assumptions about expertness and participation in research disciplines do not always make their way smoothly to curriculum design. I think that it might be only a matter of time and maybe even be something that rhetoric can help with as rhetoric learns more about digital tools. DH has yet to settle on the nature or terms of its own instability long enough to establish a pedagogical stance, but it should be wary of delay, lest administrators decide the terms for it.

For rhetoric programs, especially those located in English departments, creating trade routes seems especially important. While others might see DH's next big thing–ness attached to funding, rhetoric and composition programs located in English departments might see DH as a place to build connections: curriculum and pedagogies more in line with their own practices. Building trade routes with DH might be even more beneficial for rhetoric scholars nested in English or communication departments than for those in stand-alone units. Doing so allows for historical alliances to be maintained within home departments—and, perhaps, even improved—as those departments perceive value in digital rhetorical projects keeping curricular and administrative resources in house, as it were (Giberson and Moriarty 2010). Alternatively for rhetoric and compositionists, having alliances with other disciplines via DH may allow them to stay with whoever best supports rhetoric's curricular commitments. This may mean that uptake of DH may vary more with the pragmatic realities of administrative and organizational mandates than with any sort of internal or field-specific identity issues.

That our two fields need each other is not, I think, an exaggeration. I am aware that my new department's survival institutionally depends on making alliances with other academic units, but that is, really, just a synecdochic formation for the entire state of the humanities. While departments of rhetoric and writing are beginning to be a trend nationwide, they are hardly stable, and, despite the high-profile nature of DH work, sustainability and legitimacy continue to be issues for DH. For the sort of rhetoric of alliance in which I am asking us to engage we must go beyond reading each other's work and working on projects together. We must also understand pedagogy within our fields and engage with each other to legitimize and value the scholarship of teaching and learning as deeply important to our collective work. We have much to build and offer each other if we listen and if we do not repeat the mistakes of the past.

Notes

1. This is a story. Malea Powell (e.g., Powell 2004) begins much of her work with this same statement invoking the power of stories to shape and understand in the Native American rhetorical tradition as well as to offer respect to those rhetorical traditions and their explanatory power. I offer it in the same way Native scholars in rhetoric cited here offer their stories. Any credit for the usefulness I produce is all theirs, and any fault is my own.

2. I hold M.A.'s in both speech-communication and writing.

3. As with many humanities pursuits, there is much written about the history of rhetoric both as an academic and as a pedagogical pursuit from both a contested and a canonical perspective. In part, this is why I am limiting myself to (*a*) the twentieth century and (*b*) one particular article. For further reading, see Berlin (1987), Goggin (2000), and Hawk (2007). In particular, I found Beard (2010) particularly insightful for its take on rhetoric's changing status in one university.

4. Again, for a good tracing of how rhetoric could have moved through all these disciplinary spaces and missions in even a single university setting, see Beard (2010). I am also indebted to Beard for his use of *praxis* and *gnosis*, one that I expand on here.

5. For example, Gabriela Rios and I are working on integrating Native American rhetorics into community outreach and service learning work with the McNair Scholars program. Such work positions rhetoric and composition's history of community outreach and Native American rhetorics as equally informative and useful in the development of community engagement pedagogies.

6. I draw on the theory of rhetoric of alliance that has been a productive concept for me, allowing me to understand how and when to begin doing work together with those who are different from me. I draw on the mixed-blood Native American rhetorical scholar Malea Powell's work with rhetoric and alliance in trying to reconcile Native American rhetorical traditions with the European centered canon within the study of rhetoric (see Powell 2004, 39, 41). Powell positions rhetoric of alliance as ways that native peoples, specifically the Miami Confederacy, have traditionally responded to change and adaptation by understanding the connectedness of situationality. It comes from the practices that both Europeans and separate Native tribes engaged in by banding together in the face of aggressive European and European American imperial projects and has been a key factor in ongoing native peoples' projects of both survival and resistance in the face of change. Other than a distant claim of genetic ancestry, I make no claim to Native American culture or ways of knowing in the world other than those I have learned through listening to my Native academic elders like Malea Powell (2004) and Ellen Cushman (2011). I owe a particular debt to the digital rhetoric scholars of Native descent Angela Haas (2008) (for helping me think of intellectual trade routes focused on digital production) and Kristin Arola (2011).

7. My experience has been that scholars who identify primarily as digital humanists do not have similar conversations about whether they are or are not digital rhetoricians, though I might be able to make a case that they are (see, e.g., French and Ferster 2012). As a project, it engages and visualizes classic concerns of rhetoric such as delivery and invention in terms of persuasive impact.

8. Note also how Bjork positions composition as moving *toward* DH rather than as simply offering something to it.

9. I do not think that this is the only thing rhetoric has to offer DH in exchange for the many things DH has already offered and will continue to. For example, work in DH has been criticized from within itself for being too hegemonic in thinking in one form or another, as Bianco (2012) and McPherson (2012) point out. Those of us who balance digital and cultural rhetorics may have something to offer here (see Sano-Franchini, in this volume).

10. These tensions are something I recognized myself when I was asked to contribute to my university's DH minor.

References

Arola, Kristin L. 2011. "Listening to See: A Feminist Approach to Design Literacy." *Journal of Literacy and Technology* 12.1:65–105.

Ball, Cheryl E. 2013. "Logging On." *Kairos: A Journal of Rhetoric, Technology, and Pedagogy* 17.2. http://kairos.technorhetoric.net/17.2/loggingon/index.html.

Ball, Cheryl, Douglas Eyman, Julie Klein, Alex Reid, Virginia Kuhn, Jentery Sayers, and N. Katherine Hayles. 2011. "Are You a Digital Humanist?" Town Hall session at the 2011 Computers and Writing Conference, Ann Arbor, MI, May 21. http://vimeo.com/24388021.

Beard, David. 2010. "Dancing with Our Siblings: The Unlikely Case for a Rhetoric Major." In *What We Are Becoming: Developments in Undergraduate Writing Majors*, ed. Greg A. Giberson and Thomas A. Moriarty, 130–52. Logan: Utah State University Press.

Berlin, James A. 1987. *Rhetoric and Reality: Writing Instruction in American Colleges, 1900–1985*. Carbondale: Southern Illinois University Press.

Berlin, James A. 2003. *Rhetorics, Poetics, and Cultures: Refiguring College English Studies*. West Lafayette, IN: Parlor.

Bianco, Jamie Skye. 2012. "This Digital Humanities Which Is Not One." In *Debates in the Digital Humanities*, ed. Matthew K. Gold, 96–112. Minneapolis: University of Minnesota Press, 2012.

Bjork, Olin. 2012. "Digital Humanities and the First-Year Writing Course." In *Digital Humanities Pedagogy: Practices, Principles and Politics*, ed. Brett D. Hirsch, 97–121.

Bloom, Lynn Z. 1998. *Composition Studies as a Creative Art—Teaching, Writing, Scholarship, Administration*. Logan: Utah State University Press; Logan, VT: Open Book.

Cushman, Ellen. 2011. *The Cherokee Syllabary: Writing the People's Perseverance*. Norman: University of Oklahoma Press.

French, Scot, and Bill Ferster. 2012. "Notes on the Future of Virginia: The Jefferson Short-Letters, 1787–1826." *VisualEyes*, July 5. http://www.viseyes.org/show/?id=62287.

George, Diana, and John Trimbur. 1999. "The 'Communication Battle'; or, Whatever Happened to the 4th C?" *College Composition and Communication* 50.4:682–98.

Giberson, Greg A., and Thomas A. Moriarty, eds. 2010. *What We Are Becoming: Developments in Undergraduate Writing Majors*. Logan: Utah State University Press.

Goggin, Maureen Daly, ed. 2000. *Inventing a Discipline: Rhetoric Scholarship in Honor of Richard E. Young*. Urbana: NCTE.

Gold, Matthew K. 2012. "The Digital Humanities Moment." In *Debates in the Digital Humanities*, ed. Matthew K. Gold, xi–xvi. Minneapolis: University of Minnesota Press.

Gold, Matthew K., Kathie Gossett, Karl Stolley, Geoffrey Sauer, Liza Potts, William Hart-Davidson, and Dean Rehberger. 2012. "Why Yes, We Are Digital Humanists!" Panel presented at the Computers and Writing conference, Raleigh, NC, May 28. http://siteslab.org/cwcon.

Haas, Angela. 2008. "Wampum as Hypertext: An American Indian Intellectual Tradition of Multimedia Theory and Practice." *Studies in American Indian Literatures* 19.4:77–100.

Hawk, Byron. 2007. *A Counter-History of Composition: Toward Methodologies of Complexity*. Pittsburgh: University of Pittsburgh Press.

Hirsch, Brett D. 2012. "</Parentheses>: Digital Humanities and the Place of Pedagogy." In *Digital Humanities Pedagogy: Practices, Principles and Politics*, ed. Brett D. Hirsch, 1–30. Cambridge: Open Book.

Kill, Melanie. 2012. "Teaching Digital Rhetoric: Wikipedia, Collaboration, and the Politics of Free Knowledge." In *Digital Humanities Pedagogy: Practices, Principles and Politics*, ed. Brett D. Hirsch, 389–405. Cambridge: Open Book.

Kirschenbaum, Matthew. 2012. "What Is Digital Humanities and What's It Doing in English Departments." In *Debates in the Digital Humanities*, ed.Matthew K. Gold, 12–15. Minneapolis: University of Minnesota Press.

Mailloux, Steven. 2000. "Disciplinary Identities: On the Rhetorical Paths between English and Communication Studies." *Rhetoric Society Quarterly* 30.2:5–29.

McPherson, Tara. 2012. "Why Are the Digital Humanities So White? or, Thinking Other Histories of Race and Computation." In *Debates in the Digital Humanities*, ed. Matthew K. Gold, 139–60. Minneapolis: University of Minnesota Press.

Phelps, Louise Wetherbee. 1988. *Composition as a Human Science*. New York: Oxford University Press.

Powell, Malea D. 2004. "Down by the River; or, How Susan La Flesche Picotte Can Teach Us about Alliance as a Practice of Survivance." *College English* 67.1:38–60.

Reid, Alex. 2011. "Digital Humanities Tactics." *Digital Digs*, July 117. http://alex-reid.net.

———. 2012. "Graduate Education and the Ethics of the Digital Humanities." In *Debates in the Digital Humanities*, ed. Matthew K. Gold, 12–15. Minneapolis: University of Minnesota Press.

Selfe, Cynthia. 1988. "Computers in English Departments: The Rhetoric of Technopower." *ADE Bulletin*, no. 90. http://www.eric.ed.gov/ERICWeb Portal/detail?accno=EJ374870.

Waltzer, Luke. 2012. "Digital Humanities and the 'Ugly Stepchildren' of American Higher Education." In *Debates in the Digital Humanities*, ed. Matthew K. Gold, 335–49. Minneapolis: University of Minnesota Press.

Warrior, Robert. 2005. *The People and the Word: Reading Native Nonfiction*. Minneapolis: University of Minnesota Press.

Whitson, Roger. 2013. "Where's the Pedagogy in Digital Literary Studies?" January 17. http://www.rogerwhitson.net/?p=1947#disqus_thread.

## SIXTEEN

Tackling a Fundamental Problem: Using Digital Labs to Build Smarter Computing Cultures

KEVIN BROOKS

CHRIS LINDGREN

MATTHEW WARNER

In 2010, two of us (Kevin and Chris) began exploring what it would take to offer an after-school computer enrichment program for students from refugee families in Fargo. We were interested in the One Laptop per Child initiative and the ideas of Alan Kay (Kay and Goldberg 1977; Kay 1984), Seymour Papert (1993), and Marshall McLuhan (1964), among others. All had expressed the idea that few educators (K–16) really understood the medium of the computer: its programmability, its computational ability, and its networking capabilities. We deployed "Sugar on a Stick"—the operating system of the XO computer loaded on a USB drive—instead of the XOs themselves, and we asked, What can kids do with this operating system and minimum guidance? We did not conceive of our work as overtly rhetorical or digital humanities (DH) in nature. We were looking to create a small but powerful educational intervention in which we, as much as the students, were the learners.

In 2011, we wrote and received funding for a proposal to "build a smarter computer" in Fargo. We presented our work as a form of *civic engagement*, a term John Ackerman says "accurately name[s] the rhetorical investments of citizen-scholars in the public life of their cities" (Ackerman 2010, 76). We sought the assistance of the Computer Science Department and received help in the form of a talented undergraduate who functioned as technical support. We knew that collaborating with computer science would be essential to meeting our goals, and we understood that these sorts of collaboration were common, often essential, in large-scale DH projects.

In 2012, we found ourselves and our project immersed in the rhetoric of "Code Year" (http://www.codeyear.com). Like many digital humanists, we were trying to develop our own understanding of what it means to learn how to write code and how one might go about educating the current generation—not to be coders, necessarily, but to be what Ian Bogost would call "procedurally literate" (2005, 35). We were influenced by Bogost, Annette Vee (2010), and medium theorists from both the humanities and the sciences, as noted above. But we also found our work resonating with scholarship in DH. Matthew Kirschenbaum's conclusion to his influential definition essay "What Is Digital Humanities and What's It Doing in English Departments?" describes our project perfectly: scholarship and pedagogy that are publicly visible (we received local newspaper and television coverage), bound up in infrastructure (higher ed and K–5), collaborative (English, computer science), and online 24/7 (through our Web site and social media channels) (2012, 9).

Exploring the interplay of rhetoric and DH gives us a chance to step back from our project and consider some of the ways in which the scholarship and practice of both fields are unconsciously influencing our project. But, in stepping back, we will also generalize from our experience, offering a white paper grounded in both a broader history and tradition of rhetoric and a wider range of DH scholarship. We do believe that there is an important, even fundamental role for rhetoricians and digital humanists to play in building smarter computer cultures in their local communities. If we are not active in fostering a rich and diverse culture of procedural rhetoricians or introducing students to the expansive possibilities and unexpected practicality of DH, we see these two specializations within each field remaining specializations, rather than the fundamental way in which the next generation does its work. Community literacy programs and after-school computer clubs abound, but we think that it will take what Richard McKeon (1971, 45) calls an "architectonic productive art"—rhetoric as social architecture—to bring together multiple efforts in a single location, in turn "contribut[ing] to the formation of the culture of the modern world" at least one locale at a time.

Modules for Building Smarter Computing Cultures

A smarter computing culture is one that understands the medium of the computer, a culture that understands computers can be programmed and not simply run programs, a culture that understands computers are about networking and building communities, not just online but offline. A smarter computing culture risks further embedding our kids and our communities in a technological environment rather than encouraging unplugged activities, but the goal is to displace some repetitive game playing and passive consumption of media with production, creativity, computational thinking, procedural literacy, and collaboration.

This chapter offers strategies for embedding rhetoricians and digital humanists in local structures to build smarter local computing cultures that empower students and widen their future possibilities through humanists' critical lenses *and* computational thinking.

Engage with K–12 students, teachers, and administrators; students are immersed in the materials and media ecologies of DH (video games, Internet culture, mass culture), but we have not engaged them in our practices and ways of thinking.

Building a smarter computing culture must engage the young people of a community, and engaging them through a local K–12 system will likely lead to the highest level of institutional, social, and educational support. The National Science Foundation (NSF) offers considerable grant incentives to its higher education constituents for bringing scientific thinking and methods into the K–12 system. In 2006, the computer scientist Jeanette Wing outlined her vision for "computational thinking," which included K–12 students and teachers, inciting her discipline to "reach the pre-college audience, including teachers, parents, and students" (2006, 35). Rhetoricians and humanists reach out to the K–12 system and public through community literacy centers, citywide book reads, writers-in-residence programs, and other methods, but we also have a role to play in building a smarter computing culture.

Christine L. Borgman, a professor and Presidential Chair of Information Studies at UCLA, imagines a DH project that develops relevant skills and practices for young students: "If students can explore cultural records from the early grades and learn to construct their own narratives, they may find the study of humanities more lively. By the time they are college students, they will have learned methods of collaborative work and the use of distributed tools, sources, and services." She also asks, "What is the humanities laboratory of the 21st century?" (2009, 63), and, while she provides a number of answers, these labs are neither in the K–12 schools nor in the community, but we have found that those are rich places for experimentation and scholarship and necessary places for changing a local culture.

Identify and lessen digital divides within the K–12 system and community, a subproblem that must be tackled in order to assure more equitable development of a smarter computing culture.

NSF funding and Google Rise grant opportunities encourage innovative educational programs that will encourage girls and underrepresented minorities to consider computer science and other science fields as a career. These individual programs work toward improving individuals' skills and credentials, but, to build a smarter computing culture, it will require sustained attention to local digital divides, including a critical reexamination of the concept of digital divide. The historian of technology Rayvon Fouché explains that the continuing drop of computing costs in the early years of the twenty-first century diffused the public and academic consciousness of the digital divide (2012, 63). Fouché argues that the digital divide is not fully understood and that current economic circumstances, coupled with increased access to technology, put the responsibility back onto the individual, overlooking larger systemic issues that reinforce racial stereotypes of haves and have-nots.

The digital divide in a community might not be about technology. One of our participating schools is close to a one-to-one computer-to-student ratio and uses iPods for language learning. In our experience, the divide manifests in ways beyond access. Transportation would have become a barrier if our program was located on the university's campus instead of directly in the students' school, after school. Many participating children (and their parents/guardians) desired to boot their Sugar sticks at home, but most failed owing to a lack of knowledge about BIOS and basic troubleshooting strategies. The divide also arose when parents or siblings of our tech team would not grant access to the computers for their own children. Building a smarter computing culture is not about adding more technology to a community; it is about understanding the technosocial and political dimensions of the digital divide and addressing social barriers, not just technological barriers.

Collaborate across campus lines to bring the resources and talent of higher education to K–12 systems and communities.

The challenge of building a smarter computing culture is too large for any individual or discipline to tackle alone. David Depew's reexamination of McKeon's architectonic productive art led him to propose that "a rhetorical art with cognitive ambitions in a changing world whose cultural core is technologically permeated knowledge production will replace Cicero's and Hume's personal skepticism with a communal, constructivist, relativist, pluralist, pragmatic, transdisciplinary conception of knowledge" (Depew 2010, 47). Single disciplines may be able to offer a robotics competition or an app development class, but collaborative efforts can imagine and strengthen K–12 or community projects that involve planning, testing, and disseminating "technologically permeated knowledge."

Digital humanists need to begin to conceive of and initiate collaborations that might deliver more of these extracurricular programs, or the computer scientists will run the game-development camps, the engineers will run the robotics, and our smarter computing culture will not include the sensitivity to language, storytelling, and creative expression that will effectively balance technical camps. Such a broadening of the types of content and practices in such camps will attract, develop, and sustain new cultures and communities.

Connect existing local initiatives because you will not be the only ones working to build a smarter local computing culture.

As we developed our Sugar Labs program, we discovered a number of other related initiatives in our area, from Lego and robotics clubs, to a 4-H Tech Wizard program that is used nationally, a local "DigiGirlz" camp hosted by Microsoft, and a summer STEM camp held on our own campus. One of the architectonic roles of rhetoric, McKeon would argue, is to connect these efforts, to play the role of social architect. And, as simple as that might seem, reaching out and building community among different projects requires a deft rhetorical hand as one project might be seen as competing for the same resources or students as another or one group might be perceived as trying to control others. Patrick Svensson suggests that digital humanists replace the big tent metaphor with "meeting place" or "trading zone" imagery, concepts that fit building a smarter computing culture as well. Centralized organization will be a nightmare for the organizer and antithetical to a networked, rhizomatic culture. "By seeing the field as a trading zone and meeting place," Svensson writes, "we can acknowledge disciplinary and methodological expertise, while approaching grand challenges, relating key disciplinary discourses, supporting multiple modes of engagement with the digital, and distinctly engaging with the future of the humanities" (2012, 47). A local culture that trades ideas, points participants to related programs, and supports multiple engagements with the digital will be essential to developing a smarter computing culture. We encourage our fifth-grade students to attend the STEM camp during sixth grade and DigiGirlz during seventh grade, and by doing that we start to build an informal curriculum and sustained engagement in related topics and projects beyond the scope of our own digital lab.

Fill the gaps.

After connecting existing initiatives, the local gaps will be apparent. We encourage our students to follow up their Sugar Labs experience with STEM and DigiGirlz camps, but at this point our community has no digital arts program to support arts or humanities computing. If rhetoricians and digital humanists are collaborating with K–12 systems, they might also be able to help bridge gaps in the curriculum. Our local public school system seems to have a gap between fourth-grade keyboarding and a seventh-grade "Exploring Technology" class and another gap between the seventh-grade class and the introduction to computer science course offered senior year. The NSF is trying to fill these gaps with its Twenty-first Century Computing grants, the bulk of which are for training teachers to develop high school computer science classes. While rhetoricians and digital humanists might need to wait for the National Endowment for the Humanities and the National Council of Teachers of English to offer similar incentives or lobby successfully to push national organizations to support this kind of work, THAT Camps for K–16 teachers, professional development courses as continuing education, and other partnerships that grow out of a good working relation with K–12 can contribute to a smarter computing culture. THAT camps that focus on the needs and interests of postsecondary education will have a smaller impact on building a local computing culture and not increase K–16 collaboration. To fill the cultural, educational, and technological gaps in our communities, rhetoricians can fill the ad hoc roles, building smarter computing cultures through discursive and material means.

Sustain your own and others' practices; the local initiatives and newly generated gap fillers will need to be sustained in order to successfully build a smarter computing culture.

The public discourse of "code year" needs to be reframed as "code decade"; cultural shifts will not happen in a single year. Sustainable projects need the people power that comes with collaboration, the documentation that comes from technical writing, and the sustained vision that comes from engaged, publicly oriented scholars. The rhetorician Richard J. Selfe (2005, 2) led the field of rhetoric and composition in thinking about "sustainable computer environments," and he offered a simple formula that is entirely relevant to building a smarter computing culture: people first, pedagogies second, technology third. His work has been extended in a collection (DeVoss, McKee, and Selfe 2009) that covers the sustainability of research centers, writing centers, and writing programs but not community DH labs. Innovative possibilities now exist, like online fund-raising through CrowdRise or Kickstarter or drawing community volunteers from local Unix clubs, OLPC clubs, or Mac User Groups.

Dan Anderson (2008), among others, has advocated for a "low bridge to high benefits" that, like Selfe's position, puts people first, emphasizes agency, and aims for social change as an outcome. Our own project, Sugar on a Stick, has a human and financial cost that is not going to be sustainable and scalable without project funding (another name for cyberinfrastructure), so we, too, will need to consider some lower-cost alternatives to reach the same goals.

Conclusion

Rhetoric brings the civic engagement that has been missing in DH, and DH brings important critical perspectives and practices about the digital divide. Accordingly, a fusion of the two has much to contribute to efforts that blur disciplinary boundaries. Such actions to blur and cross lines are manifest throughout rhetoric's history as a discipline and origins as *the* humanities. McKeon talks of "continuities and revolutions" (1971, 45), and William Keith discusses the foolish expectation that rhetoric will "hold still as a stable object of theorizing," which gives contemporary justification for Aristotle's "thick manuals" of production over his "thin theoretical tomes" (Keith 1997, 231, 235). More importantly, however, it justifies the call to see the shared values and deep skill set that both parties bring to such ambitious projects to start digital labs that immerse themselves in the public sphere.

Our goals may be too ambitious. We doubted the viability of our project from the beginning, yet we had a vision and persistence, as well as some necessary funding, that have sustained us for three years. We were buoyed early on by the conclusion of Walter Bender's (2011) TedxKids talk in Brussels: a "Fail better!" chant. And we know, and find support in, the realization that what we are doing is good and meaningful even if we do not achieve our ultimate goal. David Coogan and John Ackerman conclude the introduction to *The Public Work of Rhetoric* by citing John Lucaites and Celeste Conduit's account of rhetoric's "'strategic liberation': 'the possibility of improving life within one's community in temporary and incomplete, but nonetheless meaningful ways.' This is the true grit and tumble of public life. This is where we find the space to work" (2010, 12). How we measure the success and failure of such civic engagement for social change is another matter that will develop as these projects emerge and grow. For now, we (and, we suspect, many other rhetoricians and digital humanists) want to live in smarter computing cultures, but, to make that happen, we will have to play a more significant role in building its many manifestations.

References

Ackerman, John M. 2010. "Rhetorical Engagement in the Cultural Economies of Cities." In *The Public Work of Rhetoric: Citizen-Scholars and Civic Engagement*, ed. John M. Ackerman and David J. Coogan, 76–97. Columbia: University of South Carolina Press.

Anderson, Daniel. 2008. "The Low Bridge to High Benefits: Entry-Level Multimedia, Literacies, and Motivation." *Computers and Composition* 25.1:40–60.

Bender, Walter. 2011. "Program or Be Programmed." *TEDxKids@Brussels*, YouTube.com. June 9. http://www.youtube.com/watch?v=5bUYtgLhAfo.

Bogost, Ian. 2005. "Procedural Literacy: Problem Solving with Programming, Systems, and Play." *Journal of Media Literacy* 52.1–2. http://www.bogost.com/writing/procedural_literacy.shtml.

Borgman, Christine L. 2009. "The Digital Future Is Now: A Call to Action for the Humanities." *Digital Humanities Quarterly* 3.4. http://www.digital humanities.org/dhq/vol/3/4/000077/000077.html.

Coogan, David J., and John M. Ackerman. 2010. "Introduction: The Space to Work in Public Life." In *The Public Work of Rhetoric: Citizen-Scholars and*

Civic Engagement, ed. John M. Ackerman and David J. Coogan, 1–16. Columbia: University of South Carolina Press.

Depew, David. 2010. "Revisiting Richard McKeon's Architectonic Rhetoric." In *Reengaging the Prospects of Rhetoric: Current Conversations and Contemporary Challenges*, ed. Mark J. Porrovecchio, 37–56. New York: Routledge.

DeVoss, Dànielle N., Heidi A. McKee, and Richard Selfe, eds. 2009. *Technological Ecologies and Sustainability*. Logan: Computers and Composition Digital Press/Utah State University Press.

Kay, Alan. 1984. "Computer Software." *Scientific American* 251.3:53–59.

Kay, Alan, and Adele Goldberg. 1977. "Personal Dynamic Media." *IEEE Computer* 10.3:31–41.

Keith, William M. 1997. "Engineering Rhetoric." In *Rhetorical Hermeneutics: Invention and Interpretation in the Age of Science*, ed. Alan G. Gross and William M. Keith, 225–46. New York: State University of New York Press.

Kirschenbaum, Matthew. 2012. "What Is Digital Humanities and What's It Doing in English Departments." In *Debates in the Digital Humanities*, ed. Matthew K. Gold, 3–11. Minneapolis: University Press of Minnesota.

McKeon, Richard. 1971. "The Uses of Rhetoric in a Technological Age: Architectonic Productive Arts." In *The Prospect of Rhetoric: Report of the National Development Project*, ed. Lloyd F. Bitzer and Edwin Black, 44–63. Englewood Cliffs, NJ: Prentice-Hall.

McLuhan, Marshall. 1964 *Understanding Media: The Extensions of Man*. New York: McGraw-Hil.

Papert, Seymour. 1993. *Mindstorms: Children, Computers, and Powerful Ideas*. New York: Basic.

Selfe, Richard. 2005. *Sustainable Computer Environments: Cultures of Support in English Studies and the Language Arts*. Cresskill, NJ: Hampton.

Svensson, Patrik. 2012. "Beyond the Big Tent." In *Debates in the Digital Humanities*, ed. Matthew K. Gold, 36–49. Minneapolis: University Minnesota Press.

Vee, Annette. 2010. "Proceduracy: Computer Code Writing in the Continuum of Literacy." Ph.D. diss., University of Wisconsin-Madison.

Wing, J. M. 2006. "Computational Thinking." *CACM Viewpoint* 49.3:33–35.

## SEVENTEEN

In, Through, and About the Archive: What Digitization (Dis)Allows

TAREZ SAMRA GRABAN

ALEXIS RAMSEY-TOBIENNE

WHITNEY MYERS

Historical recovery in rhetoric finds great value in digital archives and digitization projects that recover underserved figures or build exhibits of texts. Yet the most compelling aspects of digitization for rhetoric may come not from building electronic exhibits but from observing how various dilemmas surrounding location, migration, and access inspire new methodologies at the intersection of rhetorical and digital work (Buehl, Chute, and Fields 2012; Sullivan and Graban 2011; Mueller 2012). In our own work at this intersection, we view the archive as a critical rhetorical space that demands equally of its creators and users and a site for testing theories about how texts migrate among discourse communities and new practices come into being. As archives and archivally based scholarship gain critical attention within rhetorical studies, so too do questions of rhetoric's influence on both the digital archive and the concept of archive, often sparking more vital discussions of disciplinary stewardship and communal ethics. In deference to such reciprocity, we articulate a methodology for archival work that is defined by the kinds of intellectual processes that digitization (dis)allows.

(Re)Locating Digital Archives

The first piece of this methodology stems from the dilemma of creating a digital archive that encompasses the personal, institutional, or disciplinary without being beholden to physical spaces. We understand archival provenance as a function of *kairos*, where archival technologies emerge from contextualized events. Yet even digital archives simultaneously reflect ideologies and spaces since important questions of *what* and *how* to digitize cannot usurp place-based questions of authority and authorization (Biesecker 2006; Haskins 2007; Cook and Schwartz 2002; Miller and Bowden 1999). Projects such as the National Archives of Composition and Rhetoric (http://www.uri.edu/artsci/writing/nationalarchives.shtml), which collects the academic papers of field practitioners from multiple institutions within a single discipline, demonstrate our need to construct digital archives as localized research spaces—in spite of their reach—because of valuable historical connections to their hosting institution. While rhetoric and writing scholars have increasingly recognized their potential to act as both archivists and researchers (Johnson 2010; Brereton 1995; Ridolfo, Hart-Davidson, and McLeod 2011), and while technology makes enacting this dual role easier, we should consider the ramifications of smaller, decentralized archival spaces created by scholars familiar with archival protocols but not specifically trained as archivists. The decision about where to locate these archives—and how to determine *location*—is itself predicated on several complicating factors.

Because most archives house more unprocessed than processed collections and are constrained by budget or labor, the digital archive simultaneously expedites and conceals the availability of materials (Ramsey-Tobienne 2010; Yakel 2010). Rhetoricians—concerned as we are with an object's context, its use and reception through time, our relation to it, and its future historiographic perceptions—look to archival aids for unstable narratives, not stable ones. We understand and appreciate that material processes will influence both what gets archived and what historical narratives we construct from archival aids. At the same time, we feel the responsibility to not conflate personal (or institutional) research agendas with our processes of recovery. Deciding how to proceed with digitizing a collection involves determining the immediacy and context of the activity surrounding that collection and determining its "knowledge-based proximity." For Janine Solberg (2012), the "proximity" of a set of materials has a spatial orientation;

but, when those materials are digitized or digitally accessed, their proximity has a temporal orientation as well, something we observe when using powerful search engines like Google that claim to speed up a research process by privileging one set of temporally available data over another.

Solberg's proximity affects not only how researchers access digital archives but also what decisions inform their construction, particularly when deciding where such archives can or should be virtually housed. This is a unique dilemma for rhetoricians who work among or between institutional spaces, are motivated by their knowledge of the topic, and must negotiate affective, geographic, and virtual attachments to the social, cultural, or institutional context in which their topics reside (Solberg 2012, 67).[1] By introducing the question of where archival materials should be *housed*, historiographers continue to challenge our notions of archival activity for rhetoric studies. Cheryl Glenn and Jessica Enoch (2010), Deborah Mutnick (2007), Malea Powell (2002), and Liz Rohan (2010), among others, have urged rhetoric scholars to shift their sites of analysis by drawing attention outside the traditional classroom, research library, institutional archive, or memorial for emerging digital questions, thus revealing new questions and possibilities for "historiographic intervention" (Glenn and Enoch 2010, 18). Cultural centers, historical societies, personal collections, heritage foundations, and local museums inspire smaller, unintentional archives whose ensuing digital access (or digitization) offers more invigorating epistemological dilemmas.

One such dilemma is mirrored in Kate Theimer's (2012b) assertion that all users and creators of archives cannot be expected to share similar motivations or approach the archival space with similar concerns since the digital archive accommodates a broad host of them. No matter the motivation, rhetoricians and historians who build archives do more than just proliferate digital information—they participate in a larger dialogue about access, proprietary rights, the boundaries of technology, and the conflicts between personal and communal interest. As James Berlin has noted, all histories are privileged in their interpretations ("Octalog" 1988, 8), and, as Jacqueline Jones Royster and Jean Williams (1999, 564) recommend, rhetorical historians should work harder to expose the gaps of their own use of these histories. More recently, Debra Hawhee and Christa Olson (in press) encourage a stance toward "archive" that enables both long-distance and close-range histories, putting "sprawling" and "zooming" historical perspectives into critical conversation. Such dialogic practice requires a "sophisticated and extensive" knowledge of archival material to pinpoint what it is they do not yet know (Ferreira-Buckley 1999). We see a skepticism growing in scholars' knowledge of preservation or archival technologies; as a result, we negotiate concerns about what we can archive even as we decide how to (digitally) archive. Our how becomes a choice of whether to create a digital archive ourselves and house it in our own institutions or to use extant spaces that act as national clearinghouses. The choice determines our process of recovery and (re)inscription by causing us to think critically about what else the archives could do and whom else they could serve.

Kate Theimer's post "Anything New Here . . . ?" (2012a) reflects this shift by raising the question not only of *what* should be archived but also of *who* should be archiving. In responding to a National Endowment for the Humanities (NEH)–funded study of archival support service providers and its six "Recommendations to Archives," Theimer notes that those recommendations simply reinforce a predictable, unsurprising move toward centralizing online tools and enhancing archival training (Rutner and Schonfeld 2012).[2] Calling them *predictable* implies that (1) conversations around archival research already overstep the boundaries of preservation-only thinking and (2) the archivist is presumed to be a more active participant in articulating new research paradigms. Most significantly, they reinforce an urgency that Kimberly Barata (2004) has already noted—traditional archival education models are "breaking down" (68)—and they support an argument that Buehl, Chute, and Fields (2012, 277) make about the necessity of introducing early career writing studies specialists into archival processing since historiography is becoming archival at its core, that there can be rhetorical and intellectual value in documentation and encoding, long thought to be the unattractive work of service providers.

The ensuing ramifications of information control, ownership, and access are significant: they call into question *what kinds of archival content are proximate* and *to whom,* thus erasing "the boundaries between the official and the vernacular" (Haskins 2007, 405). This kind of proximity reaffirms the important role of rhetoricians in archiving their own discipline's records: it calls into question the types of documents and technologies we may find useful (Moon 2007; Kirsch and Rohan 2008). Larger archives become reconceptualized as more intimate spaces where rhetoricians can function as archivists, and vice versa, making user-centered decisions about what information is documented and how it gets displayed. In sum, rethinking digital archival spaces means recognizing rhetoricians as agents in both preservation and dissemination, without disavowing important knowledge of trained librarians and archivists in the preservation process (including the responsibilities that come with this kind of agency), and without assuming that preservation fixes a set of materials to a singular and finite location or set of beliefs.

Reaching Wider Publics

The second piece of our methodology stems from the dilemma of what Kimberly Christen (2011) calls "digital repatriation"—how issues of archival migration and an idealized public both complicate and are complicated by digital archives. When historical metadata migrate from print to online spaces, rhetoricians must (re)define *open* and *access* so as to more ethically reach wider publics. The choice of digital space and the means of archival organization are rhetorical acts deploying arguments about relations, power dynamics, and gate-keeping methodologies and should be treated as such. While most academy scholars are conversant in these arguments, the communities they grant digital access to are often not. Thus, scholars participating in digital repatriation must critically interrogate such social and political relations, even while embracing digitization's democratic potential.

Recovery scholars have long insisted on the priority of bringing previously ignored and overlooked voices to presence within academic conversation (Enoch 2008; Glenn 1997; Gold 2008; Miles 2011; Romano 2004). Yet the forms such recovery takes often delegitimize the voices found within the archive, undermined by familiar hierarchies and dominant Western methodologies or privileged by the institutions where they are housed. While each individual recovery project presents extraordinarily different ethical dilemmas, Heidi A. McKee and James E. Porter (2012), Malea Powell (2008), and Anne Frances Wysocki (2007) all insist on an essential commonality: *papers are people.* Objects have a past attached to a group of people who might not want their story told or are better able to tell it without our interference (Tuhiwai-Smith 1999). If we are not careful, our ideals about digital recovery will (re)produce the research practices that we wish to critique by closing off publics and demarcating ownership, authorship, and interpretive control.

We embrace Christen's notion of "reciprocal curation" (2011, 193)—now increasingly common in digital projects that aim to give multilayered access—because it provokes critical dialogue about how annotating the archive helps mitigate what we see as a 2.0 naïveté that digital curation is necessarily reciprocal. Most digital archival spaces provide neither "granular levels of access for various types of users, nor a way to customize protocols for access based on cultural parameters" (186). But, in co-opting Christen's term, we privilege cultural transfer and maintenance as the most important ethical components of nuanced archival recovery. Christen's work among the Warumungu Aboriginal community of Central Australia reflects "extensive user profile[s] and a rich content-tagging upload process" (186), offering dynamic access to a community while retaining its indigenous value. Similarly, the 2006 Protocols for Native American Archival Materials (PNAAM) (see First Archivist Circle 2007) have inspired a dialogue between Native and non-Native librarians, archivists, and nonspecialists who want the recognition of indigenous rights and the destruction of stand-alone academic silos when working with Native American archival materials. While the PNAAM have not escaped criticism,[3] they invite researchers to contribute and critique best practices through their Web page, thus placing archival data and their reflection in the same public space. Such framing of archival material provides a site for multiple communities to argue what is at stake when curating, annotating, and presenting. The archive's users become cocreators of knowledge, a move echoing the NEH's (2012) Code of Ethics related to research projects involving Native peoples. The archive becomes an evolving and dynamic *genre* of possibility for academic and nonacademic audiences alike.

Inventing Historiographic Methods

The final piece of our methodology stems from the simultaneously formative and determinate nature of archival work, especially in extrainstitutional spaces. Being rhetoricians in public archives involves coming to terms with our hybrid roles and recognizing how they become sites for invention. Being rhetoricians in *digital* archives means constructing archival tools that enact the kinds of invention we think possible (Biesecker 2006). In response, we recommend an archival method that reflects this hybridity—similar in respects to what Hawhee and Olson (in press) call the *archive's* multiplicity—and reinforces the relation between our decisions and their outcomes.

Digital archival work is already communal and inventive (Haskins 2007; Juby 1997; Purdy 2011), and evidence ranges from the National

Archives' "Citizen Archivist" Project (http://www.archives.gov/citizen
-archivist), to Ohio State University's "Digital Archive of Literacy Narratives" (http://daln.osu.edu), to broad-reaching data-storage projects
such as NORA.[4] Yet, in spite of a partiality toward crowd sourcing and
invention, archival methods specifically for rhetoric and writing remain principally focused on categories of work that are all centered on
traditional notions of recovery, motivated by analogue tendencies to
recover figures and texts in linear time or space. This tension between
born-digital invention and analogue archival recovery allows rhetoric
scholars to consider a different category—*metadata projects*, which provide several ways of visualizing relations among texts, topics, and subjects, thereby enabling researchers to understand historical events as
outcomes of their own archival interventions.

Metadata amplify traditional bibliographic practice (Day 2013),
are *user driven and relational* (Smith-Yoshimura and Shein 2013), and
reach well beyond the artifact, collection, or set of materials being preserved, as seen in projects like MONK (http://http://monk.lis.illinois
.edu), InPho (https://inpho.cogs.indiana.edu/), and the Writing Studies
Tree (http://writingstudiestree.org/network) whose content parameters
continue to grow with use. By learning Encoded Archival Description,
doing data visualization, and constructing topical ontologies, rhetoricians can privilege their broader motives and approaches toward diplo-
matics and histories of rhetoric. In turn, their archival tools help them
imagine new kinds of relations among texts and users rather than only
representing relations according to traditional taxonomies of storage
and use.

Metadata projects also blur stark methodological distinctions between organizing, analyzing, and using historical information. This
is significant to historiography in rhetoric because most metadata are
prevalent and shared and most historiographers are interested in metadata whether they realize it or not. Rather than resulting from pre-
scribed ways of reading and writing histories, metadata reveal how
historiographers value the histories they write and read and even approach reinstantiations of *history*. For example, each of us is interested,
to some extent, in demonstrating how much of our histories is built on
various kinds of performances in various kinds of contexts. As portfolio coordinator at Eckerd College, Alexis justifies her decisions about
archival construction of a two-decades-long writing portfolio assessment program in data gathering that is highly localized and actively in
progress. As an accidental archivist for the Albuquerque Indian School,
Whitney considers where to look for potential material of interest to

the archive and how to ensure access/ibility for sustaining open nar-ratives, not closed ones. In her development of a historical tool for tracing women's pedagogical activities throughout the Progressive Era, Tarez visualizes information about obscure texts (including their past and present locatability) as a model for question building, not for map-ping their static locations. Each of these projects reflects Patricia Sulli-van's (2012, 371) in situ archival positioning: overcoming, or not being stymied by, evidentiary gaps in our archival knowledge as we try to place persons and events. We extend Sullivan's claim to digital archival tools on the basis of our understanding that such evidentiary gaps are created anew when we merely rely on increasingly technologically rich resources to execute traditional research paradigms. This is what we urge rhetoricians to avoid.

Finally, metadata projects can change our preservation paradigms. While rhetoricians' arrangement methods have traditionally stemmed from their expectations about what things a collection can contain, and while their information literacies for historical work have tradition-ally stemmed from beliefs they hold about containment, the reading methods derived from metadata are not bound by expected relations between artifacts but are flexible and contingent. The ideal metadata tool simultaneously promotes inquiry and metainquiry, allowing users to access various categories, types, or sets of information through the same portal. It functions simultaneously as a database and an ontol-ogy, allowing users to explore algorithmic relations between keywords, even as they note simple keyword chains. Ultimately, the success of most metadata projects hinges on a paradigm shift from tools that pre-serve materials for historians to those that potentially transform what it means *to do history* in virtual spaces and with digital forms. What results are historiographic possibilities like the following:

- Users can call up data records in a variety of forms and relations, that is, not just show the origin and provenance information of a particular text.
- Users can access the geographic and disciplinary locations where other research-ers are either interested in a particular text, have contributed metadata for it, or are actively teaching its topics.
- Users can bridge a critical gap between data visualization and analysis, espe-cially when the data points that users contribute, search for, and map constitute movable targets.

These possibilities are useful for the development of research tools in rhetoric studies that aim to do more than display, revise, or correct archival histories. Ideally, they would result in the construction of databases that support multiple functions beyond searching and cataloging, toward *managing knowledge.*

Conclusion

Digital archives and their constituents are simultaneously encoded, provoking a theoretical shift in how rhetoric scholars evaluate archival movement from static to active and think about the historicity of archives and narratives therein (Biesecker 2006). With Ann Laura Stoler (2002, 87, 97), we embrace the archive as a way of identifying power dynamics and performing political critique. We also acknowledge that questions of authorization and access compel rhetoric scholars to view the digital archive as operating both within and outside various critical frames and to claim each frame as a site for historiographic invention. In response, this methodology highlights our duality as creators and users of digital archives, following Solberg's (2012, 56) advice to be always "attuned to" and ready to "critically engage" those digital spaces in which, and between which, rhetoricians reside.

Notes

1. As recovery scholars we recognize the importance of place and its relation to establishing a greater context and understanding for our research (Kirsch and Rohan 2008; Powell 2008; Sutherland 2008). Yet the "official" archives we visit are often displaced. For example, how do the records in the National Archives from Bureau of Indian Affairs off-reservation boarding schools (http://www.archives.gov/research/guide-fed-records/groups/075.html) shift and change when juxtaposed with the archival materials available in the Carlisle, PA, site of the Carlisle Industrial Indian School (http://home.epix.net/~landis)?
2. Sponsored by Ithaka Strategic Consulting and Research (Ithaka S+R), the study surveyed professional historians, archivists, and librarians in order to better gauge how their shifting or emergent practices might require new or different services.
3. The Society of American Archivists and the American Library Association have declined to endorse their recommendations.
4. Now subsumed under other data-mining projects, NORA had as its goal to produce software for discovering, vizualizing, and exploring significant patterns across large collections of full-text humanities resources in existing digital libraries.

References

Barata, Kimberly. 2004. "Archives in the Digital Age." *Journal of the Society of Archivists* 25:63–70.

Biesecker, Barbara. 2006. "Of Historicity, Rhetoric: The Archive as Scene of Invention." *Rhetoric and Public Affairs* 9:124–31.

Brereton, John C., ed. 1995. *The Origins of Composition Studies in the American College, 1875–1925: A Documentary History.* Pittsburgh: University of Pittsburgh Press.

Buehl, Jonathan, Tamar Chute, and Anne Fields. 2012. "Training in the Archives: Archival Research as Professional Development." *College Composition and Communication* 64:274–305.

Christen, Kimberly. 2011. "Opening Archives: Respectful Repatriation." *American Archivist* 74:185–210.

Cook, Terry, and Joan M. Schwartz. 2002. "Archives, Records, and Power: From (Postmodern) Theory to (Archival) Performance." *Archival Science* 2:171–85.

Day, Michael. 2013. "Issues and Approaches to Preservation Metadata." In *Proceedings from the Joint RLG and NPO Preservation Conference, September 28–30.* http://www.ukoln.ac.uk/metadata/presentations/rlg-npo/warwick.html.

Enoch, Jessica. 2008. *Refiguring Rhetorical Education: Women Teaching African American, Native American, and Chicano/a Students, 1865–1911.* Carbondale: Southern Illinois University Press.

Ferreira-Buckley, Linda. 1999. "Archivists with an Attitude: Rescuing the Archive from Foucault." *College English* 61:577–87.

First Archivist Circle. 2007. "Protocols for Native American Archival Materials." Last modified April 9. http://www2.nau.edu/libnap-p/protocols.html.

Glenn, Cheryl. 1997. "Mapping the Silences; or, Remapping Rhetorical Territory." In *Rhetoric Retold: Regendering the Tradition from Antiquity Through the Renaissance,* 1–17. Carbondale: Southern Illinois Press.

Glenn, Cheryl, and Jessica Enoch. 2010. "Invigorating Historiographic Practices in Rhetoric and Composition Studies." In *Working in the Archives: A Practical Research Guide for Rhetoric and Composition,* ed. Alexis E. Ramsey, Wendy B. Sharer, Barbara L'Eplattenier, and Lisa S. Mastrangelo, 206–19. Carbondale: Southern Illinois University Press.

Gold, David. 2008. *Rhetoric at the Margins: Revising the History of Writing Instruction in American Colleges, 1873–1947.* Carbondale: Southern Illinois University Press.

Haskins, Ekaterina. 2007. "Between Archive and Participation: Public Memory in a Digital Age." *Rhetoric Society Quarterly* 37:401–22.

Hawhee, Debra, and Christa J. Olson. In press. "Pan-Historiography: The Challenges of Writing History across Time and Space." In *Theorizing Histories of Rhetoric,* ed. Michelle Ballif. Carbondale: Southern Illinois University Press.

Johnson, Nan. 2010. "Autobiography of an Archivist." In *Working in the Archives: Practical Research Methods for Rhetoric and Composition*, ed. Alexis E. Ramsey, Wendy B. Sharer, Barbara L'Eplattenier, and Lisa S. Mastrangelo, 290–300. Carbondale: Southern Illinois University Press.

Juby, Dianne L. 1997. "Memory, Arts, Electronic Topoi, and Dynamic Databases." In *Making and Unmaking Prospects for Rhetoric: Selected Papers from the 1996 RSA Conference*, ed. Theresa Enos and Richard McNabb, 189–96. Mahwah, NJ: Erlbaum.

Kirsch, Gesa E., and Liz Rohan. 2008. *Beyond the Archives: Research as a Lived Process*. Carbondale: Southern Illinois University Press.

McKee, Heidi A., and James E. Porter. 2012. "The Ethics of Archival Research." *College Composition and Communication* 64:59–81.

Miles, John D. 2011. "The Postindian Rhetoric of Gerald Vizenor." *College Composition and Communication* 63:35–53.

Miller, Thomas P., and Melody Bowden. 1999. "A Rhetorical Stance on the Archives of Civic Action." *College English* 61:591–98.

Moon, Gretchen Flesher. 2007. "Locating Composition History." In *Local Histories: Reading the Archives of Composition*, ed. Patricia Donahue and Gretchen Flesher Moon, 1–13. Pittsburgh: University of Pittsburgh Press.

Mueller, Derek. 2012. "Grasping Rhetoric and Composition by Its Long Tail: What Graphs Can Tell Us about the Field's Changing Shape." *College Composition and Communication* 64:195–223.

Mutnick, Deborah. 2007. "Inscribing the World: An Oral History Project in Brooklyn." *College Composition and Communication* 58.4:626–47.

National Endowment for the Humanities (NEH). 2012. "Code of Ethics Related to Native Americans." http://www.neh.gov/grants/manage/code-ethics -related-native-americans.

"Octalog: The Politics of Historiography." 1988. *Rhetoric Review* 7:5–49.

Powell, Malea. 2002. "Rhetorics of Survivance: How American Indians Use Writing." *College Composition and Communication* 53:396–434.

———. 2008. "Dreaming Charles Eastman: Cultural Memory, Autobiography, and Geography in Indigenous Rhetorical Histories." In *Beyond the Archives: Research as a Lived Process*, ed. Gesa E. Kirsch and Liz Rohan, 115–27. Carbondale: Southern Illinois University Press.

Purdy, James. 2011. "Three Gifts of Digital Archives." *Journal of Literacy and Technology* 12:24–29.

Ramsey-Tobienne, Alexis. 2010. "Viewing the Archive: The Hidden and the Digital Archive." In *Working in the Archives: Practical Research Methods for Rhetoric and Composition*, ed. Alexis E. Ramsey, Wendy B. Sharer, Barbara L'Eplattenier, and Lisa S. Mastrangelo, 79–90. Carbondale: Southern Illinois University Press.

Ridolfo, Jim, William Hart-Davidson, and Michael McLeod. 2011. "Archive 2.0: Imagining The Michigan State University Israelite Samaritan Scroll Collection as the Foundation for a Thriving Social Network." *Journal of Community Informatics.* http://ci-journal.net/index.php/ciej/article/view/754/757.

Rohan, Liz. 2010. "The Personal as Method and Place as Archives: A Synthesis." In *Working in the Archives: Practical Research Methods for Rhetoric and Composition,* ed. Alexis E. Ramsey, Wendy B. Sharer, Barbara L'Eplattenier, and Lisa S. Mastrangelo, 232–47. Carbondale: Southern Illinois University Press.

Romano, Susan. 2004. "Tlaltelolco: The Grammatical-Rhetorical Indios of Colonial Mexico." *College English* 66:257–77.

Royster, Jacqueline Jones, and Jean C. Williams. 1999. "History in the Spaces Left: African American Presence and Narratives of Composition Studies." *College Composition and Communication* 50:563–84.

Rutner, Jennifer, and Roger C. Schonfeld. 2012. "Supporting the Changing Research Practices of Historians." *Ithaka S&R,* December 10. http://www.sr.ithaka.org/research-publications/supporting-changing-research-practices-historians.

Smith-Yoshimura, Karen, and Cyndi Shein. 2013. "Social Metadata for Libraries, Archives and Museums: Pt. 1, Site Reviews." *OCLC Research.* http://www.oclc.org/research/publications/library/2011/2011–02.pdf.

Solberg, Janine. 2012. "Googling the Archive: Digital Tools and the Practice of History." *Advances in the History of Rhetoric* 15:53–76.

Stoler, Ann Laura. 2002. "Colonial Archives and the Arts of Governance." *Archival Science* 2:87–109.

Sullivan, Patricia. 2012. "Inspecting Shadows of Past Classroom Practices: A Search for Students' Voices." *College Composition and Communication* 63:365–86.

Sullivan, Patricia, and Tarez Samra Graban. 2011. "Digital and Dustfree: A Conversation on the Possibilities of Digital-Only Searching for Third-Wave Historical Recovery." *Peitho* 13.2:2–11. http://cwshrc.org/wp-content/uploads/2012/01/Peitho13.2.pdf.

Theimer, Kate. 2012a. "Anything New Here for Archives? 'Supporting the Changing Research Practices of Historians.'" *Archivesnext.com,* December 18. http://www.archivesnext.com/?p=3179.

———. 2012b. "Debate: The Majority of Users Don't Care about Provenance. They Just Want Access to Information." *Archivesnext.com,* May 23. http://www.archivesnext.com/?p=2771.

Tuhiwai-Smith, Linda. 1999. *Decolonizing Methodologies: Research and Indigenous Peoples.* New York: Zed.

Wysocki, Anne Frances. 2007. "It Is Not Only Ours." *College Composition and Communication* 59:282–88.

Yakel, Elizabeth. 2010. "Searching and Seeking the Deep Web: Primary Sources on the Internet." In *Working in the Archives: Practical Research Methods for Rhetoric and Composition,* ed. Alexis E. Ramsey, Wendy B. Sharer, Barbara L'Eplattenier, and Lisa S. Mastrangelo, 102–18. Carbondale: Southern Illinois University Press.

## EIGHTEEN

Pop-Up Archives

JENNY RICE

JEFF RICE

Saturday morning, downtown Lexington, Kentucky. Farmers and vendors gather in Victorian Square for the winter farmers' market. A series of interactions and activities—selling goods, telling stories, comparing harvests with one another, showcasing the week's produce or meats, taking pictures—stands to be lost. What appears banal, in fact, represents a series of nodes in a larger network of meaning. These items, and others like them, deserve some form of preservation—from the temporary to the permanent—so that participants, observers, and other interested parties can identify patterns and connections regarding Kentucky food culture. These encounters are meetings of things, people, and moments that might offer newer understandings of Kentucky food culture.

On this particular Saturday morning, dozens of students from the University of Kentucky have set up card tables filled with digital recorders, a portable scanner, and a laptop. They are part of the Kentucky Food Project, which is an effort to trace and archive those encounters as networks of meaning. The students record stories, images, and artifacts from both longtime vendors at the market and people who are visiting for the first time. A woman strolls by the table and casually asks the students, "What are y'all doing here?" A student grabs her digital recorder. "We're recording your stories of the market! Will you talk with us?" The woman puts down her bags and begins to tell her story.

———

The archive has earned an important place within the digital humanities. The Shakespeare Quartos Archive (http://www.quartos.org), the City University of New York's Looking for Whitman (http://looking forwhitman.org), the Emory Women Writers Resource Project (http://womenwriters.library.emory.edu/about.php), and many other online sites institutionalize the storage, searchability, and arrangement of materials in archival spaces so that scholars can easily access them. The criterion of archivability, as well as the telos of an archive, has typically been *temporal endurance*. By creating an index of texts and artifacts that are worthy of preservation, archives seem to be defined by a kind of transcendent temporality. Even if archives house ephemera and texts that have disappeared from public memory, the temporal endurance of the archive itself is a constant. Explore UK (http://exploreuk.uky.edu), a library-supported archive available to us at the University of Kentucky, localizes this sense of endurance by preserving oral histories, images, and texts relevant to the history of the university so that the history remains available forever.

These kinds of efforts are found elsewhere in other digital collections whose aim is temporal endurance. The Emory Women Writers Resource Project, for example, promises that "the database will expand access to a significant facet of American and British culture. The electronic publication of women's genre fiction makes these novels widely available in searchable, digital form for the first time." The novels housed in the Emory Women Writers Resource Project are archivable both because of their endurance and because of a desire to secure their ongoing accessibility in the future. In addition, Syracuse University's National Endowment for the Humanities–funded Marcel Breuer Digital Archive (http://breuer.syr.edu) provides access to the famed architect's manuscripts, drawings, and photographs in order to prevent such work from being forgotten. Even with these examples, endurance and preservation are not givens regarding how we access and utilize such work, whether it is located in a university or a national archive. When Cara Finnegan documents her search through the Library of Congress in order to track down an elusive picture of a man standing on his porch, she describes her work as accessing the permanent and enduring national archive. Even within such permanence, however, she realizes that archival attempts to categorize can be misleading; in her case, an image search for a "man" is hampered by the archive's permanent tagging of the image as "shack." "Images in archives prompt complex rhetorical negotiations" (2006, 121), she concludes regarding this conflict over how an item is regulated to endurance. Whatever one might say about archives in the era of digital humanities, they are almost always defined by the goals, methods, and values of preservation. Those goals, however, must be tempered by negotiation. It is not a given to claim that archives must preserve forever since forever labels or placements can mislead or their meaning can shift over time.

Not all archives, however, have to make claims of permanence for themselves without recognizing such negotiations. Archives can also respond to what Jean-François Lyotard (1984, 60) calls "the quintessential form of imaginative invention," the small story (or *petit récit*), as opposed to the grand narratives that many institutional archives support (i.e., the entire Shakespeare corpus available for online access). Although the temporal endurance of the archive seems to be a constant, we can imagine what might change if this were not the case. What if we could create an archive whose aim is neither preservation nor a totalizing narrative created from accumulation but the encouragement and support of the kinds of negotiations Finnegan calls for? If we created an archive that disappeared or disintegrated after a time, would the telos of archiving disintegrate as well? How could we value an archive that eschews the significant facets of cultural narratives in favor of the *petit récit*?

In this chapter, we propose an explanation and theorization of one such archive of little stories, The Pop Up Archive Project at the University of Kentucky. The Pop Up Archive seeks to forge community connections within Lexington, Kentucky, by gathering specific public groups and undergraduate students in one place, on one day, for a temporary archival moment. The purpose of the Pop Up Archive is to create a digital space that memorializes and highlights the temporality of network connections, the fragile and momentary ways agents affect one another. In the age of networks, spaces of meaning fluctuate as new agents enter such spaces and affect other agents. The Pop Up Archive highlights how these networks work within the specific domain of archiving. Moreover, endurance or endurability is neither a criterion nor a telos for the archives created within this project. Instead, the Pop Up Archive Project reimagines archives in a digital age as performances and gestures.

The Gathering

Pop-up is not a concept new to contemporary culture. Pop-up highlights the speed of digital culture. Despite Paul Virilio's reservations that "with acceleration there is no more here and there, only the mental confusion of near and far, present and future, real and unreal" (1995, 35), speed offers unique opportunities for capturing what otherwise would be dismissed as trivial, passing, or unimportant. The pop-up restaurant, a temporary restaurant often featured in urban settings where chefs cook and serve in a borrowed space for one night, allows for a different kind of temporal experience. Unlike conventional restaurants, the pop-up restaurant exists only for a night or two. The attraction, as one *New York Times* story argues, is flexibility (Dicum 2010). Because such restaurants are defined by transience, they often embrace experimentation and innovation in ways conventional (and thus grand) dining experiences cannot; there is no dependence on return clientele the next night.

The food writer Jonathan Gold writes about his trips to LudoBites, a Los Angeles pop-up restaurant by chef Ludo Lefebvre, who opens his high-end restaurant for only a few days each year in a friend's small bakery or sandwich shop. The food is amazing, says Gold, but the experience is just as important. Writing about one's experience, as so many visitors to the pop-up do online, is important since LudoBites has quickly ended and will never be experienced in the same way ever again. Each incarnation of LudoBites comes with a numeric notation: LudoBites 8.0 is the most recent version. Flickr pages are devoted to visually documenting the LudoBites experience, and Twitter streams rumors about the next LudoBites opening. LudioBites represents a temporary, archival pop-up moment (captured by Flickr and Twitter).

The space hardly matters. The food looks amazing, but maybe that does not matter either. Chef Lefebvre (a handsome French tattooed rock-star chef) is a celebrity, but maybe even *that* does not matter. The temporal gathering matters. A gathering of temporariness. A gathering that matters because it is short-lived and will never happen again. Yet it is the memory of gathering that will transcend time. And the *writing about* that gathering matters as well.

Pop-up architecture, too, is drawing attention from urban planning, community activism, architectural theory, and neighborhood groups. Examples of pop-up architecture could be something as simple as a vendor (with or without a license) selling books and trinkets on a street corner or as complex as an art installation (with or without a license) featured in an abandoned building. In her *New York Times* opinion piece on temporary architecture, Allison Arieff (2011) writes that the pop-up's recent celebration is not "advocating an end to planning but encourages more short-term doing, experimenting, testing":

"While this may not directly change existing codes or zoning regulations, that's O.K. because . . . the practices employed 'shine a direct light on old ways of thinking, old policies that are in place.'"

In Western countries, pop-up events have taken on an aura of privilege, yet Peter Bishop and Lesley Williams remind us: "For large sections of the world's population, . . . 'permanence' is an unattainable dream. Urban poverty is often characterized by living in a temporary physical environment and in a state of extreme and challenging uncertainty" (2012, 12). The idea of architecture as a response to immediate situations—including crisis—is a vastly different view of architecture as a mode of permanence.

As pop-up restaurants and retail exemplify, there is great value in experiences that happen on the fly, in a moment, for a night or day only. In the pop-up moment, the aim is not preservation. The moment occurs and then is lost forever. These moments might serve as an example of contemporary "just in time" logics. Such logics can challenge the grand gestures and master narratives that are typically associated with institutional thinking that aims to preserve forever. If the institutional logic of archives has, up until now, been dominated by a will to permanence, then it is worth considering an archive that exists for a reason beyond preservation.

The Pop-Up Archive Project

Even in an age of digital archives, with their alternative modes of delivery and access, archival access points can still remain out of reach for academics who wish to facilitate an immediate encounter with shared topoi. For instance, university archives are understandably more interested in the permanent and grand (i.e., special collections) than in the temporary and transient. Locally, the Kentucky History Project's mobile app (http://explorekyhistory.ky.gov) maintains a logic of permanence by using its app only for viewing already archived sites, not for generating new archival material from users. In this way, such efforts work against the spirit of Michel de Certeau's concept of the tactic (as opposed to the strategy). The tactic, de Certeau writes, "cannot count on a 'proper' (a spatial or institutional localization) nor thus on a borderline distinguishing the other as a visible totality." It "depends on time—it is always on the watch for opportunities that must be 'seized on the wing'" (1984, xix). For the most part, institutional archives do not yet seize the wing.

In order to confront more directly the transient and temporary, therefore, several faculty at the University of Kentucky created a pop-up archive of the Lexington Farmers' Market. Our focus was the tactile, to seize on the wing. The pop-up archive, dubbed the Kentucky Food Project, is part of an interdisciplinary project affiliated with the University of Kentucky's Digital Distillery (http://digitaldistillery.as.uky .edu). Stakeholders in food communities across Kentucky—including almost two hundred registered farmers' markets across the state, hundreds of community gardens, and numerous longtime food festivals such as the annual Bar-B-Q Festival in Owensboro—can benefit from preserving oral histories and archival records of their beginnings and their evolution. While food communities in Kentucky have long-term stakeholders, there are also many short-term participants and stakeholder groups (including farmhands, seasonal orchard workers, ranch hands, festival attendees and workers, students in courses about food communities, and migrant groups who bring their own food traditions into Kentucky).

Although regional food projects, most notably Southern Foodways, already archive oral histories and video documentaries, such projects are not designed to archive impromptu events or interviews. During several pop-up writing events at the weekly farmers' market in Lexington, Kentucky, students set up makeshift stations filled with laptops and digital recorders. Rather than record the history of individual farmers or the market itself, the events worked to capture the little stories lost to patrons or residents of the city (or even to the farmers themselves) by creating an on-the-fly curation day.

The first pop-up writing events were held in conjunction with Jeff Rice's first-year course at the University of Kentucky, "Eating Kentucky." In this course, students worked with members of the Lexington Farmers' Market to record oral histories and scan relevant historical artifacts from longtime market vendors and farmers. Response from the farmers' market community was overwhelmingly enthusiastic. In the first pop-up event, demand was so great that farmers waited in lines to work with students. Subsequent sessions resulted in similar positive responses. All oral histories were uploaded to the Digital Distillery and shared with the Lexington Farmers' Market board members.

With this project, temporal community moments—the gathering at a market, the narration of anecdotes, the collection of photographs, the interaction by students with farmers and vendors, the selling of food and crafts, and even the pop-up moment itself—become archived for future reflection, appropriation, and other uses. The interaction between student archivist and farmer on a Saturday morning passes quickly; pop-up archiving captures a fleeting moment that might escape more institutional standards of archivability.

However, the Kentucky Food Project does not aim only to preserve ephemera or small details that might help tell a more complete story of food cultures in Kentucky. In fact, this archive's own permanence may not even be its most valuable aspect. It is possible that this pop-up archive will not remain online forever. By the time you read this, it may have grown, or it may have disappeared. While its longevity may be useful for a number of reasons, we would not consider this archive a failure if it is erased tomorrow. The pop-up archive's focus is not in preservation but in the gesture and performance of archiving moments. The moment is not preserved; instead, what is preserved is an encounter of the archivists themselves. By working in the temporary network spaces that digital media allow for, students are enacting the work of archiving. What is created is not digital archives per se but *digital archivists*.

In this spirit, we conclude by sketching out a much different kind of tool for digital archives. This tool is meant to help users and collectors of materials become digital archivists (rather than being meant to build an archive). This tool builds on existing technologies, but its use requires us to rethink the telos, or goal, of archives. We must shift from thinking of archives as spaces (physical or digital) of preservation to thinking of them more as an action that happens between two or more users. Archives as collections of material are, thus, simply the conduits or the materials that allow for this archiving action to take place.

Our own vision of such a tool for the Kentucky Food Project is a mobile app that allows for flexible, social curation in which negotiation of materials is the goal. The mobile app design in progress draws on the logic of the social media site Pinterest, which has popularized the notion that curation can be a powerful form of social networking and communication. In Pinterest, users curate on the fly, drawing on repositories of uploaded information (video, text, image) as well as their own material. Much like Pinterest's interface, the Kentucky Food Project mobile app allows users to embed images from other users into their own archival repository. Users will be able to search and navigate that repository, choose materials to include, and generate their own archive instantly. A single upload repository will store all video, text, audio, and images. But the focus is on the user who, through the navigation of found and uploaded material, becomes a digital archivist (even if for only a day, week, moment, or event).

Food studies have become an important object of study in the humanities (e.g., *College English* 70.4 [2008]; *Pre-Text* 21.1 [2013]; the University of California Press Studies in Food and Culture series), yet, in general, scholars do not have access to either the creation or the curation of material if they are not based where permanent archives exist or have funding to visit such archives. Likewise, food stakeholder communities often do not have the resources to create extensive online archives; they lack the funding, material, or know-how regarding setting up such archival spaces. One could go to an archive—if access permits—and find an item, but one cannot often use that item to build a temporary archive. For instance, when a Southern Foodways intern discovers a forgotten 1950s USDA recipe card for a peanut butter dried beef sandwich, her discovery is shared online as a narrative, but the usage of that material—despite its permanent status in the University of Mississippi's Child Nutrition Archives—can never be temporarily combined with other just-in-time moments (oral memory, photograph of said sandwich, saved newspaper clipping) by a food stakeholder or researcher (Evans 2013). The material artifact—the recipe card—is recalled but not used to create a momentary, pop-up archive as our mobile app would allow for.

Our project—a crowd-sourced, user-driven archive—provides a response to such situations. As a mobile app, material, access to material, and ability to curate material will exist via just-in-time logic. In a broader sense, the Kentucky Food Project mobile app helps develop new models of information dissemination and multimodal sharing, which is of interest to humanities-based fields. As one industry analysis of Pinterest's platform remarks: "People stare into the fire hose of information every day, and it's having an impact. They're actively seeking ways to not only filter and organize what they find, but also to less stressfully consume more content" ("Pinterest," n.d., 8). The Kentucky Food Project mobile app hopes to help users contribute more easily to the preservation of food traditions, events, stories, and artifacts. But we also hope to help those same users filter and organize what they find so that they can negotiate the complex relations information generates. Mobile archives will provide the necessary resources for visualization of the larger issues at play.

The ability to create instant archives, such as the Kentucky Food Project's pop-up archives, prompts digital humanists to theorize different kinds of archival effects, including the effects of temporality. Considering temporality in ways beyond permanence and longevity is also important when we recall that practices like crowd sourcing in archives have their own kinds of built-in transience. Specifically, the growing examples of crowd-sourced online archive projects have seen only a few users consistently contribute. In the Library of Congress's Flickr Commons project, for example, one analysis found that 40 percent of contributions were added by a group of ten individuals who were actively helping curate the images through tags and descriptions. At the same time, the analysis found that 2,518 unique users participated in the archival project (Springer et al. 2008). In short, a few people participate a lot, and a lot of people will try something once. We might define this as a participation problem, but the humanities can also define this as a design challenge for digital humanists who look to engage with both temporary moments and the individuals who might encounter such moments. The Kentucky Food Project encourages us to think about information usage in ways that go beyond the storage and preservation of spaces and material. Instead, users (those who interact with information) and time (temporality) become digital foci for archival work. In this way, we ask, How can we create tools for archiving in a way that lowers the pressure of a long-term commitment to archiving for individual users? Our response is the pop-up.

References

Arieff, Alison. 2011. "It's Time to Rethink Temporary." *New York Times*, December 19. http://opinionator.blogs.nytimes.com/2011/12/19/its-time -to-rethink-temporary.

Bishop, Peter, and Lesley Williams. 2012. *The Temporary City*. Oxford: Routledge.

de Certeau, Michel. 1984. *The Practices of Everyday Life*. Berkeley and Los Angeles: University of California Press.

Dicum, Gregory. 2010. "At Pop Ups, Chefs Take Chances with Little Risk." *New York Times*, February 11. http://www.nytimes.com/2010/02/12/ dining/12sfdine.html.

Evans, Amy Cameron. 2013. "SFA Oral History Intern Digs Up a Culinary Gem." Southern Foodways Alliance, July 24. http://www.southern foodways.org/sfa-oral-history-intern-digs-up-a-culinary-gem.

Finnegan, Cara A. 2006. "What Is This a Picture Of? Some Thoughts on Images and Archives." *Rhetoric and Public Affairs* 9:116–23.

Lyotard, Jean-François. 1984. *The Postmodern Condition: A Report on Knowledge*. Minneapolis: University of Minnesota Press.

"Pinterest: A Review of Social Media's Newest Sweetheart." n.d. *Engauge.* http://www.engauge.com/assets/pdf/Engauge-Pinterest.pdf.

Springer, Michelle, et al. 2008. *For the Common Good: The Library of Congress Flickr Pilot Project.* Washington, DC: Library of Congress. http://www.loc.gov/rr/print/flickr_report_final.pdf.

Virilio, Paul. 1995. *Art of the Motor.* Minneapolis: University of Minnesota Press.

## NINETEEN

Archive Experiences: A Vision for User-Centered Design in the Digital Humanities

LIZA POTTS

Over the past several decades, we have witnessed a race to build, archive, and distribute various scholarly materials across the digital humanities (Earhart 2012). While these systems hold a veritable treasure trove of knowledge, they are crippled by their user experiences. Instead of distributing knowledge to the public and encouraging scholarly exploration, interactions with these systems are clunky at best and irrelevant at worse. Rather than building systems that prioritize data above experience, we need to architect archives that are focused on engagement with scholars and outreach with the public. This is a call for scholar practitioners in rhetoric to engage with the digital humanities as user advocates, experience architects, and participant-centered researchers.

Many of these digital humanities systems, either by accident or by design, are focused on serving up material—images, texts, and videos—rather than engaging with participants. What these archives in practice and the digital humanities in general desperately need is a sense of audience, appeal, and interaction. Instead, these archives are often inwardly facing, aimed at their own research partners and, perhaps, their own specific field. However, these systems are live and on the public Internet, where there is a huge opportunity to interact with and create new audiences. Unfortunately, these systems often lack user-centered, rhetorically situated, contextually aware experiences. We need to build systems that are more widely accessible.

To make such a move toward accessibility, we need to build digital humanities projects that allow for more engagement with at a minimum the digital humanities specifically and a multitude of audiences more broadly. We must design and build for experience. I refer to these practices, rooted firmly in technical communication and evolving from user-centered design (UCD), as *experience architecture*. Experience architecture is an emerging practice, one that draws together issues of information design, information architecture, interaction design, and usability studies to assess and build products, services, and processes. The outcomes of a well-architected system include systems, interfaces, and policies that support participation, growth, and sustainability—in other words, building experiences that are focused on human experience, the kinds of experiences we are espousing when we discuss the application of rhetoric and digital humanities. By realigning project teams across disciplines to build user-centered experiences, we can have a huge impact on how these systems are received by their audiences.

Digital Humanities and the Hidden Users/Participants

The need for refactoring, rebuilding, and integrating experience architecture into the product life cycle of these projects is clear. When scholars in digital humanities turn to examining usability and design, it is often to comment on design rather than engage with its practice. Examining the most recent major book surveying the digital humanities (Gold 2012) shows that only two of the forty-nine chapters and printed blog posts relate even somewhat to UCD and that both are in the critique section of the text (Edwards 2012; Williams 2012). Similarly, recent publications coming out of a major digital visualization lab makes no mention of the terms *usability* or *UCD*, much less any of the necessary concepts behind building user-centered, rather than data-driven, experiences (Manovich 2012, n.d.). Searching one of the largest digital humanities hubs shows that only a minority of scholar practitioners self-identify as designers, with no category available for expertise in information architecture or usability (Digital Humanities Commons, n.d.). That said, in rhetoric there is a much stronger understanding of and skill set for UCD than is being represented in these publications. This work is already taking place. What is needed are more obvious connections between our work in technical communication and work across other fields in digital humanities. Our years of experience in UCD, information design, and experience architecture are an asset for digital humanities projects.

Collections on digital humanities scholarship contain some brief mentions of users and design. Some even suggested readings that are woefully dated, continuing to mention early works on UCD from, e.g., Norman (1989), Cooper (1995), and Nielsen (1993). We are now on the cusp of a new age, where big data, metadata, and participatory culture are set to collide. And while Norman, Cooper, and friends were certainly useful companions to help give us a foundation, we now need to pay attention to new ways of architecting, designing, managing, and developing our products. There is a wave of new work all espousing a collective discussion on how to engage users as participants, both in design and in social engagement, that I will discuss in the next section. Suffice it to say, we have moved forward in industry practice and research in our field.

Another major issue is how projects are managed. While industry practice has moved into agile methods and practices, many digital humanities projects seem to be trapped in waterfall methods of software development. Some of these projects even seem to promote this dated process. Many of the discussions of making fetishize the concept of coding, which is disconcerting for several reasons—not the least because it feels like a repeat of a era we have already lived through. These movements are, indeed, akin to the late 1990s of computing, making the above-mentioned references of dated UCD work relevant—albeit entirely out of place given current workplace practices. Rather than relive the dot-com boom and bust, we need to call for an intervention, redirecting and updating the practices in digital humanities projects. In the next section, I will define the kinds of work involved in UCD, calling on us to be the experience architects that are so woefully missing on many of these digital humanities projects.

Rather than seeing these gaps as a lack of interest, we can see this moment as an opportunity for our field. And, frankly, it is unfair to expect our colleagues in English, history, linguistics, and other humanities-focused fields to have the same backgrounds we have in information design, usability, information architecture, and other technical communication teachings. Realistically, we are the ones who have the backgrounds, teachings, and experiences to lead projects. Scholar practitioners in rhetoric are well equipped to respond to this challenge because of their deep tradition of user advocacy and empowerment design (Davis 2002; Hart-Davidson 2001; Grabill and Simmons 1998; Johnson 1998; Mirel 1996; Miller 1979). This moment in this field is one in which a shift toward participating in and researching the design of interfaces, interactions, and processes and analyzing the use of these genres and associated tools is becoming more prevalent (Spinuzzi 2003, 2007, 2013; Potts and Jones 2011; Swarts 2008). Moreover, all these developments contribute to our abilities to work effectively in complex contexts where one must address these issues of sustainability, participation, and engagement. This lack of UCD in digital humanities projects provides an opportunity for us to fill this gap, participate in these programs, and draw on our strengths to engage with these scholars and materials to refocus these projects in ways that support UCD.

Rhetoric and UCD

In making these connections between rhetoric and the digital humanities, we can focus on engagement. By *engagement*, I mean engagement both with the internal digital humanities communities as they exist today and with the external audiences for digital humanities projects. Concentrating on building systems that provide for engagement between the curators and the participants can broaden the audiences for these projects, addressing the needs of both researchers and the public. Participating in these projects as experience architects, usability experts, information architects, and information designers, we can propose early questions about audience, purpose, and scope.

These tasks are the same kind of work that we are already doing in our own practices and classrooms. Our worldview is unique to those of us trained in rhetoric in general and certainly to those of us with experience running technical projects and mentoring our students through these activities. Theory and practices for UCD are not widely known throughout the humanities. It is an opportunity and a responsibility to lead and participate in these projects because of our knowledge of how to architect, manage, and improve both the process and the building of these products and services.

We may need to clearly make the case for UCD projects, distributing the knowledge that we already have in our field to those outside it. We may find ourselves having the same arguments as we did in the 1990s (why do we need UCD?). Thankfully, we have a rich set of materials from which we can draw on old and new discussions about user interface design (Tidwell 2011), information architecture (Resmini and Rosati 2011;

Morville and Rosenfeld 2006), content strategy (Halvorson and Rach 2012; Redish 2007), agile development (Ratcliffe and McNeill 2012), project management (Berkun 2008), and team management (Lund 2011).

Engaging with users and participants, we can work on a strategy for the success of digital humanities projects. There are many excellent examples out there for guiding principles of user experience, including Morville's (2005) concept of findability, Krug's (2006) thoughts on not thinking, and Garret's (2010) levels of interaction and work flow. All three books are good for understanding the basic concepts of UCD. As another example, we can look to Halvorson and Rach's (2012) work on experience and content, where they outline three major foci: core, content, and people. Purpose, context, and audience are major concepts in rhetoric, ones that we emphasize repeatedly within our pedagogy and our practice. Looking at a combination of these components, we can discuss what UCD can and should be for digital humanities, focused squarely on creating contextualized experiences for engagement. Launching any new project—whether it is creating a new product, service, process, or whatever—requires asking questions up front to ensure successful outcomes. And, while we ask these questions in the beginning, it is important to revisit them constantly to align the project with the goals of our users and stakeholders.

Purpose

Before diving into any project, we are obligated to ask what we are trying to achieve. What is the purpose of this digital archive, this mobile application, this Web site, this kiosk, etc.? Coming to some consensus on what the end result is meant to achieve is of critical importance. There are some key purposes to digital humanities projects: to share knowledge, to educate the public, to appeal to donors, to connect to a wider research community, etc. While any project can have multiple purposes, it is important to come to an agreement on its major purpose. Aligning the team toward this goal is essential to building a product that will be user centered.

Content

There are many types of content on digital humanities Web sites and applications, including images, games, videos, text, pdfs, data sets, maps, and audio. The types of content and the ways in which it is presented all need to take into consideration the context in which our users/participants will engage with it. Many digital humanities projects are addressed and logically present their work to their peers and funders. Credibility is heavily emphasized, as evidenced by the listings of the researchers, contributors, centers, and funding agencies that contributed to the project. That said, the connection between producer and potential audience is not always as overt. If this content is of public interest, and most digital humanities research certainly can be, then how can we best present this content to these audiences? What entry points will we create to these rich materials? How can we create the kinds of appeals that connect site producers with participants (academic and the general public) who are eager to engage with this content? Building content and structures to serve that content in interactive, contextualized ways will help distribute our research and create experiences for multiple audiences.

People

Whenever we sit down to start a project, the first question I have is, Who is our audience? Understanding audience is a key skill to develop in our students. The next question is always, What is the context in which that audience will use our product/service/process? For digital humanities projects, there is a clear and strong audience of scholars. And, while that is important, there is a set of audiences out there that are interested in our work, can engage with our work, and can add value to our research. This group is composed, at a bare minimum, of the general public, prospective benefactors, and interdisciplinary researchers. So why is it that so many of these archives and projects lack any sense of audience, interaction, and appeal? By understanding our audiences, we can create interactive, useful, and rich experiences for them.

Having a grasp on these three core concepts (purpose, content, people) is essential for developing products focused on users and participants. There are many methods for developing user-centered products, services, and processes. Useful methods include landscape analysis, content inventory, focus groups, site visits, contextual inquiry, surveys, researcher participation, affinity diagramming, card sorting, prototyping, and usability testing. Stakeholder interviews can help us gain a better understanding of the problem space as well as of the goals of the project. Sitting down and discussing the reasons for the project, the hopes for new solutions, and the constraints in which the project will be deployed help focus the project. Contextual inquiry allows us to visit the spaces in which these technologies are (or will be) deployed. Observing task flows, learning about usage, and witnessing patterns of behavior can help document work flow and lead to solution discovery. Returning back to the team armed with these data, we can begin to design useful prototypes. After the prototype is built, we can conduct usability testing. The results of these tests can help us refine the final implementation as well as create wish lists for future iterations based on user feedback.

This list is by no means comprehensive, and there are countless Web sites, articles, and books on further methods that could help with our research work. I have listed the ones that have served me best and will, I think, give us a good start, but leaders will need to select the methods that work for specific projects and teams. These are iterative processes—meaning that we can design, share the design with the internal team, iterate on the design, show the users/participants the design, iterate some more, etc. Above all else, it is important to work on architecting and designing these systems before incurring the high costs of development work. To do otherwise is costly and time consuming and will certainly result in user-experience issues.

Future Work as Agents of Social Change

We can bring a vision of UCD to the digital humanities that stands on the shoulders of rhetoric's vast research on communication design, information architecture, and rhetoric. Recently, an industry contact asked me for an updated reading list and set of examples for UCD. He stated plainly that industry looks to universities to be on the cutting edge of technologies, of movements, of change. It is imperative that the products and services coming out of the digital humanities are cutting-edge. With a background in rhetoric and training in UCD, we can be the "agent of social change" (Savage 2004, 183). We must move on this moment and architect for experience, rather than simply archiving collections. Such moves will allow us to explore what Kathleen Fitzpatrick refers to as the creative tension between "making and interpreting, between the field's history and its future" (2012, 14). It is within this space that we may also see the future of digital humanities and rhetoric, one in which we can be key contributors, leading the work to "shape emerging digital culture rather than only adapt to the change it brings" (Salvo and Rosinski 2010, 111).

References

Berkun, Scott. 2008. *Making Things Happen: Mastering Project Management.* Sebastopol: O'Reilly.

Cooper, Alan. 1995. *About Face: The Essentials of User Interface Design.* Foster City, CA: IDG Worldwide.

Davis, Marjorie T. 2002. "Shaping the Future of Our Profession." *Technical Communication* 48:139–44.

Digital Humanities Commons. n.d. "Collaborators." http://dhcommons.org/collaborators.

Earhart, Amy E. 2012. "Can Information Be Unfettered? Race and the New Digital Humanities Canon." In *Debates in the Digital Humanities*, ed. Matthew K. Gold, 309–18. Minneapolis: University of Minnesota Press.

Edwards, Charlie. 2012. "The Digital Humanities and Its Users." In *Debates in the Digital Humanities*, ed. Matthew K. Gold, 213–32. Minneapolis: University of Minnesota Press.

Fitzpatrick, Kathleen. 2012. "The Humanities, Done Digitally." In *Debates in the Digital Humanities*, ed. Matthew K. Gold, 12–15. Minneapolis: University of Minnesota Press.

Garrett, Jesse James. 2010. *The Elements of User Experience: User-Centered Design for the Web.* 2nd ed. Indianapolis: New Riders.

Gold, Matthew K., ed. 2012. *Debates in the Digital Humanities.* Minneapolis: University of Minnesota Press.

Grabill, Jeffrey T., and W. Michele Simmons. 1998. "Toward a Critical Rhetoric of Risk Communication: Producing Citizens and the Role of Technical Communication." *Technical Communication Quarterly* 7:415–41.

Halvorson, Kristina, and Melissa Rach. 2012. *Content Strategy for the Web.* 2nd ed. Berkeley, CA: New Riders.

Hart-Davidson, William. 2001. "On Writing, Technical Communication, and Information Technology: The Core Competencies of Technical Communication." *Technical Communication* 48:145–55.

Johnson, Robert R. 1998. *User-Centered Technology: A Rhetorical Theory for Computers and Other Mundane Artifacts.* Albany: State University of New York Press.

Krug, Steve. 2006. *Don't Make Me Think! A Common Sense Approach to Web Usability.* 2nd ed. Berkeley, CA: New Riders.

Lund, Arnie. 2011. *User Experience Management: Essential Skills for Leading Effective UX Teams.* Burlington, MA: Morgan Kaufmann.

Manovich, Lev. 2012. "Trending: The Promises and Challenges of Big Social Data." In *Debates in the Digital Humanities*, ed. Matthew K. Gold, 460–73. Minneapolis: University of Minnesota Press.

———. n.d. "Visualizing Image and Video Collections: Examples." *Media Visualization.* http://softwarestudies.com/cultural_analytics/Visualizing-image-and-video-collections-examples.pdf.

Miller, Carolyn R. 1979. "A Humanistic Rationale for Technical Writing." *College English* 40:610–17.

Mirel, Barbara. 1996. "Writing and Database Technology: Extending the Definition of Writing in the Workplace." In *Electronic Literacies in the Workplace: Technologies of Writing,* ed. Patricia Sullivan and Jennie Dautermann, 91–114. Urbana: NCTE/Computers and Composition.

Morville, Peter. 2005. *Ambient Findability: What We Find Changes Who We Become.* Sebastopol, CA: O'Reilly.

Morville, Peter, and Louis Rosenfeld. 2006. *Information Architecture for the World Wide Web: Designing Large-Scale Web Sites.* 3rd e. Sebastopol: O'Reilly.

Nielsen, Jakob. 1993. *Usability Engineering.* San Diego: Morgan Kaufmann.

Norman, Donald A. 1989. *The Design of Everyday Things.* New York: Doubleday.

Potts, Liza, and Dave Jones. 2011. "Contextualizing Experiences: Tracing the Relationships between People and Technologies in the Social Web." *Journal of Business and Technical Communication* 25:1–21.

Ratcliffe, Lindsay, and Marc McNeill. 2012. *Agile Experience Design: A Digital Designer's Guide to Agile, Lean, and Continuous.* Berkeley, CA: New Riders.

Redish, Janice. 2007. *Letting Go of the Words: Writing Web Content that Works.* Amsterdam: Morgan Kaufmann.

Resmini, Andrea, and Luca Rosati. 2011. *Pervasive Information Architecture: Designing Cross-Channel User Experiences.* Burlington, MA: Morgan Kaufmann.

Salvo, Michael J., and Paula Rosinski. 2010. "Information Design: From Authoring Text to Architecting Virtual Space." In *Digital Literacy for Technical Communication,* ed. Rachel Spilka, 103–27. New York: Routledge.

Savage, Gerald J. 2004. "Tricksters, Fools, and Sophists: Technical Communication as Postmodern Rhetoric." In *Power and Legitimacy in Technical Communication,* vol. 2, *Strategies for Professional Status,* ed. Teresa Kynell-Hunt and Gerald J. Savage, 167–93. Amityville, NY: Baywood.

Spinuzzi, Clay. 2003. *Tracing Genres through Organizations: A Sociocultural Approach to Information Design.* Cambridge, MA: MIT Press.

———. 2007. "Guest Editor's Introduction: Technical Communication in the Age of Distributed Work." *Technical Communication Quarterly* 16:265–77.

———. 2013. *Topsight: A Guide to Studying, Diagnosing, and Fixing Information Flow in Organizations.* N.p.: CreateSpace Independent Publishing Platform.

Swarts, Jason. 2008. *Together with Technology: Writing Review, Enculturation, and Technological Mediation.* Amityville, NY: Baywood.

Tidwell, Jenifer. 2011. *Designing Interfaces.* 2nd ed. Sebastopol: O'Reilly.

Williams, George H. 2012. "Disability, Universal Design, and the Digital." In *Debates in the Digital Humanities,* ed. Matthew K. Gold, 202–12. Minneapolis: University of Minnesota Press.

## TWENTY

MVC, Materiality, and the Magus: The Rhetoric of Source-Level Production

KARL STOLLEY

The greater the range and intenseness of the opportunities for the exercising of our symbolic prowess, the greater might be our delight in such modes of action. KENNETH BURKE, *LANGUAGE AS SYMBOLIC ACTION*

Let me open with the major premise of this chapter's argument: programming is writing. I mean that literally, as I will illustrate with some limited examples from the Ruby on Rails framework in this chapter. Though I mean the phrase literally, *programming is writing* is frequently invoked as a metaphor, even among programmers. I agree with programmer Steve McConnell (2004), who dismisses writing as "the most primitive metaphor for software development" (7). However, there are some key points in his dismissal that are unsound. Among McConnell's observations on the metaphor's shortcomings:

- "[Writing] doesn't require any formal planning, and you figure out what you want to say as you go" (5).
- "Writing is usually a one-person activity" (6).
- "In writing, a high premium is placed on originality. In software construction, [originality] is often less effective than focusing on the reuse of design ideas, code, and test cases from previous artifacts" (6).

An oversimplified conception of writing forms the basis of McConnell's critique of the metaphor. True, writing may not require formal planning, but, as even the introductory-writing student quickly discovers, that is an unstudied and ineffective way to proceed. Playwrights, poets, and technical writers alike know that writing is collaborative, to some degree, always. And, from citation practices to genre features, writers have a wide foundation of reusable material on which originality is built, given a particular rhetorical occasion: to write is to engage in intelligent, ethical (i.e., nonplagiarized) reuse of previous artifacts. However, as I discuss later, richer encounters with originality that digital writers and humanists alike might otherwise experience are routinely preempted by careless reuse and outsourcing of source-level production.

To provide a glimpse into the experience of programming, I will present some of the activities involved in building a Web application using Ruby on Rails (a full Rails app is available with additional commentary via this book's companion Web site: www.press.uchicago.edu/sites/rdh/). There is not room in this chapter for a full technical description of Ruby on Rails, but it is enough for now to note that Rails is an open-source Web-application development framework written in the Ruby programming language.

Rails can be installed, invoked, and developed entirely through writing. There is no file to manually download and unzip (as with Drupal, WordPress, and other platforms as frameworks that are currently popular) and nothing to click on. Rails is installed by running a command on any system with a command-line interface (CLI; indicated here by the dollar sign, $) and a Ruby installation, as is the case for Mac OS X and many distributions of Linux:

```
$ gem install rails
```

Installing Rails does not create a Rails application. Among other things detailed below, a Rails installation includes a command-line program, conveniently called *rails*; and it is with the rails command that a project is brought into existence. All that Rails requires is a name for the project, and in this example I have chosen BeSocial, an imaginary social networking application:

```
$ rails new besocial
```

Running that command fills the CLI screen with dozens of lines of output indicating the creation of a number of files and directories as well as the installation of additional Ruby software packages, called *Gems*, that a basic Rails app depends on. Two lines written on the command line have built the foundations for a Web application developed through written programming activity. Running the rails server from within the new besocial directory, which Rails created, starts a Web server for the app. Although not much to look at yet, it can be viewed in a web browser at http://localhost:3000. I will return to the construction of the app toward the end of the chapter.

Materiality

When I claim that programming is writing, I am talking about writing source code right alongside and in service of acts of communication, including visual and interaction design. Yet, for over thirty years, point-and-click interfaces have mediated writing and other forms of digital communication and design. Despite the benefits of those interfaces, their mediation has also obscured much of the rich symbolic activity happening just beneath the apparent simplicity of something like an iPad's touch screen. Digital materiality would appear to be only screen deep.

Jay David Bolter's simple 1991 observation seems striking today: "Even a graphics program does not draw: it writes" (10). Working at a time even before the introduction of Microsoft Windows 3.1 and the mouse and graphic-user-interface (GUI) model of interaction that that operating system would make ubiquitous in ways the original Macintosh could not, Bolter could confidently proclaim as literal what now appears metaphoric: "All computing is reading and writing. The computer is therefore a technology for all writers—scientists and engineers as well as scholars, novelists, and poets" (10).

Just as McConnell oversimplified the activity of writing, so too do nonprogrammers generally oversimplify the activity of programming. To speak of programming as a vague, monolithic abstraction is no different from speaking that way of cooking or even writing. Any sustained, personal encounter with the activity reveals the vast complexity behind its abstraction. Although I am fascinated by books such as *10 PRINT* (Montfort et al. 2013) and certain other intellectual efforts emerging from the field of software studies, it is not uncommon to encounter conference presentations and scholarship—including *10 PRINT*'s focus on a single line of BASIC—that showcase truly ancient source code, divorced (as with most writing) from the lived activity of its creation. Historical treatment of source code is, of course, as important as any other history of writing and media. But it is important to note that historical examples of source code typically differ greatly from contemporary programming languages such as JavaScript, Python, or Ruby. The materiality of source code has evolved and, with it, the activity of programming.

It is no huge leap to reformulate Bolter's observation as: "All *programming* is reading and writing." Of course, outside small groups of researchers in the field of rhetoric and other areas in the digital humanities, the idea that programming is writing and, therefore, counts as intellectual work is far from accepted. It is difficult to seek acceptance for something that has not been widely practiced, argued, and made known.

Ramsay and Rockwell (2012) note that, for those digital humanists "who have turned to building, hacking, and coding as part of their normal research activity," there is a looming question of "whether the manipulation of features, objects, and states of interest using the language of coding or programming . . . constitutes theorizing" (82). Although far from arriving at any actionable answer to that question, Ramsay and Rockwell articulate the challenge that faces anyone who would claim that programming is literally writing and, therefore, a mode of inquiry and intellectual work: those who program and build are compelled "to present their own activities as capable of providing affordances as rich and provocative as that of writing" (83).

The key word there is *activities*: it is neither the created artifact experienced on screen nor even the source code behind it alone that expresses the affordances of programming as intellectual work. It is the activity of programming itself that builders, writers as programmers, must demonstrate. This activity, I believe, will ultimately present itself as theorizing, as Ramsay and Rockwell seem to hope. But the path to theorization may look different from simply demonstrating to others a "rich and provocative" set of affordances meant to *metaphorically* suggest that programming is writing.

An approach to theorizing programming activity, perhaps based in rhetoric's roots as a practical art that embraces theory as well as techne and craft, must be articulated in order to demonstrate that programming is a knowledge-generating, epistemological activity. Along those lines, Malcolm McCullough observes: "As we overcome the residual notion that computing is for objective documentation only, we must cultivate expressive sensibilities. These may result in a digital aesthetic or poetics. . . . And in the end, chances are that appropriate artifacts and descriptions will engage us through rich and transparent tools, built on newfound densities of symbolic notation and personally experienced as a medium" (1996, 219).

A digital rhetoric that would account for the intellectual work of programming (i.e., the dense symbolic notation that McCullough anticipates) has yet to emerge in the digital humanities. Ramsay and Rockwell's emphasis on a literary type of theorization privileges an established type of knowledge making, one that is not necessarily welcoming to screen artifacts or the source code behind them. The screen artifact struggles to demonstrate the intellectual work of programming; perhaps they are objects for literary-style analysis by media historians and critics. Software studies is an emerging field that similarly applies literary methods, such as close reading, to the analysis of source code. It is challenging to distinguish the intellectual work of creation when analytic modes are so well established in the humanities—even if their objects of analysis are relatively new.

Complicating matters, the personal experience of a medium that McCullough calls for is preempted by the ossifying tradition of outsourcing what could otherwise be knowledge-making work in the digital humanities. Outsource programming activity to third-party programmers, WYSIWYG interfaces, or ready-made software packages like WordPress and Drupal, and it becomes even more difficult to realize McCullough's calls for something as lofty as a digital aesthetic or poetics rooted in the symbolic materiality of programming.

For those of us who program as a crucial part of our research agendas, then, our argument must proceed by demonstrating that programming *as an activity* is genuine, humanistic inquiry that resists denigration with regard to more established knowledge-making activities grounded in the manipulation and interpretation of symbols.

The need for that line of argument draws writers and humanists as programmers in close company to the knowledge-making practices of art and design. In an obscure but important pamphlet published by the Royal College of Art, Christopher Frayling (1993/94) urges differentiating between three craft-/activity-oriented modes of inquiry: research *into* art and design; research *for* art and design; and research *through* art and design.

Rhetoric and writing, as a humanistic example, have no small body of work that researches *into* writing, often by studying writers and their contexts, such as introductory writing students in first-year composition or seasoned technical writers working in industry. The research conducted *for* writing often takes a pedagogical turn: this line of inquiry is aimed at making writing more teachable to students rather than necessarily at improving the practice of writing itself. But it is Frayling's last prepositional category, research *through* writing and rhetoric—or, as I am arguing, *through* programming as personally experienced symbolic activity—that remains an underexplored mode of inquiry.

Magic and Programming

Decades before Steve Jobs introduced to the world the iPad and proclaimed it to be a magical device, Arthur C. Clarke had already articulated what has become known as Clarke's Third Law: "Any sufficiently advanced technology is indistinguishable from magic." It is no feat of imagination to see the magic inherent in sixty-four-bit color depths, multitouch interfaces, retina displays, and other hardware-based wonders of screens introduced over the last decade.

To program and write is to act and create knowledge in the realm of the symbolic. In *Magic, Rhetoric, and Literacy*, William Covino writes that "making language has long been regarded as, in some sense, magical; as a *spell*," adding: "Spelling, even in its ostensibly nonmagical sense, denotes the visible materialization of invisible thought" (1994, 5).

The apparently magical incantation of words written in one programming language or another is what makes the symbolic activity of programming a particularly interesting problem for rhetoric and the digital humanities, even when the ends of such activity are visual. Emerging production methods such as responsive Web design (RWD; see Marcotte 2010) provide compelling evidence that the written word can trump ready-made visual production interfaces in opening up the affordances of newer screens while still accommodating the old.

Reflecting on the scene from *The Matrix* in which Neo announces to Tank from inside the Construct that he needs "guns, lots of guns," the digital designer John Maeda describes "the sense of magic that occurs when Neo expresses his wish": "The instantaneous rush of tremendous resources, as visualized in the simple special effect of this scene, epitomizes for me the experience of freedom when programming the invisible spaces of computer codes" (2004, 17).

While Maeda personally experiences "freedom," of course, other people no doubt experience the fear inherent in contemplating the magical symbolic activity of programming: "Fear of magic has always been with us, in particular the fear of magic words . . . which claim to define or alter reality" (Covino 1994, 1). It is arguably a cultural reflection of this kind of fear that *The Matrix* is set in a simulated reality created by source code that is made visible: to enter the matrix, the camera must pass through streams of code in the film's opening sequence.

In addition to favoring literary modes of inquiry, as I noted above, the digital humanities has inherited a cultural mythos of programming as a mysterious and magical activity. That mythos is probably reinforced by the intercession of so many screens and interfaces that provide both a sanctioned visual kind of magic (the GUI) and tacit promises of protection from a disruptive, unpredictable textual kind of magic (programming).

Covino's treatment accounts for those two oppositional senses of magic: as "arresting magic," programming would indeed by conjured only by a particular magus, the programmer, whose spells and incantations (realized in visual interfaces from word processors to smart phones) represent "the imposition of the powerful few upon the unquestioning many" (1994, 8). However, magic presents itself in another sense: "the practice of disrupting and critiquing articulate power: a (re)sorcery of spells for generating multiple perspectives." Noting that "generative magic enters the world it questions," Covino argues that generative magic is therefore "an amplification of the possibilities for action" (8).

Situated as I am in the study of digital rhetoric, design, and development, this is the digital humanities that I envision: research *through* programming, as a kind of generative magic, that creates knowledge that pushes the digital humanities toward a rhetorical theory of symbolic action at the source level.

Model-View-Controller (MVC) Architecture

MVC is a software design pattern that abstracts and distinguishes three core components of any digital system that will be controlled by a user-facing GUI. Originally conceived at Xerox PARC by Trygve Reenskaug and his colleagues in the late 1970s, MVC was intended "to bridge the gap between the [programmer's] mental model and the digital model that exists in the computer" (Reenskaug 2008). The View provides a visual interface to data described by the Model. The Controller exists to respond to actions occurring within the View and makes requests to the Model.

In Rails, there is no GUI: instead, there is a CLI and an application-programming interface (API). Both can be accessed only through writing (issuing commands, writing source code) and are discoverable primarily via the Rails documentation, either online at http://api .rubyonrails.org or on the command line: issuing the command gem server starts a local Web server, providing documentation for all Gems, including Rails, at http://localhost:8808. The basic documentation for the rails CLI is available by running rails -h; documentation for specific rails commands can be found by appending -h, such as "rails generate -h."

The *rails generate* command builds the basic component parts of MVC, using a number of generators that Rails makes available. Because rails generate is invoked so frequently, it has been aliased to the shorter *rails g* command. Every Rails tutorial begins with the *rails generate scaffold* command, which produces the scaffolding for MVC: a basic model; a controller that handles standard create/read/update/delete (CRUD) operations that are typical for working on data; and a set of matching views. By convention, Rails names generated views to match their corresponding controller action.

So to return to the skeletal BeSocial app that I created earlier in the chapter: regardless of what the BeSocial app enables users to do, it is clear that there will need to be users in the system. So the first scaffold that I will create is for a User model and what I think should be its corresponding properties (a username, first and last names, and a bio). This line generates a model called *User* that will consist of a username as well as first and last names, each of the string datatype (a string is roughly 255 characters), plus a biography, bio, that is of the text datatype (basically a much longer string):

```
$ rails g scaffold User username:string firstname:string lastname:string bio:text
```

On running this command, Rails demonstrates Maeda's observation of the "rush of tremendous resources" that programming calls forth:

```
invoke   active_record
create   db/migrate/20130903160957_create_users.rb
create   app/models/user.rb
invoke   resource_route
route    resources :users
invoke   scaffold_controller
create   app/controllers/users_controller.rb
invoke   erb
```

```
create     app/views/users
create     app/views/users/index.html.erb
create     app/views/users/edit.html.erb
create     app/views/users/show.html.erb
create     app/views/users/new.html.erb
create     app/views/users/_form.html.erb
```

On the basis of one command, Rails has generated this particular MVC scaffold based on my specifications for the data that will make up the User model (I have removed many lines of output that are beyond the scope of this chapter). By invoking ActiveRecord, Rails's native Object-Relational Mapping (ORM) module, it has created a recipe (called a *migration*, the file inside db/migrate) that specifies how the User object will be mapped to a database table. Unlike Drupal and WordPress, which have traditionally specified a specific database (MySQL) with predetermined columns, Rails is equipped to connect to and create in many different databases the tables specific to an app. (By default, Rails uses an embedded database called SQLite.)

The Model code that Rails generated in the app/models/user.rb file is quite minimal:

```
# app/models/user.rb
class User < ActiveRecord::Base
  attr_accessible :bio, :firstname, :lastname, :username
end
```

Just three lines that define the User class and allow the rest of the Rails app to access to the four data attributes that I specified. If someone wished to see the record for a particular user, this portion of the controller code would be invoked (for brevity, I have omitted the other CRUD actions):

```
# app/controllers/users_controller.rb
class UsersController < ApplicationController
<#>
  def show
  @user = User.find(params[:id])
<#>
  respond_to do |format|
  format.html # show.html.erb
  format.json { render json: @user }
```

```
end
end
end
```

The line that reads "@user = User.find(params[:id])" is the controller creating an instance (@user) of the User class defined in the model based on a user ID that is pulled from a URL pattern (e.g., http://localhost:3000/users/123 will attempt to look for a user with 123 as a unique identifier).

The controller makes the @user instance available to view that shows details for individual users. To output a logged-in user's username in the view, for example, show.html.erb would include lines similar to this:

```
# app/views/users/show.html.erb
<p>
  Your username is <%= @user.username %>.
</p>
```

The unusual .html.erb file extension indicates that this view file is written in Embedded Ruby (ERB). Similar to PHP and its <?php and ?> tags that are written among HTML tags, ERB requires placing Ruby code inside of <%= and %> tags. In this case, the view calls on the @user instance provided by the controller and the username method defined in the model, which is accessed via dot notation: @user.username. (Other template frameworks, particularly HAML, are cleaner than ERB, the Rails default. The example app at the companion site [www.press.uchicago.edu/sites/rdh/]shows HAML in action.)

That line of view code would, for a username johnsmith, render as HTML like this, as could be inspected by choosing View > Source from a Web browser:

```
<!— HTML source output at http://localhost:3000/users/123 —>
<#>
<p>
  Your username is johnsmith.
</p>
```

All this ready-made source code, spread among a set of files and directories generated by Rails, would appear to contradict my earlier complaints about outsourcing programming concerns to frameworks.

However, the *rails g scaffold* command serves primarily a pedagogical purpose: it illustrates both how Rails organizes an application (everything of interest here has been created inside an app/ directory, with models/, views/, and controllers/ each receiving subdirectories within app/) and minimal, skeletal code that, while functional, is hardly ready for a Web-available app.

Rails developers typically prefer to use either the stand-alone generators for models and controllers (the latter also generates corresponding views, by default) or, in the case of more advanced developers, custom generators of their own creation.

When I teach Rails in my course on Web application development, students and I build one or two throwaway apps using rails g scaffold, just to get a sense of how Rails apps are organized, and to illustrate the interactions between MVC's component parts. A small customization of the User model here, for example, might be to ensure that all usernames are unique. That is achieved by adding one line to the User model:

```
# app/models/user.rb
class User < ActiveRecord::Base
  attr_accessible :bio, :firstname, :lastname, :username
<#>
  validates_uniqueness_of :username
end
```

What I enjoy about the Rails framework is how the methods in its API (such as validates_uniqueness_of) are so close to written English: "the User model validates the uniqueness of each username." Students further introduce their own methods (and, thus, add to the API provided by Rails). For example, to make a user's full name available as a method on @user instances, the User model can be extended by writing a custom method, perhaps called *fullname*:

```
# app/models/user.rb
class User < ActiveRecord::Base
  attr_accessible :bio, :firstname, :lastname, :username
<#>
  validates_uniqueness_of :username
<#>
  def fullname
```

```
[self.firstname, self.lastname].join(" ")
  end
end
```

The view and other components of Rails immediately have access to that method: just write @user.fullname and something like "John Smith" will be output.

That is a very small taste of the lived experience of writing as programming. As the example app for this chapter shows, there is one additional piece of technology that helps capture and preserve such experiences: a version control system, such as Git. Git enables writer-programmers to record both the exact Rails command and its output as a particular moment in a project's history. Subsequent changes, such as extensions to the model, can also be recorded along with a rich, descriptive narrative of what was done and why. Authors and peer reviewers alike can read the running narrative of the programming experience, in close proximity to line-by-line representations of the changes that the narrative describes. Git, itself a CLI program, and the ongoing reflective writing required for its effective use add an additional layer of lived experience: a moment-by-moment account that, over a sustained encounter, makes a compelling argument that programming offers "affordances as rich and provocative as that of writing."

References

Bolter, Jay David. 1991. *Writing Space: The Computer, Hypertext, and the History of Writing.* Hillsdale, NJ: Erlbaum.

Burke, Kenneth. 1966. *Language as Symbolic Action: Essays on Life, Literature, and Method.* Berkeley, CA: University of California Press.

Covino, William A. 1994. *Magic, Rhetoric, and Literacy: An Eccentric History of the Composing Imagination.* Albany: State University of New York Press.

Frayling, Christopher. 1993/94. "Reseach in Art and Design." *Royal College of Art Research Papers* 1.1:1–5.

Maeda, John. 2004. *Creative Code.* New York: Thames & Hudson.

Marcotte, Ethan. 2010. "Responsive Web Design." *A List Apart: For People Who Make Websites,* May 25. http://alistapart.com/article/responsive -web-design.

McConnell, Steve. 2004. *Code Complete.* 2nd ed. Redmond, WA: Microsoft Press. Kindle ed.

McCullough, Malcolm. 1996. *Abstracting Craft: The Practiced Digital Hand.* Cambridge, MA: MIT Press.

Montfort, Nick, Patsy Baudoin, John Bell, Ian Bogost, Jeremy Douglass, Mark C. Marino, Michael Mateas, Casey Reas, Mark Sample, and Noah Vawter. 2013. *10 PRINT CHR$(205.5+RND(1)); : GOTO 10.* Cambridge, MA: MIT Press.

Ramsay, Stephen, and Geoffrey Rockwell. 2012. "Developing Things: Notes toward an Epistemology of Building in the Digital Humanities." In *Debates in the Digital Humanities*, ed. Matthew K. Gold, 75–84. Minneapolis, MN: University of Minnesota Press.

Reenskaug, Trygve M. H. 2008. "MVC: Xerox PARC 1978–78." http://heim.ifi .uio.no/~trygver/themes/mvc/mvc-index.html.

## TWENTY-ONE

Procedural Literacy and the Future of the Digital Humanities

BRIAN BALLENTINE

In his well-known critique of digital rhetoric, Ian Bogost (2007) complains that current scholarship "typically abstracts the computer as a consideration, focusing on the text and image content a machine might host and the communities of practice in which that content is created and used" (25). What is missing, according to Bogost, is a robust understanding of how computers execute processes and how coded procedures make arguments. He insists: "A theory of procedural rhetoric is needed to make commensurate judgments about the software systems we encounter every day and to allow a more sophisticated procedural authorship with both persuasion and expression as its goal" (29). Bogost's ideas have a great deal of traction in his home field of game studies, but they have also attracted the attention of rhetoric, computers and writing, and professional and technical communication scholars. Rudy McDaniel's 2009 "Making the Most of Interactivity Online Version 2.0" builds on Bogost to advance a call for "procedural literacy." An expert in asynchronous JavaScript and XML (abbreviated as AJAX), McDaniel claims that we need a new literacy that "takes into account lower-level technical rules in addition to existing conceptual understandings of both new media forms as architectural spaces and socio-organizational practices" (384).

If McDaniel's description sounds familiar to those researching within the digital humanities, it may be due to its similarities with another related field, critical code studies, which, as defined by Mark Marino, is "an approach that applies critical hermeneutics to the interpretation of computer code, program architecture, and documentation within a sociohistorical context" (2006). Similarly, in a series of short essays collected in a special issue of *Enculturation*, scholars like Mark Sample, Karl Stolley, and Annette Vee (see "The Role of Computational Literacy in Computers and Writing" 2012) begin to tackle "the role of computational thinking in computers and writing" by claiming that "code has reached a critical moment in writing studies." I agree, but, regardless of where we locate other areas of study like critical code studies, software studies, and digital rhetoric in relation to or overlapping with the digital humanities, the theoretical, practical, and definitional disputes found at their many intersections do not result in a clear consensus that pushes the digital humanities toward *requiring* a procedural literacy with code and mark-up language proficiency. Indeed, in a blog entry titled "Code? Not So Much," this collection's coeditor, William Hart-Davidson, remarked that, when it comes to writing code, digital rhetoricians "should leave that to other people" (2012). To be clear, the comments section of the blog entry proves useful as Hart-Davidson clarifies that learning mark-up languages like XHTML and understanding cascading style sheets as well as how XML functions are all "absolutely important and necessary for digital rhetoricians." Pushing even harder for code-level literacy, at the 2012 Conference on College Composition and Communication Karl Stolley gave a live demonstration on building a simple Web application in Ruby in a talk titled "No, Really: Learn to Program." While I wish to advocate for code-level procedural literacy becoming endemic to the digital humanities, I also recognize the reality that we cannot subsume computer science and its curriculum. A balance has to be struck.

While I wish to remain positive about what Katherine Hayles (2012, 24) recently described as the "contentious vitality" of the digital humanities, what is at stake, I will argue, is nothing short of rapid obsolescence. For example, in *Two Bits* (2008), Chris Kelty details the way the technically savvy—the "geeks" of his ethnographic study—make arguments within what he terms the *recursive publics* of the Internet: "They [geeks] argue about technology but they also argue through it. They express ideas but they also express infrastructures through which ideas can be expressed (and circulated) in new ways" (29). In other words, our future requires dedicated collaboration with computer science and technical communication in order to not be shut out of these important discussions (and our own interpretive practices) because we do not have the language to argue in these spaces.

The discussions and the arguments are changing because the technology and the ways we interact with software-powered devices are changing. According to Noah Wardrip-Fruin (2009): "Computational processes are an increasingly significant means of expression for authors. Rather than defining the sequence of words for a book or images for a film, today's authors are increasingly defining the rules for system behavior" (3). Additionally, he notes that we need a means to "talk about what processes express in their design—which may not be visible to audiences" (4). Digital humanists interested in participating in the design, development, implementation, and/or critique of digital texts (in short, *all* the arguments) must be able to expand to the code level.

In order to better illustrate my point, what follows is an analysis of a feature found within a software application that I was responsible for when I worked in industry. In what will amount to a compressed case study, I will demonstrate how the automated new-user help system built into a Web-based radiology software application can be developed and interpreted (successfully) only with a procedural literacy that has code-level competency. The help system in question was developed in 2001, and it clearly represents Web 1.0 affordances. What is the point of including an older system in a chapter based on the future? Beyond the very practical reason of having permission to use the design documentation in support of the system and the code, I believe that a procedural analysis makes several clear points: (1) The rules of a system have a profound effect on a user's experience, and access to and understanding of those procedural rules are necessary to develop, edit, and debate the system. (2) The analysis of an older system demonstrates the dangers (and safeguards) of attempting to control or script user experience by way of procedural rhetoric. (3) Finally, the evaluating, editing, and upgrading of these existing 1.0 systems cannot be done effectively without procedural literacy. Additionally, the implication here is that, if procedural literacy was in urgent demand for the design and development of synchronous Web 1.0 systems, it is now essential for future asynchronous 2.0 systems and beyond.

Software Requirement Specifications

In 2010, I argued that technical writers and software developers could use Software Requirement Specifications (SRS) to better anticipate user needs (Ballentine 2010). I advanced a claim for technical writing serving an epistemic function and traced the influence of the SRS I analyzed back to its respective application's code level (e.g., naming conventions for JavaScript functions and variables could be found in the contents of the SRS). For this compressed case study, I have returned to this same SRS, almost two hundred pages of documentation written in support of an advanced Web-based radiology application for a major medical company, in order to demonstrate not just how far we have come at the code level since 2001 but also how the digital humanities needs procedural literacy. This review focuses on the application's new-user help system dubbed "IntelliGuide," which attempted to provide context-based orientation for radiologists transitioning from the traditional method of reviewing X-rays, MRI, and CT scans as printed film hanging on a light board to reviewing digitized versions of those scans on screen.

The original entry in the SRS for the IntelliGuide system offered little guidance for the development team and served mostly as a placeholder reminding us that we would, at some point, need to begin the recursive process of prototyping and testing a useful and usable help system. It read:

In order to provide a quicker path to in-depth knowledge of this application, it is required that there be a number of contextual help tips made available to users. These tips provide two basic functions:

1. To guide the user through basic features of the application necessary to accomplish the workflow appropriate to the mode they are operating.
2. To present specific features which might be helpful based on actions the user performs.

This was, at least, a place to start. As an SRS develops through its many drafts and iterations, those iterations are informed by processes familiar to those in technical communication, including usability testing with prototypes, trade show demonstrations, and on-site user observations (e.g., shadowing radiologists at their workplaces to better understand their day-to-day needs). Our criteria for the help system grew within the SRS to include presenting the tips in "obvious" and "unmistakable" fashion as well as limiting each tip to no more than two actions (93).

What eluded our team at the time was that the mandate that in no way should the tips "conflict with the look and feel of the application" was technically an impossibility given our then Web 1.0 technology. AJAX makes some of the more salient differences between Web 1.0 and 2.0 technologies quite clear. Web-based technologies powered by AJAX and its asynchronous capabilities "lets an application make a server call, retrieve new data, and update the webpage without reloading all of the contents, which speeds up Web applications' performance, responsiveness, and interactivity" (Lawton 2008, 10). McDaniel populates his article with examples of AJAX-driven Web interfaces such as Google Maps, Netflix, and Amazon's "Diamond Search," all offering a rich, interactive user experience. Invoking a "conversational metaphor," McDaniel (2009, 376) demonstrates how the asynchronous capabilities of AJAX afford a fluid, dynamic, and open discussion between the user and the technology.

These are not the affordances of Web 1.0, and in 2001 our design would force asynchronous and heavily scripted interactions with the user. We would deliberately block the user's access to any of the other controls or options within the application until they engaged with the help tip. In fact, we coded the application to block the user from being able to engage with the interface at all until the help information was dealt with by the user. As shown in figure 21.1, this sample tip from the original SRS provided the option of either closing the tip by clicking on the × in the upper-right-hand corner or electing to turn off the IntelliGuide system altogether. All the other controls are "grayed out."

Additional revisions to the SRS reveal a rigid approach that desires not an "open-ended" interaction with the help system but instead our

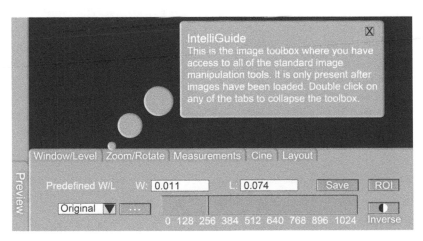

21.1. Screen shot of an IntelliGuide tip from the original software requirements specifications.

attempts to account for all possible use cases and control of them. This is not to say that to harness the Web 2.0 interactivity powered by AJAX developers must abandon user considerations; quite the opposite is true. Instead, developers must embrace the notion that users will want to manipulate their application and data in ways the development team did not necessarily intend or anticipate.

Without AJAX as an option, we set out to pin down everything we could in the help system and control each back and forth, synchronize exchange, and develop the code to make those exchanges possible. To do so, we documented exactly what radiologists believed to be the core features necessary to perform on the job. Next, we identified the specific features from our software application that could be challenging for radiologists to use and would benefit from help tips attached to them. We placed the features into a new, three-column table in the SRS. All the features requiring tips were placed in the first column, titled "Tip Description." The second column was labeled "Triggering Events," and it documented what must occur for the tip to appear. The third column was a reference to the SRS's appendix, which contained an image or screen capture of each defined tip. In table 21.1 is a single row from the table in the SRS detailing the tip for the "Image Toolbox" in figure 21.1.

As with most of the help tips, the "Triggering Events" column requires more than one event for the tip to appear. It was not until the table for the help tips was drafted that a debate was sparked over the order of the triggering events. For example, should the tip for the "Image Toolbox" still display if the user performs other activities in between opening a patient scan and "mousing over" a toolbox tab? What if the order is reversed? Ultimately, we would decide that the answer to these questions is "it depends," but I would add now that a procedural literacy at the code level helps in making more substantive decisions about how to proceed. The solution, it was decided, was that each tip would need to be labeled in such a way as to signify whether the order of events was relevant to the tip appearing. Each tip was, therefore, labeled as one of three types: sequential, linear, or random. A sequential

Table 21.1 Excerpted row from the SRS section on new user help or "IntelliGuide"

Tip description	Triggering events	Reference
Image Toolbox description	User opens a scan and mouses over an image toolbox tab	Figure 91: Image Toolbox

tip required that all the triggering events occur in order with no other actions performed in between those events. The "Image Toolbox" tip was labeled as a sequential tip, and, therefore, the user would have to open a patient scan first and then mouse over an image toolbox tab. If the user were to perform another action, for example, print the patient scan, the tip would not display even if the user were to mouse over the proper tab as the sequence would be broken. A linear tip required that the user perform all the necessary actions in a predetermined order, but it allowed for other actions to occur in between those events. Finally, it was determined that some of the tips had events that could occur in any order, and they were labeled as random.

Coding the help system benefited from the clear documentation in the SRS. Again, such documentation drafted, revised, and/or analyzed to support software requires procedural literacy for a complete picture as called for by Bogost. All the naming conventions inside the Java Script controlling IntelliGuide were propagated by the language in the SRS. For example, we kept track of the events with three different types of triggers that we named TRIGGER_TYPE_SEQUENTIAL, TRIGGER_TYPE_LINEAR, and TRIGGER_TYPE_RANDOM. Next, we determined that the most efficient way to monitor a user's actions would be to develop an event counter within the code that kept a temporary record of user activity. When a user performs an action within the application and that action is one of the many events that could display a help tip, the code performs a series of validations to determine what role that event plays in the help system. The code determines whether the event is part of a sequential, linear, or random triggered tip. In the case of a sequential tip, if the user event is the final event needed to display or "fire" the tip, the code must display the appropriate tip. Conversely, if the event breaks the necessary sequence required to display a tip, the code must reset the counter monitoring that sequence. The function that handles the display of a tip was called Trigger_fireEvent, and the function responsible for resetting a tip's sequence was called Trigger_resetEvents. Clearly, the language found in the SRS drives the construction of functions within the code, but I would add that a digital humanist either authoring or analyzing such documents needs procedural literacy, including programming knowledge, to understand the possibilities and limitations at all levels of the application. The question then becomes *how* the humanities learns to program.

I do not take it as a coincidence that many of the well-known scholars writing in (or around) digital humanities like Bogost, Hayles, Kirschenbaum, Manovich, McDaniel, Stolley, and Wardrip-Fruin also know how to program. That knowledge informs their work. They also have strong opinions on coding. For example, while Kirschenbaum is an advocate for humanists learning to program, his own reflection on learning to code shows his frustration with the "purely vocational" approach to the teaching methods in his early classes on BASIC and Pascal (Kirschenbaum 2009). I took similar courses, and they too were frustratingly devoid of context and concern for the user. The emphasis at the time was just knowing how to program a while and a for loop, with no concern for situations where a programmer would choose one over the other. For Kirschenbaum: "Programming is about choices and constraints, and about how you choose to model some select slice of the world around you in the formal environment of a computer" (2009). The rote performance of coding a loop misses the point, yet a useful procedural literacy requires programming fundamentals.

If digital humanists do intend to "understand the logic of new media," then, according to Manovich (2001), "we need to turn to computer science" (48). And, while I agree with David Berry's recent claim that we need to "introduce a humanistic approach to computer code" (2012, 17), I do not think that is possible without first engaging with computer science on its home turf. For example, Kirschenbaum (2009) recounts that he gained permission to use the programming language Perl to satisfy part of his Ph.D. program's language requirement. As of 2012, my own department's M.A. in professional writing will accept a four-credit-hour computer science course on Java to satisfy the degree's language requirement. In the summer of 2013, I attended the Java course, and that experience was exceptionally positive. The course did insist on an understanding of the fundamentals in object-oriented programming, including terms like *algorithms*, *objects*, *classes*, *inheritance*, and *methods*, but the curriculum also contained a refreshing emphasis on the importance of writing out a story for a program. What is known as *pseudocode* is used to provide context for the world the programmer wishes to create and attempts to capture the user's experiences within that world (Horstmann 2013, 23).

Even as we continue to understand the digital humanities "as broadly as possible" (Hayles 2012, 26), the unifying practice across its many disciplines is that of the act of interpretation. "Hermeneutics often dominate digital humanities scholarship," but that "practice of interpretation" remains incomplete and less useful if the code level is abstracted out (Rice 2013, 360). Our ability to unpack the nuances of "both persuasion and expression" found even in the simplest of

Web 1.0 applications will depend on procedural literacy and learning the fundamentals of programming and mark-up languages.

References

Ballentine, Brian D. 2010. "Requirements, Specifications and Anticipating User Needs: Methods and Warnings on Writing Development Narratives for New Software." *Technical Communication* 57.1:26–43.

Berry, David M. 2012. "Introduction: Understanding the Digital Humanities." In *Understanding Digital Humanities*, ed. David M. Berry, 1–20. New York: Palgrave.

Bogost, Ian. 2007. *Persuasive Games: The Expressive Power of Video Games*. Cambridge, MA: MIT Press.

Hart-Davidson, William. 2012. "Code? Not So Much." *Digital Rhetoric Collaborative*, October 17. http://www.digitalrhetoriccollaborative.org/2012/10/17/code-not-so-much.

Hayles, N. Katherine. 2012. *How We Think: Digital Media and Contemporary Technogenesis*. Chicago: University of Chicago Press.

Horstmann, Cay. 2013. *Java for Everyone: Late Objects*. 2nd ed. Hoboken, NJ: Wiley.

Kelty, Christopher M. 2008. *Two Bits: The Cultural Significance of Free Software*. Durham, NC: Duke University Press.

Kirschenbaum, Matthew. 2009. "Hello Worlds." *Chronicle of Higher Education*, January 23. http://chronicle.com/article/Hello-Worlds/5476.

Lawton, George. 2008. "New Ways to Build Rich Internet Applications." *Computer* 41:10–12.

Manovich, Lev. 2001. *The Language of New Media*. Cambridge, MA: MIT Press.

Marino, Mark. 2006. "Critical Code Studies." *Electronic Book Review*, December 4. http://www.electronicbookreview.com/thread/electropoetics/codology.

McDaniel, Rudy. 2009. "Making the Most of Interactivity Online Version 2.0: Technical Communication as Procedural Architecture." *Technical Communication* 56.4:370–86.

Rice, Jeff. 2013. "Occupying the Digital Humanities." *College English* 75.4:360–78.

Sample, Mark, and Annette Vee. 2012. "Introduction to 'The Role of Computational Literacy in Computers and Writing.'" *Enculturation: A Journal of Rhetoric, Writing, and Culture*, October 12. http://enculturation.net/computational-literacy.

Stolley, Karl. 2012. "No, Really: Learn to Program." Paper presented at the annual meeting of the Conference on College Composition and Communication, St. Louis, MO, March 21–24.

Wardrip-Fruin, Noah. 2009. *Expressive Processing: Digital Fictions, Computer Games, and Software Studies*. Cambridge, MA: MIT Press.

## TWENTY-TWO

Nowcasting/Futurecasting: Big Data, Prognostication, and the Rhetorics of Scale

ELIZABETH LOSH

As the information about an expanding number of discrete cultural producers grows dramatically to include data about geographic location, social networks, and other highly granular forms of context about the most minute characteristics of overlapping networked publics that are producing massive quantities of user-generated content, digital humanities projects will need to adapt to making sense of content at new orders of magnitude. In addition to redesigning interfaces and search engines to accommodate nonscholarly users and participants, principle investigators in the digital humanities soon may need to collaborate with a new class of information specialists who might be able to understand the statistically complex fluidities of these shifting rhetorical situations, grapple with research questions that explore the nuances of narrowcasted and invisible audiences and purposes, map assemblages of strategies and tactics for managing subtle modulations of online identities, and uncover the signatures of local devices embedded in the database artifacts that are composited into a global culture of remix.

Attempting to represent complex assemblages of authors, works, editors, recommenders, readers, publishers, technologies, media, and institutions and the systems in which persons, products, ideas, and corporations circulate in dynamic patterns of influence can sometimes be difficult, even if the action takes place in the past and the community of production is relatively well defined and closely knit. In the case of developing an "alpha prototype" or "proof of concept" for a "relationship browsing tool" to represent the collective creative output from the Yaddo retreat for artists and writers in Saratoga Springs, New York, Mickey McGee (2012) hoped to create a "very complete map of 20th century American culture" by harvesting content from other archives. However, even developing the component of this digital humanities collection that maps the personages of the Yaddo archive itself with a focus on first-degree relationships has been the work of many years. McGee also faces the challenge of representing many kinds of strong and weak ties among Yaddo agents that may be intimately entwined in a variety of kinship relationships that range from the parental surrogacy of mentorship to transgressive sexual liaisons.

These are new kinds of interpretive problems for the humanities, and our current methods of disciplinary indoctrination may do little to help emerging scholars prepare for explicating patterns in rapidly morphing objects of study. At the same time, experts in artificial intelligence acknowledge that current algorithms often fail at the simplest human tasks of recognition that could be easily completed by a child, such as perceiving that a lion is shown in a photograph surrounded by tawny grass. Furthermore, enthusiastic hyperbole about our nascent abilities to collect information about data at this scale may mask the technical difficulties of creating interpretive frameworks in the humanities with which to analyze and synthesize very large quantities of cultural information. Not only do academic departments in literature, history, philosophy, and visual studies have relatively few resources in comparison to intelligence agencies, targeted marketers, and corporations policing copyright, but cultural computation of this sort also emphasizes calculation rather than communication and an instrumental approach to objects of study.

When YouTube archives forty-eight hours of video uploaded every minute and facilitates three billion views per day and sites like Flickr and Facebook store five billion photos and three billion photos, respectively (at the time of writing), scholars creating organizational schema for the composition practices of the immediate past may find themselves, as Jeremy Douglass from the Software Studies lab at the University of California, San Diego, once said, struggling to "drink directly from the firehose" (Losh 2012b, 98). Although machine learning algorithms and very large training sets may make possible increasingly sophisticated kinds of "event detection" or "concept detection" that process material in large databases of born-digital images and video, the digital humanities remains more comfortably oriented around textual artifacts from print culture and the models of readership and authorship of the very first digital humanities projects at the dawn of literary and linguistic computing. The personalization of Web-browsing experiences and the rise of mobile Internet applications creates even more massive "digital dossiers" (Palfrey and Gasser 2008) than the ones imagined at the beginning of Web 2.0, and historical and discursive actors may effectively be "naked in the nonopticon" because those collecting data for marketing efforts do so clandestinely and without coordinating with state efforts that would bring surveillance to public attention (Vaidhyanathan 2008), and the blurring of public and private distinctions makes ethical research much more challenging. Furthermore, user agreements often prohibit scraping digital materials from the social network sites where they are posted, even if the texts, images, or videos seem obviously historically or artistically significant.

Part of our emerging profession's resistance to working with born-digital materials that are generated in real time can also be traced to an understandable desire to preserve the remainders of disciplinary convention in an already interdisciplinary field, as the digital humanities inevitably becomes more like novel forms of deep analysis with mathematically complex systems made possible by powerful computation. Lev Manovich has argued that there are a number of potentially allied disciplines outside the digital humanities that have already "adapted quantitative methods (i.e., statistical, mathematical, or computational techniques for analyzing data)," such as "quantitative schools of sociology, economics, political science, communication studies, and marketing research" (Manovich 2012b, 461). The tendency of these disciplines to operationalize or seek efficiencies in certain forms of cultural production may intensify existing institutional hostilities.

Manovich has become perhaps the most famous advocate of attention to the new paradigms of big data in the digital humanities in works on "trending" and "scale effects." In a 2012 NEH grant application, Manovich (2012a) argued that, instead of "describing the history of any media collection in terms of discrete parts (years, decades, periods), we can begin to see it as a set of curves, each showing how a particular property of form, content, and rhetoric changes over time." Thus, according to Manovich's group, "we can supplement existing rigid data classifications with new clusters that group together artifacts that share some common characteristics." Looking at what Manovich calls the *style space* of content mapped out in media visualizations with large collections of cultural content, such as hundreds of thousands of discrete files culled from databases of manga pages or user-generated vernacular digital art, he argues that it is possible to find new territory for original cultural expression or understand why certain technical forays seem to be taboo. This mapping of curves and clusters also produces visually dazzling and dynamic data sets that look less like taxonomies that archive objects of study in the remote past and more like the weather patterns of a constantly shifting contemporary aesthetics driven by fashion as much as by style. Manovich's distinctive rhetoric of magnification has even made him a figure of fun among the academic cognoscenti: an online wag has created a Twitter stream for "fake Lev Manovich" (https://twitter.com/FakeLevManovich) with rhapsodic expressions full of exclamations, exaggerations, overstatements, improbable predictions, and sweeping generalizations.

However, Manovich's diction seems to appear considerably less bombastic when humanities scholars gain attention for being willing to ask bold research questions about the nature of political, social, or aesthetic change. Much like economics or climate science, the digital humanities has been asked to become a predictive science that can foretell the cultural future. For example, digital mapping and information visualization projects by Xarene Eskandar, Gilad Lotan, and Laila Shereen Sakr (a.k.a. VJ Um Amel) show the activities of urban crowds, citizen journalists, and online participants involved in political activism in the Middle East. Although Malcolm Gladwell famously asserted that "the revolution will not be Tweeted" (2010), Eskandar and Shereen Sakr argue that the record of revolutionary activity can at least be mapped meaningfully in ways that engage the present. As digital humanities projects, Eskandar's work in Farsi and Shereen Sakr's work in Arabic provided useful expert readings of the landscape of social media and contemporary protest movements. It is noteworthy that US government officials tend to want information not only about present ecologies of political meaning but also about the shape of democratic speech acts in the future. Shereen Sakr's work actually became of interest to the State Department, which monitors trends in the Middle East. As remarks from a State Department official indicate, it is the predictive qualities of this mapping that matter.

Laila Shereen Sakr, a Ph.D. candidate at the University of Southern California, followed the Arab Spring closely, creating a massive database of Arabic-language tweets. Instead of selecting terms herself and searching the database, Sakr let a computer program aggregate data and identify patterns. While aggregating tweets from Libya, her program identified spikes in certain hashtags or selected keywords. These word spikes became a sort of pulse, an early warning identifying the fall of the town of Zawiya. A short while later, similar word spikes reappeared, allowing Sakr to identify the impending fall of Tripoli. She was accurate to within a few hours (Department of State 2011).

This desire for chronological numerical accuracy as well as the validity and reliability of results is not alien to conventional scholarly efforts to date events of the past, but seeking an "early warning system" from the digital arts and humanities seems very different from traditional work that attempts only to understand the future from a position of typology and assumed reiteration of events or according to Santayana's (1946) maxim that those "who cannot remember the past are condemned to repeat it." As Shereen Sakr herself notes: "There are no definitive economic models to study the value of our associations, our temporality, or how to quantify things in the present" (Shereen Sakr 2013).

Those who are interested in understanding the phenomenon of trending in the digital humanities often look to the work of Franco Moretti to understand the ebb and flow of textual phenomena that emerge over time and a methodology that many call *distant reading* that involves very large corpora of works. In *Graphs, Maps, Trees*, Moretti tries to look at the literary output of entire nations or historical periods to characterize the features of tens of thousands or hundreds of thousands of volumes. "Now, 'temporary structures' is also a good definition for genres: morphological arrangements that *last* in time, but always only for *some* time. Janus-like creatures, with one face turned to history and the other to form, genres are thus the true protagonists of this middle layer of literary history—this more 'rational' layer where flow and form meet" (Moretti 2005, 14). In understanding how new genres emerge, Moretti's analytic approach seems promising to those who would hope to do futurecasting, although Moretti himself admits that he often does his work of data visualization without resorting to digital tools.

However, those who have actually attempted to work in meaningful ways to rationalize into mathematical curves the seemingly random spikes of activity in certain forms of cultural production often find themselves stymied by the enormity of the tasks. Matthew Kirschenbaum catalogs the persistence of these obstacles in what he calls an "unofficial version" of the digital humanities that describes these expensive Herculean multicampus efforts. As he puts it: "All of this is very, very hard." Not only does energy need to be devoted to leveraging "several existing platforms and technologies" and stabilizing the architecture of what he calls a "loose tissue of resources and standards" that connect disassociated "datastores, text mining engine, visualization toolkit and end-user interface," but the ends can also be as challenging as the means when project participants are "spending our time trying to figure out what technologies like text mining are good for in humanities research, particularly in literary studies" (Kirschenbaum quoted in Goodwin and Holbe 2011, 32–33). According to Kirschenbaum, gaining "fluency in terms like naïve Bayesian analysis, cosine similarity matrices, features, vectors, dendograms, decision trees, and neural networks" might not have much utility since "we don't typically set out to 'solve' problems in the humanities" (Goodwin and Holbe 2011, 33–34). In the same volume of essays responding to Moretti, Cosma Shalizi argues that applying scientific rationalism to cultural production might itself be a doomed effort because "the facts are often just screwy, both about the developments to be explained: non-existent trends, non-existent causes, weirdly mis-characterized trends, trends being explained by events which happened long after the former began, etc." (123).

Necessarily any approach that focuses on trends expressed in the past also places the humanities scholar in an awkward position, one in which, as Marshall McLuhan once wrote, "we look at the present through a rear-view mirror" (McLuhan and Fiore 1967, 75) and move forward into the future only while looking backward into the past. It is interesting to note that McLuhan's metaphor makes frequent appearances in the oratory of public prognosticators about new directions in digital delivery systems that such evangelists observe are likely to be overlooked by the old guard. For example, in a conference on "the second screen," Robert Tercek (2013) uses McLuhan's rear-view mirror to point to the "blind spots" of the traditional entertainment industry.

Rather than aspire to a predictive humanities, the task of "nowcasting" rather than "futurecasting" may promise a methodology of more engaged research in which the cultural, political, literary, artistic, and material life of the present becomes the focus of attention. Although he also borrows terminology from economics and meteorology, Peter Lunenfeld (2012) has described nowcasting as an attempt "to apply design theory to emerging issues in the digital humanities" in phenomena that are radically present. Lunenfeld also insists that "communication design, interaction design, and industrial design will be vital to 21st century humanistic inquiry" and seems leery of mathematical models that might assume an absence of creative human agency as social actors design the present in real time.

Indeed, what might be most important for rhetoricians considering the ambitious and lofty claims in the discourses of the digital humanities presented by Manovich and Moretti are the ways in which these methodological manifestos present not only new ways to map time with content but also new ways to think about the concept of *kairos* in the context of knowledge making. After all, in the original Greek, the term *kairos* is used both to indicate both timeliness (exact or critical time, season, or opportunity) and appropriateness (due measure, proportion, or fitness), which can create conflict if the target for a given speech act is moving too rapidly for elegant articulation. In other words, the specific moment of "drinking directly from the firehouse" may resist the interpretative stasis necessary for meaningful expression, particularly if neither position nor direction can be simultaneously known to separate out noise from signal.

In more recent work on Instagram with Nadav Hochman, Manovich emphasizes how certain forms of visual expression in very large data sets structured by contemporary social media depend on display interfaces in which the measurement of temporality emphasizes the gap "between the present moment of launching the application and the original date of creation," so that "although the specific time in which a photo was taken exists in the software's database, its timestamp is dynamic as each image shows a constantly changing representation of time" (Hochman and Manovich 2013). Thus, an image labeled *four days ago* today will be labeled *five days ago* tomorrow. It is a temporal logic in which the present moment is nowcasted even as the past is represented.

Although there are many spatial metaphors in these digital humanities calls to action that include "distant reading," "style space," and "scale" that can be mapped, charted, graphed, and visualized, this is also a rhetoric of temporal exigency implicitly at work that involves the production of interpretive scholarship as well as the production of cultural objects of study. Such rhetoric often presents a logic of progression in which the humanities must catch up to other disciplines or keep up the pace with ones that are rapidly advancing, as Christine Borgman has asserted, when knowledge becomes "more data-intensive, information-intensive, distributed, multi-disciplinary, and collaborative." What Borgman calls "the data deluge" requires accelerated acquisition of "the technical infrastructure available to the sciences" (Borgman 2010).

Ironically, Manovich once announced the death of rhetoric in the pages of *The Language of New Media* (2002). He has since retracted this pronouncement and now discusses "database rhetorics" as essential for understanding contemporary forms of cultural production. Database rhetorics can also be deployed for giving activism more visibility, as the work of Eskandar and Shereen Sakr indicates. The work of Victoria Vesna, Sharon Daniel, and many media arts practitioners loosely allied with digital humanities initiatives may support current abolitionist movements in favor of prison reform, data privacy, and even animal rights. Digital humanities projects may have persuasive goals that are uniquely able to be expressed through computational media on distributed networks, and, thus, their greatest impact may be in making our present moment visible.

Some of these big data initiatives championed by digital humanities futurists have been criticized for their masculinist celebration of "brogrammer" unisex code cultures, particularly when *digging, mining, tools, challenge,* and *competition* function as the key terms for engagement (Nowviskie 2012; Wernimont 2012). It may be a legitimate critique when the humanities aspires to match the sciences, and it naturalizes assumptions about gender and technology, but I might argue that it is the absence of human agency and embodiment in these digital humanities documents that is often even more striking than supposed machismo.[1] Because of the distance at which such large collections of cultural objects become legible, we are reduced to being passive spectators as the map grows progressively larger than the territory. Rather than consider our own time embedded within the humanities of the digital from far out in cyberspace, I might argue that it is far more important to jump disciplines in other directions to engage with the rich tradition of participant observation or action research that comes from the social sciences or with the critical creative practices of the digital arts among hacktivists, tactical media activists, and culture jammers of all kinds (Losh 2012a).

Note

1. Of course, many feminist scholars of technology point out that the pose of neutrality and objectivity is probably inherently a masculinist one, so these two positions are not necessarily incompatible.

## CHAPTER TWENTY-TWO

References

Borgman, Christine L. 2010. "The Digital Archive: The Data Deluge Arrives in the Humanities." http://works.bepress.com/borgman/235.

Department of State. Office of Website Management. Bureau of Public Affairs. 2011. "From the Manhattan Project to the Cloud: Arms Control in the Information Age." Remarks | Remarks. *U.S. Department of State*, October 27. http://www.state.gov/t/avc/rls/176331.htm.

Gladwell, Malcolm. 2010. "Why the Revolution Will Not Be Tweeted." *New Yorker*, October 4.

Goodwin, Jonathan, and John Holbo. 2011. *Reading Graphs, Maps and Trees? Responses to Franco Moretti*. Anderson, SC: Parlor.

Hochman, N., and L. Manovich. 2013. "Zooming into an Instagram City: Reading the Local Through Social Media." *First Monday* 18.7. doi:10.5210/fm.v18i7.4711.

Losh, Elizabeth. 2012a. "Hacktivism and the Humanities: Programming Protest in the Era of the Digital University." In *Debates in the Digital Humanities*, ed. Matthew K. Gold, 161–86. Minneapolis: University of Minnesota Press.

———. 2012b. "Play, Things, Rules, and Information: Hybridized Learning in the Digital University." *LEA Leonardo Electronic Almanac* 17.2:92–108.

Lunenfeld, Peter. 2012. "Nowcasting and the Digital Humanities | Beyond the Beyond | Wired.com." http://www.wired.com/beyond_the_beyond/2009/09/nowcasting-and-the-digital-humanities.

Manovich, Lev. 2002. *The Language of New Media*. Cambridge, MA: MIT Press.

———. 2012a. "Cultural Analytics." In *Understanding Digital Humanities*, ed. David M Berry, 249–78. New York: Palgrave Macmillan.

———. 2012b. "Trending: The Promises and the Challenges of Big Social Data." In *Debates in the Digital Humanities*, ed. Matthew K. Gold, 460–75. Minneapolis: University of Minnesota Press.

McGee, Micki. 2012. *Yaddo Circles Prototype—Relationship Mapping Demo*. https://vimeo.com/36929545.

McLuhan, Marshall, and Quentin Fiore. 1967. *The Medium Is the Massage*. New York: Random House.

Moretti, Franco. 2005. *Graphs, Maps, Trees? Abstract Models for a Literary History*. London: Verso.

Nowviskie, Bethany. 2012. "What Do Girls Dig?" In *Debates in the Digital Humanities*, ed. Matthew K. Gold, 235–40. Minneapolis: University of Minnesota Press.

Palfrey, John G., and Urs Gasser. 2008. *Born Digital: Understanding the First Generation of Digital Natives*. New York: Basic.

Santayana, George. 1946. *The Life of Reason; or, The Phases of Human Progress*. New York: Scribner's.

Shereen Sakr, Laila. 2013. "Eighteen Hours to Thirty Six Hours Entering #Tripoli—R-Shief." *R-Shief.* http://r-shief.org/eighteen-hours-to-thirty -six-hours-entering-tripoli.

Tercek, Robert. 2013. "Ten Things That Should Be Obvious . . . but Apparently Aren't." Opening keynote address at the Second Screen Summit NYC 2013. https://vimeo.com/73055244.

Vaidhyanathan, Siva. 2008. "Naked in the 'Nonopticon.'" *Chronicle of Higher Education*, February 15. http://chronicle.com/article/Naked-in-the -Nonopticon-/6197.

Wernimont, Jacqueline. 2012. "Feminism and Digital Humanities." *Jacqueline Wernimont.* http://jwernimont.wordpress.com/2012/02/29/feminism-and -digital-humanities.

## TWENTY-THREE

New Materialism and a Rhetoric of Scientific Practice in the Digital Humanities

DAVID GRUBER

In English and communication departments, where rhetoric scholars most often find academic homes, the digital humanities is popularly enacted through the development of novel quantitative approaches to alphabetic texts (Kirschenbaum 2010; Muralidharan 2012). However, keeping the work of textual analysis vital to the digital humanities as enacted in rhetoric threatens to perpetuate what John Lynch calls a "logic of representation" in rhetorical theory dependent on a sign-object correspondence, ignoring the active and dynamic potentials of bodies and machines (Lynch 2009, 439). More specifically for a rhetoric of science, equating the digital humanities with mapping document data and visualizing discursive strategies of scientists overlooks the constitutive role of practice in the analysis of science and may continue to neglect scientific materiality. Put differently, the digital humanities in the field of rhetoric may be prone to focus considerable attention on discursivity at the expense of a materialist analysis of environments and practice. However, digital tools can contribute to a practice-centered, activity-based digital humanities in the rhetoric of science, one that moves scholars away from a logic of representation and toward the logic informing "New Materialism," or the rejection of metaphysics in favor of ontologies made and remade from material processes, practices, and organizations, human and nonhuman, visible and invisible, turning together all the time. That is, a New Materialism, broadly conceptualized, seeks "new ways of thinking about matter and processes of materialization" (Coole and Frost 2010, 2) while making an effort to journey beyond the semiotic turn and a human-centric mode of analysis.

A New Materialism in the rhetoric of science probably aligns most closely with science and technology studies' pursuit of "multiple ontologies" (Mol 2002) and embraces the notion, as Scott Graham and Carl Herndl put it, that "the reality you engage is determined by the kinds of actions you habitually perform and the material contexts in which you act" (2013, 110). In other words, a theory of multiple ontologies (MO) fits under the umbrella of New Materialism insofar as MO allows for multiple distributions of material relations and the investigation of many material realities—not simply a singular material reality viewed from various perspectives.[1] Taking New Materialism and, more specifically, MO seriously would reposition the rhetoric of science, at least in part, as a rhetoric of scientific practice and, accordingly, compel the pursuit of a digital humanities in the field to be about more than creative textual analysis.

I aim to show how keen use of digital resources allows rhetoric scholars to focus on practices and to see documents as important but wrapped up with machines, bodies, expectations, and institutions in a "mangle" that makes science the messy work of managing the unknown, the impractical, and the unpredictable (Pickering 1995). Three specific projects will be detailed to demonstrate what a rhetoric of scientific practice in the digital humanities might potentially look like. The first project explores the use of Arduino and the Processing programming language to make the furniture of an office or lab space aware and able to record and respond to data. The second project investigates the multiple worlds recorded by medical imaging machines and engages what Ian Bogost calls "carpentry," or the practice of building ways to better understand the "inner life" of nonhuman objects (Bogost 2012, 85). The third project uses various media to capture and animate what happens on-site in surgical rooms in hospitals in order to discover affective potentials and recover the importance of practices that would, otherwise, be lost. Overall, the chapter aims to call attention to the exciting possibilities of making the digital humanities in rhetoric, in part, about engaging material worlds and contributing to an analysis of scientific practice.

Project 1: Sentient Room

In a project developed in Dr. David Rieder's digital media class at North Carolina State University, the doctoral students Brent Simoneaux, Samara Mouvre, and Fernanda Duarte installed sensors in the seats of chairs and programmed a computer to receive the signal and then send out Twitter messages based on shifts and fluctuations of weight in those chairs (see fig. 23.1). They explained their project this way: "By sitting, wiggling, the user generates data. . . . These numbers are then passed through wires into an Arduino processor and are subsequently taken up by a computer. Those numbers then become actionable based on a

23.1. Sentient Chair Construction: Armchair, Arduino, sensors, wires. Courtesy of Brent Simoneaux.

criteria set within the computer program" (Simoneaux, Mouvre, and Duarte 2011, 3).

This sentient room project generates data from the lived (and now live) environment: "The room itself becomes an interface" (Simoneaux, Mouvre, and Duarte 2011, 4). Drawing on work by Florian Cramer and Matthew Fuller, the interface for this project is conceptualized as "a surface forming a common boundary of two bodies, spaces, phases" (Cramer and Fuller 2008, 49). Thus, the chair is positioned as the "surface" that translates among environments, humans, and nonhumans (Simoneaux, Mouvre, and Duarte 2011, 4). The act of touching, getting up, or sitting down allows private behaviors to become public and opens the protected space of an office or a laboratory to public conversation on a social networking site. Duarte et al. rightly recognize the political dimensions of this work, suggesting that a sentient room moves private activity out into what Manuel Castells calls the "global space of flows" (Castells 1996, 453). Yet sentient environments in scientific settings need not necessarily be deployed as social media experiments, surveillance technologies, or ironic art criticisms; projects like this one can be arranged to foster an inclusive, exploratory kind of analysis, discovering how the material world is involved in and influences practice.

Digital infusions like the sentient room project might be used to account for human-nonhuman relations and expose an often hidden, long scientific process that happens each day at odd times in everyday places with everyday things. Chairs, desks, lamps, filing cabinets, phones—even automatic door closers, as Bruno Latour (writing as Johnson 1988) has pointed out—make a difference to human behavior and mood, to the events that happen in the building, to the operations of other machines, and to decisions that are—pointedly here in the passive voice so common to scientific writing—ultimately made. Decisions are, of course, made, but who and/or what makes them together in an affecting and affectable milieu at any given place and time is the question. Once formed into a question of material interactions, it becomes a question for a New Materialist–inspired humanities inquiry that can be enacted through digital means. Although this kind of computational re-presenting may not entirely escape dependency on discursivity in the rhetorical analysis of scientific practice, from the perspective of the rhetoric scholar, discursive constructedness is not able to be so easily isolated, nor can it be set aside, nor should it be; the point is to make the material environment an active and reactive participant, to examine practice more closely and complexly, and to do so in a way inclusive of bodies and environments.

Projects like the one at North Carolina State University voice the environment and make material objects recognizable as "capacities" that affect humans and have effects and "do things," as Jane Bennett (2010, vii–x) puts it. If nothing else, the creation of a sentient room draws attention to nonhuman objects and their roles in human affairs. Leaving open the possibility for mundane or seemingly unimportant nonhuman objects to add to a scholar's analysis takes seriously Pickering's (1995, 3) remark that science is made with machines and instruments and social practices at a specific time and place. In fact, projects like the sentient room distribute agency "to a set of nonhuman agents (the chair and the chaise lounge)" (Simoneaux, Mouvre, and Duarte 2011, 5), and, in so doing, they not only include those objects in the scholar's analysis but also enact analysis as an unpredictable process of cobeing and invention—not always a process that chases some defined argument, but one that becomes aware of happenings and influences and spurs happenings in the world.

Project 2: Ontological Carpentry and Imaging Devices

"Carpentry" is, according to Bogost, the act of making things that might help "explain how things make their world." Carpentry can be achieved in any number of ways. It may involve making lists or Web sites or other things that speculate and describe relations between objects and their surrounding world. It is the pursuit of an "alien phenomenology" or "what it's like to be a thing" through craft (Bogost 2011, 93, 100).

An example of carpentry and what it can do is gleaned from the work of the artist Scott Short, which provides an interesting place from which to consider carpentry in the rhetoric of science. Looking at Short's work suggests that rhetoric scholars may find value in considering imaging technologies in scientific practice as objects worthy of exploration in and of themselves. Extended to a discussion of the digital humanities, Short's work inspires a hands-on method of doing *as* discovering the machine through digital tools, exploring ways of understanding how it is that things like imaging devices coconstruct some reality and contribute, in their thingness, to the making of science.

Short's works "begin with simple colored construction paper that the artist copies then re-copies numerous times on a black-and-white photocopying machine" (Adamek 2012). He then scrupulously copies the copy—every faded line and smeared detail—in black oil paint on a white canvas. Short subjects the art image to the photocopy machine, its operations and its output. In this way, he does something like what the machine does, and his art making investigates the alien life of the photocopy machine. He may not technically understand the machine's functioning or mirror it exactly, but he explores the machine in the way that he knows how. The change of medium is, thus, important insofar as painting acts as a metaphoric movement for photocopying; it is a human way to understand a machine that is, as Bogost (2012, 32–34) puts it, "alien" and able to be understood only through metaphor. What complicates the work is the way that Short's process is machinic and, thereby, interrogates a dualism supporting a strong division between him and the machine or even between agencies of creation—his own or that of the machine—and, accordingly, the work questions the independent identity of any object at all.

The point here is that the basic carpentry that Short exemplifies can be extended to other imaging technologies and to an understanding of scientific practice aided by digital tools. This is not to suggest that rhetoric scholars can be or should be off painting pictures. This is, instead, to suggest that the kind of work Short does can inspire new rhetoric scholarship under the trajectory and banner of the digital humanities. Indeed, the digital affordances celebrated in more traditional digital humanities projects can be geared toward understanding machines or practices invested in machinic design and capabilities. Understanding the magnetic field of a functional magnetic imaging machine (fMRI), for example, and the way the computer interface translates that field may well be a worthy pursuit for scholars engaging a rhetoric of scientific practice.

Appreciation for the value of carpentry in understanding scientific practice can be gained from the philosophy professor Dan Lloyd, who explored the inner workings of the fMRI machine. In seeking to contemplate the differences between people diagnosed with schizophrenia and those with so-called normal brains, Lloyd built a computer program that musically translated the numerical data of the fMRI, which is usually colored onto a brain scan image (Lloyd 2009). The activity registered by the fMRI machine became, through Lloyd's computer program, pitches of sounds.

Although originally intended to explore brain differences, Lloyd's work, more to the point here, musically expressed the numerical density of magnetic fields composed by fMRI machines as they registered the uptake of oxygen in a human brain. In other words, through computational means Lloyd's program interrogated the machine by re-expressing the relations it found and by offering an alternative way to see what the machine was doing. His work allowed a human user to reexperience relations between the machine's magnetic field and the hemodynamics of the brain. In so doing, Lloyd also throws into question the allure of brain images and highlights their rhetorical construction (the choices, colors, framing used, etc.) by constructing them differently.

Although typical modes of inquiry for rhetoric scholars are not directly associated with those of programmers or craftspersons, embracing such modes may well be, or can be, part of their exploratory job. As Bogost notes, we need "to get our hands dirty with grease, juice, gunpowder and gypsum" (2012, 34). If the digital humanities is about finding new and productive ways to use digital means to expand and revise traditional forms of inquiry in the humanities (Presner, Schnapp, and Lunenfeld 2009), then projects framed as digital art or digital play might be excellent places to locate interesting avenues for a rhetoric scholarship pursuing material worlds. Projects like Short's and Lloyd's reveal the value of carpentry and inspire creative uses of digital affordances for a scholarship that starts with machines.

Project 3: Affect and Action in Medical Settings

Invigorated scholarly interest in affect intends to upset the notion that "subjectivities are understood as more or less clearly defined positions in a semiotic field" (Gregg and Seigworth 2010) and seeks a dynamism that instigates and investigates multiple, possible relations between things. In critical cultural theory, discussions of affect inevitably build from Brian Massumi's (2002, 28–36) definition of the term, which draws on Gilles Deleuze and Félix Guattari's (1987, 288) notion of bodies as sets of relations capable of affecting others and being affected. For Massumi (2002, 25), then, an affect is any "pre-narrativized" bodily influence acting as an intensity. However, defining the term more carefully, as Lawrence Grossberg notes, can help scholars avoid using it as a "'magical' term" that does not "do the harder work of specifying modalities and apparatuses" and does not distinguish "affect from other sorts of non-semantic effects" (2010, 315). In contrast, defining affect too narrowly brings about its own difficulties since affect can be internal, unconscious, and more complex than single definitions can inscribe (Clough and Halley 2007, 28). Even so—despite definitional difficulties—accounting for affect by articulating a material organization from interforming and interfolding relations does not necessarily undo the wonder of affective potentials or suppress the significance of transforming a semiotic turn into a complex study of movement.

Accordingly, using digital tools to map affects can be both a process of reconstructing felt influences as well as a kind of "registering of potentials" (Massumi 2002, 92). It can be empirical as well as speculative and developmental. This work could be accomplished in any number of ways, but some projects offer points of suggestion for a digital humanities within a rhetoric of scientific practice. One such project is Jane Prophet's (2004) use of video to document the space and action surrounding open-heart surgeries. Prophet identifies previously unnoticed actions and persuasive forces that go unmentioned in official narratives. In so doing, her project offers viewers a sense of the situated happenings and multiple influences that, quite literally, make up the event.

To start the project, Jane Prophet sets up a video camera and records an open-heart surgery. She notices something unexpected. While the surgery is reaching its conclusion, and while the patient is still lying cut open on the operating table, Frank Wells, the surgeon, dips his tweezers into the patient's blood and draws a picture of the patient's heart on a piece of paper. He does this to explain the procedure to visiting doctors who attend to learn about Wells's innovative valve-replacement technique. Prophet describes Wells's action here as a teaching moment and an artistic practice tied, specifically, to his admiration of Leonardo da Vinci's drawings of the heart and da Vinci's attention to the shape and fluid dynamics of the body.

Indeed, as Prophet discovers, Wells draws the patient's heart for many reasons. For one, he believes that "what Leonardo was saying about the shape of the valve is important" (Prophet 2010), so drawing the shape of the heart emphasizes his point. But Wells is also unable to speak in this surgery theater setting—he wears a mask and needs to communicate with doctors who visit from overseas and know little English. Additionally, the blood acts as good ink and does not contaminate the patient. Further, since Wells recognizes irregularities in the heart by feel—squeezing the heart with his hand—drawing a picture of the heart on the spot captures something of the immediate moment and the individualized patient.

After the surgery, Prophet explains that Dr. Wells steps outside for a breath of fresh air. He tells her that he believes that the beautiful, manicured grounds of the building improve his frame of mind and help him consider the bigger picture (Prophet 2010). Prophet's video project captures these seemingly small, unnoticed affective pathways or "prepersonal intensities" (Deleuze and Guattari 1987, xvii) that influence the surgeon, and reviewing the video footage of Wells's work, before, during, and after surgery, helps Prophet discover connections between the body, artistic practice, and situated technical and scientific ways of seeing.

The concept driving this project could be extended to medical settings and bolstered by new digital affordances to enable some account of affect. Scholars pursuing a rhetoric of scientific practice might, for instance, record the experiences of those involved in a surgery such as a heart or kidney transplant and incorporate additional digital tools to emphasize material interactions; the rooms and hallways of the hospital (their temperature, smells, and sounds) could play a direct role in narratives; the people's voices could be reconfigured and compared as pitches of sounds or sets of emotional pauses; the stories could be produced in tandem with the physical computing possibilities now explored by researchers such as William Turkle (2011) or David Rieder (n.d.). A project like Jane Prophet's might, for example, be redesigned to incorporate open-source software that highlights bodily gestures made in a lab environment, to visualize the proximity between individuals and nonhuman objects in a room, or to re-present the physical movements happening in an operating theater as a line map or a heat map while allowing those involved to watch the visualization and speak about the event as it unfolds. Designing digital humanities projects like these could emphasize material, bodily interactions and help identify important human and nonhuman relations that might otherwise go unnoticed.

Conclusion

Coole and Frost open their edited collection on New Materialisms recognizing the primacy of matter and the need for ecological perspectives: "Our existence depends from one moment to the next on myriad micro-organisms and diverse higher species, on our own hazily understood bodily and cellular reactions and on pitiless cosmic motions, as well as on economic structures. . . . We now advance the bolder claim that foregrounding material factors and reconfiguring our very understanding of matter are prerequisites for any plausible account of coexistence" (Coole and Frost 2010, 1–2). Their reversal here of a traditional Western glorification of the immaterial and abstract epitomizes New Materialisms and corroborates a theory of MO, which, as Scott Graham explains it, turns away from focusing on representational issues and suggests that "the specifics of local practice create a world, or ontology, unique to that environment" (Graham 2011). Engaging these materialist ideas now circulating in academe is not so much to argue that textual analysis is always inadequate or inappropriate; it is, rather, to entertain new, alternative modes of thinking, being, and doing in a rhetoric of science that can perform differently and maybe, in some cases, recognize more with digital means and nonhuman partnerships.

Note

1.   For a further discussion of this, see Graham and Herndl (2013).

References

Adamek, Pauline. 2012. "Scott Short's Paintings at Christopher Grimes Gallery." *ArtsBeatLA*, January 18. http://www.artsbeatla.com/2012/01/scott-short-paintings.

Bennett, Jane. 2010. *Vibrant Matter: A Political Ecology of Things*. Durham, NC: Duke University Press.

Bogost, Ian. 2011. "Seeing Things." Ian Bogost Personal Web site, September 14. http://www.bogost.com/writing/seeing_things_1.shtml.

———. 2012. *Alien Phenomenology; or, What It's Like to Be a Thing*. Minneapolis: University of Minnesota Press.

Castells, Manuel. 1996. *The Rise of the Network Society*. Oxford: Blackwell.

Clough, Patricia Ticineto, and Jean O'Malley Halley. 2007. *The Affective Turn: Theorizing the Social*. Durham, NC: Duke University Press.

Coole, Diana H., and Samantha Frost. 2010. *New Materialisms: Ontology, Agency, and Politics*. Durham, NC: Duke University Press.

Cramer, Florian, and Matthew Fuller. 2008. "Interface." In *Software Studies: A Lexicon*, ed. Matthew Fuller, 149–52. Cambridge, MA: MIT Press.

Deleuze, Gilles, and Félix Guattari. 1987. *A Thousand Plateaus: Capitalism and Schizophrenia*. Minneapolis: University of Minnesota Press.

Graham, Scott. 2011. "Multiple Ontologies and Rhetorics of Health and Biomedicine." Academia.edu, April 6. http://www.academia.edu/1684282/Multiple_Ontologies_and_Rhetorics_of_Health_and_Biomedicine.

Graham, Scott, and Carl G. Herndl. 2013. "Multiple Ontologies in Pain Management: Towards a Post-Plural Rhetoric of Science." *Technical Communication Quarterly* 22.2:103–25.

Gregg, Melissa, and Gregory J. Seigworth. 2010. "Eff the Ineffable: Affect, Somatic Management, and Mental Health Service Users." In *The Affect Theory Reader*, ed. Melissa Gregg and Gregory J. Seigworth, 229–49. Durham, NC: Duke University Press.

Grossberg, Lawrence. 2010. "Affect's Future: Rediscovering the Virtual in the Actual." In *The Affect Theory Reader*, ed. Melissa Gregg and Gregory J. Seigworth, 309–38. Durham, NC: Duke University Press.

Johnson, Jim. 1988. "Mixing Humans and Nonhumans Together: The Sociology of a Door-Closer." *Social Problems* 35.3:298–310.

Kirschenbaum, Matthew. 2010. "What Is the Digital Humanities, and What's It Doing in English Departments?" *ADE Bulletin*, no. 150. http://mkirschenbaum.files.wordpress.com/2011/01/kirschenbaum_ade150.pdf.

Lloyd, Dan. 2009. "Brain Music: fMRI into Musical Sound." YouTube, February 27. http://www.youtube.com/watch?v=7tFlrPwrwKY.

Lynch, John. 2009. "Articulating Scientific Practice: Understanding Dean Hamer's 'Gay Gene' Study as Overlapping Material, Social and Rhetorical Registers." *Quarterly Journal of Speech* 95.4:435–56.

Massumi, Brian. 2002. *Parables for the Virtual: Movement, Affect, Sensation.* Durham, NC: Duke University Press.

Mol, Annemarie. 2002. *The Body Multiple: Ontology in Medical Practice.* Durham, NC: Duke University Press.

Muralidharan, Aditi. 2012. "Text Mining and the Digital Humanities." Mining humanities.com, October 9. http://mininghumanities.com.

Pickering, Andrew. 1995. *The Mangle of Practice: Time, Agency, and Science.* Chicago: University of Chicago Press.

Presner, Todd, Jeffery Schnapp, and Peter Lunenfeld. 2009. "The Digital Humanities Manifesto 2.0." Blogroll, for the UCLA Mellon Seminar, June. http://vimeo.com/13832954.

Prophet, Jane. 2004. "Swab Drawing Videos 2004." Jane Prophet. http://www.janeprophet.com/2011/09/francis-wells-surgeon-blood-heart-mitral-valve-repair-swab-drawing-videos-2004. http://www.humanitiesblast.com/manifesto/Manifesto_V2.pdf.

———. 2010. "One Person's Everyday Creativity Is Another's Extraordinary Insight." Vimeo.

Rieder, David. n.d. "Digital Rhetoric, Writing, Theory." Rieder's Website. http://www4.ncsu.edu/~dmrieder.

Simoneaux, Brent, Samara Mouvre, and Fernanda Duarte. 2011. "The Sentient Room Project." Report for Dr. Rieder, Communication, Rhetoric and Digital Media Program, North Carolina State University.

Turkle, William. 2011. "Designing Interactive Exhibits." William J. Turkel, December 17. http://williamjturkel.net/2011/12/17/designing-interactive-exhibits.

Contributors

DANIEL ANDERSON
Department of English and Comparative Literature
University of North Carolina at Chapel Hill
Chapel Hill, NC 27514
United States

CHERYL BALL
Department of English
West Virginia University
Morgantown, WV 26506
United States

BRIAN BALLENTINE
Department of English
West Virginia University
Morgantown, WV 26506
United States

CASEY BOYLE
Department of Rhetoric and Writing
University of Texas at Austin
Austin, TX 78712-1038
United States

KEVIN BROOKS
Department of English
North Dakota State University
Fargo, ND 58108
United States

CONTRIBUTORS

JAMES J. BROWN JR.
Department of English
Rutgers University—Camden
Camden, NJ 08102
United States

SHANNON CARTER
Department of Literature and Languages
Texas A&M University—Commerce
Commerce, Texas 75492
United States

DOUGLAS EYMAN
Department of English
George Mason University
Fairfax, VA 22030
United States

JENNIFER GLASER
Department of English and Comparative Literature
University of Cincinnati
Cincinnati, OH 45221
United States

TAREZ SAMRA GRABAN
Department of English
Florida State University
Tallahassee, FL 32306
United States

DAVID GRUBER
Department of English
City University of Hong Kong
Kowloon Tong
Hong Kong

SUNCHAI HAMCUMPAI
Department of Literature and Languages
Texas A&M University—Commerce
Commerce, Texas 75492
United States

RODERICK P. HART
Dean, College of Communication
University of Texas at Austin
Austin, TX 78712
United States

DAVID HOFFMAN
School of Public Affairs
Baruch College, City University of New York
New York, NY 10010
United States

NATHAN JOHNSON
Department of English
Purdue University
West Lafayette, IN 47907
United States

JENNIFER JONES
Department of Literature and Languages
Texas A&M University—Commerce
Commerce, Texas 75492
United States

KRISTA KENNEDY
Department of Composition and Cultural Rhetoric
Syracuse University
Syracuse, NY 13244
United States

NEYLA KOTEYKO
School of Languages, Linguistics and Film
Queen Mary, University of London
London E1 4NS
United Kingdom

CHRIS LINDGREN
Department of Writing Studies
University of Minnesota
Minnespolis, MN 55455
United States

CONTRIBUTORS

SETH DAVID LONG
Department of Composition and Cultural Rhetoric
Syracuse University
Syracuse, NY 13244
United States

ELIZABETH LOSH
Director of Academic Programs
Sixth College, University of California San Diego
Irvine, CA 92697-2650
United States

BRIAN MCNELY
Department of Writing, Rhetoric, and Digital Studies
University of Kentucky
Lexington, KY 40506
United States

LAURA R. MICCICHE
Department of English and Comparative Literature
University of Cincinatti
Cincinnati, OH 45221
United States

WHITNEY MYERS
Department of English
Texas Wesleyan University
Fort Worth, TX 76105
United States

LIZA POTTS
Department of Writing, Rhetoric, and American Cultures
Michigan State University
East Lansing, MI 48824
United States

ALEXIS RAMSEY-TOBIENNE
Eckerd College
St. Petersburg, FL 33711
United States

ALEXANDER REID
Department of English
University at Buffalo—The State University of New York
Buffalo, NY 14260
United States

JEFF RICE
Department of Writing, Rhetoric, and Digital Studies
University of Kentucky
Lexington, KY 40506
United States

JENNY RICE
Department of Writing, Rhetoric, and Digital Studies
University of Kentucky
Lexington, KY 40506
United States

JENNIFER SANO-FRANCHINI
Department of English
Virginia Tech
Blacksburg, VA 24061
United States

JENTERY SAYERS
Department of English
University of Victoria
Victoria, BC V8W 3W1
Canada

KARL STOLLEY
Department of Humanities
Illinois Institute of Technology
Chicago, IL 60616
United States

CHRISTA TESTON
Department of English
The Ohio State University
Columbus, OH 43210
United States

CONTRIBUTORS

DON WAISANEN
School of Public Affairs
Baruch College, City University of New York
New York, NY 10010
United States

DOUGLAS WALLS
Department of Writing and Rhetoric
University of Central Florida
Orlando, FL 32816
United States

MATTHEW B. WARNER
Department of English
North Dakota State University
Fargo, ND 58108
United States

Index

Italicized page numbers indicate illustrations.